THE
CANADIAN
ETHNIC MOSAIC

The Canadian Ethnic Mosaic

A Quest for Identity

Leo Driedger, Editor

McClelland and Stewart

Canadian Ethnic Studies Association series, Volume VI

The Canadian Publishers
McClelland and Stewart Limited
25 Hollinger Road, Toronto M4B 3G2

Printed and bound in Canada

CANADIAN CATALOGUING IN PUBLICATION DATA

Main entry under title:
The Canadian ethnic mosaic
(Canadian Ethnic Studies Association series; v.6)

A selection of papers presented at a conference held
in Winnipeg, 1975, sponsored by the Canadian Ethnic
Studies Association.

Includes index.
ISBN 0-7710-2888-1 pa.

1. Ethnology — Canada — Congresses. 2. Ethnicity
— Congresses. 3. Canada — Foreign population —
Congresses. I. Driedger, Leo, 1928-

II. Series: Canadian Ethnic Studies Association
Canadian Ethnic Studies Association series; v.6

FC104.C35   301.45'0971   C78-001118-X
F1035.A1C35

Contents

Preface

Ethnic research in Canada has been expanding enormously in recent years. However, many of us who teach courses related to ethnic relations and minority groups are still looking for more Canadian data in a theoretical framework designed for the Canadian situation. In this volume we present contributions by Canadian social scientists who are deeply involved in Canadian ethnic studies.

"The Canadian Ethnic Mosaic: A Quest for Identity" was the theme of a conference sponsored by the Canadian Ethnic Studies Association in Winnipeg in 1975. The Canadian Ethnic Studies Association has held such conferences biannually, to provide ethnic scholars with the opportunity to present their research. The 200 scholars who gathered for the Winnipeg conference came from east and west, representing the disciplines of sociology, history, anthropology, psychology, linguistics, economics, education, and numerous others. These conferences, together with the association quarterly *Bulletin* and the *Canadian Ethnic Studies* journal, are providing a context in which scholars become friends, eager to share their work and their aspirations.

At the Winnipeg conference, papers were solicited for five topics which require special study in Canada: theoretical perspectives, immigration, child development, native identity, and ethnic identification. Additional papers were solicited to provide a well-rounded discussion of these areas. This volume includes eighteen papers, all but one specifically prepared for publication in this book. Twenty-two of the twenty-three contributors are residents in Canada; the research is mostly Canadian; and most of the authors have been engaged in ethnic research in Canada for many years.

Many individuals contributed to the study conference and to this volume. Special thanks are due Rita Bienvenue, who chaired the local arrangements for the conference, and to Wsevolod Isajiw and the Executive Committee of the association, who provided valuable counsel. We also thank the chairpersons of the conference sessions, Shirin Schludermann, Richard Mezoff, Cornelius Jaenen, Howard Palmer, Jean Burnet, Pierre Laporte, and Sally Weaver. In addition, a personal thank you to a score of persons at the Universities of Manitoba and Winnipeg who helped me plan the program which has become the contents of this volume, as well as to Darlene Driedger who typed hundreds of letters and scores of manuscripts in the preparation of this publication.

The Secretary of State of the federal government assisted with special funding, which is gratefully acknowledged.

7

Introduction
Ethnic Identity in the Canadian Mosaic
Leo Driedger*

The purpose of this introduction is to orient the reader to the basic design of this volume. As the first part of the title suggests, we will concentrate in Parts One and Two on the Canadian ethnic mosaic, and on some of the factors related to ethnic pluralism. The quest for identity, as the second part of the title suggests, will be discussed in Parts Three, Four, and Five by focusing on the early development of ethnic identity, and on the patterns of identification of various ethnic groups in Canada. An introduction appears before each of the five parts of this volume to clarify the specific contents of each part. A brief discussion of the concepts of ethnic pluralism and ethnic identity follows.

PLURALISM: THE CANADIAN ETHNIC MOSAIC

The analogy of the mosaic to describe the Canadian plural society is useful in answering three questions: How are the tiles in the mosaic distributed? Do the tiles all have equal influence, or do some dominate others because of their size, or because of the way in which they cluster in the total design? Finally, what is the nature of each of the tiles in the total design, and what would be missing if they no longer remained distinctive? If the analogy of the mosaic is applied to Canadian society, the first has to do with the regional distribution of various ethnic groups, the second focuses on the status and power of the various groups within the total society, and the third is related to the cultural and institutional contributions of the various ethnic groups (to be discussed under a quest for identity). Each of these three components of the mosaic will be described, beginning with regional distribution.

*Leo Driedger is Associate Professor of Sociology, University of Manitoba, Winnipeg.

Regional Mosaic: Ecological Distribution of Ethnic Groups

Since Canada is regionally, ecologically, and demographically a highly differentiated nation, we plan to examine the mosaic of Canadian national regions, such as the Northlands, the West, Upper Canada, Lower Canada, the Atlantic provinces, and New Brunswick. The regions vary from multilingualism and multiculturalism in the Northwest to monolingualism and uniculturalism in the East. High concentrations of the Native People in the North, the "other" ethnic groups in the West, the French in Quebec, and the British in the East, provide a mix which represents differential ethnic aspirations and social organization.

The Northlands: Multilingualism and Multiculturalism. The Northlands include all of the Yukon, the Northwest Territories, and roughly the northerly two-thirds of the six most westerly provinces (British Columbia, Alberta, Saskatchewan, Manitoba, Ontario, and Quebec). This area constitutes about four-fifths of Canada's territory, though it includes a relatively small proportion of the Canadian population. Demographically, it is the area where, in 1971, 69 per cent of the population were of native origin, and 56 per cent used their native tongue at home (Vallee and DeVries, 1975: Table B-5). Vallee and DeVries illustrate that these Native Peoples perpetuate multilingual and multicultural societies, where European influences are increasing but not yet dominant.

The native residents were the people who lived here first; and they occupy the larger part of our land area. Treaties have not yet been made in much of this region. On the other hand, they are a very small percentage of our population, and they are economically and politically powerless. They are also multilingual and multicultural. The trend, however, seems to be for the natives to come south into more urban settings, and there is strong evidence that they adopt either English or French (in Quebec) very quickly. Only 33 per cent of the Native People in urban areas use their mother tongue (Vallee and DeVries, 1975: Table B-6). The Northlands could best be described as multicultural and multilingual.

The West: Anglophones and Multiculturalism. The West includes the southern portions of the four most westerly provinces (British Columbia, Alberta, Saskatchewan, Manitoba). These were the domain of the Native Peoples and were settled most recently by immigrants of European origin. This is the only region where no group is in the majority, although the British form the largest group. The region is highly rural and agricultural; it includes substantial enclaves of British, German, Ukrainian, French, and smaller ethnic groups. Although the Hudson's Bay Company, administered from Britain, traded in the area for two hundred years, from 1670 to 1870, a diversity of European ethnic groups settled the region and began social institutions.

Although many ethnic groups seek to maintain their ethnic language, the language used by the majority (85 per cent) is English (Vallee and

DeVries, 1975:17). Many promote British, Ukrainian, German, French and other cultures, because no one group dominates the region culturally.

Upper Canada: Anglophones and Multiculturalism. Upper Canada consists of southern Ontario, which until recently was English linguistically and British culturally. It was the stronghold of the British, a charter group, whose large population promoted urban industrial growth while it maintained a strong economic and financial base.

Recently, this urban industrial area has attracted many immigrants into its labour market, so that almost half of the new immigrants to Canada, during the seventies, are going to Toronto. These immigrants represent many cultures from northern and southern Europe as well as the Third World. Thus, the urban areas of Ontario are changing from highly British cultural areas to multicultural areas, which involve the use of a diversity of languages. However, because these new immigrants are competing for jobs they are learning English. Although the British culture is not threatened in Upper Canada, multiculturalism is certainly on the rise.

In Ontario, 75 per cent of the people use English at home (Vallee and DeVries, 1975:16), whereas only about 5 per cent speak French at home. Although Ontario has made some efforts to become bilingual (French and English), it appears that English lingualism is dominant, and other languages constitute a small minority. This region could best be described as English linguistically with strong multicultural trends.

Although the linguistic and cultural condition of the West and Upper Canada seem to be the same, the historical trends vary. The West has been strongly multilingual and multicultural throughout its short history. However, since it is less industrialized than southern Ontario, new immigrants do not seem to be streaming into this area. Consequently, its cultural diversity is not increasing. In Ontario, however, with a very strong influx of new immigrants, multilingualism will likely increase and will be reinforced by multiculturalism.

Lower Canada: Francophones and Multiculturalism. Lower Canada, the southern portion of Quebec, could be designated francophone; French is spoken by a large majority. English spoken in the home seems to be declining (Vallee and DeVries, 1975:16). One of the reasons that English has persisted in Quebec is the economic elite, who tended to be English, and the influence of their industrial connections with the larger North American scene. But as there is some evidence that Toronto may become Canada's dominant financial and industrial base, this may mean that slowly, but increasingly, business headquarters and offices will shift to Ontario. Therefore, the power of the English business elite in the province of Quebec may decline, and French lingualism may increase.

A second factor which may cause greater French lingual and cultural influence in Quebec is provincial legislation which favours the French language. This may lead toward greater French lingualism rather than towards bilingualism. The influence of the Québécois and French nationalists may result in English interests leaving Quebec, thereby increasing the French emphasis.

The five million French Canadians living in Quebec represent the largest ethnic regional block in Canada. With their long Canadian history, their new-found drive for French identity, the desire to promote French language and culture in Canada, and provincial legislation to do so, it is likely that this will remain the strongest single ethnic region.

The Maritimes: Anglophones and Anglo-culturalism. The three most easterly Atlantic provinces (Newfoundland, Nova Scotia, Prince Edward Island) represent British unilingualism and uniculturalism. Ninety-five per cent of the residents in this area speak English at home (Vallee and DeVries, 1975). Their long history is largely British, and demographically they are British. Very few immigrants enter these provinces, which will likely mean that they will remain highly British. This region represents only 6 or 7 per cent of the Canadian population so its impact on the total mosaic is small. It is also highly unlikely that residents of this region will push for a heterogeneous mosaic. Their native population is very small, their Black population is English-speaking and small, and other ethnic groups are hardly represented.

New Brunswick: Bilingualism and Biculturalism. New Brunswick is really the only region in Canada that is bilingual and bicultural. It contains only about 2 or 3 per cent of the total population. About one-fourth speak French at home, and about two-thirds speak English. Other languages are spoken in the home by less than 10 per cent (Vallee and DeVries, 1975). According to Joy (1972), the likelihood that the French in New Brunswick will retain their language is high, since they are part of the bilingual belt adjacent to the French province of Quebec. Thus, bilingualism (English and French) seems to be assured. Biculturalism is also evident because other cultures are not represented in large numbers.

Our regional analysis of linguistic and cultural realities suggests that Canada is a regional mosaic. The differences between the multilingual and multicultural Northwest and the unilingual and unicultural East are great.

Vertical Mosaic: Status, Prestige, and Power Differentiations
John Porter (1965) describes Canada as a vertical mosaic, with vast differentiations in social stratification. Whereas the regional mosaic focuses on ecological distribution of ethnic groups, the vertical mosaic has to do with the vertical strata of status and prestige. Some ethnic groups are much more heavily represented in the upper strata of the power elite, while other groups are more heavily represented in the lower classes. Such factors as charter group status and entrance status apply (Porter, 1965).

Charter group status. The British North America Act of 1867 gave the founding groups of Canada (British and French) what has been termed by some (Porter, 1965) as charter group status. The act legalized the claims of the two original migrating groups for such historically established privileges as the perpetuation of their separate languages and cultures. The Royal Commission on Bilingualism and Biculturalism (1970) continued to support and encourage the charter group status of the French, even though by 1971, immigrants of other ethnic origins comprised over one-fourth of the Canadian population. Although legally of equal status, the French have always been junior partners in the alliance with the British. Though the charter group status of the French was legally secure, they nevertheless had difficulty matching the numerical, economic, and political strength of the British. They came to rely on regional segregation and their institutions and culture as means of counteracting British dominance, and devoted their energies to them.

The dominance of the charter groups has never been seriously challenged because of French natural increase and high levels of British immigration. Also, the ethnic structure of a community in terms of its charter and non-charter groups is determined early and tends to be self-perpetuating (Porter, 1965). The French still comprise about 30 per cent of the Canadian population (although that figure declined slightly to 28.7 per cent by 1971), while the British have always been the largest ethnic group, although their proportion of the population has been steadily dropping–to 44.6 per cent in 1971 (Canada Census, 1971).

At the time of confederation, the British and French in Upper and Lower Canada and the Maritimes (representing almost 90 per cent of the population) formed a bilingual and bicultural nation, with few representatives from other countries (Porter, 1965). This is slowly changing, however, and in 1971, about one-fourth (26.7 per cent) of the Canadian population was neither British nor French. The status of these immigrants who came to Canada needs some discussion, as it is these immigrants who are in the process of changing Canada from a bicultural to a multicultural and plural society.

Entrance group status. The position to which ethnic groups are admitted, and at which they are allowed to function in the power structure of a society, is described as entrance status by Porter (1965). In Canada, this position, for most ethnic groups, is characterized by low status occupational roles and a subjection to processes of assimilation laid down by the charter groups. Less preferred immigrants were allowed to enter Canada but were channelled into lower status jobs, and because of their later entrance into Canada were often left with marginal farmlands (Driedger, 1976; Driedger and Peters, 1977).

In 1881 inhabitants of British and French origin made up almost 90 per cent of the Canadian population; others, predominantly of German origin, made up about 7 per cent (Porter, 1965). German, Dutch, Jewish, and Scandinavian immigrants entered Canada earlier than many of the others, so that they can be considered older entrance-status groups. Many Germans, such as the ones who settled in the Berlin (now Kitchener-Waterloo) area have been here two hundred years, and those who formed the large settlements in Manitoba have been here over one hundred years. Many of these earlier immigrants have moved out of an entrance status into higher educational, income, and occupational status. The Jews, for example, placed great value on education and entered higher status occupations, so that they are, on the average, of higher status than any of the other groups, including the charter groups.

Porter (1965) suggests that the idea of an ethnic mosaic, opposed to the idea of a melting pot, impedes the process of social mobility. "The melting pot, with its radical breakdown of national ties and old forms of stratification, would have endangered the conservative tradition of Canadian life, a tradition which gives ideological support to the continued high status of the British charter group" (Porter, 1965:71). This seems to be changing, however, as many former entrance groups are gaining status educationally, occupationally, and economically, and are nevertheless retaining many of their ethnic characteristics. The Jews are an excellent example of high upward mobility with high maintenance of ethnic identity (Driedger, 1975).

The political and economic power elite, however, are still largely British. The British elite (Porter, 1965) dominate the Canadian economic system with a strong influence in urban industrial Ontario, with emerging strength in Alberta but declining strength in the Maritimes. The French dominate the political structure in the province of Quebec, the British dominate in Ontario and the East, and other ethnic groups are increasingly becoming politically influential in the West. Any theory of Canadian ethnic relations must deal with these multidimensional regional, economic, and political status structures in order to account for the push and pull factors which will influence the Canadian mosaic, and also the identity of individual ethnic groups (Driedger, 1975).

ETHNICITY: A QUEST FOR IDENTITY

In our discussion of pluralism we sought to speak to the two questions: how are the various Canadian ethnic groups distributed regionally? and what is the status and influence of various groups within the total society? In our discussion of ethnic identity in this section, we wish to speak to the third question: to what extent do various ethnic groups in Canada adhere to a distinctive heritage, culture, and institutions, that differentiate them from the rest? Once we have discussed all three, the analogy of the mosaic should apply: 1) how are the tiles in the mosaic distributed? 2) do the tiles all contribute equally, or are some dominant? and 3) what are the distinctive features of the ethnic tiles in the total design?

Gordon (1964:24) defines an ethnic group as a group of individuals with a shared sense of peoplehood based on presumed shared sociocultural experiences and/or similar physical characteristics. This would include racial, religious, national, and linguistic groups. Dashefsky (1976:8) defines group identification as "a generalized attitude indicative of a personal attachment to the group and a positive orientation toward being a member of the group. Therefore, ethnic identification takes place when the group in question is one with whom the individual believes he has a common ancestry based on shared individual characteristics and/or shared sociocultural experiences." As Erikson has suggested, "Identity is not the sum of childhood identifications, but rather a new combination of old and new identification fragments" (1964:90).

"Identity may best be understood if it is viewed first as a higher order concept, i.e., a general organizing referent which includes a number of subsidiary facets" (Dashefsky, 1972:240). Dashefsky (1976:7) has reviewed some of the literature on identity and identification which illustrates the many dimensions of identification:

Foote (1951) and Lindesmith and Strauss (1968) have suggested that identification involves linking oneself to others in an organizational sense (as becoming a formal member of an organization) or in a symbolic sense (as thinking of oneself as a part of a particular group). Stone (1962) argues further that identification subsumes two processes: "identification of" and "identification with." The former involves placing the individual in socially defined categories. This facilitates occurence of the latter. In Stone's terms it is "identification with" that gives rise to identity. Finally, Winch (1962:28) follows the interactionalist approach to define identification as the more or less lasting influence of one person on another.

Rosen has gone further in arguing that an individual may identify himself (herself) with others on three levels (1965:162-66). First, one may identify oneself with some important person in one's life, e.g. parent or a friend (i.e. significant other). Second, one may identify oneself with a group from which one draws one's values, e.g. family or co-workers (i.e. reference group). Last, one may identify oneself with a broad category of persons, e.g an ethnic group or occupational group (i.e. a social category). It is on the third level that ethnic identification occurs.

In our discussion of ethnic identification we shall touch on six identification factors: identification with an ecological territory; identification with an ethnic culture; identification with ethnic institutions; identification with historical symbols; identification with an ideology; and identification with charismatic leadership. We suggest that these factors are some of the basic components that constitute an ethnic community, which Gordon (1964) referred to as a group of individuals with a shared sense of peoplehood.

Identification With a Territory

Both Joy (1972) and Lieberson (1970) argue that the maintenance of a language and culture is not possible unless there is a sufficiently large number of a given ethnic group concentrated in a given territory. Joy demonstrates how in Quebec the French were in control of the provincial territory, and thus perpetuated their language and culture through religious, educational, and political institutions. When minorities wish to develop means of control over a population in a specific area, they need to control a territory in which their offspring pass on their heritage through socialization and voluntary identification. Space becomes a crucible in which ethnic activities take place.

The Hutterites are one of the best examples of a rural enclavic ethnic community, characterized by extensive boundary maintenance and controlled systemic linkage with outsiders (Hostetler and Huntington, 1967). Indian reserves also demonstrate ethnic territorial segregation. Most minorities cannot maintain such exclusive control over a territory; however, it is a model to which many minority groups seem to aspire. Ethnic block settlements, especially in the West, are common. The French have been highly concentrated in Quebec; the Germans were heavily concentrated in the Kitchener-Waterloo area in Ontario; and the Ukrainians settled in the Aspen Belt, stretching from the Manitoba Inter-Lake region to Edmonton – to name a few. Rural hinterlands often supplied immigrants to the city who tended to perpetuate the urban villager way of life, as best illustrated by the Northend of Winnipeg, until recently the stronghold of Ukrainians, Poles, and Jews (Driedger and Church, 1974; Driedger, 1978). Richmond (1972) also found extensive residential segregation in Toronto. Territory is an essential ingredient of any definition of a community. Individuals can identify with a territory, and it is the ground within which ethnic activity can take place.

Ethnic Institutional Identification

Breton (1964) argues that "the direction of the immigrant's integration will to a large extent result from the forces of attraction (positive and negative) stemming from three communities: the community of his ethnicity, the native (receiving) community, and the other ethnic communities." These forces are generated by the social organization of ethnic communities and their capacity to attract and hold members within their social boundaries. Ethnic integration into their own ethnic community, supported by institutional completeness of their group, would reinforce solidarity.

The rationale for institutional completeness is that when a minority can develop a social system of its own with control over its institutions, the social action patterns of the group will take place largely within the system (Driedger, 1977; Comeau and Driedger, 1978). Breton (1964) suggests that religious, educational, and welfare institutions are crucial, while Joy (1972) adds the importance of political and economic institutions. Vallee (1969) confirmed Breton's claims by summarizing the need for organization of group structures and institutions which influence socialization and ethnic community decision-making. Driedger and Church (1974) found that in Winnipeg the French and the Jews maintained the most complete set of religious, educational, and welfare institutions compared to other ethnic groups in the city. These two groups were also the most segregated in St. Boniface and the Northend, respectively, where they had established their institutions. Residential segregation and ethnic institutional completeness tended to reinforce each other. The French and the Jews identified with both territory and ethnic institutions.

Identification With Ethnic Culture
Kurt Lewin (1948) proposed that the individual needs to achieve a firm, clear sense of identification with the heritage and culture of the ingroup in order to find a secure "ground" for a sense of well-being. We assume that a minority culture can be better groomed within the territorial enclave where an ethnic group can build a concentration of ethnic institutions. The territory becomes a crucible within which ethnic institutions can be built, and the ethnic culture should flourish within its boundaries.

Ethnic cultural identity factors have been studied by numerous scholars: Segalman, 1967; Geismar, 1954; Rinder, 1959; Dashefsky, 1976; Royal Commission on Bilingualism and Biculturalism, 1969; Lazerwitz, 1953; Driedger, 1975, 1977b; Levinson, 1962; and many others. Driedger (1975) found at least six cultural factors which tended to differentiate group adherence to culture: language use, endogamy, choice of friends, participation in religion, parochial schools, and voluntary organizations. The French and Jews in Winnipeg, who also were more residentially segregated and maintained their ethnic institutions to a greater degree, also ranked high on attendance of parochial schools (79 and 74 per cent); endogamy (65 and 91 per cent); and choice of ingroup friends (49 and 63 per cent) (Driedger, 1975). This would seem to support use of the French language at home (61 per cent) and attendance in church (54 per cent). Other ethnic groups such as the Germans, Ukrainians, Poles, Scandinavians, and British supported their ingroup cultures less actively.

Examination of territorial, institutional, and cultural identity factors suggest that these three tend to reinforce each other, so that when individuals of a given ethnic group identify with their ingroup along these dimensions, they tend to remain more distinctive. This blocks tendencies toward assimilation. Such maintenance of distinctive ethnic features is necessary if the Canadian ethnic mosaic is to remain a distinct reality.

Identification With Historical Symbols

Minority rural villagers may perpetuate their social structure and community as an end in itself, without much reference to where they came from or their future purpose. A knowledge of their origins, and pride in their heritage, would seem to be essential for a sense of purpose and direction among ethnic urbanites (Driedger, 1977). Without such pride and knowledge the desire to perpetuate tradition rapidly diminishes. The Jews have ritualized their history, which they place before their youth in the form of special days, fastings, candles, food habits—symbols of their past history. Such historical symbols can create a sense of belonging, a sense of purpose, a sense of continuing tradition that is important and worth perpetuating. Although tragic for the Jews, the Nazi holocaust in the 1940s and the present struggles in the East may be a sharp reminder of the conflict which is a part of their historical past (Driedger, 1977).

A comparison of identity of seven ethnic groups in Winnipeg, using a Worchel-type scale, indicated strong French and Jewish ingroup affirmation and low ingroup denial, while Scandinavians scored low on both (Driedger, 1976). Jewish and French students were proud of their ingroups, felt strongly bound to them, wished to remember them, and contributed to them. Their ingroups were positive symbols. The French, especially, indicated low ingroup denial. They did not try to hide, nor did they feel inferior about, their ethnicity; they seldom felt annoyed or restricted by their identity (Driedger, 1976). The Ukrainians, Poles, and Germans felt less positively about themselves and at the same time were more inclined to deny their ethnicity. The ethnic heritage of the past can be a positive or negative influence on identity.

Identification With an Ideology

A religious or political ideology can rally followers to a goal beyond cultural and institutional values (Glazer and Moynihan, 1970). For many of the younger generation, territory, culture, and ethnic institutions seem to be means rather than ends to be perpetuated indefinitely. As urban ethnic youth becomes more sophisticated, it is doubtful that enclavic means will hold them within an ethnic ingroup orbit. A political or religious ideology, however, provides a purpose and impetus for values which are considered more important than cultural and institutional means (Driedger and Form, 1976).

In our study of Winnipeg clergymen, we found doctrinal belief, for example, to be an important factor in differentiating attitudes toward a variety of social issues (Driedger, 1974). Beliefs had an independent effect on positions taken on issues related to social control, personal morality, use of power by the elite, civil liberties, minority rights and welfare support. Absolutist clergy with a conservative, other-worldly focus were reluctant to change society; clergymen who were more doctrinally liberal

18

were open to change. There is often a very strong correlation between religion and ethnicity: French and Polish Roman Catholics, Orthodox and Catholic Ukrainians, Scandinavian Lutherans, German Lutherans and Baptists, Jews, and British Anglicans and United Church adherents.

Identification with religious beliefs or a political philosophy provides a more social psychological dimension, which may often ask again, what is the meaning of this territory, these institutions, and this ethnic culture, and why should it be perpetuated or changed?

Charismatic Leadership and Identification

The importance of charisma is demonstrated in a variety of new minority movements including Martin Luther King and Malcolm X among the Blacks in the United States; the leadership of René Lévesque among the Québécois; and Harold Cardinal's Indian movement in Alberta; to name a few. Individuals with a sense of mission often adapt an ideology to a current situation, linking it symbolically with the past, and using the media to effectively transform the present into a vision of the future (Driedger, 1977).

Most religious movements began with charismatic leaders (Buddha, Confucius, Abraham, Jesus, Muhammed). The importance of leadership in the beginnings of the Lutherans (Martin Luther), Reformed (John Calvin), Mormons (Joseph Smith), Mennonites (Menno Simons) illustrates this also. The same is true of political movements, including Ho Chi Minh, Mao, Lenin, Hitler, Mussolini, Churchill, Castro, Tito, Gandhi, Lincoln, and Lévesque.

Such charismatic leaders usually use social psychological means of gaining a following, designed to create trust with which they mold a cohesive loyalty to both leader and ingroup. They are true believers in a cause which is passed on to their followers, resulting in new potential for change. Whereas in the beginning they may be less oriented to territory, institutions, culture and heritage, slowly, as the movement matures, such structural features become more important.

Although there may be many more ethnic dimensions with which minorities identify, we have suggested that territory, institutions, culture, heritage, ideology, and leaders are important. Studies show that different ethnic groups identify more with some of these dimensions than others, and some are more successful in their maintenance of a distinct community. The Hutterites are perhaps one of the most successful groups who have survived in a rural setting, and the Jews have done so effectively in cities for centuries. The task in this volume is to explore the various dimensions and foci of ethnic identification in which various ethnic groups are involved. It will not be possible to explore all of these dimensions with each group. All we can do is provide a small sample of studies to illustrate the multidimensional and multilinear complexity of the ethnic mosaic.

Part One will deal with the various perspectives which can be taken in studying a plural society. Part Two deals with immigration and is designed to illustrate how the Canadian mosaic developed, and how it is changing today. Part Three focuses on the social psychological factors of socialization and identification. In Part Four the authors discuss some of the dimensions of Native Peoples' identification, such as conflict, territorial segregation, and status. Other dimensions of ethnic identification are explored in Part Five, such as the Mennonite heritage, Jewish socialization, Italian community maintenance, and French-Italian community conflict.

References

Breton, R.
  1964 "Institutional Completeness of Ethnic Communities and Personal Relations to Immigrants." *American Journal of Sociology* 70:193-205.
Comeau, L., and L. Driedger
  1978 "Ethnic Opening and Closing in an Open System: A Canadian Example." *Social Forces* 57:z.
Dashefsky, A.
  1972 "And the Search Goes On: Religio-Ethnic Identity and Identification in the Study of Ethnicity." *Sociological Analysis* 33:239-245.
Dashefsky, A.
  1976 *Ethnic Identity in Society.* Chicago: Rand McNally.
Driedger, L.
  1974 "Doctrinal Belief: A Major Factor in the Differential Perception of Social Issues." *Sociological Quarterly* 15:66-80.
Driedger, L.
  1975 "In Search of Cultural Identity Factors: A Comparison of Ethnic Students." *Canadian Review of Sociology and Anthropology* 12:150-162.
Driedger, L.
  1976 "Ethnic Self-Identity: A Comparison of Ingroup Evaluations." *Sociometry* 39:131-141.
Driedger, L.
  1977a "Toward a Perspective on Canadian Pluralism: Ethnic Identity in Winnipeg." *Canadian Journal of Sociology* 2:77-95.

Driedger, L.
1977b "Structural, Social and Individual Factors in Language Maintenance in Canada." in W.H. Coons (ed.) *The Individual, Language, and Society in Canada.* Ottawa: The Canada Council.
Driedger, L.
1978 "Ethnic Boundaries: A Comparison of Two Urban Neighbor-
hoods." *Sociology and Social Research* 62:2.
Driedger, L., and G. Church
1974 "Residential Segregation and Institutional Completeness: A
Comparison of Ethnic Minorities." *Canadian Review of Sociology
and Anthropology* 11:30-52.
Driedger, L., and W.H. Form
1976 "Religious Typology and the Social Ideology of the Clergy." *International Journal of Comparative Sociology* 17:1-18.
Driedger, L., and J. Peters
1977 "Identity and Social Distance: Towards Understanding Simmel's
'The Stranger'." *Canadian Review of Sociology and Anthropology*
14:158-173.
Erikson, E.H.
1963 *Childhood and Society.* New York: W.W. Norton.
Foote, N.
1951 "Identification as the Basis for a Theory of Motivation." *Ameri-
can Sociology Review* 15:14-21.
Geismar, L.
1954 "A Scale for the Measurement of Ethnic Identification." *Jewish
Social Studies* 16:33-60.
Glazer, N. and D.P. Moynihan
1963 *Beyond the Melting Pot.* Cambridge, Mass.: MIT Press.
Gordon, M.
1964 *Assimilation in American Life.* New York: Oxford University
Press.
Hostetler, J.A. and G.E. Huntington
1967 *The Hutterites in North America.* New York: Holt, Rinehart and
Winston.
Joy, R.J.
1972 *Languages in Conflict.* Toronto: McClelland and Stewart.
Lazerwitz, B.
1953 "Some Factors in Jewish Identification." *Jewish Social Studies*
15:24.
Levinson, B.M.
1962 "Yeshiva College Sub-Cultural Scale: An Experimental Attempt
to Devise a Scale of the Internalization of Jewish Traditional Values." *Journal of Genetic Psychology* 101:375-399.
Lewin, K.
1948 *Resolving Social Conflicts.* New York: Harper and Brothers.

Lieberson, S.
  1970 *Languages and Ethnic Relations in Canada.* New York: John Wiley and Sons.
Lindesmith, A.R. and A.L. Strauss
  1968 *Social Psychology* (3rd ed.). New York: Holt, Rinehart and Winston.
Porter, J.
  1965 *The Vertical Mosaic.* Toronto: University of Toronto Press.
Richmond, A.H.
  1972 *Ethnic Segregation in Metropolitan Toronto.* Toronto: Survey Research Center, York University.
Rinder, I.D.
  1959 "Polarities in Jewish Identification: The Personality of Ideological Extremities." Pp. 493-502 in Marshall Sklare (ed.) *The Jews: Social Patterns of an American Group.* New York: Free Press.
Rosen, B.C.
  1965 *Adolescence and Religion.* Cambridge, Mass.: Schenkman.
Royal Commission on Bilingualism and Biculturalism
  1969 *The Cultural Contributions of Other Ethnic Groups.* Ottawa: Queen's Printer.
Segalman, R.
  1967 "Jewish Identity Scales: A Report." *Jewish Social Studies* 29: 92-111.
Stone, G.P.
  1962 "Appearance and the Self," in Arnold M. Rose (ed.) *Human Behavior and Social Processes.* Boston: Houghton Mifflin.
Vallee, F.G.
  1969 "Regionalism and Ethnicity: The French-Canadian Case." Pp. 19-25 in Card (ed.) *Perspectives on Regions and Regionalism.* Edmonton: University of Alberta Press.
Vallee, F.G. and J. DeVries
  1975 *Data Book for the Conference on Individual, Language and Society.* Ottawa: The Canada Council.
Winch, R.F.
  1962 *Identification and its Familial Determinants.* Indianapolis: Bobbs-Merrill.

PART ONE

Perspectives on Ethnic Pluralism

PART ONE

Perspectives on Ethnic Pluralism

The approach to ethnic studies in Canada is crucial for an understanding of an industrial society which has evolved over the centuries in the shadow of three major national forces–the French, the British, and the Americans. To what extent has Canada been moulded by the three major groups, and to what extent do a majority of Canada's citizens conform to any one of these groups? To what extent has a new national identity emerged which is distinctly Canadian? We propose in this volume, as the title suggests, that Canada is a pluralist society, made up of a multitude of historical influences, regional patterns, and ethnic collectivities. It is a mosaic of many histories, regions, cultures, ideologies, and communities. A diversity of perspectives must be used to comprehend and describe the many structures.

Some perspectives to consider include: the influence of technology on minority groups; theories about how Canadian society is changing, and the future of ethnicity; and the manner in which the structures of power and ethnic collectivities are being designed. In Part One, three authors address themselves to these issues.

Technology and Ethnicity
The technological society tends to bring groups together for the purpose of mass production. Industry attracts people to jobs which are usually more numerous in cities. It is logical that persons of a variety of ethnic backgrounds will be drawn together to find work. Will they be integrated into the larger society? How will this major diversionary force of technology affect maintenance of ethnicity? In the first essay, Professor Isajiw addresses himself to the influence of technology on ethnicity.

The technological society is also based on power systems and stratified status relationships. Where will minorities of lower status find themselves in these social structures, and how will it affect their relationships? Olga is a member of a minority entrance status group, a person who left her country to live in an advanced technological society where Alice and Pierre have lived for a long time. Canada is a wonderland of opportunities–or is it? What will be the relationship between Olga and Alice? How will these two people get along together? Has the majority-minority situation been so structured that she will indeed be accepted as an equal, or will the power structures and the status systems militate against her opportunity to compete fairly? The majority-minority atmosphere Isajiw creates is optimistic: the Canadian wonderland could indeed be what it appears to be; there may be a place for Olga. It looks like she will be invited to the birthday party–but was she only invited to wash the dishes?

Theoretical Perspectives on Pluralism
Giant industrial technological societies, such as Canada, stimulate change and tend to engulf ethnic enclaves into a mainstream nationalism. What happens to new immigrants who enter Canada? Do they assimilate into the melting pot? Some groups may wish to assimilate and may be permitted to do so; others may wish to assimilate but the majority will not accept them; other minorities may resist assimilation, and seek to maintain their distinctive identity; and still others may wish to relate to the larger society, but are only in part willing to change and adjust their culture and institutions. The potential for conflict in an ethnic mosaic is evident when minorities wish to assimilate but are not given equal opportunities to do so. Conflict is also evident when other minorities attempt to maintain their distinct identity in a society unable to allow such aspirations.

William Newman provides a review of the potential perspectives available in a discussion of ethnic relations. In addition to the three theories summarized by Gordon (1964) (assimilation, amalgamation, and pluralism), Newman includes the approaches of Milton Gordon and Glazer and Moynihan. Gordon provides the context within which we can begin to analyze the multidimensional aspects of stratification. He suggests that assimilation will tend to take place within the economic, political, and educational institutions, but that pluralism may be maintained in religious, family, and recreational institutions. However, Glazer and Moynihan point (beyond the melting pot) to a modified pluralism. Newman views the five theories employed in the past as depictions of a linear process through which different groups move, and he wishes to challenge this assumption. Thus, he feels it necessary to offer an alternative theory of pluralism which 1) will not presume unilinearity, and 2) will not assume that all groups seek the same type of assimilation or pluralism.

The failure to understand intergroup relations in structural terms has been one of the most serious weaknesses of assimilation theory. Newman expounds on some structural postulates on which pluralist theories agree: 1) ethnic diversity is a basic structural aspect of most societies; 2) these relationships derive from social stratification; and 3) group differentiation and social stratification are neither strange nor non-normative. These postulates prepare the ground for a perspective of ethnic relations as a form of social conflict. Thus, most societies have at least some ethnic diversification, the resulting groups will be concentrated in lower or higher strata, and the potential for competition and conflict will be a natural result. The task within the conflict perspective is to study the structures of Canadian society, to examine the stratification and institutional system, and to explore where within the system ethnic groups are located.

Group Structures and Ethnic Relationships

Whereas Isajiw discusses majority-minority relations in general theoretical terms, and Newman describes macro-theories of the processes and changes of social structures, Breton examines the social structures of some of these groups, and the social relationships that they tend to perpetuate. Newman already suggested that a diversity of ethnic structures will create potential for conflict, and Breton continues this discussion by examining some of the existing alternative structures and relationships.

Breton's presentation focuses on three dimensions of the structure of relationship between ethnic collectivities: 1) the different types of ethnic organization; 2) the conditions under which people form groups on an ethnic basis; and 3) the institutions which emerge to accommodate this ethnic diversity.

To examine ethnic organization, Breton discusses ethnic segmentation and ethnic heterogeneity. All societies have, within their boundaries, sub-societies or sub-cultures of people with unique social characteristics, which distinguish them and sometimes set them apart. These social collectivities form the different patterns of the ethnic mosaic in Canada. The social boundaries of some of these groups are more distinct than others, and some are also more effective than others in the maintenance of these collectivities. Heterogeneity deals with the extent to which an individual is able to identify with a society that is relatively homogeneous or heterogeneous. The industrial technological society tends to create diversity and heterogeneity, where persons cannot always respond as whole persons, but must begin to perform a variety of roles in a variety of social situations. In such situations the person's identity tends to become fragmented.

If the industrial society tends to fragment relationships, then to what extent and in what form can ethnicity be a basis for social organization and integration? How social relationships are structured is the second dimension explored by Breton. This discussion raises the question of whether belonging to an ethnic ingroup is an asset or a liability in economic, political, social, or psychic terms. Some may be ambivalent about their ethnic identity, while others may have little choice in the matter, as is the case with racial groups.

How, then, do various groups organize to act? Breton discusses the Québécois independence movement, the multiculturalism movement, and the "red power" movement as illustrations of three sets of social groupings organized on an ethnic basis for social action. This volume will also include studies of other ethnic groups and the diversity of social organization and social action in which they are involved. What role does ethnicity play in the attitudes and behaviour of Canadians? Is Canada indeed a dynamic ethnic mosaic, and will it continue to be a diversified society with a variety of enclaves?

1

Olga in Wonderland: Ethnicity in a Technological Society

Wsevolod W. Isajiw*

The question of the relationship of technology to ethnicity has been raised in social scientific literature primarily in regard to the developing countries of Africa and Asia. As these countries have been going through the process of modernization, a basic issue has been the introduction of technology into traditional ethnic societies. The point of interest has been how these societies adapt to the importation of technological culture. The question I want to raise concerns ethnic groups in North American societies, particularly in Canada. My basic issue is not the introduction of technology into traditional ethnic societies, but the reverse, that is, the process by which ethnic groups are introduced into, and remain part of, technological societies.

"Ethnic group" can be defined as a group of people who share a distinct culture, or as descendants of such people who identify themselves, and/ or are identified by others, as belonging to the same group (Isajiw, 1974). This definition suggests two types of ethnicity. The first type concerns the people who share a distinct culture, i.e., people who have gone through the primary process of socialization in their culture and no other. ("Culture" is used here in the anthropological sense of the word, meaning a totality of behaviour patterns.) Ethnicity, in this sense, can be said to include both what Robert Redfield has called the "little tradition" and the "great tradition." The great tradition is the culture of the unreflective many (Redfield, 1960:41-42). The former includes the so-called "fine" arts–poetry, music, scholarly thought, manners, etc.; the latter includes the folk arts, the folklore, and the folkways. Ethnic groups today contain both traditions, though not necessarily in identical proportions. It

* Wsevolod W. Isajiw is Associate Professor of Sociology, University of Toronto, Ontario.

29

is the little tradition, however, that makes the ethnic group distinct; the great tradition is part of this distinctiveness only inasmuch as it articulates the elements of the little tradition.

The second type of ethnicity refers to people who are descendants of the first type of ethnic group, but who have gone through the primary process of socialization in a different culture. In a limited way, some of these people might have gone through a partial process of socialization in some aspects of their ancestral culture, but the main link that binds them to the ancestral group is not the sharing of its culture; rather, it is a feeling of identity with them. This identity may take various forms, but it is at the root of this type of ethnicity.

I will also speak of Olga and Alice; the old Olga and the new Olga. Olga is my name for the non-British and non-Quebec French ethnic groups in Canada. Some of the things said about these groups, however, will also be applicable to the Quebec French. Alice represents the Angloceltic groups. Admittedly, there are dangers in speaking about these groups in a univocal manner. But my intention here is not to describe any of them in detail; rather, it is to capture several processes which I think all of the groups have been going through.

The old Olga represents ethnic groups of the first type. She is either the ethnic first generation, i.e., the immigrants who have come to Canada as adults; or, she is the old generation in those groups who have lived in the rather isolated manner of community life, and in so doing have preserved their ethnic institutions. Groups in rural settlements such as the Indians on reserves, the Hutterites, Ukrainians, and others, and perhaps some settlements of the French outside Quebec, would be included in this ethnic type. The new Olga represents ethnicity of the second type, particularly involving the third, and to some extent the second, generations. However, later generations may also be included. Again, these are not necessarily only the generations of people whose grandparents or parents were immigrants; they are also the generations whose ancestors lived in comparatively isolated ethnic community life, but who have been immersed in the larger society.

It is my contention that on the one hand technology and the technological culture bring ethnic groups together; yet on the other hand, and in an indirect way, they contribute to the persistence and perpetuation of ethnicity in North American societies.

Technology and Technological Culture as Integrating Factors
In his classic definition of plural societies, Furnivall states that the market-place is what brings ethnic groups together (1939). The social market-place, according to him, is the only factor which works to integrate ethnic groups into one society. I am not implying that technology is the only influence in our society, but technological culture and institutions, more than any other, have been integrating ethnic groups into the society

30

at large. Technology has been doing this in industry and related occupations; technological culture does this by means of values and patterns into which ethnic groups assimilate. The role which societal educational institutions play in regard to the ethnic groups is essentially related to both industry and technological value-patterns.

It is probably trite by now to say that industry is a great mixer of people. As Everett Hughes has pointed out, in no considerable industrial region of the world has an indigenous population supplied the whole working force (1952). It should be emphasized, however, that bringing people of different ethnic backgrounds together, and integrating them into societies via industrial institutions, has not meant integration of all ethnic groups into society on an equal basis. On the average, some groups have come to occupy better positions in the socio-economic structure than others. Typical examples are occupational domains in which different ethnic groups have concentrated in industries, or in related institutions, on different levels. It has been in this fashion that the influence of industry and its related institutions has been two-sided. On the one hand, they have served as avenues of social mobility, and are thereby a means of integrating ethnic groups into society at large. On the other hand, they have contributed to the development and persistence of inequalities among ethnic groups, resulting in a system of ethnic stratification.

What I want to discuss in more detail, however, is the technological culture–rather than industry itself–and its relation to ethnicity. Why focus on technological culture? Because it is something that Canadian ethnic groups seem to share more than anything else. The basic issue here is that of cultural assimilation. If ethnic groups assimilate, what do they assimilate into? Which ethnic features do they drop, and which do they retain? The process of assimilation has not yet been studied in enough detail. The assumption often made is that there is one unified body of Angloceltic culture into which immigrants assimilate, and which, except for Quebec, integrates the members of society. However, this assumption is misleading. Contemporary Canadian culture involves at least seven layers: 1) the technological culture, i.e., a culture which is common to all modern industrial societies, and which puts a premium on standardization and homogeneity; 2) the Angloceltic culture, which is rooted in Protestantism and the British historical experience, and which has imprinted itself on Canadian national institutions; 3) the Quebec French culture; 4) other ethnic subcultures; 5) regional subcultures which represent modifications of the Angloceltic culture; 6) popular subculture, i.e., the current in-patterns of relatively short duration which are characterized by successive change; and 7) counterculture, i.e., patterns developing as a result of rebellion against all the other layers of culture, and centring around the use of socially forbidden drugs, radical political and social ideals, religious ideals taken from other, radically different cultures, and the like.

To what extent all these cultural layers work together, and to what extent they are contradictory and conflicting, is an interesting empirical question. It appears, however, that the layer of culture which is shared more widely than any other by communities and individuals in our society is that of the technological culture. Central to this culture is the value placed on access to, and use of, the products of technology, and on contact with people who have such access and use. This is the modern value of success; it does not, however, necessarily imply any elements of the Protestant ethic. Although there are variations among ethnic groups in the emphasis placed on this value, and variations in the way it is legitimized, it appears to be quite widely accepted, especially among the consecutive ethnic generations (Maykovich, 1975).

I repeat, of all the layers of culture, it is the technological culture that is most readily accepted and shared by ethnic groups. The common language itself is learned and used less as a symbol of identity with society as a whole than as a practical means of attaining the products of the technological culture.

Persistence of Ethnicity
In spite of the strong acculturation process, ethnicity has persisted in North America. This is not something that has to do only with the first ethnic generation, the old Olga, although every year there are probably between 15 and 20 per cent of the total Canadian population who represent the first ethnic generation (Kalbach and McVey, 1971:133). Persistence of ethnicity is an important matter for the new Olga. Many writers have noted revivals of ethnicity, or a "new ethnicity," among those ethnic generations who presumably have been (or should have been) assimilated (Greeley, 1974, 1975; Novak, 1971; Glazer and Moynihan, 1975; Dashefsky, 1972; Stein and Hill, 1973). We do not know the numbers or proportions of those among the second, third, or consecutive generations who have retained or regained ethnic identity. Goering's recent study gives support to the third generation return hypothesis (1971). O'Bryan et al's (1975) study showed that in a Canadian national sample, on the average, over 40 per cent of the second, and over 30 per cent of the third generation identified themselves as ethnic or hyphenated ethnic Canadians. Richmond's (1974) study showed that in the third generation from 54 to 58 per cent, and in the second generation 68 per cent of the sample, identified themselves as ethnic or hyphenated ethnic Canadians. Whether these are adequate measures of ethnic persistence is doubtful. As Driedger (1975) has pointed out, the measure of ethnic identification may vary according to the criterion used to measure it.

Another way of measuring retention (or rediscovery) of ethnicity in the consecutive generations is to ascertain the involvement of these generations in ethnic organizational activities, such as the civil rights movements, the multiculturalism movement, or activities which emphasize creative development of elements of ethnic cultures. Here the measure is not the numbers of people involved, but the intensity of activity undertaken and the support, moral or financial, given by other members and groups in the ethnic community. There do not seem to be any systematic studies of these activities. A review of the multicultural grants given by the federal government indicates that there are quite a number of such organizations made up of young people, and that the activities of these groups, to a large extent, are aimed at society at large in order to gain public recognition of their demands or of their ethnic cultures.

My conclusion is that since this re-emergence of ethnicity has been taking place among most, if not all, ethnic groups in Canada and the United States, institutions within ethnic groups alone, such as ethnic schools, or the ethnic family socialization process, are insufficient to account for this phenomenon. There must be factors operating in society at large that produce this form of ethnic persistence.

What are these factors? A number of commentators have suggested answers to this question. Michael Novak (1971) notes that an increasing ethnic consciousness among the "white ethnics" is related to their feelings of being rejected by the establishment; this has been previously identified by Milton Gordon (1964) as cultural assimilation without structural assimilation. J. Goering (1971) believes that the re-emergence of ethnicity is related to a growing scepticism about the "American dream," and resentment of unattained promises. Ethnic consciousness is seen by him as being stimulated by a sense of threat from (or jealousy of) such groups as the Blacks, who are seen as undeserving of the privileges they are claiming. Hence, the third generation returns to ethnicity as the basis for organizing discontent and racial confrontation. Similarly, Daniel Bell (1975:171) states that the upsurge of ethnicity "is best understood *not* as a primordial phenomenon in which deeply held identities have to re-emerge, but as a strategic choice by individuals who, in other circumstances, would choose other group membership as a means of gaining some power and privilege."

It is quite probable that a combination of these things is accountable for the persistence or rediscovery of ethnicity. To these I would add another factor: occupational competition among socially mobile members of ethnic groups. Recent analysis of occupational mobility among Canadian ethnic groups indicates that there has been a tendency toward equalization of occupational distributions between a number of ethnic groups (Reitz, 1978). Occupational mobility, especially on the higher occupational levels, is connected with increased competition. Alongside the criterion of performance, intensified competition tends to bring into awareness ascriptive characteristics of the competing parties. And one of the most common ascriptive characteristics is ethnic background. Thus, intensified occupational mobility, or, in general, increased social mobility, may evoke increased awareness of ethnicity and rediscovery of ethnic identity.

To say, however, with Daniel Bell (1975), that rediscovery or persistence of ethnic identity is purely a rational strategic choice in a political game, or that it is nothing but a rational basis for organizing political confrontation, is misleading. It fails to take into account much of the nature of the phenomenon. The phenomenon of ethnic persistence has very important affective dimensions, dimensions which cannot be explained on purely rational grounds. Ethnic group identification involves a positive affective orientation. As Rose and Rose (1965) have put it: "It involves not only a recognition that because of one's ancestry one is a member of a racial or religious group, and a recognition that the majority group defines one as belonging to that racial or religious group; it also involves a positive desire to identify oneself as a member of a group and a feeling of pleasure when one does so (1965:247; Dashefsky, 1976:8)." To explain the persistence of this desire in any sector of our modern society, one should go back to the technological culture.

Technological Culture and Ethnic Identity

What is important to understand about ethnicity is that it has a time dimension. Ethnicity connects with patterns of life which go back very far into history, and perhaps even into prehistory. André Varagnac (1948) in his perceptive work on the traditional civilization and the style of life, has suggested that underneath the aristocratic or bourgeois culture of the higher classes, underneath the refined culture of the priests and the scientists, there always existed a much older tradition which reached back into protohistory, into the neolithic age, and which, according to him, remained virtually unbroken up to the 1870s, when for the first time the scientific and industrial revolution began to seriously affect the everyday life and work of rural people. Peasant society, Varagnac tells us, has preserved through the ages cultural traits which are extremely old. These traits are not isolated remnants of past cultures, but functioned as a living whole in Europe as late as the last century (Stark, 1953). Today the "old ethnicity," i.e., the rural, total, ethnic culture–the "little tradition"–has simply been disappearing within the technological culture; in North America, in fact, it has already disappeared as a unified whole.

As unified ways of life, the rural ethnic culture and the technological culture are antithetical in their essential features. Technological culture is componential; reality is seen as made up of units which, at least potentially, can be broken down into sub-units and rearranged. Rural ethnic culture is wholistic; reality tends to be seen in organic terms as something given and unalterable. Technological culture is made up of man-made objects, manipulated and manipulatable by tentative, rational techniques. Ethnic rural culture is a world of natural, living entities, related to by means of ritual or long established ways. Technological culture tends to be impersonal; rural ethnic culture is always personal. Finally, technological culture is informed by a pragmatically rational form of thought, whereas ethnic culture is informed by religion and belief.

The fact is that, in the New World, the old Olga has thrown herself eagerly into the technological wonderland, picking up toy after toy as she has been moving up the wonderland's social-status escalator. Hence, to-day, in North American societies, ethnic cultural traits do not form a way of life and do not function as a whole anymore.

Yet whatever metamorphoses they might have gone through, many of the traits which have been extracted from the "little tradition," and re-tained by the younger ethnic generations, are not mere carryovers, but actually have a life in connection with and in relation to the technological culture. If we examine those ethnic patterns to which second or third generations go back, they seem to be those which link up with the remote ethnic past. Such are the rituals which many persons or families practise in relation to the calendar, to the seasons of the year, to the events in one's life cycle, to marriage ceremonies, and to burial ceremonies. All these are rituals which kept ancestors in contact with nature. The same can be said of the ethnic dances, the art objects, and the crafts: their artistic motifs go back to origins lost in history. On the more reflective level, the interests of the younger ethnic generations hearken back to the first rural settlers, the *habitants* the archaeological discoveries in Israel, the tribal life-styles in Africa, the ancient mythology of the Inuit, etc.

It is this link with the past that is central to our understanding of the persistence of ethnicity within technological society. Whatever symbolic meanings these extracted ethnic patterns may or may not have to those who are involved in them today, they share one thing: feelings of identity. Ethnic patterns, even if completely torn out of their original social and cultural context, become symbols of an individual's roots. Such symbols are necessary for the support of a person's identity. Hence, in any search for identity, ethnicity becomes relevant because through its ancestral time dimension a person can, at least symbolically, experience belonging.

Rather than provide strong feelings of identity, the technological cul-ture, on the contrary, tends to foster anonymity and impersonal social relationships. As Peter Berger (1973:31-33) has pointed out, the tech-nological process, at the very least, introduces a dichotomy into the individual's consciousness of others, who are seen as both concrete func-tionaries, and anonymous substitutable functionaires. Berger further states that this consciousness of others carries over into the experience of oneself and a process of self-anonymization occurs, by which it becomes easier for an individual to think of himself in terms of his external roles–as a worker, professor, manager–rather than in terms of the con-crete qualities of his personality.

Many events and processes in society, such as strikes, ideological movements, and cultic movements, can be seen as defensive reactions, both collective and individual, against the anonymization pressures of the technological culture. As such, they represent a search for identity

(Klapp, 1969). Hence it can be said that in an indirect way, the techno-logical culture heightens identity needs and creates identity search. Ethnic rediscoveries or "new ethnicity" is one significant direction that this search takes.

As previously stated, the "new ethnicity" is not a total culture: it is a phenomenon of identification with selected ethnic cultural patterns. There are persons who have gone through the basic process of socializa-tion, not in the culture of their ancestors, who have experienced intergen-erational social mobility within the larger society, but whose feeling of identity with their ancestral group has actually increased rather than de-creased. The turn to the past is symbolic. Some elements of the heritage come to be known, practised, or glorified. What is significant is that there is a process of selecting items, however few, from the cultural past—pieces of ethnic folk art, folk dances, music, a partial use of language, knowledge of some aspects of the group's history—which become symbols of ethnic identity (Isajiw, 1975). The "new ethnicity" is ethnicity which has adapted itself to the technological culture. As an identity phenomenon it complements the technological culture by, as it were, filling in the gaps, and the needs created by it.

Further, ethnicity is the process of a search for identity of both the minority and the majority. But the search takes different forms in the two types of groups. In the majority group, it takes the form of nationalism. Like the new ethnicity, nationalism involves a symbolic turn to the past. But the heritage that is glorified, in Canada and the United States, is part of the Angloceltic background and history. There is probably a relation-ship between heightened nationalism and "ethnic rediscoveries," i.e., tendencies in support of Canadian or American identity also produce ten-dencies supporting ethnic identities and vice versa.

Privatization and De-privatization of Ethnicity

There is another way in which ethnicity has emerged in the technological society. I have already mentioned that the technological process produces a dichotomy in social relationships, but this dichotomy goes further: it produces a type of pluralism which I think is at the basis of ethnic plural-ism in our society. This pluralism derives from the dichotomy of private and public spheres. In modern society, the individual is typically con-scious of a sharp division between the world of his private life, and the world of large public institutions to which he relates in a variety of seg-mented roles. By the word "public" I do not mean "governmental," but "societal," pertaining to society as a whole.

Ethnicity in North American societies has come to be relegated to the private sphere, the sphere defined by society as that formed by the indi-vidual's own choices, wishes, and relations, with which society presuma-bly does not have to be concerned. The problem is that ethnicity is not simply a matter of individual choice; it is a matter of ancestry, and a matter of membership and belonging. In other words, ethnicity is a matter of community. In the technological society, however, community itself becomes a matter of the private sphere. The technological society has no one *societal* community; rather, it has many private communities.

To say that ethnic community has become a matter of the private sphere is not to say that all ethnic communities are removed from the public sphere to the same degree. If we look at society as if it were a circle with a centre and a periphery, the centre being the public sphere, then some ethnic communities are closer to the centre and others closer to the periphery. To a large extent, this is a question of power and influence in society. That is, the more power an ethnic group has in society, the closer it will be to the public sphere. Alice's home is closer to the centre; Olga's home is closer to the periphery. The old Olga did not mind this too much for her privatization of ethnicity was satisfying, and she often preferred to live in a segregated manner. The new Olga, however, does not seem to be happy with this arrangement. The new Olga is intent on bringing ethnicity out of the private sphere and into the public sphere. The multiculturalism movement, as a political movement, seeks public recognition for ethnic groups as part of the total society. Hence, what the ethnic rediscoverers are doing, in effect, is attempting to bring community itself out of the private sphere. Theoretically, they wish to establish a societal community for all, a community in which all ethnicities participate equally and are recognized as equal members. The ideology set forth by the proponents of multiculturalism takes seriously the idea of unity in diversity; it articulates the notion that people are different even though they are alike. But the differences are not intended to mean that some are superior and others inferior. The ideology of multiculturalism is not related to the old nationalistic idea of superiority of one's own culture. On the contrary, it is a pluralist ideology where all cultural differences are seen as good, and all are to be respected. To be human is to be different (Canada, 1971; Yuzyk, 1970; Krawchenko, 1970).

The new Olga wants the enchanted societal circle rearranged so that the centre is closer to the periphery; to achieve this she has exerted pressures on the governmental institutions. However, her success depends on whether Alice will co-operate in this endeavour.

References

Bell, D.
   1975   "Ethnicity and Social Change," in *Ethnicity, Theory and Experience*. N. Glazer and D.P. Moynihan (eds.). Cambridge: Harvard University Press.

Berger, P.
1973 *The Homeless Mind, Modernization and Consciousness.* New York: Random House.
Dashefsky, A.
1972 "And the Search Goes On: The Meaning of Religio-ethnic Identity and Identification." *Sociological Analysis* 33:239-45.
Dashefsky, A. (Ed.)
1976 *Ethnic Identity and Society.* Chicago: Rand McNally.
Driedger, L.
1975 "In Search of Cultural Identity Factors: A Comparison of Ethnic Students." *The Canadian Review of Sociology and Anthropology* 12:150-162.
Furnivall, J.S.
1939 *Netherlands India: A Study of Plural Economy.* Cambridge: Cambridge University Press.
Glazer, N. and D.P. Moynihan (eds.)
1975 *Ethnicity, Theory and Experience.* Cambridge: Harvard University Press.
Goering, J.M.
1971 "The Emergence of Ethnic Interests: A Case of Serendipity." *Social Forces* 49:379-84.
Gordon, M.
1964 *Assimilation in American Life.* New York: Oxford University Press.
Government of Canada
1971 Federal Government's Response to Book IV of the *Report of the Royal Commission on Bilingualism and Biculturalism.* Document tabled in the House of Commons on October 8 by the Prime Minister. Ottawa: Queen's Printer, pp. 8580-8581.
Greeley, A.M.
1974 *Ethnicity in the United States, A Preliminary Reconnaissance.* /New York: John Wiley and Sons.
Greeley, A.M.
1975 *Why Can't They Be Like Us? America's White Ethnic Groups.* New York: E.P Dutton and Co., Inc.
Hughes, E.C., and H.M. Hughes
1952 *Where People Meet: Racial and Ethnic Frontiers.* Glencoe, Illinois: Free Press.
Isajiw, W.
1974 "Definitions of Ethnicity." *Ethnicity* 1:111-124.
Isajiw, W.
1975 "The Process of Maintenance of Ethnic Identity: The Canadian Context," in *Sounds Canadian, Languages and Cultures in Multi-Ethnic Society.* Toronto: Peter Martin Associates.

Kalbach, W.E. and W.W. McVey
1971 *The Demographic Bases of Canadian Society.* Toronto: McGraw-Hill Co. of Canada, Ltd.

Klapp, O.E.
1969 *Collective Search for Identity.* New York: Holt, Rinehart and Winston.

Krawchenko, B.
1970 "Toward a Development of Multi-Culturalism," in *Multi-Culturalism for Canada.* Report of the Conference at University of Alberta.

Maykovich, M.K.
1975 "Ethnic Variation in Success Value," in *Socialization and Values in Canadian Society,* Vol. II. R.M. Pike and E. Zureik (eds.). Toronto: McClelland and Stewart, Ltd. Carleton Library No. 85, 158-179.

Novak, M.
1971 *The Rise of the Unmeltable Ethnics.* New York: Macmillan and Co. Inc.

O'Bryan, K.G., J.G. Reitz and O. Kuplowska
1975 *Non-Official Languages, A Study in Canadian Multi-Culturalism.* Ottawa: Ministry Responsible for Multi-Culturalism.

Redfield, R.
1960 *The Little Community and Peasant Society and Culture.* Chicago: University of Chicago Press, Phoenix Books.

Reitz, J.G.
1978 *Urban Ethnic Communities.* Toronto: McGraw-Hill Ryerson. In preparation.

Richmond, A.
1974 "Language, Ethnicity and the Problem of Identity in a Canadian Metropolis." *Ethnicity* 1:175-206.

Rose, A., and C.B. Rose
1965 *Minority Problems.* New York: Harper and Row.

Stark, W.
1953 "Peasant Society and the Origins of Romantic Love." *Sociological Review* I (New Series).

Stein, H.F. and R.F. Hill
1973 "The New Ethnicity and the White Ethnic in the United States." *Canadian Review of Studies in Nationalism* 1:81-105.

Varagnac, A.
1948 *Civilisation Traditionelle et Genre de Vie.* Paris: Albin Michel.

Yuzyk, P.
1970 "True Canadian Identity–Multi-Culturalism and the Emerging New Factor in the Emerging New Canada," in *Multi-Culturalism For Canada.* Report of the Conference at University of Alberta.

2

Theoretical Perspectives for the Analysis of Social Pluralism
William M. Newman*

The Ethnic Studies Revival

Science, like most everything else in society, is subject to trends and fads. The social scientific community today is witnessing a revival of interest in the area of study variously called intergroup relations, majority-minority relationships, and ethnic studies. This trend is itself an inherently interesting social phenomenon. Why such a revival? and why such a revival at this particular time? are important questions for a sociology of science and, more so, a sociology of knowledge. Yet my concern here is not so much with the fact of this revival but with its consequences for the sociology of intergroup relations.

Upon close inspection, the current revival of interest in ethnic group studies appears to be something more than just that. It is not simply a rekindling of intellectual interest, but a reformation of the basic conceptual and theoretical tools with which the interactions of diverse social groups, and the societies in which they dwell, are understood. We are beginning to see the emergence of what Kuhn (1962) for the sciences generally, and Friedrichs (1970) for sociology in particular, have called a new "paradigm." The current revival of ethnic studies has signalled the formation of a fundamentally new perspective from which research and theory about intergroup relations may be conducted.

Long before the important contributions of Kuhn and Friedrichs, Karl Mannheim provided some essential insights into the processes of intellectual change in societies. Mannheim (1928, 1929) suggests that idea systems change in relation to one another. Specifically, new ideas and concepts arise out of competition with old ones. These basic lessons imply

*William M. Newman is Associate Professor of Sociology, University of Connecticut, Storrs.

that even in science, the excesses of the past are likely to be replaced by the excesses of the future. Under normal circumstances it is not so much that our understanding of social reality becomes better or more finely tuned, but simply different from what it was. It is my purpose here to suggest that perhaps an awareness of these tendencies may allow us to prevent them.

Even a cursory review of the literature shows that there exists today a confrontation between two powerful theoretical perspectives for the analysis of ethnic group relations. Moreover, it is clear that the perspective employed may have consequences not only for social theory but also for social policies regarding ethnic groups (for a summary of these debates see Hraba and Richards, 1975). I am referring, of course, to the long-established theory of assimilation, and the recently emergent theories of social pluralism. While I, too, have criticized the predominance of the assimilation model (Newman 1973), I am fearful that the social sciences may totally discard a one-sided theory of assimilation and replace it with an equally one-sided pluralist view. The greater challenge, it seems to me, lies in attempting to draw upon the insights of both of these perspectives.

The creation of what van den Berghe (1967), Schermerhorn (1970), and I (1973), among others, have called a "dialectical" perspective is not a simple task. On the one hand, we must provide some corrective measures for assimilation theory as we have traditionally known it. On the other hand, different varieties of pluralist theory abound in our literature. Some important issues that distinguish one brand of pluralist theory from the next must be resolved. This essay shall address these two issues: first, what correctives may be applied to the theory of ethnic assimilation? and second, which avenue of pluralist theory seems most fruitful? However, before addressing these issues, it will be useful to review the several theoretical perspectives that have led us to the present juncture.

Theories in Retrospect
No one has yet provided a definitive analysis of the historical trends in the theory of intergroup relations. Even if such a history were available, it is likely that each generation would reinterpret and rewrite it from its own vantage point. From my perspective, it seems reasonable to distinguish seven major contributions to the theory of intergroup relations. As Milton Gordon has shown (1964), the first quarter of the twentieth century witnessed the emergence of three distinct social doctrines about ethnic pluralism in the United States. I refer, of course, to the notions of assimilation, amalgamation, and cultural pluralism. Each of these doctrines attempted to interpret the meaning of mass immigration for American society, and each in turn has had an impact upon our social scientific thinking about socially pluralistic societies.

The doctrine of assimilation contends that a cultural consensus will be obtained through the absorption of minority groups into the majority group. In the American case, this has been expressed as "anglo-conformity." While contemporary assimilation theorists argue that social power and economic relationships account for this process when it occurs, the original Social Darwinist doctrine of assimilation relied upon the assertion that the dominant group's culture is socially superior. Much research has demonstrated that assimilative processes do occur in many societies. Yet the assumption that ultimately minority cultures disappear has not been empirically validated. Moreover, the Black Power movement, the "red power" movement, and the white ethnic revivals of the 1970s have led social scientists to reject the idea that cultural assimilation is cumulative and linear. Rather, there is a growing perception that processes of intergroup alliance and coalition, and fluctuating assimilative and divergent relations between groups are normal. It is no longer possible to understand group differences as temporary lapses in an unbending route to assimilation.

The doctrine of amalgamation, or "the melting pot," provided a slightly different, though still basically Social Darwinist, set of predictions. Rather than contending that the majority culture is superior, the "melting pot" idea stipulates that all ethnic cultures have desirable elements. The new social amalgam is said to result from a selective merging of the superior traits of the various ethnic cultures that contribute to it. As a social theory, the idea of amalgamation has been fruitfully employed by anthropologists to explain events in such places as Trinidad and Brazil. Amalgamation has also been the focus of sociological analyses of both Mexico and Hawaii. It is typically argued that amalgamation is both a biological and cultural consequence of trading and economic alliances between peoples. Yet few contemporary theorists would argue that amalgamation is a central process in modern, socially pluralistic, nation states. While one can point to isolated examples of amalgamation even in the United States (such as Spanish Harlem in New York City), it is not a characteristic process.

A third doctrine, expressed most eloquently by the late Horace Kallen (1915, 1924), is that of cultural pluralism. Yet it is important to realize that Kallen's notion of cultural pluralism—a pluralism in which everyone lives "happily every after" in peaceful coexistence—is a Utopian dream, far removed from the realistic power-conflict theories emerging today. Kallen argued that social diversity has been an inherent aspect of American society from its beginning. His doctrine of cultural pluralism was intended to combat the doctrine of assimilation and to relieve the threat that a white-Protestant-dominated America saw in the immigrant cultures.

These three ideas, assimilation, amalgamation, and cultural pluralism, provided alternative perspectives from which both society and social science could interpret the history of the United States and other nations. In modern sociology, assimilation theory and modifications of it, have prevailed. There are three such modifications that are worthy of mention: the work of Robert Park, of Milton Gordon, and of Nathan Glazer and Patrick Moynihan.

The earliest scientific approach for which one can identify a clear tradition of authorship is the so-called Park-Wirth school of race relations. Robert Park's (Hughes et al., eds., 1950) theory of a race-relations cycle had a powerful effect upon other Chicago-based sociologists, such as Louis Wirth (1928) and W.I. Thomas (1904, with Zanecki 1918). Similarly, the writings of E. Franklin Frazier (1947, 1949, 1957) and Lloyd Warner (with Srole 1945) may be seen as a dialogue with, though not a validation of, Park's theory. Park argues that all intergroup relations undergo four evolutionary phases: contact, conflict, accommodation, and assimilation. As Stanford Lyman (1973) has shown, Park's own students readily demonstrated the fallacy of assuming that assimilation was inevitable. Today both Park's evolutionism and the Social Darwinism on which it is based are largely rejected. While Park's four phases have not been empirically validated, his work is nonetheless important because of the research to which it gave impetus.

Milton Gordon's work, *Assimilation in American Life* (1964), was the first important conceptual advance in the theory of assimilation in the contemporary period. He neither adopts Park's cyclical view nor treats assimilation as a simple unitary process. Rather, he posits four distinct types of assimilation. His variables are: cultural assimilation (adoption of dominant group culture, values, and life-style); structural assimilation (entrance into dominant group institutions, clubs, and cliques); amalgamation (defined and measured by intermarriage rates); and identificational assimilation (minority group members think of themselves as American, Canadian, Mexican, etc.). In addition to these four types of assimilation, he argues that assimilation may be measured by the absence of three phenomena: prejudice, discrimination, 'and power or value conflicts between groups.

Gordon's ideas, more than any other recent work, have had a significant impact upon empirical research. Numerous studies have demonstrated the utility of his assimilation variables. Yet the two most important theoretical propositions that emerge from Gordon's work have not been validated. First, the idea that all groups enter a linear and cumulative process of cultural assimilation has been shattered by ethnic consciousness and even separatist movements in the United States, Canada, Ireland, Southeast Asia, Africa, and elsewhere. Second, the contention that assimilation culminates through the onset of structural assimilation has not been validated. As I have argued in *American Pluralism* (1973), the most dramatic cases of minority social mobility in the United States appear to have been facilitated through the creation of minority-group-controlled parallel structures, not through structural assimilation. While

Gordon's work provides empirically useful concepts, it suffers from the erroneous assumption that total assimilation inevitably occurs.

There were of course numerous studies over the years, especially in the area of American race relations, that depicted not assimilation but continuing intergroup conflict. Among the better known studies of this type are Dollard's *Caste and Class in a Southern Town* (1937), Myrdal's *An American Dilemma* (1944), and Killian and Grigg's *Racial Crisis in America* (1964). Yet Glazer and Moynihan's *Beyond the Melting Pot* (1963), rev. 1970) was the first major study to eschew a strict assimilationist approach for the analysis of white immigrant ethnic groups. In that work, it is argued that ethnicity must be understood not as a residue of the period of mass immigration, but as a "new social form." While Glazer and Moynihan refrain from predicting a point of complete assimilation, they do emphasize ethnic group political organization as the primary mechanism of both assimilation and social mobility. Moreover, as they lament in the second edition of *Beyond the Melting Pot*, the original study did argue that ethnicity would disappear as a significant social variable once the process of political, and therefore economic, assimilation had taken place.

It is clear, then, that the theory-building enterprise in the area of intergroup relations has been a rather limited undertaking. Beyond the original three theories of assimilation, amalgamation, and cultural pluralism, most theory building, notably the works of Park, Gordon, and Glazer and Moynihan, have aimed at a more detailed understanding of assimilation processes. I have suggested that the recent attempts at a pluralist approach represent a new and different perspective. Yet it is obviously premature, at this time, to claim that the pluralist position is a single, distinct theory. Rather, we have several different approaches, all of which claim that total assimilation is far from inevitable and that group diversity is a permanent fixture of many modern societies. The most useful way to explore the various pluralist theories is to consider them in the context of their confrontation with the assimilation model.

Assimilation and Ethnic Culture
It is precisely the competition between the assimilationist and pluralist models that allows each of them to be seen a bit differently than might otherwise be the case. If assimilation theory is examined through pluralist glasses, it is seen that while the latter is a structural type of theory, the former understands social reality in cultural terms. Of course, both culture and social structure are equally important metaphors for describing social reality. Yet the confrontation between these two perspectives in intergroup studies prompts a re-examination of the way in which the cultural dimension of ethnic relations has been understood in the theory of assimilation.

It is indeed culture that distinguishes one social group from the next. Ethnic culture becomes valued (or more properly, disvalued) and in turn places the ethnic group somewhere in the continuum of status ranks in society. In other words, ethnic culture at once serves as a criterion for value differentiation and for social stratification. Yet the theory of assimilation has traditionally maintained that the weakening and eventual disappearance of ethnic culture is the key to dominant-subordinate relationships. Even when the effects of dominant group prejudice and discrimination have been acknowledged, it is argued that ethnic group cultures prevent "adjustment" to the host society. Those ethnic groups that experience the greatest "adjustment," and therefore the greatest social mobility, are the ones that allegedly cease being ethnic groups. Assimilation theory has only understood the problem of social mobility in cultural terms. Groups fail to obtain a share of society's rewards because they fail to assimilate to dominant values.

As I have already noted, Glazer and Moynihan's well-known *Beyond the Melting Pot* (1963, rev. 1970) provided only a limited departure from this otherwise pervasive feature of assimilation theory. Except for their depiction of ethnic groups as salient political entities, Glazer and Moynihan disregard their own insights. The message of *Beyond the Melting Pot*, like most of the literature of the 1960s, is that social mobility is dependent upon cultural assimilation. Glazer and Moynihan simply added the proviso that this process works only for those groups that organize politically for a long enough time to allow infiltration into the existing political structures.

What is required is an understanding of the processes through which ethnic group cultures change without disappearing; the ways in which malleable ethnic cultures promote assimilation and social mobility without disintegrating; the ways in which changing ethnic identities become vehicles through which groups and individuals participate in culturally mixed social structures. For instance, sociologists have consistently overlooked the fact that as minority groups organize to promote their own social mobility, they are at the same time creating new social associations that preserve and symbolize their group distinctiveness. To be sure, the Italian-American Civil Rights League is different from the older Italian-American Athlete clubs, the Jewish Defence League differs from the American Jewish Committee, the recently formed Ethnic Millions Political Action Committee seems different from the older ethnic labour organizations. Yet all of these phenomena embody ethnic distinctiveness in the United States. While the newer ethnic organizations clearly symbolize a changed set of ethnic identities, they are nonetheless ethnic. It is indeed likely that cultural distinctiveness and assimilation occur simultaneously, and that the two processes facilitate each other in different ways.

Historically, social scientists have assumed that an ethnic group either assimilates or remains locked into a position of limited social status. Groups that attain social mobility but fail to assimilate, usually through some form of self-segregation, have always been treated as exceptions to the rule. I would argue that there are many more such instances than social scientists have bothered to study. For instance, the examples of such Asian American groups as the Chinese, Japanese, and Koreans, seem less unique when examined alongside such groups as the Scandinavian, Hutterite, and Mennonite communities in the midwestern states, the Mormons in Utah, French Canadians in Maine, and the recently arrived Cuban American community in southern Florida. Similarly, American scholars have long overlooked the development of separatism, not only by the French, but by indigenous Indian populations and European immigrants in Canada. In each of these cases, we see degrees of cultural segregation and autonomy that are firmly woven into the fabric of modern societies.

As is always the case, theory building must be linked to concrete research findings. There has been little research that traces ethnic cultures, and changes in them, past the mythical third generation of "Hansen's Law" (1937). For instance, the authors of a recent historical treatise on ethnicity in the United States write:

> The old immigrants, those coming in large numbers between 1840 and 1890 from northern and western Europe, have largely assimilated and lost much of their original culture. The new immigrants, coming after 1880 and now producing a fourth generation, have assimilated...It does not appear likely today that any minority culture, except for small and dedicated groups like the Amish and Hutterites, can hold its own in the United States indefinitely (Dinnerstein and Reimers 1975:139-140, 156).

From this work and others like it, one must conclude that the myth of assimilation is far from dead. Allegedly, once the third generation has experienced a romanticized revival of its grandparents' ethnic heritage, the ethnic culture will rapidly disintegrate. Even such a recent sociological work as Light's *Ethnic Enterprise in America*, (1972)–a book that depicts the positive functions of ethnic culture for certain Asian American groups–ends its narrative once the period of alleged "adjustment" has ended. What is known of the cultural patterns and "identity kits" of Light's Asian Americans once they have experienced social mobility? What is known some thirty years later about the children of the ethnics studied by Warner and Srole in *Yankee City* (1945)? What is known today of the Jews studied by Gans (1951, 1958) in Park Forest, who even during the 1950s created new suburban religious institutions, as an expression not of religious fervour, but of ethnic solidarity? Obviously, little is known of these post-third generation ethnic populations because the assimilation of ethnic culture has simply been assumed.

The absence of empirical research on the persistence of ethnic culture reflects both a substantive and a methodological dilemma. The increasing availability of survey research data files for secondary analysis has drawn social scientists away from the very research strategies that are most likely to provide answers to questions about ethnic culture and identity in contemporary community life. Consider, for instance, Andrew Greeley's recent work, *Ethnicity in the United States* (1974). Working with data collected by one of the largest American survey research facilities (the National Opinion Research Center), Greeley warns of the "weaknesses" of secondary analysis and the "preliminary" and "tentative" nature of his findings (1974:16). My own guess is that such methods as the community study, the in-depth interview, and the recently developed techniques of oral history will bring social science closer to an understanding of ethnic culture than will the more prevalent quantitative research techniques. Longitudinal rather than cross-sectional research is required. To the extent that stratification and social mobility have become important issues, the European tradition known as "political economy" may well provide a model for the next decade of research in the area of intergroup studies. The various works of Max Weber, as well as those of his teacher, Theodore Mommsen, demonstrate the utility of a balanced historical scrutiny of both ideological and economic forces in enlightening our understanding of the formation and life chances of status groups in changing societies.

Ethnic culture, then, like all other culture, is capable of changing both its meaning and its functions. It is capable of revealing both adaptability and resistance to social change. A new understanding of ethnic groups as groups that possess an enduring though changing culture is a first step in setting a new research agenda. Just as Gordon (1964) has argued that assimilation must be viewed as a set of subprocesses, so I would argue that social science must examine the discrete segments of ethnic culture that in different ways both promote and resist assimilation and change.

Intergroup Relations as Social Structure
The failure to understand intergroup relations in structural terms has been one of the most serious weaknesses of assimilation theory. In place of a structural depiction of ethnic relations, assimilation theory has provided two complementary pathologies of group life. One of these, of course, is the pathology of "backward" ethnic culture, a culture that is "deviant" and ultimately retards social mobility. The other is the pathology of group or individual prejudice. I stress the term "pathology" here because in both instances these phenomena are seen as non-normative. On the one hand, social mobility fails to occur because of the strange victimization of minority groups through dominant group prejudice; on the other hand, the ethnic group's culture is itself something strange to the social milieu. In neither instance are intergroup relations described in truly relational terms, or seen as part of the normative processes of social intercourse between groups.

There are at least three basic structural postulates upon which most pluralist theories appear to agree. First, ethnic diversity and the relations between ethnic groups are a major structural aspect of many, though not all, societies. Second, these relationships derive primarily, though not exclusively, from social stratification; that is, the ranking, competition, and coalition of groups in terms of the distribution of valued social resources. Third, neither of these processes, group differentiation or social stratification, are non-normative. Rather, they constitute a major segment of what social scientists commonly call social process and social structure.

The linking of intergroup studies with the study of social stratification has both positive and negative consequences. On the positive side, ethnic relations are now viewed as an important component in the social theory-building enterprise. The study of intergroup relations has been removed from a limited "social problems" perspective. The development of sophisticated social theories about intergroup relations will not only have value in its own right, but probably represents the most reliable route to a genuine understanding of the social problems aspect of the subject. On the other hand, the joining of social theory and ethnic studies means that the latter has become embroiled in some long-standing controversies of the former. The question of which brand of stratification theory best explains ethnic relations is now a paramount issue. Some would characterize these debates in terms of Marxist and non-Marxist approaches. It is less ideologically complex simply to distinguish those theories that emphasize respectively the three major stratification variables: class, status, and power.

The argument for ethnic relations as a form of social-class conflict was made by the late Oliver Cox in his classic *Caste, Class, and Race* (1948), and is a central theme of John Leggett's *Class, Race, and Labor* (1968). In the hands of more polemical authors, such as Fanon in *The Wretched of the Earth* (1961), the social-class argument is explained in terms of capitalist exploitation and nationalist imperialism. Regardless of whether the organizing concept is class or caste, the message is that ethnic relations are based upon economic exploitation and competition.

The social class variable seems to have yielded in more recent literature to a social power perspective. Both Schermerhorn, in *Comparative Ethnic Relations* (1970), and more so Wilson, in *Power, Racism and Privilege* (1973), argue that ethnic relations are derived from the struggle between groups for social control. This approach has the advantage of bringing both sociologists and political scientists into the same theoretical framework. It has also provided a linkage between studies of ethnic relations and comparative studies of development, modernization, and social change (see, for instance, Enloe, 1973).

A third perspective, represented by Shibutani and Kwan (1965), the late Judith Kramer's *The American Minority Community* (1970), and my own work (Newman 1973), stresses the importance of social status distinctions as the essential mechanism of ethnic stratification. It is argued that while ethnic conflicts and coalitions may readily focus upon class and power rewards, the initial placement of an ethnic group in a social rank is based upon the specification of value, that is, social status, honour, and prestige differences. Obviously, where any one of these theories is weak, one of the other two is strong. No one of them alone will provide a comprehensive theory of intergroup relations. For instance, the economic competition model is indeed a powerful explanatory tool for understanding many historical situations. Yet its plausibility weakens under at least two circumstances. As Wilhelm suggests in *Who Needs the Negro?* (1971), economic exploitation is not a sufficient rationale for discriminating against populations that are functionally marginal to an economic system. In the reverse case, as Max Weber predicted would prevail in the so-called "modern" nation-states (1922), once different groups attain some degree of social class parity, intergroup conflicts and coalitions tend to revolve around status and power resources. Here again, the class conflict argument explains relatively little. Similar examples could easily be found for weaknesses in both the power and status approaches.

A theoretically mature stratification approach to the problem of social pluralism clearly requires enough comparative research to produce two kinds of analytical tools. First, a theory of the genesis of ethnic stratification must distinguish typologically the social conditions that produce different instances of stratification by class, status, and power. Second, patterns of change in the bases of stratification must also be understood as different types of normative processes. In other words, in place of a theoretical dispute between advocates of the class, status, and power approaches, we need careful comparative research that identifies the types of social conditions that prevail when these different forms of ethnic stratification are produced. Similarly, we must scrutinize the typical processes through which one form of stratification relationship between groups is superimposed upon or transformed into another.

Three additional issues are involved in the creation of a structural theory of social pluralism. Each of these issues has strong ideological overtones. First, there is the question of whether race is a special case, empirically and therefore theoretically distinct from other variables that create ethnic stratification. The last decade of theory and research on American Blacks was informed by an ideology that stressed the uniqueness of race relations. It is significant that during a period when most research focused upon assimilation processes, the few major structural concepts employed were focused upon racial discrimination, so-called institutional racism. Given the view that race relations somehow differ from other intergroup situations, it is not surprising that the study of institutional racism did not produce a broader theory of all intergroup discrimination as a normative structural feature of the social order.

This admittedly complex substantive issue has been made even more difficult to resolve by the emergence of a fierce methodological dispute.

As evidenced by the debate over Fogel and Engerman's *Time on the Cross: The Economics of American Negro Slavery* (1974), (Bryce-Laporte 1975, Record and Record, 1975), there is apparently little agreement concerning the reliability and appropriateness of different kinds of historical data that may be used to characterize and analyze the American race situation and race relations in general. I would not impugn the genuineness of these methodological debates. However, I do believe that the analysis of race relations can be incorporated in a broader theory of intergroup relations. The crucial question is whether race relations differ from other intergroup situations by degree or by type. I am inclined to think that the difference is one of degree, and that important similarities between race, ethnic, religious, and other forms of cultural stratification exist. If, on the other hand, we are to view race relations as typologically different, then it should be possible to provide a complete typological schema within which other important status variables may be placed. Regardless of which position ultimately dominates, it is clear that theoretical closure in the field of intergroup studies will not easily be obtained without some resolution of this volatile issue.

A second important issue, that has plagued sociology since its founding, has now become vitally significant in the study of intergroup relations. Are societies more controlled by ideological, especially political, factors or do material, especially economic, factors play the leading role in the determination of the social structure? This, of course, is the classic debate between Marx on the one hand, and Durkheim, if not Weber, on the other. It is the dispute between the class, power, and status arguments at yet a higher level of analysis. Richard Schermerhorn (1970) provides a useful preliminary approach to the problem in his distinction between "ec-pol" and "pol-ec" types of societies. In other words, he argues that situations in which polity dominates over economy will produce dramatically different consequences from those in which economy dominates over polity. As I am sure Schermerhorn is aware, it is not so much a question of whether a given society is inherently of the pol-ec or ec-pol type. Rather, a theory of social pluralism must depict the "sequences," to use Schermerhorn's apt term, through which material and ideological forces shape the social structure.

The third issue that must be addressed concerns the relative emphasis that should be placed upon conflict as opposed to co-operative efforts between dominant and subordinate groups. As I suggested in *American Pluralism* (1970:101-103, 116-117), while the conflict dimension of intergroup relations has been too long overlooked, an exclusive focus on conflict is equally undesirable. There is a distressing tendency for a stratification approach to be equated with a conflict approach. Obviously, the distribution of social resources and the negotiation of a social order involves both intergroup struggles and coalitions. An understanding of the balancing of these two fundamental social processes might well be one

50

of the more important theoretical achievements of the next decade of research on intergroup relations.

Prospects for the Theory of Social Pluralism

This essay began with the observation that science undergoes fads, that scientific inquiry responds to trends in the social structure. Some would argue that this fact reveals the essential inability of the social sciences to develop objective theory about those same social structures. I would argue quite the reverse. A social science that does not respond to the social issues of its day will be of little humanistic value. There is indeed a difference between a social science that bases its research agenda upon the problems of the social structure, and a social science that adopts its theoretical perspective from the ideology of that social structure.

This essay also began with the observation that the sociology of intergroup relations appears to evidence what Thomas Kuhn has called a situation of competing paradigms (1962). Yet, as Robert Friedrichs correctly observes (1970), Kuhn never claimed that the syndrome of competing paradigms he documents for the natural sciences is also an inherent feature of social science. In fact, Friedrichs suggests that while the history of sociology surely exhibits such a pattern, current theoretical developments point to the possibility of some sort of "paradigmatic consolidation." Moreover, Friedrichs suggests that this type of merger or dialectic exchange between previously competing theoretical perspectives may be taken as an indication of the increasing maturity of social science itself.

I would like to think that the present revival of ethnic studies, and the theoretical disputes it has precipitated, are leading to a point of paradigmatic consolidation. If we are to understand the pluralism of social groups in dialogue with one another, we must develop an ability to employ different social theories in dialogue with one another. My purpose here has been to suggest a few of the central issues around which that dialogue may be emerging.

References

Bryce-Laporte, R.S.
1975   Review of Robert Fogel and Stanley Engerman's *Time on the Cross: The Economics of American Negro Slavery*, in *Contemporary Sociology*, 4:4 (July), 353-361.
Cox, O.C.
1948   *Caste, Class, and Race: A Study in Social Dynamics*. Garden City, New York: Doubleday.

Dinnerstein, L., and D.M. Reimers
1975 *Ethnic Americans: A History of Immigration and Assimilation.* New York: Dodd, Mead and Company.
Dollard, J.
1937 *Caste and Class in a Southern Town.* New Haven: Yale University Press.
Enloe, C.H.
1973 *Ethnic Conflict and Political Development.* Boston: Little, Brown and Company.
Fanon, F.
1961 *The Wretched of the Earth.* (American edition 1968) New York: Grove Press.
Fogel, R.W. and S. L. Engerman
1974 *Time on the Cross: The Economics of American Negro Slavery* and *Time on the Cross: Evidence and Methods.* Boston: Little, Brown and Company.
Frazier, E.F.
1947 "Sociological theory and race relations," *American Sociological Review,* 12:265-271.
Frazier, E.F.
1949 *The Negro in the United States.* New York: Macmillan.
Frazier, E.F.
1957 *Race and Culture Contacts in the Modern World.* Boston: Beacon Press.
Friedrichs, R.W.
1970 *A Sociology of Sociology.* New York: The Free Press.
Gans, H.
1951 "Park Forest: birth of a Jewish community," *Commentary,* 11:330-339.
Gans, H.
1958 "The origin and growth of a Jewish community in the suburbs: a study of the Jews of Park Forest," *The Jews,* Marshall Sklare (ed.). New York: The Free Press, 205-248.
Glazer, N., and D.P. Moynihan
1963 *Beyond the Melting Pot* (rev. ed. 1970). Cambridge, Mass.: MIT Press.
Gordon, M.
1964 *Assimilation in American Life.* New York: Oxford University Press.
Greeley, A.M.
1974 *Ethnicity in the United States.* New York: John Wiley and Sons.
Hansen, M.L.
1937 *The Problem of the Third Generation Immigrant.* Rock Island, Ill.: The Augustana Historical Society.
Hraba, J., and R.O. Richards

1975 "Race relations, social science, and social policy: a comment on two articles," *American Journal of Sociology*, 80:6 (May), 1438-1447.

Hughes, E.C. et al. (eds.)
1950 *Race and Culture, Volume I, The Collected Papers of Robert Ezra Park* Glencoe: The Free Press.

Kallen, H.
1915 "Democracy versus the melting pot." *The Nation*, 100 (Feb. 18-25); 190-194, 217-222.

Kallen, H.
1924 *Culture and Democracy in the United States*. New York: Liveright.

Killian, L., and C. Grigg
1964 *Race Crisis in America*. Englewood Cliffs, N.J.: Prentice-Hall.

Kramer, J.
1970 *The American Community*. New York: Appleton Century Crofts.

Kuhn, T.
1962 *The Structure of Scientific Revolutions*. Chicago: The University of Chicago Press (rev. ed. 1970).

Leggett, J.
1968 *Class, Race, and Labor*. New York: Oxford University Press.

Light, I.H.
1972 *Ethnic Enterprise in America: Business and Welfare among Chinese, Japanese and Blacks*. Berkeley: The University of California Press.

Lyman, S.M.
1973 *The Black American in Sociological Thought*. New York: Capricorn Books.

Mannheim, K.
1928 "Competition as a cultural phenomenon," *Essays on the Sociology of Knowledge*, (Paul Kecskemeti ed.). London: Routledge and Kegan Paul Ltd., 191-229.

Mannheim, K.
1929 *Ideology and Utopia*. London: Routledge and Kegan Paul.

Myrdal, G. et. al.
1944 *An American Dilemma*. New York: Harper and Row.

Newman, W.M.
1973 *American Pluralism: A Study of Minority Groups and Social Theory*. New York: Harper and Row.

Record, W., and J. Cassels Record
1975 Review of Robert Fogal and Stanley Engerman's *Time on the Cross: The Economics of American Negro Slavery*, in *Contemporary Sociology*, 4:4 (July), 361-366.

Schermerhorn, R.A.
1970 *Comparative Ethnic Relations: A Framework for Theory and Research*. New York: Random House.

Shibutani, T. and K.M. Kwan (eds.)
1965 *Ethnic Stratification*. New York: Macmillan.
Thomas, W.I.
1904 "The psychology of race relations," *American Journal of Sociology*, 9 (March), 593-611.
Thomas, W.I., and F. Zanecki
1918 *The Polish Peasant in Europe and the United States*. Chicago: University of Chicago Press.
Van den Berghe, P.L.
1967 *Race and Racism*. New York: John Wiley and Sons.
Warner, L., and L. Srole
1945 *The Social Systems of American Ethnic Groups*. New Haven, Connecticut: Yale University Press.
Weber, M.
1922 "The distribution of power within the political community: class, status, party," in *Economy and Society* (Guenther Roth and Claus Wittich eds., 1968). New York: Bedminster Press, 926-939.
Wilhelm, S.
1971 *Who Needs the Negro?* Garden City, New York: Doubleday and Company.
Wilson, W.J.
1973 *Power, Racism, and Privilege*. New York: The Macmillan Company.

3

The Structure of Relationships Between Ethnic Collectivities
Raymond Breton*

There are several dimensions to the structure of relationships between ethnic collectivities. One dimension that has received considerable attention, and rightly so, is the degree of inequality and the occurrence of conflict among people of different ethnic or racial origins. But there are three other dimensions that have perhaps not received the attention they deserve. First, it is quite evident that ethnic collectivities differ considerably from each other in their social organization. But relatively little has been done toward the development of conceptual frameworks that could be used for the analysis of the various types of collectivities found in Canadian society, and of how such variations affect the ways in which the ethnic collectivities relate to one another. Second, we know little about the conditions under which people establish relationships and form groups on an ethnic basis. In a way, our ethnic origin is always with us, but it is not always operative in determining social behaviour and in shaping social organization. Third, attention needs to be given to the variations in institutional arrangements that emerge (or fail to emerge) to accommodate the existing ethnic diversity, and to the particular forms of the institutional accommodations. It is such arrangements that structure and regulate inter-ethnic relationships; it is also such arrangements that become at times the object of inter-ethnic conflicts and of social change.

In the following pages, these three issues are explored. Only selected aspects of the issues are discussed, however. In the first section, an attempt is made to contrast two basic kinds of situations, that of ethnic segmentation and that of ethnic heterogeneity. Next, the question of ethnic group formation is examined, or more generally, the conditions under

*Raymond Breton is Professor of Sociology, University of Toronto, Ontario.

which ethnicity becomes a basis of social organization as a phenomenon which is important for the structure of inter-ethnic relationships. Finally, three social movements are discussed–social movements which are an expression of ethnic aspirations and which have implications for the possible restructuring of the institutional arrangements within which inter-ethnic relationships take place. The movements in question are the multiculturalism movement, the "red power" movement, and the Québécois independentist movement.

1. Ethnic heterogeneity and ethnic segmentation

One way of approaching situations of ethnic diversity is to examine the circumstances at the origin of the diversity. First, a distinction can be made between situations arising from migrations and those arising from the amalgamation of contiguous territories either from the drawing of or changes in political boundaries. For example, when European states established their colonial empires in Africa, "they subdivided the whole continent arbitrarily among themselves, usually proceeding from the coast and its natural harbors into the interior, cutting across all traditional boundaries" (Duchacek, 1970:25). As a result, the units formed tended to enclose different African ethnic groups. And these units, which initially represented zones of European sovereignty and colonial administration, provided, in many cases, the territorial basis of multi-ethnic independent African countries. The Austro-Hungarian Empire is an example of ethnic diversity resulting from annexation of contiguous territories through dynastic agreements and marriages, and through wars of conquest (Jaszi, 1929).

An essential characteristic of amalgamation of contiguous territories is that it is a process that brings together groups that already exist as societies, each having their own social and institutional systems (Hughes and Hughes, 1952). In such situations, the character of the inter-ethnic relationships–at the political, economic, social and socio-psychological levels–is likely to be substantially different than in other types of diversity.

On the other hand, ethnic diversity which arises out of migrations can be quite varied, depending on factors such as the motives for migration, the intentions of the migrants with respect to their new environment and its native population, the socio-economic characteristics of the migrants, and the mode of implantation into the new environment.

One set of characteristics of migrants are those that pertain to their capacity to create the political and economic milieu suitable for establishing their own institutions. Lieberson identifies a number of variables in this connection, but two appear particularly important: "When the population migrating to a new contact situation is superior in technology (particularly weapons) and more tightly organized than the indigenous groups, the necessary conditions for maintaining the migrants' political and economic institutions are usually imposed on the indigenous population" (1961:12-13). By means of such assets and other factors such as a substantial flow of immigrants, the migrants establish their own social organization parallel[1] to the ones already existing on a given territory. Canada offers a good example of such a process, first with the French establishing an institutional system parallel to that of the Indians, and then the English establishing a third institutional structure.[2] "Migrant superordination," to use Lieberson's expression, is a situation that resembles amalgamation of contiguous territories in at least one respect: in both instances, the resulting diversity involves groups that tend to be institutionally complete, that is to have their own institutional systems.

The other type of migration is characterized by the fact that the migrants are not in a position to set up a full-fledged institutional structure, or may not wish to do so. They may have migrated with the intention of integrating as rapidly as possible into the receiving society. Sometimes, the migrants do not wish to integrate, or are prevented from doing so by various kinds of circumstances, e.g., language difficulties or rejection by members of the receiving society. In such instances, some sort of community will form itself, but it will tend to be limited in scope and function. By and large, except for British immigration, immigration in Canada since the conquest has been of this type.[3] British immigration, at least up to well into the nineteenth century, has been "settlement immigration" aimed at establishing and expanding an English institutional system; that is to say, it was part of the process of establishing a parallel and dominant institutional system.

The first type of diversity can be referred to as segmentation and the latter as heterogeneity. Canadian society contains both types of diversity.

a) Ethnic segmentation
Although agreement is not complete as to what constitutes a segmented or "pural society," as opposed to unitary social systems, there seems to be a certain consensus with regard to two points. Societies are segmented insofar as they exhibit, to a greater or lesser degree, 1) an enclosure of social networks along ethnic lines; and 2) "a social structure compartmentalized into analogous, parallel, non-complementary but distinguishable sets of institutions" (van den Berghe, 1969:67).

Social enclosure, in the present context, refers to the structure of social relations among the members of a society; to the existence of separate networks of social relations. It refers to the existence of social boundaries between groups and to mechanisms for the maintenance of these boundaries.[4] It also refers to a particular pattern in the contours of such boundaries. Indeed, enclosure involves a certain superimposition of social boundaries, or, perhaps more accurately, the containment of the many networks of social affiliations within the boundaries of an inclusive system of ethnic boundaries. In an ethnically segmented society, the limits of various social networks tend to coincide with the more inclusive ethnic boundaries. Group memberships may overlap considerably within the segments, but the resulting criss-crossing of social affiliations does not extend over the basic ethnic line of social division.

Again, as Barth mentions (1969:9-10), the existence of a boundary does not mean that there is no interaction between the members of each segment, nor does it mean that there is no mobility between them. What enclosure means is that the interaction and mobility that takes place is regulated in such a way as to preserve the boundaries between the segments.

If enclosure refers to the structure of social relations, compartmentalization refers to the related structure of institutions and corresponding organizations.

Each segment has a set of institutions of its own. This does not necessarily imply culturally distinct institutions and practices. For example, both English and French in Canada operate within a variant of the British parliamentary system. Compartmentalization is not a statement about cultural pluralism; rather, it is a statement about the locus of the institutional authority and clientele. For example, parallel educational structures refers to the fact that there are at least two sets of educational organizations serving different clienteles and under the control of different elites, not to their cultural differences. Since both the clientele and the elite are defined in terms of the lines of social segmentation, the processes of institutional compartmentalization and of social enclosure reinforce each other. Of course, both aspects of segmentation are a matter of degree; they are not all-or-none phenomena.

b) Ethnic heterogeneity

The situation of ethnic heterogeneity, on the other hand, is quite different. It is a differentiation that does not entail the degree of social enclosure and of institutional compartmentalization discussed above. Rather, this type of ethnic differentiation tends to occur within the social and institutional systems common to the society.

One approach to the phenomenon of ethnic heterogeneity draws—implicitly or explicitly—from the sociological analysis of a more general phenomenon, namely the difference in the patterns of social affiliations in different types of social structures. In the more "traditional" society, persons tended to identify themselves as members of a group, their "people," and "this 'peoplehood' was, roughly, coterminous with a given rural land space, political government...a common culture..." (Gordon, 1964:23). On the other hand, in medieval society, according to Simmel (1955), the individual is enveloped in a set of concentric circles. That is to say, participation in the smallest social unit implied participation in larger ones as well. Such a pattern:

...had the peculiarity of treating the individual as a member of a group rather than as an individual, and of incorporating him thereby in other groups as well...In the Middle Ages affiliation with a group absorbed the whole man. It served not only a momentary purpose, which was defined objectively. It was rather an association of all who had combined for the sake of that purpose while the association absorbed the whole life of each of them. If the urge to form associations persisted, then it was accompanied by having whole associations combined in confederations of a higher order. [Thus] cities allied themselves first of all with cities, monasteries with monasteries, guilds with related guilds. (Simmel, 1955: 139, 149).

One feature of the "traditional" and of the "medieval" patterns is that social relationships within them tended to be involuntary. There is little room for individual choice in social structures based on localized relationships, on kinship ties or on groupings which do "not permit the individual to become a member in other groups, a rule which the old guilds and the early medieval corporations probably illustrate most clearly" (Simmel, 1955:140).

Furthermore, in such social structures, the individuals tend to act as whole persons. Of course, people perform different types of activities and, in this sense, perform different roles. But since the various role relationships tend to involve the same set of persons, there is little discontinuity in their social lives. As a consequence, their identities do not tend to be compartmentalized on the basis of different roles and role relationships.

The so-called "modern" type of society, on the other hand, is characterized by a structure of social relations that is highly differentiated and consists of juxtaposed groups: instead of exhibiting a pattern of concentric circles, social affiliations follow a pattern of intersecting circles, with the individual at the point of intersection. What we have is a "social organization based on roles rather than on persons" (Coleman, 1970:163). Modern social structure involves a large number of organizations which structure the different segments of our lives: work, recreation, religion, politics, and so on. Our social personalities are thus segmented into roles and role relationships occurring in a series of organizational domains. And even within the organizations, the relationships through which the organization functions are to a substantial extent "relationships between roles, not the persons who occupy them" (Coleman, 1970:163). In short, we have a kind of social organization in which people perform more or less segmented roles usually involving relationships with different sets of people. In Simmel's terms, "the groups with which persons affiliate are juxtaposed and 'intersect' in one and the same person" (150).

Moreover, in a differentiated social structure, roles and role relationships involve an element of individual choice. For instance, a person's network of relationships is not completely determined by the kin groups in which he happens to be born or by the guild to which he belongs. Relationships are formed on affection, necessity, or interest rather than being "given" (Geertz, 1963; Simmel, 1955).

In such a structural situation, a person's identity tends to be fragmented or "partialized" rather than unitary and total. Mazrui illustrates the difference between a total and a partial identity in the following way: "A tribe in a relationship of bare coexistence with other tribes has a total identity of its own. But the Hotel Workers Union in Uganda or the American Political Science Association is only a partial form of identity. The process of national integration is a partialization of group identities—as the tribes or communities lose their coherence as distinct systems of life" (1969:335). The situation of ethnic heterogeneity (as opposed to segmentation) is one in which the ethnic grouping tends to involve "a partial form of identity." The question can be explored further by examining the differences between ethnically homogeneous and heterogeneous societies. A *homogeneous* society, ethnically speaking, is one in which virtually everyone shares the sense of a common origin, the sense of belonging to the same "people." In such a society ethnicity takes the form of nationalism. Fishman points out that "nationalism is made up of the stuff of primordial ethnicity; indeed, it is transformed ethnicity with all the accoutrements for functioning at a larger scale of political, social and intellectual activity" (1965:72-73). There are two kinds of nationalism: territorial and ethnic. Territorial nationalism occurs when the relevant collectivity is defined in terms of a territorial unit, while ethnic nationalism "seeks to extend the ethnic by securing economic integration and political rights, through self-government and autonomous legislation" (Smith, 1972:14). Nationalism in a homogeneous society is both ethnic and territorial; the boundaries of the ethnic national collectivity and of the territorial national collectivity are the same. In such a situation, ethnic identity is a "total identity"—total in the sense that it is supported by all the cultural and organizational components of the society. It is total in the sense that there is a continuity of identity throughout all the spheres of social relationships and activities, and in the sense that there is no institutional domain, social activity, or network of relationships in which people have to meet different ethnic assumptions for the definition of the situation. In both the "traditional" and the "modern" homogeneous society, then, ethnicity is a total, all-encompassing phenomenon, although in different ways in the two types of situations.

In the ethnically *heterogeneous* society, ethnicity tends to become fragmented or partialized rather than being total. And this tends to be the case, but in varying degrees, at the cultural, relational, and organizational levels as well as at the level of the individual identity. Only certain areas of a person's life involve his or her ethnicity. Ethnically specified social expectations tend to be restricted to a few limited aspects of behaviour such as, for example, those pertaining to the role of spouse or parent.

Ethnicity becomes partialized as a result of the process of social differentiation which involves, as we have seen, a social organization based on roles. Individuals behave differently in different roles and in different contexts; they change "social personality" from one to the other. In this kind of social organization, it is primarily roles and role relationships rather than entire institutional domains that become ethnically defined. Some segments of the lives and identities of individuals become "de-ethnicized," while others remain within the confines of ethnic definitions and expectations. In this kind of social organization, a person's identity or position in the system becomes a divisible quality in the sense that identity choices are not mutually exclusive or in opposition to each other. In Parenti's (1969:283) words, "A person experiences cumulative and usually complementary identifications, and his life experiences may expose him to some of the social relations and cultural cues of the dominant society while yet placing him predominantly within the confines of a particular minority subculture." The reverse may occur: a person may be exposed to some of the social relations and cultural cues of a particular ethnic sub-culture while placing him predominantly within the mainstream society.

As far as the structure of social relations is concerned, it tends to consist in "individual-based coalitions" (Wolf, 1966) rather than in closed ethnic networks. Friendships, marriages, business relationships, and so on, are formed in a multiplicity of directions; "members of the ethnic group cease to have a single focus of alliance with their fellow-members" (Zenner, 1967:111). Ethnic ties characterize a limited number of the "intersecting circles" to which a person belongs. Ethnicity may characterize, for example, his kinship and friendship ties, but not his occupational, religious, and political affiliations. A person's ethnic ties may be even further specialized in the sense of being limited to membership in ethnocultural associations. In such instances, ethnic networks are virtually completely dissociated from other types of social affiliation.

At the institutional level, a parallel phenomenon occurs: the network of organizational structures is fragmented or partial. It involves structures for limited aspects of social life (e.g. religious, recreational, professional services).

The fragmentation of ethnicity is a phenomenon that occurs in ethnically heterogeneous societies. But it is important to note that ethnic heterogeneity, as opposed to segmentation, is possible only to the extent that a society is differentiated; that is, to the extent that certain roles are performed in separate organizational contexts. A "social organization based on roles" is a type of social organization that allows ethnic heterogeneity because it permits its members to establish at least a few basic functional role relationships independent of their ethnic identities. A social organization based on whole persons could not enclose members of different ethnic groups without assimilating them completely, or treating them as

61

strangers existing at the periphery of the group. ⌋

Heterogeneity involves some degree of fragmentation whereby the cultural, social, and institutional elements of ethnicity become dissociated from each other (at the individual and collective levels), and whereby some of the elements lose their importance and even disappear. But all groups in a heterogeneous society are not equally subject to the process of partialization. The ethnicity of dominant groups, for instance, usually maintains a higher degree of integration, in the sense discussed here, than that of subordinate groups. As Zenner points out, "one development in the modern world has been the constitution of the dominant ethnic group in a state as a corporate ethnicity" (1967:110). Corporateness pertains to the capacity of a collectivity to maintain its social and institutional boundaries, and to define the rules and conditions of membership. Dominant corporateness is a characteristic that tends to prevent the partialization of the ethnicity of the group.

Finally, the fragmentation of ethnicity varies not only in degree but also in the particular combinations of areas of social life which remain subject to ethnic expectations and social definitions, and of those who become "de-ethnicized."

The situations of heterogeneity and of segmentation are structurally quite different. Because of this, we would expect the character of inter-ethnic relationships also to be quite different under the two types of situations. For instance, the institutional forms of economic equality and inequality would differ as well as the institutional expressions of differentials in political power. The condition of socio-economic mobility would be somewhat different under the two structural conditions. The issues over which conflict would occur as well as the forms of the conflict would also differ.[5] In short, the nature of the relationships between ethnic collectivities cannot be properly understood without taking account of the overall structural context in which they occur.

It should be emphasized by way of conclusion that this section deals with overall patterns of ethnic differentiation. There is a need to identify and analyze the variety of subpatterns that can occur within each of these broad patterns. Moreover, these two patterns are not exhaustive of all the possible broad patterns of ethnic differentiation.

2. Ethnicity as a basis of social organization

In order to understand the structure of relationships in a multi-ethnic community or society, another question that must be raised is the extent to which, and the ways in which, ethnicity becomes a criterion of group formation, that is, the ways in which it delimits the boundaries of social networks. Much of our thinking about inter-ethnic relationships assumes the existence of ethnic groups. That is to say, the very phenomenon that is problematic is frequently taken as a given. Fishman has pointed out that we "all too frequently ask *which* ethnic *groups* exist in a particular area (or

62

what is the ethnic background of informant X) rather than inquire of the extent to which ethnicity is apparent in behavior" (1965:78), and in the institutional structure. In the previous section, the concern was with two societal patterns of ethnic differentiation. But within these broad patterns, certain social relationships and structures are defined as ethnic while others are not; or a given role relationship (e.g. employer-employee) is sometimes defined in its non-ethnic and sometimes in its ethnic dimensions. These patterns of variation need to be accounted for.

The variations are considerable: variations for people with different objectively defined ethnic backgrounds; variations from one institutional context to another; variations from one historical period to another; variations from one social situation to another.

It is important not to restrict the question of ethnic group formation to the formation of ethnic associations within the so-called ethnic communities. Group formation, or the establishment of social relationships on an ethnic basis, can occur in many other circumstances: commercial networks may be formed along ethnic lines; financial transactions can occur within ethnic channels[6]; contracts and subcontracts can be negotiated within particular ethnic networks; informal work groups in an organization can follow ethnic identifications; levels of authority can be defined in ethnic terms[7]; political parties or subgroups within parties can have an ethnic basis; and so on. In fact, it is possible to imagine a society in which ethnicity permeates the entire social organization but which has very few specifically ethnic voluntary associations.[8]

In a way, ethnicity is always there in the sense that we all have an ethnic origin. As van den Berghe points out, "ethnicity is an absolutely fundamental and ineluctable aspect of social reality. We are all ·human, not in the abstract or by virtue of our membership in a biological species but as carriers of a specific culture, speakers of a specific language, and so on" (1971:41). But ethnicity, or at least several elements of one's ethnicity, can remain latent; it may have little significance in defining one's identity and behaviour and no relevance for the structuring of social relationships. On the other hand, under certain kinds of circumstances, it may acquire meaning for certain categories of people and become relevant for the organization of their personal lives, of their occupational activities and networks, of their communities, or of the institutions of the society. A basic question, then, is under what conditions or in what circumstances does ethnicity acquire such a role in behaviour and social organization?

In order to deal with such a question, a few propositions need to be taken into consideration, even though they are almost truisms. First, depending on the circumstances, ethnicity may be an asset or a liability, or it may be indifferent for those involved. In other words, it may be to one's advantage to keep one's ethnicity latent, hidden in the background, or it may be to one's advantage to do the very opposite, to bring one's origin and identification to the fore, to define the relationship, the social situation, in ethnic terms. When I say an asset or a liability, I do not mean in economic terms necessarily; it may well be so in psychic, social, political, or economic terms.

It is important to emphasize that ethnicity may or may not be consistently a liability or an asset for a particular category of people. It can be a liability in particular roles and social contexts and an asset in others. It can be a liability in relation to certain categories of people or an asset in relation to others. For most people, there is a lack of complete consistency in this area, and because of this, I would hypothesize that a considerable number of people are to some degree ambivalent about their own ethnicity: in some ways they see it as a positive element in their lives; in other ways, it is something they would prefer be ignored.

Second, particular categories of people may or may not have much choice in the definition of their behaviour and social relationships in ethnic terms. This depends on the character of the social climate in the community-at-large, or in particular contexts; it also depends on the definitions that other parties bring into the situation.

Multiculturalism as a government policy has been criticized on grounds related to the question of choice. It has been argued by some that an official policy fostering the maintenance of ethnicity is likely to make it more difficult for individuals to keep their ethnicity latent if they so wish. Others argue the opposite: that the policy makes it easier for people to define themselves ethnically if they so choose. Whatever the case may be, this debate suggests that the social context is very much related to the degree of choice that particular categories of people may have in manifesting or keeping latent their ethnic identifications, whether this context has been defined historically, or defined by official policies, by ethnic group leaders, by the activities of certain organizations, by the mass media, or otherwise.

Of course, there may be some degree of ambiguity as to whether or not ethnicity is an asset or a liability, or as to the degree of choice that can be experienced in particular contexts. There may be uncertainty as to the advantages and disadvantages of defining the situation in ethnic terms.

The variations on the extent to which ethnicity is an advantage, or on the extent to which it is a matter of choice, depend on several factors:

a) The condition of segmentation that I have described above leaves less choice than a situation of heterogeneity. When people from different segments interact, the situation tends to be defined in ethnic terms, at least to some degree. A cabinet minister from French Quebec is likely to be seen not as a cabinet minister, but as a French cabinet minister, that is, one acting as a representative of the ethnic segment with which he is identified. Also, under conditions of segmentation, ethnicity is more likely to be consistently either an asset or a liability; in situations of heterogeneity, it will vary much more with the position one occupies in the social structure, with the role relationships involved, with the organizational context, and so on.

b) It also depends on the particular ethnic origins involved and the historical antecedents each carries with it. The weight of the historical background should not be underestimated in the definition of contemporary ethnic configuration of assets and liabilities, and the degree of choice in resorting to one's ethnicity.

c) The extent to which a collectivity is given an explicit, formal recognition in society will also affect the configuration of advantages and disadvantages and the extent of choice in making reference to one's ethnicity.[9]

d) It depends on the particular institutional context and the person's location in it. As a result, people of the same ethnic origin may experience a different set of advantages and disadvantages, and a different amount of choice depending on the circumstances.

What the foregoing comments are intended to underscore is that the structure of inter-ethnic relationships in particular social contexts can be best understood through an examination of the conditions under which people form groups, associations, or organizations on an ethnic basis, and the conditions under which their ethnicity remains latent or is kept in the background. People form groups in order to deal with problems they are encountering or in order to take advantage of certain opportunities. People attempt to define situations to their advantage and to resist the definitions that they perceive as being to their disadvantage. When does ethnicity come to define the configuration of problems and of opportunities?

In this perspective, inter-ethnic relationships are not necessarily the relationships between ethnic communities. Rather, inter-ethnic relationships are those that occur between whatever ethnic groupings happen to be formed in particular institutional contexts or social situations.

3. Societal organization as an object of social action

In recent years, Canada has witnessed the emergence of three sets of social groupings organized on an ethnic basis, articulating ethnic interests and advocating types of policies bearing on the condition of ethnic collectivities. These three sets of groupings can be referred to as the Québécois independentist movement, the multiculturalism movement, and the "red power" movement. Even though each set is heterogeneous, it is possible to refer to them as movements because of their overall thrust. For example, there were at one time over a dozen separatist organizations in Quebec, each with its own political philosophy and program of action. Since the formation of the Parti Québécois, the number appears to have decreased, but there is still not a unique organization representing a unique approach. Even within the Parti Québécois there are factions with differing views as to what the orientation of the party should be. But in spite of this diversity, the groupings are related to each other at least in their basic definition of the problem, and on overall orientation to its solution. Because of this, we can refer to the set as a movement.

The situation is similar in the case of the multiculturalism and "red power" movements. They also involve a variety of groups and associations in different parts of the country. From the point of view of the rest of the society, they do not constitute a series of isolated groups with activities occurring at random. Each has in common a problem and a general thrust.

Each of the three movements represents a mobilization designed to modify or transform the social order in certain ways.[10] There are perhaps more differences than similarities among the three movements in their societal situation and in the modifications they advocate. For instance, two of the movements are occurring within a "societal segment" which, historically, have had a very different relationship with the dominant segment. Both show a certain mobilization towards redefining that relationship. On the other hand, the multiculturalism movement is occurring in the context of heterogeneity rather than in the context of segmentation. Also, as indicated above, there are considerable differences of orientation within each movement. But in spite of their diversity, there is one factor that they appear to have in common: they represent the beginning of a basic change in orientation vis-à-vis the institutional system.

Touraine has indicated that such an orientation toward the social organization is a phenomenon that appeared with the advent of industrial civilization in which economic achievement and growth became a paramount goal to the pursuit of which the institutions of the society had to be used and thus shaped to satisfy such a requirement. The very organization of the society, and of its institutions, came to be seen as objects of invention, experimentation, and social action (1965: 119-132).

A similar kind of orientation may now be slowly appearing in regard to the role of ethnicity in social organization. That is to say, political rules and structures, educational organizations and programs, mass communication facilities, and even occupational and economic organizations are beginning to be seen as being modifiable in such a way as to take account of ethnic diversity and even facilitate its expression. Traditionally, the institutional order was taken as given; the questions raised had to do with the integration or assimilation into it of newcomers or of people who were somehow defined as alien (e.g. because of their colour, language, or culture); the view was the adaptation of people to the existing structures. The functionalist and conflict approaches did not differ markedly in this regard: both took the institutional system as given; they differed especially in the ways in which individuals and groups increase their participation in it, one approach stressing value consensus, the other the confrontation between established and emerging interests.

The traditionally dominant ideology in our society, an ideology which is far from having disappeared, views the institutions of the society as functioning better if ethnic differences are ignored, and preferably eliminated. In this perspective, ethnicity is relegated to the private sphere–to family life, interpersonal relationships, and voluntary associations. It is interesting to note that the trend toward the de-ethnicization of the social organization appears to have paralleled the trend toward secularization in which religion was also relegated to the private sphere.

One variation of this traditional view has been analyzed in a very insightful fashion by Blumer (1965). In this variation, the modern industrial personality is essentially non-ethnic; whatever ethnicity remains is a remnant of a traditional past and will eventually disappear under the powerful forces of the industrial and post-industrial civilization whose institutional forms are based on rationality, something seen as almost the opposite of ethnicity. If ethnic elements remain, it is only the result of a cultural lag. Blumer argued that this view constituted an ideology with little basis in reality. Industrialization may be a solvent of pre-established patterns of ethnic organizations and social relations, but with it ethnic boundaries assumed new social forms and frequently lines of ethnic differentiation that were not salient before industrialization appeared in social organization.[11]

Industrialization was pushed forward on an individualistic ideology in which the attachments to one's ethnic origin, one's religion, one's community of origin were seen as detrimental to the mobilization of labour for economic development. They were also seen as detrimental to the formation of the nation-state. Indeed, the ideology underlying the nation-state held that only one kind of nationalism was valid: territorial nationalism. Nationalisms based on culture or region were seen as a threat to the nation-state, as a menace to the integration of the political community. The social philosophy that accompanied these developments was one in which individuals, not collectivities, had rights.

In this context, ethnicity is also considered as an essentially individual attribute. Ethnicity and ethnic identity are seen as a "heritage," as "cultural baggage," as a set of values and sentiments, as a feeling of common origin. Of course, many people may have these attributes, share in the heritage, and have a sense of common origin; but these attributes are individual. Under a philosophy of individual rights, they have to be respected. But they are not attributes that could serve as a basis of social organization except perhaps in the private sphere. Ethnicity should intrude as little as possible in the organization of public institutions.

The prevalence of this ideology is not an accident. Its role in the institutional evolution of our society is certainly very complex. But an important aspect of this phenomenon should be alluded to. It appears that the prevalence of this ideology accompanied the appropriation by one ethnic collectivity–the English–of as large a portion as possible of the institutional system of our society. It is also striking that in the process, that particular ethnic group has, by and large, succeeded in defining itself as "non-ethnic." In other words, it appears that the ideology of an ethnicity-free social organization played an important role in the process whereby an ethnic collectivity assumed the control of the major social institutions, a process requiring that it define itself as non-ethnic.

Historically, the attempt was to make Canada an English society, to give its institutions and way of life a definite ethnic (English) character.[12] This involved a valuation of English culture and language and a devaluation of other cultures and languages as "alien," "minority," "traditional," and less adapted to the industrial civilization. It also involved a particular usage of the word "ethnic"—a word which became part of the very language of devaluation. The success of this ideology in organizing our way of thinking is reflected in the fact that a substantial proportion of Canadians find it impossible to think of the English in Canada as an ethnic collectivity and of an important segment of the Canadian institutions as institutions which, to a large extent, were moulded by and reflect the culture of a particular ethnic group.

What has been happening in recent years is the emergence of a different view concerning the relationship of ethnic diversity and social organization—a view in which it is possible to mould the institutions of the society to take into account ethnic differences. Rather than seeing the ideal social organization as ethnicity-free, social institutions are seen as objects of creativity and experimentation for the purpose of best incorporating ethnic diversity. This is the basic significance of the three social movements that have emerged recently.

I am not saying that this orientation is well established; on the contrary, it is only an emerging one. I am not saying either that it will eventually become the prevailing attitude in our society; it may be a temporary, transitory phenomenon. Certain groups may perceive its results as having such high social and economic costs for themselves that they will oppose it with varying degrees of success. The potential implication of this social perspective for the patterns of inter-ethnic relationships are such that it is a phenomenon that we cannot ignore; nor is it a phenomenon we can be content to be for or against. We need to study its dynamics and the ways in which it is affecting the structure and functioning of our institutions.

We need to study the specific orientations of the movements, the social forces underlying them, their internal organization and conflicts, and the social and institutional responses to them. For instance, Touraine (1965:151-163) points out that a social movement involves a principle of identity that is a definition of its interests, goals, and character; a principle of opposition that is a definition of the obstacles that have to be overcome, obstacles that are usually embedded in conditions controlled by other groups in the society; and, finally, a principle of totality that is a view of the place that the group or collectivity is to have in the organization of the society.

It would be quite worth while to compare the three movements in regard to these three parameters: identity, opposition, totality. For example, if we consider the principle of totality, we sense that the independentist movement does put forward a model of organization of the socio-political system, although the model does evolve with time. The "red power" movement is now in the process of formulating its own model of how it is to fit in the institutional system of the society as a whole. It represents a dissatisfaction with the present arrangement and a rejection of the individualistic integration model which negates ethnic communal values and structures. The multicultural movement, however, does not offer as clear an image as to which ethnic collectivities are to be incorporated in the social organization and in what institutional form they would be.[13] It represents a certain dissatisfaction with the place that has been given to the "other" groups in our society; but it is not clear what institutional arrangements are contemplated. There is a good deal of uncertainty and concern about multiculturalism in Canada. The most frequent questions raised about it are "What does it mean in practice? What does it mean other than folklore?" Such questions may appear superficial, but I think they are quite fundamental. What is asked is what does multiculturalism imply for the organization of society and of its institutions? These questions reflect an uncertainty as to the kind of institutional arrangements–at school, at work, in politics, and so on–that are intended or that are implicit in the orientation of the multicultural movement.

In short, we need to study carefully the theory or theories concerning the way the society as a whole, or particular institutions, should be organized and put forward by each social movement either implicitly or explicitly. It is essential to analyze theories if we are to understand the role of the movements in generating social change, in restructuring the relationships between ethnic collectivities in our society. We also need to study the internal organization and dynamics of movements as well as the social and institutional responses to them. Such responses are crucial in determining the kind of impact, if any, that the movements will eventually have.

In short, these movements represent attempts to modify, in varying degrees, the institutional arrangements that define the position of the ethnic segments *vis-à-vis* each other and regulate their interaction, as well as the arrangements that determine the modes of incorporation into our society of the existing ethnic heterogeneity.

Conclusion

The aim of this paper is to show that the structure of inter-ethnic relationships is the result of at least three broad categories of factors. One pertains to the socio-historical circumstances at the origin of inter-ethnic contact and to the type of ethnic differentiation that emerges. Two types were discussed: segmentation and heterogeneity. Another stems from the notion that although categories of people may be identifiable in terms of their ethnic origin, it does not mean that groups are necessarily formed and social relationships established on an ethnic basis. That is, ethnicity may or may not be a basis of social organization. The conditions under which it does must be studied. Also, ethnicity may take many different social forms, and such variations must be accounted for.

The third class of factors has to do with the theories and designs that groups generate for the structuring or restructuring of institutional arrangements in which inter-ethnic relationships take place, with the organizations that set up to pursue those clear objectives, and with the response that other groups and institutional elites make to them.

Notes

1. Parallel does not mean that the institutional systems are independent of each other; they do interact and have an impact on each other.

2. Situations of migrant superordination or dominance exhibit a wide variety of patterns. See Mason (1970), especially Part II, for a discussion of different patterns and of the factors related to their emergence.

3. There are exceptions such as the Hutterites and Mennonites. Such groups have followed a different pattern which suggests yet another type of ethnic differentiation that is not discussed here.

4. For a discussion of ethnic boundaries and their maintenance, see Barth (1969: ch. 1).

5. For a discussion of some differences in patterns of inter-ethnic relationships under the conditions of segmentation and of heterogeneity, see Breton (forthcoming).

6. The role of ethnicity in shaping commercial and financial networks is shown in Handlin (1956), Kriesberg (1955), and Cohen (1969).

7. Examples of the role of ethnicity in occupational structures can be found in Collins (1946) and Carlin (1966).

8. Campbell (forthcoming) argues that this is the case in Nova Scotia, where there are few associations to maintain ethnic identities and social boundaries since the social structure is sufficiently organized along ethnic lines to provide such support as a matter of course, so to speak.

9. For an analysis of the impact of formal legitimation in the case of religious educational institutions in Canada, see Westhues (1976).

10. Smelser defines a social movement as a collective attempt to restore, protect, modify, or create norms or values in the name of a generalized belief. Participants may be trying either to affect norms or values directly or induce some constituted authority to do so. It is a mobilization on the basis of a belief which redefines social action (1963: slightly adapted from pages 8, 270, 313).

11. The continuing role of ascription in "modern" societies and the particular role it plays in them is well argued by Mayhew (1968).

12. The historical resistance of the French to these attempts is also well documented, a resistance that had some degree of success.

13. Multiculturalism as a set of ideas does not appear to explicitly recognize differences among the various collectivities that it presumably encompasses. It does not appear to be formulating different modes of incorporation in the institutional system for the various ethnic collectivities. As an ideological tool, it runs the risk of imposing the same framework on all types of ethnic groupings. Thus, while being an ideology in favour of diversity, it may be ignoring much of the existing ethnic diversity.

References

Barth, F.
1969   *Ethnic Groups and Boundaries.* Boston: Little, Brown.
Blumer, H.
1965   "Industrialization and Race Relations." Pp. 220-253 in G. Hunter (Ed.), *Industrialization and Race Relations.* New York: Oxford University Press.
Breton, R.
        "Ethnic Segmentation and Ethnic Heterogeneity: Some Social and Institutional Characteristics." (Forthcoming).
Campbell, D.
        "The Ethnic Literature and the Nova Scotia Experience." Unpublished paper.
Carlin, J.E.
1966   *Lawyers' Ethics.* New York: Russell Sage Foundation, Ch. 2.
Cohen, A.
1969   *Custom and Politics in Urban Africa.* Berkeley: University of California Press.
Coleman, J.S.
1970   "Social Inventions." *Social Forces* 49:163-173.
Collins, O.
1945   "Ethnic Behavior in Industry: Sponsorship and Rejection in a New England Factory." *American Journal of Sociology* 51:293-298.

Duchacek, I.D.
1970 *Comparative Federalism: The Territorial Dimension of Politics.* New York: Holt, Rinehart and Winston.

Fishman, J.A.
1965 "Varieties of Ethnicity and Varieties of Language Consciousness." *Georgetown University Monographs* No. 18.

Geertz, C.
1963 *Old Societies and New States.* New York: The Free Press of Glencoe.

Gordon, M.
1964 *Assimilation in American Life.* New York: Oxford University Press.

Handlin, O., and M. Handlin
1956 "Ethnic Factors in Social Mobility." *Explorations in Entrepreneurial History* 9:1-7.

Hughes, E.C., and H.M. Hughes
1952 *Where Peoples Meet.* Glencoe, Illinois: The Free Press.

Jaszi, O.
1929 *The Dissolution of the Habsburg Monarchy.* Chicago: University of Chicago Press.

Kriesberg, L.
1955 "Occupational Controls Among Steel Distributors." *American Journal of Sociology* 61:203-212.

Lieberson, S.
1961 "A Societal Theory of Race and Ethnic Relations." *American Sociological Review* 26:902-910.

Mason, P.
1970 *Race Relations.* New York: Oxford University Press.

Mayhew, L.
1968 "Ascription in Modern Societies." *Sociological Inquiry* 38 (Spring), 105-120.

Mazrui, A.A.
1969 "Pluralism and National Integration." Pp. 333-349 in L. Kuper and M.G. Smith, (eds.), *Pluralism in Africa.* Berkeley: University of California Press.

Parenti, M.
1969 "Ethnic Politics and Persistence of Ethnic Identification." Pp. 267-283 in H.A. Bailey, Jr. and E. Katz, *Ethnic Group Politics.* Columbus, Ohio: Charles E. Merrill.

Simmel, G.
1955 *Conflict and the Web of Group Affiliations.* Glencoe, Illinois: The Free Press.

Smelser, N.J.
1963 *Theory of Collective Behavior.* New York: The Free Press.

Smith, A.D.
  1972 "Ethnocentrism, Nationalism and Social Change." *International Journal of Comparative Sociology* 13:1-20.

Smith, M.G.
  1969 "Institutional and Political Conditions of Pluralism." Pp. 26-65 in L. Kuper and M.G. Smith (eds.), *Pluralism in Africa*. Berkeley: University of California Press.

Touraine, A.
  1965 *Sociologie de l'Action*. Paris: Editions du Seuil.

Van den Berghe, P.
  1971 "The Benign Quota: Panacea or Pandora's Box." *The American Sociologist* 6:40-43.

Van den Berghe, P.
  1969 "Pluralism and the Polity: A Theoretical Exploration." Pp. 67-81 in L. Kuper, and M.G. Smith, (eds.), *Pluralism in Africa*. Berkeley: University of California Press.

Westhues, K.
  1976 "Public Versus Sectarian Legitimation: The Separate Schools of the Catholic Church." *The Canadian Review of Sociology and Anthropology* 13:137-151.

Wolf, E.R.
  1966 "Kinship, Friendship, and Patron-Client Relations in Complex Societies." *The Social Anthropology of Complex Societies* (Conference on New Approaches in Social Anthropology), Vol. I.

Zenner, W. P.
  1970 "Ethnic Assimilation and Corporate Group." Pp. 105-113 in M. Kurokawa (ed.), *Minority Responses*. New York: Random House.

PART TWO

Ethnic Migration
and Immigration Policy

PART TWO

Ethnic Migration and Immigration Policy

Immigration is an important feature of continued pluralism in any country. Immigrants replenish the old ethnic stock within the country, and contribute to its change and renewed identity. New immigrants also create continual change in the relative sizes of the groups. Sometimes large numbers of new immigrants added to a relatively small resident ethnic group, such as the recent Italian immigrants in Toronto, create a new pluralist dimension to a city or region. The somewhat greater recent influx of non-Europeans into Canada will add to the cultural and racial heterogeneity of the country.

When immigration is severely regulated, or even shut off (as has been the case for a much longer time in the United States), then a society tends increasingly to homogenize. When the flow of fresh cultural perspectives and differentiated styles of life is truncated, a society is inclined to integrate and increasingly assimilate its residents. New immigrants have, for most of the history of Canada, added a dynamic quality to Canadian society. And although this dynamic quality may be somewhat difficult to control and regulate, it makes the overall environment more stimulating. Thus, the continuation of significant inflows of immigrants into Canada seems to be a factor which is important for Canadian pluralism.

Ethnic Distribution in Canada
Warren Kalbach reviews the growth and distribution of ethnic populations in Canada during the past one-hundred-year period (1871-1971). He illustrates how immigration has always been an important factor in Canada, but that these influxes have tended to evolve in cycles over the years.

During each of the first five decades, over a million immigrants entered

Canada, while in the 1930s immigration dropped to 150,000. The ethnic origin of immigrants was heavily northern European for most of this period, but those proportions have changed recently with more southeastern and southern Europeans entering Canada. The source countries of immigrants have also been changing with the result that the number of immigrants from countries outside of Europe has been rising. However, approximately one sixth of the population has always been foreign-born.

Immigrants have also, at various times, been attracted to different regions. In the early years, the major founding groups (the British and French) settled in the eastern and central parts of Canada. During the early part of the century large numbers helped open up the prairies and the West; and recently the influx has been into large urban centres such as Toronto, Montreal, and Vancouver.

Thus, the ethnic patterns and concentrations in the Canadian mosaic vary by regions. The high British concentrations in the three most easterly Atlantic provinces, the concentration of the French in Quebec, and the high concentration of other ethnic groups in the prairies add to the interesting national mosaic. It should not be surprising that some regions of Canada should be more concerned with uniculturalism, others with biculturalism, and still others with multiculturalism. As Kalbach demonstrates, ethnic patterns and concentrations are also influenced by the rural-urban shift. Whereas many immigrants used to go to farms, they now tend to congregate in urban centres: almost half of the recent immigrants to Canada have gone to Toronto. Undoubtedly, the Canadian ethnic demographic history has been a varied one which has stimulated and changed the Canadian mosaic in various places at different times.

Canadian Immigration Policy
During the past century the Canadian government has had a fairly open immigration policy, although there have always been some restrictions, depending on the time period and the ethnic groups in question. In the early years, northern Europeans were highly favoured; they were encouraged to come through immigration offices in Britain, France, Germany, and other European countries. The British came in large numbers, while the French tended to be reluctant to emigrate. Asians were never greatly encouraged, and occasionally they were excluded from immigration policy. But continued pressure to give residents of other countries an opportunity to come to Canada resulted in revised immigration laws.

Anthony Richmond describes the different categories under which applicants may enter Canada: independent applicants, nominated relatives, and sponsored dependents. Independent applicants are subject to a points system which was designed to be impartial so that immigrants compete for entrance into Canada regardless of country of origin. Richmond discusses the problems involved in applying this system. Since this new system has been in operation, there has been a decline in northern European immigrants, and an increase in non-Caucasian immigrants, which, although allowing a more heterogeneous immigrant influx, seems to have some Canadians worried.

Recently the government prepared to review Canadian immigration policy by publishing a Green Paper on immigration in preparation for a new act. Richmond reviews some of the issues discussed in the Green Paper, including the recent immigration experience, economic implications, language implications, the points system, and the present immigration act. He tends to support extensive immigration in the future, but he fears that because of the pressures of Canadians to protect jobs and to consolidate the dominance of the northern European stock in Canada, "the outcome will probably be an unsatisfactory compromise between long-run ideals and short-run economic interests." In Richmond's opinion, such an outcome would not be the best for Canada in the long run. Whatever the immigration policy may be, it will affect the Canadian ethnic mosaic.

Immigration and the Canadian Economy
The economic factor seems to be one of the most crucial factors in determining immigration policy, and it is to this question that Professor Allen addresses himself in the third paper of this section, concerning immigration. He discusses economic goals, saying that Canada should adhere to an international perspective which views migration as good and encourages free mobility of labour. On the other hand, the nationalist perspective is concerned with the well-being only of the residents of a particular nation. Allen suggests that the authors of the Green Paper take the nationalist view because they claim that immigration will reduce wages and the amount of goods and services available for residents in Canada, and that it should be tightly controlled for the benefit of Canadians. Allen strongly supports the need for world interdependence and mutual concern for the welfare of all nations and, in short, criticizes the narrow nationalist perspective.

In a comparative study of a Canadian immigrant sample and a mass layoff sample of Canadians, Allen shows the ability of immigrant workers to compete in the job market despite the fact they are handicapped in many respects. In every measure used, the Canadian immigrant groups showed a more successful experience than the mass layoff control group. The immigrants had a lower unemployment rate than the control group, and they fared no worse in job mobility and earned income. Allen concludes that the labour market experience of both independent and nominated immigrants is remarkable, given that their labour market situation and employability characteristics were inferior to those of the mass layoff control group. He does not agree that immigrants pose an economic burden to Canada, and, more important, he feels that improvement in the lives of the immigrants is a concern often ignored. Through the eyes of an international economic model, Allen feels that immigrants are an important asset to Canada. Many expect Canada to share its abundant space and resources with others; immigration affords an opportunity to do so. In addition, immigration will maintain Canada as an ethnic mosaic, perhaps even more heterogeneous than before. Canada's immigration policy may result in potential conflict, but then some conflict serves to keep Canada a dynamic and growing nation.

Attitudes of Canadians Toward Immigrants
More comprehensive surveys need to be made of Canadian attitudes toward immigrants. Friedenberg does provide us with an assessment of Canadian attitudes toward American immigrants, the second largest group of immigrants to enter Canada recently. He suggests that although Canadians have decried American racial discrimination, some Canadians are hardly less prejudiced against Americans. While the Canadian Bill of Rights Act declares that there shall be no discrimination by reason of race, national origin, colour, religion, or sex, Friedenberg does not give Canadians high marks for following these ideals with regard to Americans.

Americans, he writes, like Jews, have been regarded as predators, and many Canadians who dislike Americans feel that they need to be protected against them because Americans are a threat to Canadian society. What is the source of this perceived threat? Friedenberg suggests that "Immigrants usually attract hostile notice if they are 1) sufficiently different culturally to seem shocking to their hosts, 2) so numerous as to be highly visible, or 3) appear to be an economic threat." The first and second reasons do not seem to be the true concern; rather, it appears to be the American economic threat that Canadians fear. It is to this matter that the author addresses himself at considerable length.

This article is but one of many studies which need to be done in Canada. Prejudice and discrimination in Canada seem to be lurking in the background, and, there is much work for scholars in studying this phenomenon as diligently in Canada as has been done in other countries. If Canada continues to open its doors to large numbers of immigrants, Canadians need to be willing to accept newcomers.

As more and more Asian, African, and southern European immigrants arrive in Canada, the northern European stock may feel increasingly threatened. This could lead to ugly consequences. What kind of a mosaic is Canada willing to create? Are we creating a fairly homogeneous northern European mosaic (which may be limited in heterogeneity), or highly diversified patterns of culture, race, religion, and colour? How extensively will the founding peoples (British and French) attempt to control a limited mosaic? Will the attitudes of Canadians tolerate a highly diversified mosaic, or will it need to be a limited pattern of differentiation?

The Kalbach survey suggests that over the past one hundred years, the

Canadian mosaic has been designed to include largely northern European stock. Richmond's discussion of immigration policy suggests that the Canadian government is seeking to develop a policy that is open to all sources of immigrants who can compete, but it is also worried about changes in the balance of majority-minority powers. Allen shows that the economic factor is a major force to contend with, because it can be used as a regulator of immigrant flows, and also as a means to control the selection of immigrants. Friedenberg warns that Canadian attitudes may be more prone to prejudice and discrimination than we are willing to admit. He challenges Canadians to live up to their high ideals as recorded in the Bill of Rights; however, he finds evidence that, at best, Canadians may be willing to build only a very limited ethnic mosaic.

4
Growth and Distribution of Canada's Ethnic Populations, 1871-1971

Warren E. Kalbach*

The national decennial census is the only source of data with sufficient scope and depth to permit an historical analysis of the population of Canada in terms of its ethnic and cultural origins. Data have been collected for over a century which have significance for the social, economic, and political development of Canada's regions and communities; and an impressive body of data, relating to the cultural origins and present composition of Canadian society, has resulted from the consistent inclusion of questions in the census asking for information on cultural and related characteristics of individuals permanently residing in Canada. The analysis of the growth and distribution of Canada's population presented in this paper focuses on two of these basic data series (nativity and ethnic origins), which have particular importance for the understanding of the ethnic character of Canadian society, and provide a more general perspective from which to view the other papers in this volume.

POPULATION GROWTH

The Foreign-born Population
The growth of the foreign-born population, which depends primarily on the influx of immigrants in relation to emigration and mortality, has reflected the succession of waves characteristic of the immigrant streams to Canada over the past century. The two periods of greatest immigration, one prior to the First World War and the other following the Second, are reflected in the increased percentage of foreign-born population reported in the Census of 1911 and again in 1961. Even though the estimated net

* Warren E. Kalbach is Professor of Sociology, University of Toronto, Ontario.

migration for the post-Second World War period was higher than that estimated for either of the decades prior to or including the First, the actual effect of immigration on the overall population was less because of the much larger size of Canada's present population.

Table 1 clearly shows that periods of high immigration were also periods of high growth rates for the total population. The foreign-born population was the largest, relative to the total, at the time of the 1921 Census, when it comprised 22.3 per cent of Canada's population. Post-Second World War immigration arrested the declining trend in the proportion of foreign-born, which took place through the economic recession years of the 1930s and the war years, and peaked at 15.6 per cent at the time of the 1961 Census following a period of rapid economic growth. As may be seen in Table 1, the relative size of the foreign-born population remained fairly constant during the 1960s, declining slightly to 15.3 per cent in 1971. With the exception of the 1930s, the foreign-born population has always managed to achieve some increase in numbers during each decade of the past hundred years, but its rate of growth has not always kept up with that of the native-born.

Children of the Foreign-Born

Data on the foreign-born alone do not reveal the full extent of their contribution to the growth of the national population. Children born in Canada to foreign-born residents are generally included with all native-born persons in census publications, so that it is not possible to estimate their direct contribution to total growth. Only twice in recent decades have data been collected on the nativity of the parents that would permit an examination of the generational components and their relative sizes. These data, from the 1931 and 1971 censuses, identifying three generational groupings of the population, are presented in Table 2.

It is apparent that the foreign-born make an additional and highly significant contribution to the population in the form of the second generation. In 1931, the children of the foreign-born made up approximately one-quarter of the population, whereas the two groups combined comprised almost one half of the total. While the numbers of first and second generation Canadians increased from 4.7 million in 1931, to 7.1 in 1971, their combined relative size actually declined to 33 per cent during this period. Nevertheless, in both years the total contribution of the foreign-born to the nation's population was actually more than twice as much as it would have been had the estimates been based on the proportions of foreign-born alone, as is usually the case.

Ethnic Populations[1]

The French were the first to establish a good foothold for themselves in that part of the New World destined to become Canada. Even after the

Table 1

Population Increase, Immigration, and The Foreign-Born Population

Canada, 1871-81 to 1961-71

Decade	Population		Immigration		Foreign-Born	
	Total Population[a]	Estimated Average Annual Rate of Population Increase	Number of Immigrants	Per Cent of Average Decade Population	Total Foreign-Born[a]	Per Cent Foreign-Born
	('000)	(%)	('000)		('000)	
1871-1881	3,605	1.60	353	8.8	602	16.7
1881-1891	4,325	1.12	903	19.7	603	13.9
1891-1901	4,833	1.06	326	6.4	644	13.3
1901-1911	5,371	2.98	1,759	28.0	700	13.0
1911-1921	7,207	2.00	1,612	20.2	1,587	22.0
1921-1931	8,788	1.68	1,203	12.6	1,956	22.3
1931-1941	10,377	1.04	150	1.4	2,308	22.2
1941-1951	11,507	1.72	548	4.4	2,010	17.5
1951-1961	14,009	2.68	1,543	9.6	2,060	14.7
1961-1971	18,238	1.70	1,429	7.2	2,844	15.6
1971-	21,569	–	–	–	3,296	15.3

Source: Dominion Bureau of Statistics, Censuses of Canada, 1851 to 1961; Statistics Canada, 1971 Census of Canada, Ottawa: Information Canada; Kalbach, W.E., The Effect of Immigration on Population, The Canadian Immigration and Population Study, Department of Manpower and Immigration, Ottawa: Information Canada, 1974, Tables 1.1 and 2.6.
[a] Population at the beginning of the decade.

Table 2

Population by Generations, Canada: 1931 and 1971

Generation[a]	1931		1971	
	Number	Per Cent	Number	Per Cent
1st generation	2,234,600	21.6	3,177,200	14.7
2nd generation	2,509,500	24.2	3,986,700	18.5
3rd[b] generation	5,615,600	54.2	14,404,400	66.8
Total:	10,359,700	100.0	21,568,300	100.0

Source: Dominion Bureau of Statistics, *1931 Census of Canada*, Ottawa: The Queen's Printer, Vol. III, Table 27, and Vol. IV, Table 15. Statistics Canada, *1971 Census of Canada*, Bulletin 1.3-6, Ottawa: Information Canada, 1974, Table 46.

[a]Generations are defined as follows: 1st generation are the foreign-born with foreign-born parents; 2nd generation are the native-born with one or both parents foreign born; 3rd and subsequent generations are the native born with native-born parents. This also includes some who were born outside Canada to native-born parents, of which there were 69,500 in 1931, and 118,300 in 1971.

[b]The 1931 total excludes 17,136 persons for whom nativity of parents was not stated.

British finally secured political control after the Seven Years War, the majority of the population was still French speaking. Not until the emigration of British Empire Loyalists from the American colonies after the American Revolution were the British able to establish a population base sufficiently large for the ultimate achievement of numerical superiority in addition to the political control they had won earlier. By the time of Confederation, just under two-thirds, or 60.5 per cent, of the population were of British origins, while almost one-third, or 31.3 per cent, were French. The remaining population was predominantly German, with some Dutch and a scattering of Scandinavians, Russians, and Italians.

The British have managed to maintain their numerical dominance throughout the century; yet, on the other hand, the population of French origin has continued to be the single largest homogeneous cultural group in Canada. On only two occasions were the numbers of French exceeded by another relatively homogeneous group. In 1921, and again in 1971, the English were ranked first in size. However, because of the difficulties in obtaining reliable estimates of the population by ethnic origins over time, it would be ill-advised to attach too much significance to the occasional exception to pervasive historical trends.[2]

The breakdown of the British origins group, provided in Table 3, underscores the greater heterogeneity of the British *vis-à-vis* the French. According to these data, the Irish tended to have numerical superiority over the English until 1901. But after the heavy influx of immigrants

Table 3

Population[a] of British Isles, French and Other Selected Origins, Canada
1871, 1881, and 1901–1971

Ethnic Group	1871[b]	1881	1901	1911	1921	1931	1941	1951	1961	1971
Total[c]	3,486	4,325	5,371	7,207	8,788	10,377	11,507	14,009	18,238	21,568
British Isles	2,111	2,549	3,063	3,999	4,869	5,381	5,716	6,710	7,997	9,624
English	706	881	1,261	1,871	2,545	2,741	2,968	3,630	4,195	6,246
Irish	846	957	989	1,075	1,108	1,231	1,268	1,440	1,753	1,581
Scottish	550	700	800	1,027	1,174	1,346	1,404	1,547	1,902	1,720
Other	8	10	13	26	42	62	76	92	146	86
French	1,083	1,299	1,649	2,062	2,453	2,928	3,483	4,319	5,540	6,180
Other European	240	299	458	945	1,247	1,825	2,044	2,554	4,117	4,960
Austrian, n.o.s.	–	–	11	44	108	49	38	32	107	42
Belgian	–	–	3	10	20	28	30	35	61	51
Czech & Slovak	–	–	–	–	9	30	43	64	73	82
Finnish[d]	–	–	3	16	21	44	42	44	59	59
German	203	254	311	403	295	474	465	620	1,050	1,317
Greek	–	–	–	4	6	9	12	14	56	124
Hungarian[e]	–	–	2	12	13	41	55	60	126	132
Italian	1	2	11	46	67	98	113	152	450	731
Jewish	–	1	16	76	126	157	170	182	173	297

Lithuanian	—	—	—	—	2	6	8	16	28	25
Netherlands	30	30	34	56	118	149	213	264	430	426
Polish	—	—	6	34	53	146	167	220	324	316
Roumanian[f]	—	1	—	6	13	29	25	24	44	27
Russian[g]	1	5	20	44	100	88	84	91	119	64
Scandinavian	2	—	31	113	167	228	245	283	387	385
Ukrainian	—	—	6	75	107	225	306	395	473	581
Yugoslav	—	—	—	—	4	16	21	21	69	105
Other	4	6	5	7	18	9	10	36	88	195
Asiatic	—	4	24	43	66	85	74	73	122	286
Chinese	—	4	17	28	40	47	35	33	58	119
Japanese	—	—	5	9	16	23	23	22	29	37
Other	—	—	2	6	10	15	16	19	34	129
Other	52	174	177	158	153	158	190	354	463	519

Source: Dominion Bureau of Statistics, *1961 Census of Canada*, Bulletin 7:1-6, Ottawa: The Queen's Printer, 1966, Table 1 and Table I; Statistics Canada, *1971 Census of Canada*, Bulletin 1.3-2, Ottawa: Information Canada, 1973, Table 1; Kubat, D., and D. Thornton, *A Statistical Profile of Canadian Society*, Toronto: McGraw-Hill Ryerson Ltd., 1974, Table f-10.
[a] Numbers rounded to the nearest 1,000.
[b] Four original provinces only.
[c] Excludes Newfoundland prior to 1951.
[d] Excludes Estonian prior to 1951.
[e] Includes Lithuanian and Moravian in 1901 and 1911.
[f] Includes Bulgarian in 1901 and 1911.
[g] Includes Finnish and Polish in 1871 and 1881.

during the early twentieth century, they were exceeded by both the English and the Scotch. Perhaps the other most significant aspect of this particular period of time was the rising prominence of the "other" ethnic-origin populations in the Canadian mosaic. The British declined from about 61 per cent in 1871 to 45 per cent in 1971, and the French component remained relatively constant at about 30 per cent. All of the other ethnic groups combined increased from a negligible 8 per cent, in 1871, to a substantial 27 per cent in 1971.

The predominance of the Germans and Dutch in this residual group prior to the 1900s has already been mentioned. With the opening of the prairies for settlement, and the events in Europe leading up to the First World War and its aftermath, the numbers of eastern and southern Europeans in the Canadian population began to increase significantly. Of the two previously mentioned, only the Germans have consistently maintained their relative numerical position, and are still the largest ethnic origin population in Canada after the British and French.

Components of Population Change

Fertility, Immigration, and Population Growth. The actual levels of fertility for the decades following Confederation, and through the first twenty years of the twentieth century, are still subject to considerable debate. Nevertheless, whichever estimates are taken as most correct, it is clear that births have had, and continue to have, greater significance for population growth in Canada than immigration. For the decade of heaviest immigration, i.e., 1901-11, births exceeded immigrants by over 170,000. Data in Table 4 clearly show that fertility, measured in numbers of births, has consistently exceeded estimates of the numbers of immigrants for each of the ten decades.

The effective contribution to population growth by births is mitigated by the number of deaths; and, similarly, the direct effects of immigration are reduced in proportion to the number of emigrants who leave the country. While the later component is extremely difficult to estimate accurately, data from the census, immigration records, and vital statistics show that the net gain from natural increase during the 1901-11 decade exceeded net immigration by at least 220,000. Estimates for other decades consistently show the greater contribution of natural increase over net immigration. For certain single years, the significance of net immigration has occasionally increased dramatically, but for the years following the Second World War, its net effect never reached 50 per cent of the annual population increase. In 1951, an estimated net immigration of 184,000 accounted for 41 per cent of the population increase for that year. The highest net immigration, which occurred in 1956, and amounted to 200,000, contributed somewhat less, or 38 per cent, to that year's growth; and, in 1966, an estimated 131,000 net immigrants contributed 36 per cent of that year's increase. At no time during the post-war period did net immigration ever achieve the distinction of contributing the major share of the country's growth.[3]

Table 4

Components of Population Change, Canada: 1891-1971

Decade[a]	Births	Natural Increase	Immigration	Estimated Net Immigration
	('000)	('000)	('000)	('000)
1871-1881	1,477	723	353	- 87
1881-1891	1,538	714	903	-206
1891-1901	1,546	718 (670)[c]	326 (250)[c]	-180 (-130)[c]
1901-1911	1,931	1,120 (1,030)	1,759 (1,550)	716 (810)
1911-1921	2,338	1,230[b] (1,270)	1,612 (1,400)	351 (310)
1921-1931	2,415	1,360	1,203	229
1931-1941	2,294	1,222	150	- 92
1941-1951	3,186	1,972	548	169
1951-1961	4,468	3,148	1,543	1,081
1961-1971	4,063	2,703	1,429	627

Source: Department of Manpower and Immigration, *1972 Immigration Statistics*, Ottawa: Information Canada, 1974, Table 1.
[a]Data for intercensal years.
[b]Includes war deaths.
[c]Corrected estimates in P. Camu, E.P. Weeks, and Z. Sametz, *Economic Geography of Canada*, Toronto: Macmillan of Canada, 1964, Table 3.

Fertility, Immigration, and Ethnic Composition. As fertility and immigration both contribute to numerical changes in the population, so too can they produce changes in the ethnic composition of that population. In short, the ethnic composition of the total is the weighted average of the ethnic make-up of the native-born and the foreign-born. Differences in fertility along ethnic lines will clearly affect the ethnic composition of the native-born population, while shifts in the source countries of immigration will directly affect the ethnic character of the foreign-born, and indirectly the composition of the total population. Again, fertility will probably have the greatest effect, but this would be more difficult to show than it was in the case of population growth alone. While changes in the character of the immigrant stream can produce significant shifts in the ethnic composition of the foreign-born in a relatively short period of time, their effects are greatly reduced when combined with the native-born population, because of its small size relative to the latter population. Similarly, whatever the fertility differentials might be among the foreign-born by ethnic origins, the annual cohort of births contributed by the foreign-born has already been shown to be rather small, hence their overall effect on the ethnic composition of the total population would be relatively slight.

It is a well-established fact that the French-origin population has maintained its relative position in Canada through its traditionally high fertility rather than through dependence upon immigration, as has been the case for the British-origins group. Both the data and the analyses of the 1961 Census, as well as the data from the 1971 Census, show that the fertility of women who have never been married is still generally higher for those of French origin than those belonging to the other ethnic groups. The exceptions are to be found among younger married women, under 25 years of age, and women from some Protestant groups, e.g., Hutterites, Mennonites, Mormons, etc.[4]

Fertility levels in Quebec have been falling since 1957, as they have generally for the nation as a whole. However, it is significant that they have been falling faster in Quebec than elsewhere, and by 1968 Quebec had the lowest crude birth rate of any province in Canada. In addition, Quebec was the only province whose gross reproduction rate had fallen below 1.0 by 1970,[5] a level somewhat below that required for maintaining a zero growth situation in the absence of a positive net immigration. For obvious reasons, these trends have caused concern among Quebec politicians and others concerned with the province's future. If Quebec can neither reverse the present trend in fertility nor succeed in attracting French-speaking immigrants, it will have to pursue more drastic measures to preserve the French Canadian culture and language for future generations.

Changes in the source countries for immigrants have been the primary factor underlying the gradual decline of the British-origins population since Confederation. The increase in immigrants from other western and northern European countries was not seen as a problem by the dominant British-origins group because of their cultural similarity. However, the increasing influx of "new" immigrants, during the 1900s, from eastern and southern Europe began to cause concern among the "old" immigrants, who felt that the increasing numbers from non-traditional source areas might have deleterious effects on the established Canadian way of life.

Between 1926 and 1966, the proportions of immigrants of northern and western European origins, including British, declined significantly. The proportions of central and eastern European origins also declined, but the relative numbers of southern and southeastern European origins increased dramatically. While the latter group constituted only 4.5 per cent of all the immigrants coming to Canada between 1926 and 1946, their proportion jumped to 15 per cent during the immediate post-war period, and then doubled to 30 per cent for the 1956-66 period. Those of Asian origins also showed a significant increase, from under 1 per cent before the war to 6.5 per cent during the same period, although their numbers were relatively small. These data are summarized in Table 5.

Table 5

Immigration by Ethnic-Origin Groups for Canada

1926-45, 1946-55, and 1956-66

Ethnic-Origin Group	1926-45	1946-55	1955-66
British Isles	47.8%	34.1	32.9
Northwestern European	24.4	30.2	20.7
Central and East European	19.1	15.1	7.7
Southeastern and South European	4.5	15.3	29.9
Jewish	3.4	3.5	2.2
Asian and Other origins	0.8	1.7	6.5
Total: Per Cent	100.0	100.0	100.0
Number	950,944	1,222,318	1,476,444

Source: Department of Manpower and Immigration, Annual immigration reports; Royal Commission on Bilingualism and Biculturalism, *The Cultural Contribution of the Other Ethnic Groups*, Book IV, Ottawa: The Queen's Printer, 1970, Table A-1; and, Kalbach, W.E., *The Effect of Immigration on Population*, The Immigration and Population Study, Department of Manpower and Immigration, Ottawa: Information Canada, 1974, Table 2.1.

Ethnic-origin data were not collected after 1966, but parallel trends can still be seen in data on "country of last permanent residence" which the Department of Manpower and Immigration continues to collect. The proportion of immigrants coming from Asian and other non-European countries increased, doubling from 6 to 12 per cent between 1955-60 and 1961-65. This trend extended into the next five-year period with their proportion almost doubling again to 23 per cent, and reaching approximately 35 per cent during the last year of this period.[6] However, it should be pointed out that between 1967 and 1971, immigration dropped from a peak of 223,000 to 122,000. What made this particular period especially notable was that the numbers of immigrants from non-European areas were steadily increasing at a time when those from European areas were

91

dropping significantly. The net effect on the character of the immigrant stream is also illustrated by the changes which have occurred in the list of ten leading source countries of immigrants since 1951 given in Table 6.

Table 6

Ten Leading Source Countries of Immigrants

Selected Years

1951	1960	1968	1973
Britain	Italy	Britain	Britain
Germany	Britain	United States	United States
Italy	United States	Italy	Hong Kong
Netherlands	Germany	Germany	Portugal
Poland	Netherlands	Hong Kong	Jamaica
France	Portugal	France	India
United States	Greece	Austria	Philippines
Belgium	France	Greece	Greece
Yugoslavia	Poland	Portugal	Italy
Denmark	Austria	Yugoslavia	Trinidad

Source: Manpower and Immigration, *Highlights from the Green Paper on Immigration and Population*, Canadian Immigration and Population Study, Ottawa: Information Canada, 1975, p. 28.

Much of this shift to non-European countries can be attributed to the elimination of restrictions against potential immigrants on the basis of race and ethnicity in 1967, and to the increasing pressure for emigration in many of the third world countries. Faced with a commitment to maintain a non-discriminatory policy during a period of increasing interest in immigration to Canada, the government has been seeking the ways and means to either restrict or more closely regulate immigration in relation to the needs of the economy. The government's extensive review of its policies and practices undertaken as a prelude to a possible revision of its Immigration Act, is set forth in its Green Paper on immigration and population.[7]

POPULATION DISTRIBUTION

Regional Patterns
The Foreign-born: 1901-1971. The patterns of residential location exhibited by immigrants, like their growth rate, have been uneven through this period of Canadian history. The heavy immigration of the early twentieth century coincided with the opening and settlement of the prairies, and the

foreign-born concentrated heavily in this western region. The proportion of the foreign-born locating in the prairie provinces doubled in the first decade, and it was not until after 1921, with continuing immigration and a shift in the pattern of settlement to other areas, that their heavy concentration in the prairies began to show signs of erosion. In Table 7, it is evident that by 1961 the distribution of foreign-born had almost returned to what it had been at the beginning of the present century. The life cycle of the early settlers seems to have been almost completed. They have raised their families, and many of those who have not already passed on have moved away from their farms in retirement. By 1971, more than half of all the foreign-born remaining in Canada were located in Ontario. Quebec and British Columbia were the only other major regions to show net gains in their relative share of foreign-born over this seventy-year period. In contrast, the Atlantic provinces, the Yukon, the Northwest Territories, and the prairie provinces all showed declines, but only in the prairies did the *number* of foreign-born actually decline during the last intercensal period.

Native-born Generations. Distributions of the population by generations for the provinces in 1931 and 1971 are shown in Table 8. In 1931, there was a very clear east-west distinction in the balance between the first generation Canadians and their children, and the third and subsequent generations of native-born population with native-born parents. Quebec and the eastern provinces were dominated by the latter generational groups. In no case did the foreign-born and their children amount to more than 20 per cent. While Ontario's population was almost evenly divided, the western provinces were almost equally dominated by the combined first and second generation populations.

By 1971, the picture had changed radically in the West as a result of the aging of the foreign-born, changing patterns of internal migration, and the high post-war fertility of the native-born. A majority of every province's population, except that of British Columbia, were native-born of native-born parents. Even in British Columbia, with 53 per cent of its population still first or second generation, its decline from 80 per cent in 1931 was both significant and consistent with the overall trend.

Ontario's first and second generation population declined from 60 to 42 per cent during this forty-year period in spite of the heavy influx of post-war immigrants to that province. The balance changed very little in Quebec, and both Quebec and Ontario were somewhat unique in that, unlike the other provinces, their first and second generations were approximately the same—reflecting, no doubt, the lower fertility of the foreign-born who have settled in these areas. The proportions of third and subsequent generations in the populations of the Atlantic provinces continued to climb, with only Nova Scotia failing to exceed the 90 per cent level. The significance of these changes in generational composition of the population would appear to be different for the Atlantic provinces

Table 7

Canada's Foreign-Born Population
by Region: 1901 to 1971

Nativity and Region	1901	1911	1921	1931	1941	1951[a]	1961[a]	1971*[a]
Foreign-Born	%	%	%	%	%	%	%	%
Atlantic Provinces	6.7	3.6	3.4	3.0	3.2	2.7	2.3	2.2
Quebec	12.7	9.2	9.7	10.9	11.1	11.1	13.6	14.2
Ontario	46.3	32.0	32.8	34.9	36.3	41.2	47.6	51.8
Prairie Provinces	20.3	40.8	40.7	37.3	34.2	28.4	21.4	16.5
British Columbia	11.3	14.1	13.3	13.8	15.1	16.5	14.9	15.1
Yukon and N.W.T.	2.7	0.3	0.1	0.1	0.1	0.1	0.2	0.1
Total:								
Percentage	100.0	100.0	100.0	100.0	100.0	100.0	100.0	99.9
Number ('000)	700	1,587	1,956	2,308	2,019	2,060	2,844	3,296

Source: Censuses of Canada, 1901 to 1971.
[a]Includes Newfoundland in 1951, 1961 and 1971.

than for the western provinces. In the first case, where there is a high proportion of British origins, a continuing decline in the foreign-born could work to strengthen the culture of the dominant group. In the latter case, the same trend could easily work towards reducing the ethnic distinctiveness of those non-British origin groups that settled in Canada's West.

Ethnic Populations. The French population in Canada has compensated, in part, for its smaller size by maintaining a singularly high degree of regional concentration. Had they been more evenly distributed throughout Canada, they would not have been able to achieve the numerical dominance in any one region that they have in Quebec today. In 1971, slightly more than three-fourths of the French-origin population lived in Quebec, and almost 80 per cent of that province's population was French. Those of British origin, less regionally concentrated, numerically dominated the French in every province outside of Quebec. Yet, only in Nova Scotia, Prince Edward Island, and Newfoundland could one find the proportions of British as high, or higher, than the concentration of French in Quebec. In this sense, only Newfoundland, with a 94 per cent British

Table 8

Population by Generation for Canada and Provinces, 1931 and 1971

Generation	Canada	Nfld.	P.E.I.	N.S.	N.B.	Que.	Ont.	Man.	Sask.	Alta.	B.C.
1971				(per cent)							
1st Generation	14.7	1.5	2.4	4.0	2.9	7.3	21.6	14.6	11.5	16.8	22.2
2nd Generation	18.5	2.7	5.8	8.8	7.0	7.2	22.0	27.4	29.4	30.7	30.9
3rd$^+$ Generation	66.8	95.7	91.7	87.2	90.2	85.5	56.4	58.0	59.1	52.5	47.0
Total:	100.0	100.0	100.0	100.0	100.0	100.0	100.0	100.0	100.0	100.0	100.0
1931											
1st Generation	21.6	—	2.2	7.4	5.0	7.8	23.0	33.4	33.9	41.4	45.5
2nd Generation	24.2	⊤	8.3	12.1	10.6	8.5	27.9	40.1	42.2	39.0	34.9
3rd$^+$ Generation	54.2	—	89.5	80.5	84.4	83.7	49.1	26.5	23.8	19.9	19.5
Total:	100.0	—	100.0	100.0	100.0	100.0	100.0	100.0	100.0	100.0	100.0

Source: See Table 2.

population, and Prince Edward Island with 83 per cent, are more British than Quebec is French.

Ethnic origins, other than British or French, tend to show higher relative concentrations west and north of Ontario. Among the Europeans, the Italians and Jews tend to be exceptions, in that the former are highly concentrated in Ontario, while the latter are found in disproportionately greater numbers in Manitoba, Quebec, and Ontario. Asians are concentrated in British Columbia, but are also found in above average numbers in Alberta and Ontario.

Less detailed information on the ethnic composition of the population by provinces for the year 1901 is also included in Table 9, along with the larger number of ethnic-origin groups shown for 1971. These data permit a consideration of the changes in proportions of provincial populations in relation to changes in the proportions of the national population for specific ethnic-origin groups at two points in time. Such a comparison indicates that the net effect of differential growth rates, and shifts in the distribution of Canada's ethnic populations over this seventy-year interval, have produced a greater relative concentration of British in the Atlantic provinces, as well as in the western portion of the country. Comparisons of the combined "other" ethnic groups indicate that a decrease in their relative concentration has occurred in Manitoba and further west, even though their proportions of the provincial populations have increased or remained about the same. Significant increases can be observed in Ontario and Quebec, although in the latter case the "others" are still underrepresented to a considerable degree. Their small representation in the remaining provinces to the east produced a further decline in their relative concentration in these areas.

Overall, there do not seem to have been any startling shifts in the relative concentrations of these major ethnic-origin groups for Canada's major regions. The basic pattern of the geographical ethnic mosaic would seem to have been laid down fairly early in Canada's history by the two founding groups, and their relatively large size would tend to resist the effects of rapid shifts caused by recent migrants responding to the increased opportunities found in Canada's largest metropolitan centres. In the long run, however, the tendency for more rapid industrial and economic development to occur in central Canada and in the far West will channel recent immigrants, as well as internal migrants of differing origins into these areas. If this is in fact the case, Canada's ethnic patterns will, in time, shift accordingly.

The Rural-Urban Shift

Since Confederation the rural-urban distribution of Canada's population has almost completely reversed itself. In 1871, eight out of every ten persons lived in rural areas. By 1971, only 24 per cent were still classified as rural. Urbanization continued throughout the entire period at a steady

96

Table 9

Percentage Composition of the Population by Ethnic Origins for Province of Residence, Canada: 1901 and 1971

Ethnic Origin	Total	Nfld.	P.E.I.	N.S.	N.B.	Que.	Ont.	Man.	Sask.	Alta.	B.C.
1901 British	57.0		85.1	78.1	71.1	17.6	79.3	64.4	43.9	47.8	59.6
French	30.7		13.4	9.8	24.2	80.2	7.3	6.3	2.9	6.2	2.6
Other	12.3		1.5	12.0	4.1	2.2	13.4	29.4	53.2	46.0	37.9
Total:	100.0		100.0	100.0	100.0	100.0	100.0	100.0	100.0	100.0	100.0
1971 British	44.6	93.8	82.7	77.5	57.6	10.6	59.4	41.9	42.1	46.8	57.9
French	28.7	3.0	13.7	10.2	37.0	79.0	9.6	8.8	6.1	5.8	4.4
Other	26.7	3.3	3.6	12.3	5.3	10.4	31.0	49.3	51.8	47.4	37.7
German	6.1	0.5	0.9	5.2	1.3	0.9	6.2	12.5	19.4	14.2	9.1
Dutch	2.0	0.1	1.1	1.9	0.8	0.2	2.7	3.6	2.1	3.6	3.2
Scandinavian	1.8	0.2	0.2	0.5	0.6	0.1	0.8	3.6	6.4	6.0	5.1
Polish	1.5	0.1	0.1	0.4	0.1	0.4	1.9	4.3	2.9	2.7	1.4
Russian	0.3	0.0	0.0	0.0	0.0	0.1	0.2	0.4	1.1	0.6	1.1
Ukrainian	2.7	0.0	0.1	0.3	0.1	0.3	2.1	11.6	9.3	8.3	2.8
Italian	3.4	0.1	0.1	0.5	0.2	2.8	6.0	1.1	0.3	1.5	2.5
Jewish	1.4	0.1	0.1	0.3	0.2	1.9	1.8	2.0	0.2	0.4	0.6
Other Europe	3.9	0.2	0.2	0.8	0.4	2.0	6.1	3.8	4.1	4.1	4.5
Asiatic	1.3	0.3	0.3	0.6	0.4	0.7	1.5	1.0	0.8	1.6	3.6
Other & N.S.	2.4	1.7	0.5	1.8	1.2	1.0	1.9	5.6	5.2	4.2	3.9
Total:	100.0	100.0	100.0	100.0	100.0	100.0	100.0	100.0	100.0	100.0	100.0

Source: Dominion Bureau of Statistics, *Census of Canada, 1921*, Vol. I, Ottawa: The King's Printer, 1924, Table 23. Statistics Canada, *1971 Census of Canada*, Bulletin 1.3-2. Ottawa: Information Canada, 1973, Table 3.

97

pace, and by 1921 the population was almost evenly divided between rural and urban areas. The surprising fact is that the heavy influx of immigrants to the prairies in the first decade of the twentieth century did not slow the process at all. The rural population did increase by over half a million at this time, but the urban population grew by one and a quarter million, causing the proportion of the population that was rural to decline from 63 to 55 per cent.

The Foreign-born Population. The settlement of agricultural lands in the West, at a time of heavy immigration, suggests that the foreign-born would be found in the rural areas in disproportionately larger numbers. While this may have been the case during the early decades of Confederation, by 1921 a larger proportion of the foreign-born were to be found in urban areas than of the native-born. Data presented in Table 10 show that this has not only continued to be the case, but also that the difference between the native- and foreign-born has continued to increase. In 1921, the proportion of foreign-born residing in urban areas was 56 per cent, compared to 48 per cent for the native-born. Fifty years later, the proportions for the foreign- and native-born were 88 and 74 per cent respectively.

Not only have the foreign-born urbanized to a greater extent than those born in Canada, but they have also shown a greater preference for the larger urban centres. In 1971, while 43.8 per cent of the native-born were located in urban places of 100,000 or more, 68 per cent of the foreign-born were similarly located. Furthermore, the more recent the time of arrival in Canada, the greater the attraction of large cities appears to be to the immigrants. As Table 11 indicates, 73 per cent of all post-war immigrants were living in urban centres of over 100,000 in 1971. For the most recent arrivals, who came in 1969 and 1970, the proportion was 77 per cent.[8]

Urbanization of Ethnic Populations. Some ethnic populations have been traditionally urban in their settlement patterns, while others have remained entrenched in rural areas. As early as Confederation, two-thirds of the population of Jewish origins resided in urban areas, and by 1971 almost all, or 99 per cent, were urban residents. At the other extreme are such ethno-religious groups as the Hutterites, who have always lived in rural colonies in Canada, and the native Indians, who have generally found themselves on the outside of the white man's municipal boundaries. In 1971, only 30 per cent of native Indians and Eskimos were living in urban areas.

From the data presented in Table 12, it may be seen that the two founding groups have charted a course between the extremes mentioned above. Those of British origins have generally been more urbanized than the French, but the two groups have been slowly converging over the years as the nation itself has become more urbanized. In 1971, for the first time, both the British and French showed the same proportion, or 75.9 per

Table 10

Per Cent Urban[a] for Foreign- and Native-Born Populations

in Canada, 1921—1971

Year	Foreign-Born	Native-Born	Total
1921	56.4	47.6	49.5
1931	59.9	52.0	53.7
1941	60.5	53.0	54.3
1951	71.0	60.0	61.6
1961	81.4	67.5	69.6
1971	87.8	74.1	76.2

Source: Statistics Canada, Censuses of Canada, 1921 to 1971.
[a]Definition of "urban" is the one in effect at each census.

Table 11

Percentage Distribution of Native- and Foreign-Born

Population by Type of Rural and Urban Residence,

Canada, 1971

Locality	Total	Native-Born	Foreign-Born Total	Foreign-Born Post-War Immigrants
Rural Farm	6.6	7.1	3.5	2.5
Rural Non-Farm	17.2	18.7	8.7	6.7
Urban: Under 10,000	11.6	12.5	6.6	5.3
10,000—29,000	8.1	8.5	6.1	5.7
30,000—99,999	9.0	9.4	6.6	6.4
100,000 & over	47.5	43.8	68.4	73.4
Total: Per Cent	100.0	100.0	100.0	100.0
Number ('000)	21,568	18,273	3,296	2,342

Source: Statistics Canada, *1971 Census of Canada*, Bulletin 1.3-6, Ottawa: Information Canada, 1974, Table 35.

Table 12

Per Cent Urban[a] for Selected Ethnic-Origin Populations in Canada

1871 to 1971

Year	Total	British	French	German	Italian	Jewish	Nat. Ind. and Eskimo
1871	19.6	22.3	18.8	11.1	53.5	67.2	1.7
1881	25.7	28.8	23.1	16.4	61.3	79.5	0.6
1901	37.5	41.8	33.7	28.0	65.4	94.2	5.1
1911	45.4	50.4	40.9	33.5	69.8	94.0	3.7
1921	49.5	53.7	47.7	33.2	79.3	95.7	3.7
1931	53.7	57.5	54.0	36.9	81.6	96.5	3.9
1941	54.3	58.3	54.9	36.4	80.9	96.0	3.6
1951	61.6	65.7	59.9	44.2	88.1	98.7	6.7
1961	69.6	71.2	68.2	61.8	94.7	98.8	12.9
1971	76.2	75.9	75.9	68.8	96.6	98.8	30.1

Source: Censuses of Canada
[a]Definition of "urban" is that in effect at the time of the particular census.

Table 13

Percentage of the Total Population of Canada Living in
Census Metropolitan Areas[a] by Ethnic Group, 1941-71

Ethnic Origin Group	1971	1961	1951	1941
British Isles	51.5	46.2	43.7	41.0
French	45.4	39.3	35.8	34.1
Other European	62.5	49.9	39.4	32.2
German	49.5	39.4	27.5	21.9
Italian	84.8	75.2	63.1	61.0
Jewish	93.4	94.0	93.0	89.9
Dutch	46.0	35.0	24.0	19.8
Polish	61.8	55.6	46.3	35.7
Russian	48.4	46.1	35.3	22.7
Scandinavian	45.7	36.8	29.2	21.1
Ukrainian	57.8	44.5	35.2	21.9
Other	73.3	56.5	43.8	33.6
Asiatic	78.7	68.6	59.9	57.8
Other Origins[b]	35.7	33.1	30.8	11.2

Source: Statistics Canada, *1971 Census of Canada*, Special tabulations; Dominion Bureau of Statistics, *1961 Census of Canada*, Bulletin 7:1-6, Ottawa: The Queen's Printer, 1966, Table VIII.

[a] 1971 data according to the 1971 census definition of census metropolitan areas. For 1961 and earlier years, the data are for the census metropolitan areas as defined in 1961.

[b] Includes ethnic origins not stated.

cent, living in urban areas. The remaining ethnic groups show considerable variability. The Italian ethnic-origin population is rapidly approaching the degree of urban concentration exhibited by the Jewish, as may be seen in Table 12. Among the other ethnic groups not included in Table 12, only the Dutch show a disproportionately low number of urban residents. The Ukrainians appear to have experienced a rather significant increase since 1961, and with 75 per cent living in urban areas, they were very close to the average for Canada as a whole. All of the major ethnic groups experienced increasing urbanization while generally retaining their relative positions with respect to each other through the 1961-71 decade.

Additional data on residence by urban size categories, or by Census Metropolitan Area residence, do not change the picture materially. By either standard, the Jewish, Italian, and Asiatic, origin groupings rank first, second, and third, respectively, in regard to their attraction to the larger urban centres. Those who tend to be underrepresented in the metropolitan areas also tend to be overrepresented in the rural-farm populations, e.g., the Dutch, Germans, Ukrainians, and Scandinavians.[9] Those of British and French origins, who are now almost identical in terms of their urban, rural non-farm, and rural-farm distributions, still differ significantly with respect to their attraction to the census metropolitan areas. The percentage of the British living in census metropolitan areas has been consistently greater than that of the French by about seven percentage points ever since 1941, as may be seen in Table 13. However, as the proportions have increased for both groups, their relative differentiations are converging.

It would seem that much of the difference in urbanization which has characterized the various ethnic populations in Canada could be attributed to differences in their time of arrival, educational and occupational skills, and in the specific opportunities for settlement and work that were characteristic of that particular period. As the country continues its development as a post-industrial society, the differences arising from these initial conditions and experiences which have differentiated these groups in the past should gradually diminish. Groups showing the least change will be those, such as the Hutterites, who voluntarily isolate themselves from the changes occurring in the larger society, and those who continue to be rejected by society, such as our native Indians and Eskimos.

Notes

1. Data in this paper relating to ethnic populations are based on the "ethnic origin" question included in the Census of Canada. The data are not necessarily indicative of the respondent's ethnic identity, or the strength of his feelings about his identity. The census question on ethnic and cultural origins aims at establishing the respondent's ethnic or cultural background, i.e., the ethnic or cultural group that the respondent, or his ancestors, on the male side, belonged to on first coming to this continent.

2. The problems associated with the collection and interpretation of ethnic-origin data have long been recognized. Unexplained deviations from long-term trends or other apparent anomalies in the data should alert the reader, or user, of ethnic-origin or other census data to possible problems. For example, in Table 3, the rather large increase in the population of Jewish origins between 1961 and 1971 is largely the result of changes in the 1971 Census editing procedures. Specifically, individuals who reported their religion as Jewish were automatically included in the Jewish ethnic-origin population regardless of the origin reported. Other changes in the census schedules and enumeration procedures may partly

account for the larger than expected increase in numbers of English origin and declines in the other British Isles-origin groups. These and other problems are discussed in the "Introduction" to Volume 1, Part 3, of the *1971 Census of Canada*. Also, see Jacques Henripin's discussion concerning the changes in British and French origins revealed in the 1971 Census in his *Immigration and Language Imbalance,* The Immigration and Population Study, Department of Manpower and Immigration, Ottawa: Information Canada, 1974, Appendix A.

3. Kalbach, W.E., *The Effect of Immigration on Population,* The Canadian Immigration and Population Study, Department of Manpower and Immigration, Ottawa: Information Canada, 1974, Table 3.2.

4. Henripin, Jacques, *Trends and Factors of Fertility in Canada,* 1961 Census Monograph, Ottawa: Information Canada, 1972, Table 6.11; Statistics Canada, *1971 Census of Canada,* Bulletin 1.5-11, Ottawa: Information Canada, 1974.

5. Statistics Canada, *Vital Statistics, 1971,* Volume I, Ottawa: Information Canada, 1974, Tables 5 and 10.

6. Kalbach, W.E., *op.cit.,* Table 2.2 and Chart 2.3.

7. Department of Manpower and Immigration, *The Green Paper on Immigration,* Volumes I-IV, The Canadian Immigration and Population Study, Ottawa: Information Canada, 1974.

8. Statistics Canada, *1971 Census of Canada,* Bulletin 1.3-7, Ottawa: Information Canada, 1974, Table 50.

9. Statistics Canada, *1971 Census of Canada,* Bulletin 1.3-2, Ottawa: Information Canada, 1973, Table 3.

References

Department of Manpower and Immigration
1974 *The Green Paper on Immigration,* Vols 1-4. Ottawa: Information Canada.
Henripin, J.
1974 *Immigration and Language Imbalance.* Ottawa: Information Canada.
Henripin, J.
1974 *Trends and Factors of Fertility in Canada.* Ottawa: Information Canada.
Kalbach, W.E.
1974 *The Effect of Immigration on Population.* Ottawa: Information Canada.

Statistics Canada
1973 *1971 Census of Canada*, Bulletin 1.3-2. Ottawa: Information Canada.
Statistics Canada
1974 *Vital Statistics, 1971*, Volume I. Ottawa: Information Canada.
Statistics Canada
1974 *1971 Census of Canada*, Bulletin 1.3-7. Ottawa: Information Canada.
Statistics Canada
1974 *1971 Census of Canada*, Bulletin 1.5-11. Ottawa: Information Canada.

5

Canadian Immigration: Recent Developments and Future Prospects

Anthony H. Richmond*

In 1971 Canada had a population of 21.5 million people inhabiting nearly four million square miles of territory. Geographically, it is the largest country in the Western Hemisphere, and the second largest in the world. This fact has led many people to regard it as an underpopulated country capable of absorbing a vastly increased population. However, this expansionist view is now being seriously questioned. It is recognized that much of the land is mountainous or subject to an Arctic climate that makes it inhospitable to settlement. The developed land is not more than one-third of the total, and permanent settlement makes up only about 10 per cent of the total area. The great majority of the population of Canada lives along a narrow strip within 650 miles of the American border. One area of continuous settlement, within 270 miles of the United States border, is only 2.2 per cent of the total area of Canada, but contains its eight largest cities, and 36 per cent of the population (*Canada Year Book*, 1973:1). Overall, Canada's average population density ranks among the lowest in the world, at approximately six persons per square mile, in 1971. However, on the basis of density per square mile of occupied agricultural land, it is 79 per square mile. The provinces of Ontario and Quebec come closer to the densities of Europe as a whole, being nearer to 290 per square mile. However, even the large cities and metropolitan areas of Canada are not as heavily populated as the major urban conurbations of Britain and Europe (Kubat and Thornton, 1974:6).

From the beginning of European settlement in the early seventeenth century, natural increase and net immigration have both contributed to a rather rapid growth of population; Canada is now more than seven times

*Anthony H. Richmond is Professor of Sociology, York University, Toronto, Ontario.

its size at the first census in 1871. A distinctive feature of the Canadian population is the persistence of a French-speaking proportion of under one-third. Until recently, the growth of this Francophone population was attributable mainly to a high rate of natural increase, and very little to net migration. Immigration was more important in maintaining the growth of the rest of the population, mainly of British and other European ethnic origin, whose birth rates, until recently, were much lower than those of French Canadians. The annual growth rate of the Canadian population reached a peak of 3.3 per cent per annum in 1956-1957 (Kalbach and McVey, 1971:31-69). Between 1961 and 1971 the growth rate averaged 1.7 per cent per annum, falling to 1.2 per cent in 1971-1972. It has risen slightly since then as a consequence of some increase in net migration.

Future growth will depend upon both fertility and migration trends. The gross reproduction rate has now fallen below the replacement level; it was 0.937 in 1973 (*Population Projections*, 1974:13). It is not known whether this trend will be maintained or whether it represents a deferment of births by some young couples. However, a fertility rate close to the replacement level does not mean that Canada will soon reach zero population growth. Even if immigration ceased, it is estimated that the population would continue to grow until about the year 2040. This is due to the high proportion of young women in the child-bearing age groups (*Population Projections*, 1974:64).

The contribution of immigration to population growth is the net result of both inward and outward movements. Between 1946 and 1971, Canada admitted approximately three and a half million immigrants–ostensibly for permanent settlement–but only 2.3 million were still resident at the time of the census (*1971 Census of Canada*, 1974: Advance Bulletin 9:1). At the same time, there was some emigration of those born in Canada. Unfortunately, accurate statistics of outmigration from Canada are not available. Between 1951 and 1961, the net gain by migration was a little over one million, compared with only 722,000 in the decade up to 1971. On this basis, net migration contributed only 21.7 per cent of the total growth in the decade (*Canada Year Book*, 1973:208). Although immigration policies have been the focus of increasing concern in Canada recently, it seems likely that the birth rate will continue to be the most important factor influencing future growth. However, it is a fact that the migration element lends itself more directly to political and administrative control than does natural increase.

SELECTION OF IMMIGRANTS

Until recently, admission to Canada as an immigrant was determined by the Immigration Act, 1952, as amended in 1966-1967 and 1967-1968, and by the immigration regulations formulated under the terms of that act. The act itself gave the Minister of Immigration extensive powers to regulate the criteria of selection and admissibility to Canada by Orders in Council. All persons admitted to Canada had to pass a health check and they could not belong to one of the "prohibited classes." These included sufferers from various physical and mental disabilities, those with a criminal record, alcohol or drug addicts, potential subversive individuals or spies, etc., together with anyone who might become a public charge. These provisions will be modified and liberalized when a new immigration bill (before Parliament at the time of writing) is passed. There had been general agreement that the physical and mental health restrictions were too stringent in the light of advances in medical knowledge, and that deportation for becoming a "public charge" was anachronistic in the age of the "welfare state."

When the new legislation comes into force, new regulations will be introduced by Order-in-Council. Between 1967 and 1977, the Regulations distinguished independent immigrants, sponsored immigrants, and nominated immigrants. The category "refugee" cut across the above classification and, in immigration statistics, refugees were included in one of the above categories. However, special policies and procedures applied to the admission of refugees, and these will be discussed below (C.I.P.S. 2: 99-118).

Independent applicants are those prospective permanent settlers who expect to become self-supporting and successfully established in Canada by virtue of the skills, knowledge, or other qualifications they possess. This category also includes the spouse and unmarried children less than twenty-one years of age, if they are assessed at the same time as the independent applicant. The Regulations of 1967 established nine criteria against which independent applicants were assessed. These are summarized in Table 1, where the range of assessment for each category is indicated.

Education and training receives the greatest weight, up to twenty points for each year of formal education, apprenticeship, and vocational, trades, or professional training successfully completed. There is some overlap between this category and that of "occupational skill" which is assessed on a scale up to ten points. Selection officers may add or subtract one unit to reflect evidence of particularly high or low skill attained by the applicant. Another important criterion is "occupational demand" which varies from time to time, and by region of Canada, according to information supplied from offices across Canada to the Department of Manpower and Immigration. Age is another factor. It is generally assumed that there is a negative association between age of migration and adaptability. Therefore, applicants over thirty-five lose one unit for each year of age up to a maximum of 10 points, i.e., up to forty-five years. Older immigrants may still be admitted so long as they are able to accumulate points on other criteria.

"Arranged employment" means that a definite job through a specific

107

employer has been provided for the applicant, prior to admission to Canada. The employment must be long term and the working conditions and wages must be consistent with other similar employment in Canada. Since 1974, prospective immigrants are now awarded points in this category only when the Department of Manpower and Immigration certifies that suitably qualified Canadian citizens, or permanent residents, are not available to fill the jobs concerned. Closely related to this is the category "designated occupation," also first introduced in 1974. Certain occupations are so designated when there is a persistent, unfillable shortage in particular localities of Canada. Points will be earned only when the applicant indicates his willingness to take such employment in the specific area concerned. This factor is related to the "area demand" factor which may earn up to an additional five points for those immigrants going to an area where job opportunities are most abundant. Further factors include an assessment of applicant's knowledge of English and/or French, together with a personal assessment by the selection officer of the personal qualities of the potential immigrant. Emphasis here is placed upon factors such as adaptability, motivation, initiative, and resourcefulness, although the brief nature of the selection interviews makes this assessment, in many cases, a difficult one. In the last resort and, subject to the concurrence of a designated senior officer, a selection officer may exercise discretion to approve a person who does not have enough points or to reject one who does, but this discretion is used very rarely. Finally, the law requires each independent applicant to have "the means to maintain himself and his immediate family until he is established." This means that independent immigrants must have some funds with them on arrival in Canada to assist them in the initial adjustment process. Depending upon the size of family, and whether or not there is pre-arranged employment, the sum of money involved may range from $200 to more than $1,000 (C.I.P.S. 2:49).

Sponsored dependents include the close relatives of a Canadian citizen or landed immigrant in Canada. Citizens or landed immigrants may sponsor a husband or wife; a fiancée; an unmarried son or daughter less than twenty-one years of age; a parent or grandparent sixty years of age or more (or younger if widowed or incapacitated); an orphan brother, sister, nephew, niece, or grandchild less than eighteen years of age; an unmarried adopted son or daughter less than twenty-one years of age, provided that the adoption took place before the child reached eighteen years of age; an orphan, abandoned child, or other child placed with a welfare authority for adoption, who is less than thirteen years of age and whom the sponsor intends to adopt. In addition, a person who has no close relatives in Canada, and no relative abroad for sponsorship, may sponsor, once in his lifetime, one relative of any degree, to come to Canada and be with him as a companion, heir, etc. Apart from the health check, the sponsored immigrant does not have to meet any other requirements, but the sponsor in Canada must be at least eighteen years of age and be capable of supporting the relative financially.

Nominated relatives are credited with up to a maximum of thirty units of assessment, according to the degree of closeness of the family relationship with the nominator, but must meet the other admission requirements on a similar basis to independent applicants. They may fall into any of the following categories: sons and daughters, irrespective of age or marital status (i.e., those not eligible to be considered as sponsored dependents); parents and grandparents less than sixty years of age; brothers and sisters (including half-brothers and half-sisters); grandchildren; uncles and aunts; nephews and nieces. In each case, a nomination includes the spouse and unmarried sons and daughters less than twenty-one years of age of the relatives named. Anyone nominating relatives to come to Canada must be more than eighteen years of age and promise to provide care and maintenance to the nominated relatives, from his own resources, for a period of five years. However, should he fail to do so, they would not be eligible for other forms of welfare, and the nominator would be expected to provide the necessary financial assistance. Theoretically, any immigrant may be deported from Canada for becoming a "public charge." In practice, this regulation is rarely enforced (C.I.P.S. 3:98-101).

Between 1967 and 1972, Canada permitted visitors to Canada to apply for "landed immigrant status," i.e., for permanent settlement, after arrival in Canada. While the majority of immigrants continued to go through the selection process and obtain the necessary documentation abroad, an increasing proportion took advantage of the opportunity to by-pass these selection processes, entering Canada as non-immigrants initially. In 1967, less than 6 per cent of all immigrants received the necessary approval for settlement after arrival, but by 1973, a third of all immigrants were processed administratively after arrival. Although permission to apply for permanent residence from within Canada was withdrawn in 1972, applications from people already in the country before that date were still being processed in 1975. The Canadian government was compelled to withdraw the privilege of applying for permanent residence after arrival because the increasing number of people taking advantage of this procedure could not be handled administratively, and an injustice was being caused to those who applied from abroad through the regular channels (C.I.P.S. 2:35-37). The situation was aggravated by the fact that, also in 1967, an appeal procedure against deportation had been instituted.

The Appeal Board was established on the assumption that the number of cases of deportation to be dealt with annually would be quite small. However, in practice, visitors to Canada who initially failed to qualify for permanent settlement (because they did not accumulate enough points on the basis of education, occupation, etc.), appealed against deportation. Meanwhile, they remained in Canada and were permitted to seek employment, rather than become public charges. By 1973, the number of appeals

Table 1

Summary of Factors Used for
the Selection of Immigrants to Canada.

Independent Applicants

Long-Term Factors	Range of Units of Assessment That May be Awarded
Education and Training	0—20
Personal Qualities	0—15
Occupational Demand	0—15
Occupational Skill	1—10
Age	0—10
Short-Term Factors	
Arranged Employment/Designated Occupation	0 or 10
Knowledge of English and/or French	0—10
Relative in Canada	0 or 3 or 5
Area of Destination	0—5
Potential Maximum	100

Nominated Relatives

Long-Term Factors (as for independent applicant)	1—70
Short-Term Settlement Arrangements Provided by Relative in Canada	15, 20, 25 or 30
Potential Maximum	100

Sponsored Dependents

Close Relative in Canada Willing to take Responsibility for Care and Maintenance	Units of Assessment not Required

Source: Department of Manpower and Immigration (C.I.P.S. 2:59-60).

1. Independent Applicants and Nominated Relatives, to qualify for selection, must normally earn 50 or more of the potential 100 units of assessment. In addition, they must have received at least one unit for the occupational demand factor or be destined to arranged employment or a designated occupation.

2. In unusual cases, selection officers may accept or reject an Independent Applicant for Nominated Relative notwithstanding the actual number of units of assessment awarded.

3. Entrepreneurs are assessed in the same way as Independent Applicants except that they receive an automatic 25 units of assessment in lieu of any units they might have received for the occupational demand and occupational skill factors.

4. A change in the Regulations was made in October 1974. The present Regulations stipulate that from the total points awarded either an independent or nominated applicant, 10 are

against deportation had risen to astronomical proportions and would have taken the tribunal up to ten years to deal with.[1] At this point, a special adjustment procedure was adopted, together with an amnesty for those who were in the country illegally. As a consequence, large numbers of people who had come to Canada as visitors were allowed to settle permanently on the basis of much less stringent criteria than those who had hitherto applied. Subsequently, new and stricter regulations were introduced which were designed to limit the number of people who would be eligible for admission to Canada as landed immigrants.

In order to understand the crisis that faced the Canadian immigration authorities in 1972, it is necessary to recognize the importance of tourism in the present-day world economy. Canada, like many other countries today, has a substantial economic interest in the encouragement of tourism, and in facilitating the movement of people into and out of the country for recreational and temporary business purposes, such as conventions of management or professional groups. Therefore, the government is reluctant to impose upon airlines or other transportation companies, travel agents, or the visitors themselves the burden of too much bureaucratic control at the points of entry and exit. In 1972, non-resident travellers entering Canada numbered 38.2 million, more than the total population of the country. Of these, 37.2 million were from the United States and one million from all other countries. Residents of Canada re-entering from abroad totalled 33.0 million, indicating multiple journeys by many travellers. It is estimated that total receipts from the United States and other travellers entering Canada were over 1,200 million dollars. (*Travel* 1974:80). It is not surprising that the government does not wish to offend the clients of such a lucrative industry. Canada does not have a system of alien registration. Neither the native nor the foreign-born population is required to give notice of any change of address or employment. Until recently it was comparatively easy for anyone, whether a visitor, landed immigrant, or even an illegal resident, to obtain a social insurance number. Such a number is a prerequisite for employment, but until 1975, employers had no obligation to ascertain whether a potential employee had permanent resident status or permission to obtain work in Canada.

Prior to 1972, independent immigrants were required to earn fifty or more of the potential one hundred units of assessment. Special administrative measures in 1972 and an "adjustment of status program" in 1973 permitted many applicants in Canada to be given landed immigrant status on very much relaxed criteria. These measures were designed to clear up the backlog of applications and appeals in Canada. By the end of 1974,

---

deducted unless the applicant shows evidence of bona fide arranged employment, or is going to a job where persistent regional shortages are known to exist (i.e. a "designated occupation"). The applicant will receive credit for arranged employment only when it has been established that no Canadian citizen or permanent resident is available to fill the vacancy.

nearly 50,000 immigrants had been admitted (either in the independent or nominated categories) who would not normally have met the selection criteria. The distribution of immigrants to Canada 1968-1974, by admission category and labour force status, is shown in Table 2. It should be noted that the figures include some persons given permanent resident status after arrival in Canada, but exclude those on temporary employment visas.

Changes in regulations in 1974 imposed more stringent conditions of admission. No matter how many points for other reasons (age, education, destination) a would-be immigrant may receive, he or she cannot enter Canada as an immigrant at present unless they have *either* a) at least one "point" for an occupation needed in Canada; *or* b) willingness and ability to work in a "designated occupation" (severe local shortage); *or* c) arranged employment with a bona fide Canadian employer (if no Canadians are available to fill the position). In addition, in every case, after totalling all the points to which an applicant is entitled, the immigration officer will deduct ten points unless the applicant has satisfactory evidence of arranged employment or is coming to a "designated occupation." In other words, with these exceptions, the required number of points for admission to Canada has been raised from fifty to sixty (C.I.P.S. 2:59-60).

These restrictive measures reflect on the one hand a deteriorating economic situation in Canada and the anticipated high unemployment in 1974 and 1975, and on the other hand the increasing potential supply of immigrants to Canada from many parts of the world.[2] The revived interest in migration to Canada evident in 1973 and 1974 is itself a reflection of world demographic and economic conditions. It has been influenced in part by the reduced opportunity to emigrate to other traditional receiving countries, such as Australia, New Zealand, and some countries in Europe, which have imposed limits on the number of permanent or temporary workers they will accept.

In addition to introducing more stringent regulations in 1974, the Department of Manpower and Immigration adopted administrative procedures to determine what it called "global priorities." Selection officers were instructed to give first priority to all applications for sponsored immigrants, i.e., immediate dependents of persons already in Canada. Second priority was given to independent and nominated immigrants destined for occupations in need of employees (occupations earning eight points or more on the occupational demand scale) or those who had pre-arranged employment. Third priority was given to entrepreneurs expected to create employment in Canada by investing capital and starting their own businesses. Lowest priority was given to all other independent and nominated immigrants who came on a "first come, first served" basis, but after the higher priority categories had been dealt with. In practice, this means a slowing down in the flow of many independent and nominated immigrants to Canada. However, the new regulations, introduced in February

112

Table 2

Immigration[a] to Canada by Category and

Labour Force Status 1968-1976.

Year	LABOUR FORCE (Percentages)			NON-LABOUR FORCE			TOTAL				
	Spon-sored	Nomi-nated	Inde-pendent	Spon-sored	Nomi-nated	Inde-pendent	Spon-sored	Nomi-nated	Inde-pendent	Number	Percentage Approved after Arrival
1968	3.3	10.4	38.3	17.6	8.7	21.9	20.8	19.1	60.1	183,974	5.8
1969	4.1	13.6	34.6	16.7	10.6	20.4	20.8	24.2	55.0	161,531	9.0
1970	4.5	13.3	34.9	17.3	10.5	19.5	21.8	23.8	54.5	147,713	12.2
1971	6.1	13.8	30.4	21.3	10.3	18.1	27.4	24.1	48.5	121,900	14.4
1972	6.4	14.4	28.0	20.7	11.0	19.5	27.1	25.4	47.5	122,006	28.6
1973	4.9	13.1	32.1	17.9	11.2	20.8	22.8	24.3	52.9	184,200	33.9
1974	n.a.†	n.a.	n.a.	n.a.	n.a.	n.a.	24.8	24.4	50.8	218,465	20.2
1975	7.9	12.9	22.4	26.3	12.1	18.4	36.2	25.0	40.8	187,881	11.7
1976	11.0	13.3	16.8	30.4	12.5	16.0	41.6	25.8	32.8	149,429	15.9

Source: Department of Manpower and Immigration
[a]Landed immigrants only, excluding temporary workers.
†n.a. indicates figures not available.

and October 1974, were not applied retroactively to potential immigrants who had already filed formal applications, although these applicants were subject to the global priority scheme. As a consequence, the total number of immigrants approved for permanent residence in Canada in 1974 (including those who had first come to Canada as visitors) reached a near record total of 218,465. Since the end of the Second World War, the only other years in which the number of immigrants admitted to Canada exceeded 200,000 were 1957 and 1967 (C.I.P.S. 3:31). It is notable that these years were characterized by substantial refugee movements. Since 1974, admissions have declined substantially.

Refugee Movements
Since the end of the Second World War, Canada has admitted more than a quarter of a million refugees. The large majority of these arrived in the first five years after the war. However, a series of international emergencies since then has resulted in a continued flow of refugees and of expellees who, while not technically refugees in terms of the United Nations' definition, nevertheless have left their countries for reasons of political persecution. Since 1968, 16,320 refugees have been admitted to Canada, together with an additional 7,000 Asian expellees from Uganda. The largest single group were those from Czechoslovakia. In 1967 and 1968 a total of nearly 19,000 Czechoslovakian refugees were admitted. Other special movements in recent years have included 228 Tibetans and 1,400 persons from Chile (C.I.P.S. 3:46).

Despite the number of refugees admitted, Canada was slow to accede to the United Nations convention on refugees and did not do so until 1970. Provision is made for the admission of refugees who cannot meet the usual selection criteria so long as the authorities are satisfied that there is sufficient private or government assistance available in Canada to ensure successful establishment. For example, in 1973, 72 per cent of the 405 refugees were admitted on relaxed criteria and in 1974, 69 per cent of the 547 refugees admitted that year did not achieve the necessary units of assessment under the usual selection factors. In theory Canada has agreed to sponsor up to fifty handicapped refugees and their families annually, in connection with the special Handicapped Refugees Program of the United Nations. In practice, the numbers admitted are generally much smaller. In 1973 and 1974, the combined total of handicapped refugees was only four. One of the obstacles to a more generous program of admissions for handicapped immigrants is the necessity of co-operation between the federal and provincial governments in Canada, together with the voluntary agencies. Nevertheless, the special arrangements made for the reception of refugees and expellees under emergency conditions, along with the special programs designed to facilitate the social adjustment of such refugees, have provided organizational models which many people consider should be extended to the reception and services provided for all immigrants to Canada (Hawkins, 1972:369). Unfortunately, the expense of such programs makes it unlikely that the government will be willing to provide the necessary funding on a permanent basis.

TRENDS IN IMMIGRATION AND TEMPORARY WORKERS

The year 1967 was a major turning point in Canadian immigration. The introduction of the "points system" of selection, and the abolition of specific racial, ethnic and national criteria of preference, resulted in a significant shift in the sources of immigration by country. The distribution of Canadian immigration offices abroad constituted the only residual basis of discrimination and this was modified with the opening of new offices in Asia, Africa, and South America.[3] Although Britain continued to rank among the most important sources of immigration to Canada, the proportion coming from that country declined, from more than 25 per cent in 1946-1967, to less than 12 per cent in 1971, recovering to nearly 19 per cent in 1975, and falling to 14 per cent in 1976. In part, the decline in British immigration was compensated by an increase in the numbers coming from the United States. There has been a steady decline in the proportion from European countries. The latter constituted 56 per cent of all immigrants before 1967, but were only 23 per cent in 1974. The major increase has been in immigration from Asia, which has risen from less than 4 per cent to 30 per cent in 1976, and from the Caribbean and Central America, which averaged 3 per cent before 1967 and was nearly 13 per cent in 1971, and 11 per cent in 1976.

A high proportion of immigrants entering Canada each year has already made one or more previous international moves and is not coming directly from the country of birth. The percentage of persons immigrating from a country other than their own birthplace or citizenship varies from country to country.[4] When weighted by the actual size of immigration from these countries, it may be estimated that more than 12 per cent of all immigrants had previous experience of emigration. It must be remembered, also, that many immigrants re-migrate or return to the former country after admission to Canada. Although exact figures are not available, "settler loss" from Canada is probably close to 30 per cent, which is probably higher than the Australian figure. Return migration is particularly high to the United States and Great Britain. The transitory nature of international migration is further emphasized by the increasing use of temporary workers recruited from abroad.

Temporary Employment Visas
Since 1972, Canada has been using the system of temporary employment visas. These enable non-immigrants to be admitted to the country for a period of up to twelve months for employment, without obtaining permission for permanent residence. Such employment visas are supposed to

115

be issued only when the Department of Manpower and Immigration is satisfied that suitably qualified Canadian residents (Canadian-born or landed immigrants) are not available for the employment in question. The maximum period for which a temporary employment visa may be issued is twelve months; it is not known how many workers successfully apply for a renewal of the permit when it expires, but it is likely that many remain in Canada longer than twelve months.

In 1973 and 1974, the number of temporary employment visas came close to the total number of persons admitted to the country for permanent residence who intended to enter the labour force. (Approximately half the permanent immigrants admitted to the country each year are dependents, not immediately expected to enter the labour force.) In 1973, 92,228 labour-force immigrants were admitted (including those already in the country who were given landed immigrant status). This compares with the 80,934 temporary employment visas issued that year. In 1974, 87,353 temporary employment visas were issued, compared with 106,083 immigrants who were destined for the labour force. In 1976, the figures were 92,200 temporary visas and 61,461 labour-force immigrants.

It is interesting to compare the countries of origin and the intended occupations of those admitted for permanent residence with those admitted on temporary employment visas. Whereas Britain and the United States almost tied for first place among the source countries for permanent immigration, the United States is the largest supplier of temporary workers. Great Britain is the second largest supplier, but falls considerably behind the United States in this respect. When Jamaica, Trinidad, Barbados, and other Caribbean countries are combined, they exceed Britain in the proportion of temporary workers.

There is a demand, both continuing and seasonal, for relatively unskilled workers in the many industries and localities in Canada that is difficult to fill with Canadians or immigrants with permanent resident status. This is true despite relatively high levels of unemployment in Canada and appears to be due to the low wages, poor working conditions, and remote areas in which such employment is available. These factors make such employment unattractive, when unemployment insurance benefits and welfare services are available to the unemployed who have established entitlement through previous employment and insurance contributions.

Some of the non-immigrant workers come under block movements approved by the federal government following an agreement between Canada and another country. Most of these movements involve agricultural workers. For example, the Caribbean Seasonal Workers Program is governed by agreements between Canada and the governments of Jamaica, Barbados, Trinidad, and Tobago. Employers must meet minimal standards of wages and accommodations and contribute to transportation costs. These workers are employed for a few months at the height of the agricultural harvest season in cropping or food canning operations. In 1974, a similar agreement was signed with the Government of Mexico to provide temporary harvest labour. There are also special movements of students and other young people to Canada during the summer months. Under these schemes, approximately 2,600 young people come to Canada annually for purposes other than academic training. Foreign students in Canada may not normally take jobs unless they qualify for employment visas in the same way as any other non-immigrant. The major exception are those for whom employment forms an integral part of their course of study. However, students already in Canada, before the implementation of the temporary employment visa scheme, have been permitted to obtain employment until the termination of their studies. In the future, students will have to be self-supporting.

So far, Canada has avoided the worst abuses associated with the "guest worker" system common in some European countries. However, there has been criticism of the inadequate housing, health, and welfare services available to temporary workers. There is some concern regarding the consequences of bringing in unattached male workers, and the possible social problems that may be created in the future, if the numbers were to increase substantially. Although there are some obvious benefits to non-immigrants who are allowed to work in Canada temporarily, there are also significant disadvantages. Generally speaking, non-immigrants pay taxes and contribute toward the costs of unemployment insurance and other social services, without deriving any benefit from these payments. Few of the countries concerned have reciprocal agreements with Canada, which means they cannot collect social benefits after their return. Although some non-immigrants may have their temporary employment visas renewed, the system appears to be evolving into one of "rotational employment," and is subject to the various criticisms that have been directed toward this system in Europe (Böhning, 1974).

FUTURE PROSPECTS

In 1973 the federal government instituted the Canadian Immigration and Population Study, which led to the publication, in 1975, of the Green Paper on Immigration. Unlike a "White Paper," which is a statement of government policy, a "Green Paper" is designed to provide a factual background and to stimulate public discussion of a major policy question, prior to the formulation of new legislation. The four volumes of the Green Paper, together with a number of technical reports prepared by consultants and published separately, review Canada's experience of immigration in recent years in the light of contemporary demographic and economic conditions, in Canada and abroad (C.I.P.S. 1-4, 1975). After extensive public debate and further examination by a Joint Parliamentary Committee of the House of Commons and Senate (Riel and O'Connell,

117

1975), a new Immigration Bill (c.24) was introduced in 1977. The new legislation will lay the foundations for major revisions in Canadian immigration policy which will be implemented by new regulations likely to come into force in 1978.

The following are some of the significant features of the new legislation. Part 1, section 3, sets out the objectives of Canadian immigration policy as follows:

a) to support the attainment of such demographic goals as may be established by the Government of Canada from time to time in respect of the size, rate of growth, structure and geographic distribution of the Canadian population; b) to enrich and strengthen the cultural and social fabric of Canada, taking into account the federal and bilingual character of Canada; c) to facilitate the reunion in Canada of Canadian citizens and permanent residents with their close relatives from abroad; d) to encourage and facilitate the adaptation of persons who have been granted admission as permanent residents to Canadian society by promoting co-operation between the Government of Canada and other levels of government and non-governmental agencies in Canada with respect thereto; e) to facilitate the entry of visitors into Canada for the purpose of fostering trade and commerce, tourism, cultural and scientific activities and international understanding; f) to ensure that any person who seeks admission to Canada on either a permanent or temporary basis is subject to standards of admission that do not discriminate on grounds of race, national or ethnic origin, colour, religion or sex; g) to fulfill Canada's international legal obligations with respect to refugees and to uphold its humanitarian tradition with respect to the displaced and the persecuted; h) to foster the development of a strong and viable economy and the prosperity of all regions in Canada; i) to maintain and protect the health, safety and good order of Canadian society, and; j) to promote international order and justice by denying the use of Canadian territory to persons who are likely to engage in criminal activity.

Part 1, section 7 provides that:

The Minister, after consultation with the provinces concerning regional demographic needs and labour market considerations and after consultation with such other persons, organizations and institutions as he deems appropriate, shall announce annually the number of immigrants that the Government of Canada deems it appropriate to admit during any specified period of time.

In introducing this provision, the Minister of Manpower and Immigration pointed out that immigration in Canada is a joint responsibility of the federal and provincial governments, although the former has primacy. He indicated that this provision would enable Canada to manage its immigration movement in conformity with economic and other short-run requirements as well as establishing long-run immigration targets that would be a framework for demographic planning. Initially, he anticipated that immigration would probably continue at an average of about 150,000 persons annually.

Among the other important provisions of the new legislation is the definition of admissible classes as families, refugees, and other applicants, comprising immigrants selected on the basis of a "points system." The nominated category which existed under previous regulations disappears, but the family class corresponds to the former sponsored dependents, expanded to include parents of any age sponsored by a Canadian citizen. For the first time in Canadian law, the obligations Canada assumed as a party to the United Nations Convention and Protocol on Refugees are confirmed and new procedures codified to determine the status of those claiming to be refugees. The majority of the old "prohibited classes" disappear in the new act, including the absolute bar against epileptics, idiots, imbeciles, and morons. Henceforward, exclusion on health grounds will be based solely on danger to public health or safety, or excessive demands on health or social services. A new objective standard for inadmissibility on criminal grounds is established on the basis of the sentence imposable for equivalent offences under Canadian law. Thus, homosexuality ceases to be an absolute bar.

An innovative provision of the new legislation enables the government to influence the location of initial settlement of immigrants. It does this in three ways. First, it provides for "deferred landing" which means that a potential immigrant will not have permission to settle permanently until he has located at a specified destination instead of being given landed immigrant status at port of entry. Second, additional points will be awarded to some immigrants who indicate an intention to locate in "designated communities" which will be chosen for their employment opportunities and growth potential. Generally, these will be away from the larger metropolitan areas where immigrants tend to settle. Third, an immigration officer may attach certain conditions to the award of permanent residence status. Specific employment and residence requirements may be imposed for a period of up to six months in the case of an immigrant who has been selected as a result of the award of such additional points. Such special conditions will expire automatically after six months and, if reasonable grounds exist, an immigrant may seek relief from or changes in the conditions imposed. It should be noted that some concern has been expressed over the possible threat to civil liberties of instituting a category of "third-class citizens" subject to special conditions even for a period as short as six months.

Among other provisions of the new legislation are those designed to combat illegal immigration. These include bonding and security deposit provisions, fingerprinting of a limited category of persons where there is doubt about identity or possible involvement in criminal activity, and powers given to immigration officers to refuse admission when there are reasonable grounds to believe that the person in question is likely to engage in criminal activity. It is intended that this clause shall be used to deal with persons who, although never convicted for any offence, are known to be closely connected with organized crime. However, it is evident that such a clause, which requires only suspicion, not proof, could be abused. For those who are only technically in breach of immigration requirements, such as those overstaying a visitor's visa, provision is made for a "requirement to depart," which is less severe than a deportation order and does not prevent the person from re-applying for admission at a later date.

The Minister of Immigration, in introducing the bill at second reading in March 1977 stated, "I am convinced that this legislation will provide a strong and imaginative foundation on which to conduct Canada's immigration program in the future."

The Global Context of Immigration
Many Canadians feel themselves to be victims of American economic and cultural imperialism. They are sensitive to the quasi-colonial relationship which Canada has with the United States, due to extensive American ownership of Canadian industry and the pervasiveness of American cultural values through the mass media. However, Canada is also an imperialist country in its own right. It is not only a wealthy country with vast resources, but its relationship with the Third World is just as exploitative as that of other western countries. From a sociological point of view, international migration must be placed in the broader context of the differential distribution of resources, capital, and income both within and between countries.

Some economists and sociologists have suggested that the external investment policies of western capitalist countries, and so-called "aid" to Third World countries, have simply increased dependency and systematically retarded development (Frank, n.d.). As a result, a pool of surplus labour has been created which can be drawn into the economics of more advanced societies when required and quickly ejected again when no longer needed. It has been argued that in order to understand questions of international migration today, attention must be paid to forms of stratification, division of labour, and conflict within the domestic metropolitan context, and also to the patterns of social relations of the latter with dependent colonial and quasi-colonial societies (Rex, 1973:154).

Whether one accepts these interpretations or not, it is evident that the rapid growth of population in the Third World, combined with the relative lack of opportunities for occupational and social mobility in those countries, will create an increasing supply of people looking to emigration as a solution to their needs and ambitions. The scale of population growth throughout the world is such that the world population crisis cannot be solved merely by redistribution. Nevertheless, there will be pressure on more advanced countries, particularly those with low population densities, such as Canada, to accept more immigrants. However, the economies and social systems of western societies are based upon assumptions of national sovereignty and the desire to maintain existing levels of wealth and privilege. Policies designed to reduce unemployment and maintain minimum levels of health and welfare involve some degree of economic and social planning, even in those countries dedicated to capitalism and free enterprise. The idea of a "welfare state" necessarily implies some control over population and labour-force growth. A completely uncontrolled flow of immigrants is out of the question if the economic and social stability of a modern society is to be maintained. At the same time, immigration itself is increasingly of a transient and often rotational character.

Within the advanced countries, upward social mobility, through the educational system, has created new aspirations and expectations which these countries are having difficulty in fulfilling for all their citizens. Traditionally, opposition to immigration came from the manual working classes who saw immigrants as sources of cheap labour, undermining the bargaining position of labour unions. However, an educationally selective immigration policy, such as that conducted by Canada in recent years, now threatens the middle classes and those who are upwardly mobile. Recent public opinion polls in Canada suggest that although higher education is still associated with a more favourable attitude toward immigration, there is less variation between the different education levels now than in the past. There has been a substantial drop in support by the university-educated for the idea that Canada needs immigrants (Tienhaara, 1975:26). Clearly, there are many conflicting interests that the Canadian government must endeavour to reconcile as it formulates an immigration policy for the last quarter of the twentieth century. Like most political decisions, the outcome will probably be an unsatisfactory compromise between long-run ideals and short-run economic interests. Whatever the decision, it will influence the type of ethnic mosaic Canada will be in the future.

Notes

1. In a Parliamentary address on the second reading of an act to amend the Immigration Appeal Board Act on June 20, 1973, the Minister of Manpower and Immigration stated that the backlog of appeals against deportation had increased at the rate of 1,000 a month and had reached a total of over 17,000, while the capacity of the board to handle cases was

only 100 a month. The new legislation was designed to eliminate the backlog by special adjustment procedures and more lenient admission criteria, for those whose cases were pending; the act also increased the capacity of the board to deal with future appeals promptly. At the same time, the right of appeal against deportation in Canada was revoked for all those who were not already landed immigrants in Canada or in possession of immigrant or non-immigrant visas, issued abroad, when they arrived.

2. The increased interest in migration to Canada was reflected in the number of *pre-application* enquiries and questionnaires completed at Canadian immigration offices abroad. According to official sources, there were 122,476 such enquiries in 1974, which was a 46 per cent increase over the previous year. Due to the stringent criteria being adopted, 76 per cent of these were discouraged by immigration officers and did not result in a formal application for admission to Canada being submitted. There were 148,370 pre-application questionnaires completed, of which 91 per cent were discouraged.

3. In 1966, Canada had 122 immigration officers abroad, of whom 93 were in Britain and Europe, 12 in the United States, 4 in the Middle East and 13 in Asian countries. By 1974, there were 174 officers, of whom 86 were in Britain and Europe, 25 in the United States, 15 in the Caribbean, Central and South America, 14 in Africa and the Middle East, 30 in Asian countries and 4 in Australia (C.I.P.S. 3:107-109).

4. For example, of those who gave Britain as the country of last permanent residence, 16 per cent were not born there, and 10 per cent were not citizens of that country. The figures for Belgium were 47 per cent, and 44 per cent respectively; Hong Kong 48 per cent, and 47 per cent; United States 17 per cent not the same birthplace, and 7 per cent not citizens of the United States.

References

Böhning, W.R.
  1974 "Immigration Policies of Western European Countries." *International Migration Review* 2:155-164.
Canada Year Book
  1973 Ottawa: Minister of Industry Trade and Commerce, and Information Canada.
Canadian Immigration and Population Study 1 (C.I.P.S.)
  1975 *Immigration Policy Perspectives*, Ottawa: Department of Manpower and Immigration and Information Canada.
Canadian Immigration and Population Study 2
  1975 *The Immigration Programme*, Ottawa: Department of Manpower and Immigration and Information Canada.

Canadian Immigration and Population Study 3

1975 *Immigration and Population Statistics*, Ottawa: Department of Manpower and Immigration and Information Canada.

Canadian Immigration and Population Study 4

1975 *Three Years in Canada: First Report of the Longitudinal Survey on the Economic and Social Adaptation of Immigrants.* Ottawa: Department of Manpower and Immigration and Information Canada.

Census of Canada

1971 *Advance Bulletin, AP-9, Population by Birthplace.* Ottawa: Statistics Canada and Information Canada.

Frank, A.G.

n.d. *The Sociology of Underdevelopment and the Underdevelopment of Sociology.* Copenhagen.

Hawkins, F.

1972 *Canada and Immigration: Public Policy and Public Concern.* Montreal: McGill-Queen's University Press.

Kalbach, W.E., and W.W. McVey

1971 *The Demographic Basis of Canadian Society.* Toronto: McGraw-Hill.

Kubat, D., and D. Thornton

1974 *A Statistical Profile of Canadian Society.* Toronto: McGraw-Hill Ryerson.

Rex, J.

1973 *Race, Colonialism and the City.* London: Routledge and Kegan Paul.

Riel, M., and M. O'Connell (Joint Chairmen)

1975 *The Special Joint Committee of the Senate and the House of Commons on Immigration Policy.* Ottawa: Queen's Printer.

Statistics Canada

1974 *Population Projections for Canada and the Provinces, 1972-2001.* Ottawa: Information Canada.

Statistics Canada

1974 *Travel Between Canada and Other Countries, 1972.* Ottawa: Information Canada.

Tienhaara, N.

1975 *Canadian Views on Immigration and Population,* (Canadian Immigration and Population Study). Ottawa: Department of Manpower and Immigration and Information Canada.

6

The Economic Factor in
Canadian Immigration Policy
Jeremiah Allen *

PRESENT POLICY

The existing immigration policy in Canada is one of relatively open admission, provided that the aspiring immigrant meets the criteria specified in the Immigration Act. The act defines three different classes of immigrant, and the criteria for admission differ for each class. A Canadian citizen or landed immigrant may sponsor the immigration of a dependent relative–this is the class of *sponsored dependents*. The other two classes of immigrants must meet criteria related to the labour market. People applying for immigration to Canada are assigned points for characteristics which, in the general population, correlate positively with success in the labour market, i.e., with relatively low rates of unemployment. These characteristics are divided into two categories: "Long-Term Factors," which can contribute a possible seventy points and "Short-Term Factors," which allow a possible thirty points.[1]

Immigrants entering Canada under this "points system" make up two classes–*nominated* and *independent*–and to be admitted must achieve fifty of the possible one hundred points, *and* receive at least one point for occupational demand *or* have a job arranged before entering Canada. For the independent class, the Short-Term Factors are related to the ability to get settled quickly in Canada; for nominated immigrants, the Short-Term Factors are the presence of a relative in Canada willing to provide help after immigration. Thus, the nominated class is in between the sponsored dependent class and the independent class, since having relatives is part of the admissibility criterion; the independent class must achieve the nec-

*Jeremiah Allen is Assistant Professor of Economics, University of Lethbridge, Lethbridge, Alberta.

essary fifty points solely on the basis of their personal characteristics.

Long-Term Factors. Applicants are allowed one point for every year of formal education, training or apprenticeship. If they are within the highly employable ages of eighteen to thirty-five, they receive ten points, and one point is deducted for every year of age above thirty-five. Occupations are rated for skill by the Department of Manpower and Immigration, and are assigned points ranging from one to ten on the basis of that rating. Personal quality points are assessed by the immigration selection officer after his interview with the applicant, and are given for such items as: possessing a steady source of income which would enable the applicant to live comfortably in Canada, even without finding employment; or having been promised help and support by a church in Canada. Occupational demand points are assessed on the basis of job vacancy surveys carried out by Statistics Canada and are updated monthly. The ratio of job vacancies to total employment is computed for a number of occupations; those with the highest ratios warrant fifteen points and those with the lowest warrant one point. No points are allowed if there are no vacancies in a given occupation.

Short-Term Factors. Area destination points are assessed mainly on the unemployment rate in the area, running from no points if it is over 10 per cent to five points if it is below 5 per cent. If an immigrant has employment arranged before he lands in Canada, he is given ten points; he may also receive the ten points without prearranged employment if his occupation is a "designated occupation." An occupation becomes "designated" when, in a given locality, the quantity of workers demanded for this occupation has been persistently greater than the quantity of workers available, and is likely to continue that way for at least a year. Normally this means that job vacancies in that occupation average more than 100 for a year.

The justification for allowing the nominated class to substitute relatives willing to help in the settlement process for the labour-market-oriented, Short-Term Factors, is that information provided by friends and relatives is normally the way people find jobs most quickly. Also, with relatives willing to provide food and shelter while the immigrant searches for work, it is unlikely that the immigrant will become a charge of the state.

This "points system" makes it clear that immigration policy is geared toward ensuring a highly skilled labour force in Canada, and toward maintaining an adequate supply of labour in specific occupations and regions.

ECONOMIC MODELS AND IMMIGRATION

The Department of Manpower and Immigration published its Green Paper on Immigration in 1972.[2] It summarizes Canadian immigration policy and, in the process of ostensibly opening a debate on a national population policy, details the possible benefits and problems which could arise from a continuation of, or an expansion of, existing levels of immigration. It is this latter aspect of the Green Paper that has received the most attention, and it is the Green Paper's treatment of the potential problems associated with immigration that has attracted the most substantial and most vitriolic criticism. There are two economic models which can be applied to the question of migration and which can help to clarify the debate.

The first is a simple labour-market model. It shows that if individuals move from low-wage areas to high-wage areas—and empirical findings have consistently confirmed this assumption—the supply of labour will fall in the low-wage area and rise in the high-wage area. This will increase wages in the low-wage area and reduce them in the high-wage area until the wage differential is so small that it will induce no further migration. If the labour-market areas being modelled are nation states, there are two ways of viewing this process: the international perspective and the nationalist perspective.

From the international perspective, migration is good and free mobility of labour should be encouraged. Since wages reflect productivity, migration, by shifting labour from nations where its productivity is low to nations where its productivity is high, will increase world-wide productivity. This will increase the quantity of goods and services produced and available for distribution, and thus increase international well-being.

The nationalist perspective, however, is concerned with the well-being only of the residents of a particular nation. If the nation happens to be a high-wage area, like Canada, migration may appear detrimental to national welfare, since it will reduce wages and reduce the amount of goods and services available for distribution to the residents of that nation. This is clearly the position taken by the authors of the Green Paper. The Green Paper rejects out of hand any notion that immigration to Canada be considered a policy to equilibrate wages on an international scale. Given the numbers involved on both sides, which would result in a Canadian wage at least half that of the present if immigration were uncontrolled, it seems clear that very few groups in Canada would favour this.

Another economic model, which has some bearing on the question of immigration, is the welfare economic model. Applied to migration, this model assumes that, if an individual moves freely and permanently from location A to location B, then he must prefer location B to location A and therefore his total welfare is higher in location B. At the simplest level, then, migration increases social welfare, since it increases the welfare of the individual making the move without decreasing the welfare of others. (The wage effect noted earlier is customarily ignored, since the overall effect is to increase the total product available for distribution.)

Economists, however, especially in recent years, have become more conscious of interdependence in the social world, and of the fact that the actions of one person may have a significant influence on the welfare of

126

others. Economists refer to these situations as "externalities"; an externality is positive if the action associated with it increases the welfare of someone else, and it is negative if it decreases another's welfare. Migration, like any human action, has externalities associated with it.

Again, there are two ways of identifying these externalities, from the international perspective and from the nationalist perspective. From the international perspective, one identifies the positive and negative externalities in both the sending and receiving countries. If the sum of the negative externalities outweighs the sum of the positive externalities, plus the initial increase in the welfare of the individual making the move, then migration should be discouraged. Otherwise, it is considered good, since it increases total social welfare, and should be encouraged.

From the nationalist perspective, considering only immigration, one must compare the sum of the negative externalities to the sum of the positive externalities in the receiving nation only. A question that arises is whether to include the welfare gain of the immigrant as part of the benefit accruing to the receiving nation. A *broad* nationalist perspective would include it, and the question would be whether the sum of the negative externalities outweighed the sum of the positive externalities plus the welfare gain to the immigrant. If so, migration should be discouraged; if not, then it should be encouraged. From a *narrow* nationalist perspective, the decision should be based only on the net welfare gain accruing to people who resided in the receiving country before immigration takes place; thus, only the externalities should be compared and the welfare gain to the immigrant ignored.

The Green Paper (C.I.P.S., 1, 2, 3, and 4) is mainly a compendium of positive and negative externalities, and, in the process of compiling them, the authors of the Green Paper do three things which have provoked much of the stronger criticism and which can be related to the previous discussion. First, while the authors of the Green Paper deliberately avoid taking a firm position, it is clear that theirs is a narrow nationalist perspective. The Green Paper not only contains no mention of the possible benefits to the immigrants themselves from living in Canada, but even ignores the benefits that the Canadian relatives of potential immigrants receive from having those relatives nearby, and the benefits that Canadian ethnic communities receive from having new members enter those communities.[3]

Second, it identifies many of the social problems, or negative externalities which occur from increasing population and, more particularly, increasing urbanization with immigration. It is true that immigration in Canada, which has had consistently high levels of immigration, does increase the population, and as the Green Paper adequately documents, immigrants are attracted to urban centres. It is also true that the selection process itself encourages immigrants to urban areas, since unemployment rates are lower there and demand for the more highly skilled worker is higher. It can be argued, however, that the problems associated with increased urbanization should be dealt with separately from the question of immigration, and that to consider reduced immigration as even a partial solution to such problems as racial violence, urban blight, increasing crime rates and increasing welfare rolls, is to ignore the real bases of these problems.

Third, the authors of the Green Paper have identified as negative externalities attitudes that are considered to be immoral and therefore unworthy of consideration in government policy-making. A Canadian resident may automatically dislike an immigrant who is non-white, solely because of the immigrant's skin colour. While this must be considered a negative externality, it has shocked and outraged some groups that this attitude could be accepted by the government in making policy. Surely, if any one feature of the Green Paper has opened it to charges of being "racist," this is it.

LABOUR MARKET ANALYSIS AND METHODOLOGICAL ERRORS

The Green Paper recognizes that since Canada's immigration program is, with the exception of the sponsored dependents, based on the potential employability of the immigrant, the actual labour-market experience of Canadian immigrants is an essential element in measuring the success of the program. This recognition is evident in the space devoted in the Green Paper to the analysis of this experience, which comprises most of one volume (C.I.P.S., *Three Years in Canada*, 1974), and is a major point of emphasis throughout the others. One theme clearly emerges as this analysis is discussed in the Green Paper: that the experience of the nominated immigrants is distinctly inferior to that of the independent immigrants and that the experience of the nominated immigrants is unsatisfactory. There appears to be a concerted effort in the Green Paper to make this class of immigrants appear to be a group which will be an economic burden on the rest of Canada.

For example, from the conclusion to the chapter "The Working Immigrant":

It is important to note, however, that the Longitudinal Survey and other studies have yielded evidence that...economic reasons, not a desire to join their relatives, are the chief motive behind the decision to emigrate on the part of most members of the nominated group. The Longitudinal Survey has also established the greater employment difficulties nominated immigrants have encountered on arrival in Canada, particularly those for whom occupational demand is marginal (C.I.P.S. 1, 1974:34).

And from the conclusion to the chapter "Recent Immigration Patterns":

Much less certain, however, is the extent to which this concept (the concept of nominated immigrants) has furthered another basic objective of immigration policy: the matching of the total immigration movement as closely as possible with domestic economic conditions, especially the requirements of Canada's labour market. There is ample evidence that the primary motivation to migrate on the part of those who have qualified for selection as nominated immigrants has been economic in character. At the same time, the data suggest that a significant proportion of nominated immigrants entering the labour force have not possessed the skills most likely to permit their rapid integration. The fact that members of this category have too frequently been unqualified for jobs in high demand has meant that *their employment experience in Canada has often been unsatisfactory* (C.I.P.S. 2, 1974:96-97).

The Green Paper includes the Longitudinal Survey (C.I.P.S. 4, 1974) which presents a summary of data concerning the economic and social adaptation of a sample of immigrants over a three-year period. The economic findings were that, by the end of the second year in Canada, the immigrants, both independent and nominated, had a lower rate of unemployment, a higher income, and a lower incidence of poverty than the national averages. From this finding, it may seem strange that the authors of the Green Paper could infer that nominated immigrants represent a potential economic burden. However, immigrants are, at least partly, chosen for qualities which correlate positively with economic success, and cannot necessarily be compared fairly to the Canadian population as a whole. For example, immigrants tend to be in the prime-age category (eighteen to twenty-five), while poverty and unemployment are more heavily concentrated in the old. In order to determine if the immigrants will not be a relatively heavier economic burden than the native population, it is necessary to compare them to a group the same age. Thus, a sample, referred to as the Canadian control group, which matched the immigrant sample in age, sex, occupation and geographical location, was selected by the authors of the Green Paper to compare to the immigrant sample.

When compared to the Canadian control group, the immigrants did not fare as well. Both classes of immigrants, by the end of three years in Canada, still had not achieved as low an unemployment rate as the control group, and had lower incomes and a higher incidence of poverty than the control group as well. In each of these three categories—employment, income, and poverty—the independent immigrants met greater economic success than the nominated immigrants. It is these findings that are used to buttress the argument that, particularly with the nominated class, immigrants represent a potential economic burden for Canada.

I have three major criticisms of the methods used in the Longitudinal Survey, however, and any one of the three is enough to invalidate most of the inferences drawn by the Green Paper as quoted above. The first involves the use of occupation as one of the characteristics of the immigrants matched to the control group. After all, occupational demand is one of the criteria used for selecting immigrants, precisely because there is felt to be an excess demand for certain occupations. Immigrants are therefore automatically going to be concentrated in occupations with low unemployment rates; that is why Canada allows them in, because their productivity will be high and the positions cannot be easily filled by the domestic labour force. Their addition to the Canadian labour force represents an improvement in the quality and productivity of that labour force. The fact that their unemployment rates are slightly higher than those of native Canadians pursuing the same occupations is irrelevant from a broad economic point of view.

The second criticism is of the comparison of the nominated immigrants to the independent immigrants in the sample, and the comparison of each to a single control group. The reason for choosing the control group for comparison was precisely because the immigrant sample possessed more of the characteristics that are positively correlated with economic success than the labour force as a whole. But, considering the differences in meeting the criteria necessary for immigration, clearly the independent immigrants possessed more of these characteristics than did the nominated immigrants. If one is interested in obtaining a picture of the various types of immigrants' relative economic experience, then there must be two control groups, one for the nominated immigrants and one for the independent immigrants. It is not possible from the analysis in the Green Paper to infer that the nominated immigrants represent a greater potential economic burden than a comparable group of native Canadians.

The third criticism also involves the selection of the Canadian control group and is perhaps the most serious criticism of all. While it is true that the control group matches the immigrant sample reasonably well with respect to the four characteristics: age, sex, occupation, and geographical location (C.I.P.S. 4, 1974:146-147), the two groups differ dramatically with respect to one characteristic which is of crucial importance in determining labour-market experiences. This characteristic is the employment state of the sample, or group, at the beginning of the study period. The immigrant sample had an unemployment rate of 75 per cent (C.I.P.S. 4, 1974:6), while the control group had a zero unemployment rate (C.I.P.S. 4, 1974:22).

This is an enormous difference, with effects of surprisingly lengthy duration; its importance cannot be overemphasized. For instance, one summary of over thirty-five studies of workers unemployed in mass layoffs found that for periods of up to five years after the layoff, not one group had achieved the national unemployment rate (Miernyk and Britt, 1965). It is common for mass layoff groups, starting with a 100 per cent unemployment rate on the date of the layoff, to have employment rates of two and three times the national average for periods of two to three years after the layoff. To an economist familiar with the effects of mass layoffs on employment patterns, the labour-market experience of both the independent and nominated immigrants to Canada, as presented in the Longitudinal Survey, appears to be one of outstanding success. As a defence of this statement, I have prepared a comparison of the labour-market experience of the Canadian immigrant sample with that of a sample of workers unemployed in a mass layoff.[4]

As Table 1 indicates, the age, sex, and occupational composition of the mass layoff sample was superior to that of the immigrant sample. The mass layoff occurred in 1965; thus the mass layoff group was seeking employment, over the period it was studied, in an expanding labour market. In fact, it was the tightest labour-market situation in the United States since the Korean War. The Canadian immigrant sample was studied during a period of rising unemployment in Canada. It is impossible to compare the geographical locations of the mass layoff sample to the Canadian immigrant sample, since mass layoff occurred in the United States. It might be assumed that the poor labour-market conditions in the location of the mass layoff would overcompensate for the national labour-market situation, and thus invalidate a comparison between the mass layoff and Canadian immigrants. To correct for this, the two Canadian immigrant groups are compared to that portion of the mass layoff sample that moved from the local labour market following the layoff, and called the "layoff control group." The mass layoff sample that moved had an unemployment rate of about 80 per cent at the beginning of the period (Allen, 1969: 105), and thus was entering the labour market in roughly the same employment state as the Canadian immigrants.

Table 2 presents the comparison of several measures of the employment experiences of the two samples. In every measure on Table 2, the two Canadian immigrant groups show a substantially more successful experience than the mass layoff control group. While both Canadian immigrant groups had an unemployment rate less than the national average within two years, the unemployment rate of the mass layoff group was significantly higher than the national average two years after the layoff. As mentioned above, this is not an anomalous finding for the mass layoff group. In fact, the mass layoff control group, because of its exceptionally high "employability characteristics," and the fact that it consists only of people who migrated following the layoff, had one of the most successful re-employment experiences to be found in the literature.

The Canadian immigrant sample had more success in other economic respects as well. In terms of job mobility, the Canadian immigrant sample was more stable, with 52 per cent holding more than one job over three years compared with more than 55 per cent holding more than one job over a single year in the mass layoff control group (C.I.P.S. 4, 1974:40 and Allen, 1969: 105). During its second year in Canada, the immigrant

Table 1

Personal Characteristic Comparison

	Sample of Canadian Immigrants[a]	Sample of Laid-Off Workers[b]
Median Age	29 years	31 years
Per cent Male	86	88
Per cent with more than 14 years' education	26.5	48
Per cent in Professional, Technical, and Managerial Occupations	37.1 (intended)	49.8 (before layoff)
Per cent in Unskilled Occupations	5.8 (intended)	2.1 (before layoff)

[a]C.I.P.S., *Three Years in Canada*, Vol. 4, 1974.
[b]Allen, 1969:15.

sample earned income equal to 88 per cent of that of the Canadian control group. The 85 per cent of the mass layoff control group *that was employed* was earning a salary equal to 87 per cent of its salary before the layoff, at the beginning of the second year following layoff (C.I.P.S. 4, 1974: 54; and Allen, 1969: 105).

The data above lead me to conclude that the labour-market experience of both independent and nominated immigrants is, in fact, remarkable. The labour-market situation and the employability characteristics of the immigrants were inferior to that of the mass layoff control group, yet they did as well as or better in every category—employment, job stability, and income. When one considers the cultural hurdles that face the immigrant to Canada in the labour market, hurdles that the mass layoff control group did not face, the success becomes even more remarkable. Any inference that the performance of either class of Canadian immigrants is in any way unsatisfactory must be considered invalid.

In conclusion, I feel that the attempt by the authors of the Green Paper to imply that the negative externalities associated with immigration on the present scale are significant enough to call the existing policy into question, has been unsuccessful. The analysis, which is intended to demonstrate that immigrants, particularly sponsored immigrants, represent a po-

Table 2

Employment Experience Comparison

	Sample of Canadian Immigrants[a]		Layoff Control Group[b]
	Nominated	Independent	
Mean time to first job in weeks	5.5	3.3	14.5
Unemployment rate:			
1 year from immigration/ layoff	9.0 (+3.0)	5.5 (-0.5)	14.6 (+10.)
2 years from immigration/ layoff	6.5 (-0.5)	4.0 (-3.0)	7.3[c] (+3.3)
(difference between group rate and national rate in parentheses)			
Mean time spent unemployed during 2nd year after immigration/ layoff in weeks	4.6	2.9	6.0[c]

[a]C.I.P.S. *Three Years in Canada*, Vol. 4, 1974, chapters 1 and 2.
[b]Allen, 1969: 15, chapter 6.
[c]These numbers are based on extrapolations of laid-off workers' actual experience over a period which varied from 8 to 16 months. These are not simple linear extrapolations, but are derived from a stochastic Markov process. This process is described in Chapter IX of Fishman, Allen, Bunger and Eaton, *op cit.*
Reprinted from Taylor, Bassili, and Aboud, 1973.

tential economic burden to the taxpayers of Canada, is faulty, and simply does not demonstrate that point. Finally, the improvement in the lives of the immigrants themselves is simply ignored. It is not especially relevant to compare their economic and social situation to that of Canadians in the same class. What is meaningful is to compare the economic and social situation of the immigrants to the situation they would have faced without the opportunity to move to Canada.

Notes

1. This "points system" is elaborated in the fourth volume of the four volumes published by the Department of Manpower and Immigration, Information Canada, 1974, entitled: *Immigration Policy Perspectives; The Immigration Program; Immigration and Population Statistics; and Three Years in Canada*, which are referred to as the Green Paper on Immigration.

2. For a relatively mild treatment of the Green Paper see the discussions in *Canadian Public Policy*, 1:3 (Summer, 1975) and in *Canadian Ethnic Studies*, VII: 1 (Special Issue, 1975). A number of groups, ranging from students to radical groups to the Canada Young Women's Christian Association, have branded the Green Paper as "racist."

3. See Gunther, 1975, for a very competent elaboration of this point.

4. A complete description of this mass layoff group's experience, as well as that of two other groups, can be found in Fishman, L., Allen, J., Bunger, B., and Eaton, C., Reemployment Experiences of Defense Workers, Report # E-113. U.S. Arms Control and Disarmament Agency. Washington, D.C.: U.S. Government Printing Office, 1968. Most of the data presented are derived from Allen, 1969.

References

Allen, J.
  1969 "The Return to Human Migration: A Case Study of a Mass Layoff." Unpublished Ph.D. Thesis. University of Colorado.
Canadian Ethnic Studies Association
  1975 *Canadian Ethnic Studies* 7:1. Special Issue on Immigration. Canadian Immigration and Population Study 2, 1974. *The Immigration Program*. Ottawa: Department of Manpower and Immigration.
  Canadian Immigration and Population Study 3, 1974. *Immigration and Population Statistics*. Ottawa: Department of Manpower and Immigration.
  Canadian Immigration and Population Study 4, 1974. *Three Years in Canada*. Ottawa: Department of Manpower and Immigration.
Fishman, L., J. Allen, B. Bunger, and C. Eaton
  1968 "Reemployment Experience of Defense Workers, Report E-113." U.S. Arms Control and Disarmament Agency. Washington, D.C.: United States Government Printing Office.
Gunther, P.
  1975 "Canada's Immigration Policy: Some Comments." *Canadian Ethnic Policy* 1:580-583.
Miernyk, W. and R. Britt
  1965 *Empirical Labor Market Studies—a Summary and Synthesis*. Bureau of Economic Research, University of Colorado.

7

Changing Canadian Attitudes Toward American Immigrants
Edgar Z. Friedenberg*

The June 1975 issue of *Canadian Forum* carried an article by David Lewis Stein entitled "'Some of My Best Friends,' Americans as Canada's Jews." Mr. Stein, a Canadian Jew, is disturbed at the development of attitudes toward Americans in Canada which he sees as ominously similar to those that prevailed against Jews in Canada twenty years ago. His piece opens with these observations:

> Americans are becoming Canada's Jews. The qualities that popular wisdom once discerned in Jews are now ascribed to immigrants from the United States. And the bigots are blooming like spring flowers.
>
> Americans are everywhere, they say, taking over everything. Americans are overbearing and oversensitive. Americans are easily distinguished in a crowd of true Canadians (unless of course a Canadian wants to show his liberal tolerance by remarking, "But you don't talk like an American"). Americans are serenely confident that they are better than the rest of us. And they have this uncanny ability always to come out ahead of us in any enterprise we undertake together.
>
> What is best of all for smart Canadians, hating Americans is now socially acceptable...Almost everywhere, knowing little cracks about Americans are as fashionable as cracks about Jews once were.

The hostility, in fact, goes a bit beyond cracks. Mr. Stein notes particularly an article by Heather Robertson (1975) in her regular space on the back page of *Maclean's* in which she put forth, among other genial comments, "I confess to a desire to toss a hand grenade into every American camper I pass on the highway." In Toronto an organization of presumably self-ap-

---

*Edgar Z. Friedenberg is Professor of Education, Dalhousie University, Halifax, Nova Scotia.

pointed patriots protect their country by selling stickers saying "Yankee, Go Home" to people who apply them to the windshields of vehicles bearing American licence plates. This is still a long way short of a *Kristallenacht* but it seems fairly extreme for a society, like that of Canada, which so strongly decries and represses spontaneous acts of violence by unauthorized personnel and which cites as a major item in its indictment of the American way of life the supposed proneness of individual Americans, as well as of their government, to violence and vandalism.

The attitude of Canadians toward ethnic minorities in the nation is both varied and ambivalent. While the Canadian Bill of Rights Act begins by declaring that "It is hereby recognized that in Canada there have existed and shall continue to exist without discrimination by reason of race, national origin, colour, religion or sex" rights for all; the rights referred to subsequently in the bill have not been administered justly to all. Native Peoples, as they are called to distinguish them from various types of "new Canadians," must sooner or later tire of trying to nourish themselves on Drybones. Such legislation as has actually proved effective, at least occasionally, in limiting the operation of prejudice against the ethnic groups disliked by Canadians who are in a position to harm them, is provincial rather than federal; and not all the provinces have, like Nova Scotia, established human rights commissions or the equivalent. And while the protections afforded by such legislation cannot constitutionally be denied to Americans, most Canadians would surely be disagreeably astonished if Americans tried to avail themselves of these rights.

The very idea of anti-discrimination legislation is itself patronizing–the more so, the more necessary such legislation may be–and envisions the discriminated-against minority as less competent than those native-born of standard ethnic stock to deal with the problems of life in an unfamiliar land: by local standards, "disadvantaged" if not inferior. But Americans are regarded, as Jews have been, as predators. Canadians who dislike Americans feel that they need protection, not from a lot of slitty-eyed exotics willing to work for slave wages and accept a standard of living that Canadians would scorn, but from an aggressive, cunning, and domineering people who constitute by their very presence a fundamental threat to Canadian culture. Some Canadians have come to doubt that a distinctively Canadian culture can even be maintained against the combined effects of American inundation, and the tendency of successful Canadians to expand their careers southward when they have a chance. Still, you won't find grape-nut ice cream anywhere else; a fact which Lévi-Strauss would have regarded as significant.

On normative grounds, Americans constitute a rather unlikely target for Canadian ethnocentricity. Immigrants usually attract hostile notice if they are 1) sufficiently different culturally to seem shocking to their hosts; 2) so numerous as to be highly visible; or 3) an economic threat. Americans do not, apparently, meet the first criterion very fully. If they did,

Canadians who emigrate to the United States would certainly be a conspicuous ethnic minority. From 1951, until the peak years of disenchantment with the American way of life in the early 1970s, more immigrants came to the United States from Canada than from any other country; and far more than emigrated from the United States to Canada (*U.S. Census, 1974*).

The United States is, of course, a much larger and more diverse country demographically, and not an easy one on which to make an impression by conspicuous behaviour in any case. It is as easy for Canadians as for Americans to get lost in it, among the millions of people seeking their identity. But that is not the only reason why Canadians are so easily assimilated. Most Americans, I believe, either think Canada is part of the United States or, at least, feel that it would be tactless to remind Canadians that it is not. Europeans and Asiatics are unlikely to blame themselves for not being Americans–they never had the chance–while Africans, having been Americanized through abduction and enslavement, can hardly be expected to be enthusiastic about the opportunities thus afforded them. But Canadians had every opportunity to get in on the start of a good thing, and they blew it voluntarily. For an American to look for differences between himself and his northern neighbours was, until the Asiatic wars, a little embarrassing, like meeting relatives who turned down your offer to share in an investment that has made you rich. The tendency is to play down the differences and praise them for having retained their grip on the earthy, natural, *human* things while Americans are being driven–yes, *driven*–by the responsibilities associated with their wealth and importance. Being driven is better than walking.

Not many Americans can still retain their former exuberant confidence in the superiority of their social system; in fact, they may now be overdoing the *corruptio optima pessimi* bit. But in any case, Americans have fallen into the custom of underestimating the very real, though subtle, differences between the two cultures; this would not have been possible if those differences were gross. Canadians, moreover, have not usually regarded them as gross. Thus, in the Metropolitan Toronto Survey of householders conducted in 1970, which gathered data from 3,218 respondents, Americans ranked first in order of acceptability on a Bogardus social-distance scale, ahead even of French Canadians (Richmond, 1974). Whether these results are representative of attitudes elsewhere in Canada, or whether they could be replicated today, I do not know. There has surely been some decline in our social acceptability, as any American who has lived in Canada these past five years must have noticed for himself. But it still seems a bit much that we should have passed in that short time from most-favoured-nation status among Torontonians to that of the only culturally-differentiated group which it is not only okay, but chic, to vilify in the mass media as well as at cocktail parties that probably haven't changed much since Mordecai Richler immortalized the cultural life of

137

Toronto in *The Incomparable Atuk.*

Turning to the second possible source of intercultural friction, Americans hardly seem numerous enough among immigrants to Canada to justify especially intense hostility. Of the nearly four million people who immigrated to Canada from 1946 to 1973, just under a million came from the United Kingdom as their last country of permanent residence. As commonwealth citizens, moreover, they were entitled until June 26, 1975 to vote in Canadian federal elections. During the same period, just under half a million came from Italy–80,000 more than came from the United States (Information Canada, 1975). Emigration from Italy to Canada, of course, peaked in the fifties but more recent figures have been smaller than American figures, which in the year 1972 surpassed emigration from the United Kingdom to Canada, although that regained its previously unbroken superiority in 1973 (World Almanac, 1975).

Looked at from a slightly different perspective, the proportion of persons of American birth permanently resident in Canada has remained almost constant at 10 per cent–it fell slightly, in fact–from the 1961 to the 1971 census, while the proportion of those of Italian and other southern European birth rose from 20 to 25 per cent. The proportion of what the Canadian Immigration and Population Study calls "Major European" (northern Europe excluding France) origin fell from 30 to 25 per cent, and the percentage of those born in the United Kingdom, but residing in Canada, fell from 34 to 28 per cent (Kalbach, 1974). Over the same decade, the proportion of Canadian residents whose country of birth is given as "Asian and others" rose from 4.3 per cent in 1961 to 10.8 in 1971, which makes them more numerous as well as, presumably, more visible than those of American birth. The fact that this proportion is likely to continue to increase unless opposed by a deliberate and–in consequence if not intent–racially discriminatory policy is, of course, the source of the basic issue underlying current and acrimonious discussions of the Green Paper.

On purely demographic grounds, Americans ought then to rank relatively low among those who are threats to Canadian ethnic and cultural purity, much lower than the British, unless the Canadian people still think of themselves as really and truly British, except for a dwindling proportion of licenced Francophones. And that does not really seem to be the case. Most Toronto people would surely feel more at home in Chicago than in London–they wouldn't like it as well, but who does, whatever his national origin? The Great Lakes region is one thing, and the Lake Country quite another. And certainly Vancouver is more like San Francisco than it is like London, though more economically active than either.

There remains, then, the question of Americans as an economic threat, and this is a much more complicated issue. It cannot be rationally denied that since the Second World War the Canadian economy has come to be dominated by American-based interests. This fact is properly regarded as

138

a major premise in any discussion of the Canadian cultural condition. But a major premise is not a syllogism, and what follows from it is by no means so clear.

Whatever advantages or disadvantages may have accrued to the Canadian people and their economy in consequence of American fiscal enterprise–and the costs of allowing outsiders to undertake the development of the economy are indeed usually enormous, as the Native Peoples of Canada can attest–they are not associated in any direct way with the presence of large numbers of American immigrants in Canada. The American imperial centre depends for its power on fiscal controls, potential military threat, and the use of hired mercenaries abroad. It does not rely on the infiltration of other countries by Americans, or on the cultivation of disruptive groups of disaffected American ethnics in the manner of Hitler's manipulation of the Sudeten Germans in Czechoslovakia. In fact, American residents in foreign countries are usually severely and justly criticized for clannishness; they build midwestern-type suburbs at kilometer six, shop at the PX when permitted, and send their children to American schools as Germans do not. This does not make us more popular, but it certainly reduces our salience as role-models. If there were ever American compounds of this kind in Canada, they are gone now; in fact, Premier Moores of Newfoundland seems to have got into a rare old temper when he finally realized that the United States government really does not intend to renew its lease on facilities in Goose Bay when the present lease expires, though one would have thought that the closure of American bases would be welcome in the present Canadian mood.

American residents in Canada, in short, are not the agents of American economic hegemony; they did not come in the service of American corporate interests, and their removal would not embarrass those interests. When America has dirty work to do in Canada it is easy, and safer, to hire Canadians to do it; it is harder, but not impossible, to effect the removal of Canadians bent on blocking American interests. Until recently, when things got rather out of hand, Salvador Allende Gossens does not seem to have been subjected to pressures from Washington very different from those John Diefenbaker had experienced earlier, and for much the same reason. And nobody had to leave the States and go live in Chile or Canada in order to put the program into effect; by now, it's probably all stored in a computer at Camp David or somewhere, and called Operation Ready–aye, Ready!

The fact that American immigrants play a negligible role in the administration of American policy-interests in Canada does not, however, exhaust the ways in which they may nevertheless be an economic or social threat to Canadians. And I think that they manifestly *do* constitute such a threat, and one which is especially infuriating to many Canadians in a relatively good position to make their fury felt. What makes Americans even more of an irritant is that Canadian immigration policy, like that of most countries, is designed to guard the country against prospective immigrants as unlike most American immigrants as possible. The Department of Manpower and Immigration—the fact that the two are grouped together pretty well says it all—perceives the problem in a way that leads it to guard against admitting too many persons of novel and distinctive appearance, rather than against potential cultural imperialists. This is especially true if the prospective immigrant is very poor or has been spared many years of schooling. Not many Americans are permitted to meet the latter condition, while those who meet the former are unlikely to view Canada or any other country as promising greater economic opportunity than their own.

Restrictions on immigration are usually designed to exclude persons whose prospects of supporting themselves without public assistance in their new home are thought to be poor; or who, by doing so, would make it notably harder for the present inhabitants to get and hold jobs, thus forcing more of them into becoming charges on the public treasury. This is the conventional way of looking at basic immigration policy, and also the reason why conventional immigration policy is inherently not merely conservative but reactionary. It isn't simply a matter of immigration policy being designed to safeguard the interests of incumbent citizens as opposed to those beyond—especially if insufficiently beyond—the pale. It is rather, and much more seriously, a matter of how those interests are defined.

Immigration policies, not only in Canada but in most industrialized countries with existing or potential unemployment problems, are based on the assumption that the existing economic structure ought to be nurtured and encouraged; that those who find places within it are "contributing to the economy"; and that those who do not are "welfare bums." David Lewis's efforts a few years ago to turn this phrase against corporate giants, especially those of infamous international reputation who themselves subsist on massive public subsidy while contributing, though dubiously, to the general welfare, seemed to me most apt. And if Lewis had been widely understood, this imagery might have considerably deepened public understanding of how the Canadian economy operates. But I don't think this got across. Most people, apparently, still think that IT&T makes jobs, but that the Atlantic provinces, and especially their poorer people, just live off the government. It would be more sensible to invert the argument and hold that existing economic arrangements keep most people east of Toronto from making themselves useful, fulfilling their potential, personal and economic, and thus enriching us all, and that the fact that this happens less frequently in Alberta, does not prove that people are more valuable to the nation if they work for oil companies than if they catch fish or cultivate their gardens.

The government has no resources of its own. It is an administrative device for organizing the economy and legitimating the development and exploitation of resources, human and otherwise. In practice, this means that it functions to service and maintain existing institutions, and to conceal or deny legitimacy to alternative arrangements that might prove more fruitful. This, it seems to me, is the proper criticism to level against the Green Paper, not that it is racist or discriminatory. It is no more racist or discriminatory than Canada itself. The establishment of educational criteria for awarding "points" toward admission, though presented as an independent factor, of course compounds the difficulty, since education is defined in terms of years of schooling in the kind of graded system that only industrially developed states use to socialize most of their young into the industrial way of life and stigmatize others out of the market. But in any case, employability on existing terms remains the decisive criterion for eligibility to immigrate to Canada.

This kind of policy has had a curious effect in shaping and intensifying the economic threat posed by American immigrants. They come schooled and factory- or office-broken; they are not usually seeking the kind of employment that is in shortest supply. According to the longitudinal study, *Three Years in Canada*, (1974), Americans also begin at and maintain, though by a decreasing margin, the highest economic level of immigrants to enter Canada from any country. The sample cohort of 1970 entrants made about 60 per cent more than the average immigrant during the first years–though only about 40 per cent more during the third– remaining, during all those years, at the top of the list of immigrants classified by country of previous residence. Family income for American immigrants in this sample also exceeded the mean income for the Canadian control group by nearly 30 per cent in 1971; this margin had decreased to about 15 per cent in 1972, as the Canadian group gained income more rapidly than the American. For 1972, the third year of the study, the average income reported for all immigrant families in the study was $10,111; for the Canadian control group, $12,115; and for the Americans, $13,992 (*Three Years in Canada*, 1974).

These data indicate that the thrust of American competition is felt primarily by white-collar groups and professionals, petty or otherwise. This helps to explain the peculiar correspondence that David Stein noted between anti-American and anti-Semitic feeling in Canada, as Jews, too, make their competition felt in these areas, and are notably successful, though not as successful as their adversaries like to think. The data also help resolve the contradiction implied by the favourable attitude toward Americans manifested in the Metropolitan Toronto Survey. American immigrants are not perceived as "gooks"; they are respectable. Even the hippy-types are familiar from television and local emulation; we don't cause much culture shock. Our adversaries are to be found in the media and in the universities more than in the streets; and it is there that we make our presence felt.

But what is feared, or at least complained of most, is not our competition but our prospective cultural domination of the Canadian scene. Robin Mathews and James Steele (1968) put the issue quite clearly in the opening statement of their book *The Struggle for Canadian Universities*:

American university teachers have contributed much to Canadian universities. They are *not* a majority in Canadian universities, not even a majority among non-Canadians. They probably account for not more than 10% to 20% of the total university-teacher population. American professors do, however, constitute by far the largest group of professors immigrating recently to Canada, and the rate of their entry is increasing rapidly... Moreover, Americans appear to be heavily concentrated in the highly sensitive social science and humanities disciplines, where their influence is greatly enhanced by the extensive use made of American textbooks. In a broader context, the influence of American scholars is even further accentuated by the vast power which non-academic American citizens wield in Canadian life.

They do, indeed; but those who wield most do not live in Canada, and may never have been here – their subordinates go south to report. In the years since this book was published, the bottom has fallen out of the academic job-market in both countries, and the struggle has taken on a much uglier tone, in which the role of economic competition is much more conspicuous, while the claims of nationalism, cultural and otherwise, have become even more strident. But the issue of cultural hegemony remains, and fear of cultural domination is still an explicit, and apparently major, factor in the increasingly hostile attitudes of Canadians toward American immigrants and, especially those who are intellectuals. Does this fear have a realistic basis?

This is a more subjective question than those we have been discussing so far; and the answer cannot be based solely on data. To approach this question, I will have to consider certain differences between the two cultures on which observers doubtless disagree, as they do on the very question of whether there is such a thing as national character. But I believe there is – not, of course, in the form of an absolute difference applicable to all members of the groups being compared, but as a fairly reliable central tendency. Are there systematic differences between Canadians and Americans which threaten to alter Canadian institutions? I think so, and God knows, I hope so. I should think some of you might hope so, too.

As evidence, albeit subjective, that such a difference does indeed exist, I must include my use of pronouns in this article. When I came to Canada, I could not possibly have written about myself as an American openly, if not exactly proudly, in the first person. Not the least of many benefits I have enjoyed as a consequence of the privilege of Canadian residence is that of straightening out and learning to accept my own national identity. I do not mean at all to imply by this that I wish or expect to return to the United States to live.

In this respect, too, the comparison to Jews may be apposite; we are called clannish, but some of us are more comfortable where we are not the dominant social group, and the hell with the country club! The Jewish faith, as such, does not proselytize, but we do feel a certain obligation to go around being Jewish, so that people who have not enjoyed all our cultural advantages will realize that is possible, at least for a time. Americans are rarely aware that they feel the same way, and are sometimes more offensive about it than they would be if they were conscious of their attitude. Moreover, through most of the world the American contribution has largely been destructive, as it has been, in certain ways, in Canada. If our influence has not made Canadian culture worse, it has certainly made it bad in different and less appropriate ways. But I think we have some important values to contribute, and that these, too, play a role—and a predictable role—in arousing Canadian hostility. It is this process that I wish to consider in the balance of this paper.

One element common to American and Jewish culture, and very different from Canadian, is a highly sceptical attitude toward authority. Jewish attitudes toward authority also differ from American, in certain fundamental respects, though not nearly as much as they did forty years ago. But their attitudes are similar in ways that might very easily evoke the similarity in hostile response that Stein notes. This entire issue has become of such fundamental importance to me during my residence in this country that I wish to discuss it very explicitly here. It affects, very fundamentally, relations between Canadians and Americans from either side of the border as well as within Canada.

Like Canadians, and unlike Americans, Jews think of themselves as respecters of the lawgivers and of the law itself. Americans tend rather to be legalistic—a contrasting attitude which sees the law as a device that defines the ways in which power may be exercised, but confers no suggestion that lawgivers are especially trustworthy, or endowed with moral authority—on the contrary, as Watergate clearly showed. There is one exception: the Constitution, and the nine learned priests who interpret it, are expected to be venerable rather than venal. The buck may stop at the desk in the oval office, as H.S. Truman stated, but it is not even allowed to enter the Supreme Court. (In Canada it does, though in a way that suggests crassness rather than corruption: having $10,000 or more at stake gives you the right to be heard there, though no issue involving mere liberty, without cash value attached, does.)

But neither Jews nor Americans see the law as benign in either origin or intent. An amiable personality is not among Jehovah's attributes; if He is said to be just, it is rather in the manner of an Alabama judge trying black people in a nineteenth-century court. He may be just in applying the law to their quarrels among themselves, but not in matters that affect His authority. He guards that with jealous wrath, and He expects His people to

143

respect not only His commandments but their own lesser rights as well; we are to be a stiff-necked people. The most heart-rending moment in the crucifixion comes with Jesus' cry, "My Lord, My Lord, why hast thou forsaken me?" for Jesus was Jewish enough to know the answer to that already. One does not arouse Jehovah's sympathy by allowing oneself to be nailed to a cross. Or screwed.

As a consequence, God is not thought of as loving or beloved, though He does try to protect His people out of a sense of military necessity. The incidents in the Old Testament that seek to modify God's image into something more tender are ghastly and repellent, as no one has shown more clearly than Leonard Cohen in his marvellous song about Abraham and Isaac. (What would modern Quebec be without its Jews; its Richler, its Cohen, its Morgentaler, who, each in his own way, has done so much to illuminate the dark question of the nature of personal freedom in Canada?) Jewish attitudes toward authority are reflected in their attitudes toward public figures and public life which are, by and large, unsentimental. Discretion may be the better part of revolt, but nothing is gained by glorifying a real or potential oppressor–even one who likes to think of himself as a Liberal, as by now Jehovah perhaps does.

Of the Canadian Liberal leadership the converse, I fear, has by now become true. And these men do not appear content with the kind of morose and argumentative acquiescence that is the most Jewish people provide even God, much less their leaders. And we have gotten a lot worse about this in the past two generations. The inconvenient obverse of the Jewish attitude toward authority is that it is, of course, authoritarian. We do not worship authority–that is a Christian vice–but we used to be *enthusiastic* about it, in the literal sense of the word to which Northrop Frye has drawn our attention: "To be enthusiastic is to have incorporated a God within–in the Jewish case, God the Lawgiver."

But the law is now the gift of the national state. Our experience of that throughout history has not been such as to inspire reverence either for it or for its functionaries. Our history as a people has given us little enough reason to regard policemen as our friends; or to think prisoners more dangerous than their guards; or to feel safer when capital punishment is restored. But whatever respect we might have accorded legitimate governments, by virtue of the fact that they *are* legitimate, Hitler kindly relieved us of.

For Americans, less reverent of the law to begin with, the Indochina War–and its aftermath–have performed something of the same function; and if less thoroughly or reliably, even more corrosively. For we were the perpetrators of that war, not its victims; and we managed it *within* the limits of our legal system and *despite* the constitutional checks on executive arrogance we had built into it, which malfunctioned under pressure. We now know what the law is worth when matters of grave principle conflict with what the constituted authorities have chosen to deem the national interest. The result has been a pervasive sense of the state's inherent treachery. Guilt has nothing to do with it–though there is that, too; but *Kriesgsentschuldigung* is not what I am discussing. Neither is rebellion, though as Thomas Jefferson pointed out, while Canadians were not listening, it sometimes becomes necessary in the course of human events. What I'm talking about is simple, alert distrust, of the kind you might have for an old truck you were dependent upon to get around, and had even developed an affection for through the years, but whose brakes and cooling system you knew from bitter experience to be no damn good.

This is the cultural resource American immigrants are ready to share with you; and to find that one is offering it to the only white folks left in the world who are still fussing about nationalism is disheartening and even ridiculous. But I can see easily enough why the offer should make our presence threatening. Even though it is true that the American concept of freedom has done much to damage the quality of life in the United States, and has led to havoc abroad, it is still appealing; and many Canadians, I believe, find it seductive, and therefore respond both angrily and fearfully to our presence among them.

This is a different matter from the quite legitimate anger and fear that Canadians direct against the fact of American economic domination. Even the fear of cultural domination from across the border seems to me relatively legitimate; though less so, because that is effective only because many Canadians really prefer the American artifact. I cannot imagine a revolution in Canada, but if anything would bring it about it would surely be denying Canadians access to any television but their own. And even though *Time*'s special tax-position is withdrawn, *Maclean's* will, I expect, experience some Owen Glendower trouble in calling Canadian consumers from the vasty deep at their advertisers' behest. But we are discussing immigration and responses to it, so it is our personal qualities that are at issue. Canadians, apparently, see us as more egotistical and aggressive and shiftier than themselves; pushier and more inclined to impose our personal moral imperatives on situations that they have already defined differently; openly, rather than ironically, contemptuous of established institutions; and insensitive and abusive to established norms of good taste.

There is something terribly wrong with a community or a nation that can respond to the depths of rebellious despair only by getting tough, cracking down, imposing stricter controls; never questioning the role authority has played in bringing about disasters through its own intransigence, but egging it on to become more and more insupportable. Canadian society, I believe, is suffering from the social equivalent of leukemia. In that disorder, the cells whose function is to protect the organism against invasion or infection multiply beyond all reason until it is they who eat the body alive. It is a very ugly way to die, and spontaneous remission and recovery are rare. But it can be treated, once the patient gets it through his head that those protectors are, in fact, what are now threatening him–the American Senate finally came to this realization regarding the CIA. The object is not to eliminate the leucocytes, which would also mean death, but to keep the body from mobilizing them into a massive abscess in response to every pinprick, and to keep them from dominating other metabolic functions and thus obstructing and arresting those functions. People who fail to accomplish this measure of restraint soon find that capital punishment begins at home.

References

Department of Manpower and Immigration
    1975 *Highlights from the Green Paper on Immigration and Population.* Ottawa: Information Canada.
Kalbach, W.E.
    1974 *The Effect of Immigration on Population.* Ottawa: Information Canada.
Mathews, R., and J. Steele
    1968 *The Struggle for Canadian Universities.* Toronto: New Press.
Newspaper Enterprise Association, Inc.
    1975 *The World Almanac.*
Richmond, H.
    1974 *Aspects of Absorption and Adaptation of Immigrants.* Ottawa: Information Canada.
Robertson, H.
    1975 "Robertson Column." *Maclean's* (April).
Stein, D.L.
    1975 " 'Some of My Best Friends:' Americans as Canada's Jews." *Canadian Forum* (June).
United States Bureau of the Census
    1974 *Statistical Abstract of the United States,* 95th Edition. Washington.

PART THREE

Psychological Development
of the Ethnic Child
and Adolescent

PART THREE

Psychological Development of the Ethnic Child and Adolescent

In Part One we presented the development of the Canadian mosaic through a series of theories showing how these processes and structures of majority and minority groups are formed. In Part Two the authors described how Canada became an ethnic mosaic through immigration, and dealt with the matters of immigration policies, economic needs, and the attitudes that Canadians may have toward newcomers. Beginning with Part Three, we turn from a discussion of the general macro-patterns of the mosaic to a closer look at how different ethnic groups in Canada fit into these macro-trends. Part Three is the first of three parts which will deal with ethnic identification. We begin with the psychological development of the ethnic child, youth, and adult.

If ethnic groups in Canada wish to maintain their identity in a pluralist society, they will need to pass on their distinctiveness to their offspring. In the process of individual development, the child needs to adopt a set of motivations, attitudes, and personality traits moulded within the context of a sub-culture and society. Insofar as an individual's personality develops in a social context, it is important to examine the characteristics of several ethnic groups to see how attitudes and personalities are developed.

The three papers written by developmental psychologists in Part Three are addressed to different aspects of the problem. Taylor and his associates focus on the child-rearing attitudes and practices of French- and English-speaking Canadians in Montreal to see whether their attitudes toward child training differ significantly. Early childhood would seem to be an important stage in development if the child is to identify with his heritage and ingroup. How do the two charter groups differ with respect to training in an urban setting? Next, the Schludermanns select a minority ethnic group (the Hutterites) to examine the types of motivation and attitudes toward the formation of personality development when individuals are placed in a segregated rural ethnic enclave. The Hutterite communal society is ideal for the study of personality development in a highly controlled social environment. Finally, MacArthur's comparative study of youth, in four different ecological and cultural environments, explores whether these different environments affect the cognitive development of youth. Differential abilities relative to the ethnic environment in which the youth is socialized could be expected.

Child-Rearing Attitudes

It is appropriate that Taylor, Frasure-Smith, and Lambert should compare the child-rearing attitudes of English and French Canadians who represent the two charter groups, and also form the two largest ethnic groups in Canada. As social psychologists, they are interested in how cultural habits are developed and shaped by significant social agents, and how these habits are maintained through the generations. The nuclear family and ethnic reference groups are discussed.

They were surprised to find that there were a greater number of differences in child-rearing values between working- and middle-class parents than between English and French Canadians. Working-class parents were more severe, and more restrictive in the child's bid for autonomy than middle-class parents. The child-rearing values of English and French parents of the same social class seemed in many ways very similar to each other. These observations would seem to confirm Porter's contention that social class is a more important factor in predicting social differentiations than is ethnicity.

There were, however, some ethnic differences. A major difference was that English parents tended to place more restrictions on privileges, and reacted more harshly to insolence. Generally, though, there were only a few significant differences; for a number of other values tested, these differences appeared to be less significant. Perhaps the attitudes of English parents in Montreal are not typical, since they are a minority in Quebec. To what extent the English-French differences are influenced by social class is a question which must also be considered.

Personality Development and Ethnicity

In contrast to the previous discussion of the child-rearing practices of the urban industrial parents of the two charter groups, the Schludermanns discuss personality development within the *gemeinschaft*-like ethnic commune of the rural Manitoba Hutterites. Hutterites have long recognized the importance of the systematic teaching of the young in order to preserve their way of life. The Schludermanns have "systematically studied Hutterite socialization in relation to social role perception, adolescent attitudes towards self and others, adolescents' perception of parent behavior, as well as attitudes of Hutterite parents toward child rearing."

The Schludermanns discuss Hutterite ideals, attitudes, and personality traits, by using three different samples.

In their study of the ideals of 272 Hutterite adolescents, the Schludermanns found that the boys most frequently selected as ideals parental substitutes, if not the parents, from within the colony, but girls most frequently chose non-professional persons from outside of the colony, presumably because colonies offer a greater variety of ideals for boys, but very few for girls. Both boys and girls rated highly expressive social traits and good looks as ideals.

The study of the attitudes of 107 young Hutterite adolescents showed that the frequency of positive responses to Hutterite life increased with age, and that there were greater sex differences during adolescence than during adulthood. These observations would suggest that, with time, the youth increasingly identify with their Hutterite ways.

The study also assesses the general personality characteristics of normal Hutterite children to see what might be the "model personality" in Hutterite colonies. A sample of seventy-two children showed variations along five dimensions: Hutterite boys, but not Hutterite girls, performed at a substantially lower level on intellectual ability tests than American youth; Hutterite children were more "tender-minded" and less "tough-minded" than American youth; they were more sober and less happy-go-lucky than American norms; Hutterite boys, but not the girls, were more apprehensive and less self-assured than the norms; and Hutterite girls, but not the boys, were more circumspect and internally restrained than the norms. The Schludermanns conclude that Hutterite attitudes, behaviour development, and personality patterns are intimately linked to Hutterite socialization practices, values, social organizations, and ideologies.

Culture and Cognitive Development

The authors of the previous two papers have laid the ground for the exploration of the effect of ecology and culture on the development of particular abilities. To proceed from this point, MacArthur asks two questions: "1) what intellectual abilities are least and most related to differences in cultural backgrounds? and 2) what particular cultural influences are related to the development of what intellectual abilities?" For a study of these questions, 750 subjects in four ethnic groups (Central Canadian Inuit, Nsenga Zambians, West Greenlander Eskimos, and Alberta Whites) were compared.

MacArthur argues that certain characteristics of adaptation are developed by different groups for survival. This adaptation for people living in subsistence-level economies involves the development of minute perceptual and cognitive discrimination within their life space, their family upbringing, which stresses self-reliance, and their loose societal structures for flexibility. He suggests that hunting peoples, such as the Inuit, will

151

develop the characteristics listed above, while people living in more urban, industrial societies, such as Whites in Alberta, will demonstrate less proficiency in these areas.

The study shows that the cognitive abilities of the four groups studied vary considerably. The Eskimo samples clearly showed greater cognitive strengths in spatial and field-independence abilities, while their strengths in the areas of non-verbal and spatial abilities seemed to be effective for resistance to social conformity required in a more complex urban industrial society. Thus, their culture seemed to provide a cognitive means of maintaining boundaries between their Inuit pattern of life and that of the more urban Canadian Whites.

Unfortunately, the many aspects of child development and its effect on ethnic identity cannot be sufficiently dealt with in a few pages. The three selections demonstrate that the socialization of children and youth is crucial for the development of ethnic identity. Some groups devote a great deal of energy to child rearing, and it appears to be effective. There also appear to be a variety of ways in which ethnic identification can be accomplished.

8

Psychological Development of French and English Canadian Children: Child-Rearing Attitudes and Ethnic Identity

Donald M. Taylor, Nancy Frasure-Smith, and Wallace E. Lambert*

There seems to be a tendency among social scientists to approach research on the matter of culture with strong expectations that cultural groups differ, and that properly conducted research on cultural-group comparisons will necessarily turn up contrasts of one sort or another, including contrasts in personality styles. This tendency is very evident in research about Canada's two charter groups, and the types of differences, and the interpretations offered for these differences, have been numerous and varied. For example, Richer and Laporte (1973) explored differences in values and cognitive style between English Canadians and French Canadians and concluded that English Canadians are oriented more to the present and collective. McClelland (1961) reported different levels of achievement affiliation and power needs in English Canadian and French Canadian children's readers. Rosen (1959), following up on achievement motivation differences, found that French Canadian immigrants to the USA had relatively low achievement needs. Garigue (1962), through a set of structured interviews, has uncovered what he claims to be the distinctive and unique role relationships that characterize the French Canadian family.

In the industrial sphere, Kanungo and Dauderis (in press) found that French Canadian managers tended to emphasize "extrinsic" job factors—comfortable working conditions, respect, recognition, and fringe benefits—more than English Canadian managers, who were more concerned with such "intrinsic" job factors as the interest value of the job and opportunities for showing responsibility, independence, and achieve-

*Donald M. Taylor, Nancy Frasure-Smith, and Wallace E. Lambert, are Associate Professor, Assistant Professor and Professor of Psychology, respectively, McGill University, Montreal.

ment. Finally, Breton (1971) has studied cultural differences between English- and French-speaking Canadians in degree of aspiration, and Yackley and Lambert (1971) studied French and English Canadian boys' aspiration levels in a competitive task. Breton found moderate aspirations on the part of English Canadians compared to French Canadians, who had extremely high or low aspiration levels. Yackley and Lambert concluded that their French Canadian children were more unrealistic in setting aspiration levels in competitive tasks.

Although these illustrative studies all report cultural differences, they nonetheless leave important questions unanswered. In the first place, each of these researchers apparently expected to find cultural differences, and very likely topics were chosen on the basis of the probability of finding differences. Thus, differences may have been accentuated or exaggerated while similarities may have been overlooked or slighted. For example, in a recent study by Kanungo (1976) a number of similarities emerge, but they are not given the same weight or discussed in the same detail as the differences. Furthermore, Garigue's study of the French Canadian family was not comparative, and hence gives the reader no way of determining whether the findings are unique to French Canadians.

In the second place, it is very difficult to untangle the specific causes for obtained differences in the studies mentioned. What are often interpreted as cultural differences could in many cases be merely social class differences, or reliable accompaniments of social class status. For instance, the children in the Yackley-Lambert research could have differed in self-assurance. Or in the Rosen (1969) study, it is not clear whether the need-achievement differences are a function of culture (French Canadian vs. American) or religion (Catholic vs. Protestant).

Finally, even when differences do emerge, we can still ask whether we are dealing with a fundamental cultural difference that goes to the personality level or whether the outcomes rest rather on some superficial difference in the way a basic tendency takes different expressive forms. This reservation is relevant for most studies concerned with "culture and personality" and "national character."

In this paper, too, we will be comparing French and English Canadians, but we will try to take a more cautious approach in our attempts to interpret our findings. In particular, we will be very cautious about attributing the differences that do turn up to fundamental personality differences between the two "cultural" groups. As social psychologists we are professionally interested in the genesis of culturally distinctive habits, especially in cases where these are moulded and differentially developed by significant social agents. The two social agents we will be concerned with here–the nuclear family and ethnic reference groups–are of particular importance to children who have to function in a multi-ethnic milieu. A comparison of the effects of these social agents on the lives of French Canadian and English Canadian children should help us better understand

154

how members of two major ethnic groups in Montreal adjust to the complex network of cultures and languages which help characterize life in Canada. It may also help us better understand what is meant by "culture" and "cultural" differences.

FRENCH AND ENGLISH CANADIAN CHILD-REARING ATTITUDES

Do English- and French-speaking Canadians differ substantially in their attitudes towards child training or do the similarities outweigh the differences? This question underlies an ongoing investigation of cultural and social class variations in the child-rearing values of Canadians living in the Montreal area (Lambert, Frasure-Smith, and Hamers, 1975). Although we have studied Greek and Italian immigrant parents, as well as working- and middle-class English and French Canadians, the present discussion will focus on the English Canadian and French Canadian part of the study.

In examining parental child-rearing practices, there are three general methodological options available: asking children how their parents behave; asking parents how they themselves behave; or observing parent-child interactions. Each option has problems that are all too familiar to researchers investigating parents and children. Direct questioning requires that one ask the right questions in the right way so as not to bias responses. In addition, respondents may answer in what they feel is a socially desirable manner, or take the easy way out and develop a set response to all questions. Beyond the fact that observational data in normal day-to-day settings are very difficult to obtain, this approach lacks controls and is often biased by the influence of the observer on the behaviour of the people being observed. In an attempt to avoid some of these difficulties we have employed a novel method which tries to capitalize on the best features of both the interview and the observational techniques. The method is a modification of that used by Rothbart and Maccoby (1966) and involves eliciting spontaneous parental reactions to a tape recorded version of a six-year-old child in various familiar interaction episodes. The child makes a number of comments or demands of the parent; the parent's task is to imagine that the statements are being made by his or her six-year-old child and to respond accordingly. All the parents in the study do have six-year-old children and most react to the tape spontaneously and with amazing naturalness.

The episodes on the tape cover a wide range of parent-child interactions: incidents where the child repeatedly asks for help with a toy; seeks comfort for a small injury; asks to have a friend come over to play; and asks to be allowed to cross the street alone. Incidents involving temper tantrums, quarrels with a sibling and a guest, and insolence toward the parent are also included. Rothbart and Maccoby feel that parental responses obtained in this fashion closely parallel actual parental behaviour, and pilot work done by Lambert, Yackley, and Hein (1971) indicates that the procedure can be extremely sensitive and powerful.

Parental responses to each of the child's requests are coded in terms of a lenience-harshness dimension. For example, when the child says, "Ow, baby stepped on my hand!" a parental response of "Poor dear, let me kiss it to make it better" would be coded near the lenient end of the scale, while a response like "You should watch where you put your hands" would be coded somewhat near the centre of the scale. Each statement is coded independently by two judges and all disagreements are resolved through discussion. The coding categories have been simplified until very high inter-judge reliability is reached. Thus, for each taped statement we have a measure of harshness or lenience for each parent representing a particular ethnic and/or social class group.

We have interviewed forty sets of English Canadian and forty sets of French Canadian parents. Half the parents from each ethnic group are working class and half are middle class. Within each ethnic-social class group there are an equal number of parents with six-year-old boys and with six-year-old girls. The mother and the father in each family are interviewed independently. This design enables us, through the use of analysis of variance, to study the effects of ethnic group, social class, sex of child, and sex of parent as well as the various interactions of these factors.

All parents came from the Montreal area and all were interviewed in their own homes. To be considered as English Canadian, both parents of the six-year-old child had to have been born in Canada with English as their mother tongue. At least three of the four grandparents also had to be native English Canadians. Similar birth restrictions were placed on French Canadians and all had to have French as their mother tongue.

Before discussing results, it is important to point out some of the limitations of the data. First, we are dealing here with attitudes, *not* behaviour, and although making the logical jump to statements about how parents actually behave is appealing, it may be erroneous. Second, although we do have some evidence of the replicability of our data, we have not yet broadened the base of our Canadian study beyond Quebec, or beyond the urban context of Montreal. Thus, our findings can be considered only suggestive of what a wider range study might show.

The Influence of Social Class
What about our results? Perhaps the most unexpected finding involves social class: we observed a greater number of differences in child-rearing values between working- and middle-class Canadian parents than between English and French Canadians. Working-class Canadian parents were more severe than middle-class parents in their reactions to temper outbursts, whether the temper was directed towards a toy, a sibling, a guest, or the parents themselves. In addition, working-class parents were

more restrictive of the child's bids for autonomy and requests to have a guest over to play. It is noteworthy that these social class differences, as powerful as they are, only appear in episodes related to disciplining or restricting the child's independence, and do not appear in those episodes involving nurturance, aid, or comfort-giving. Most important, the influence of social class on parents' discipline-related attitudes seems to cut across linguistic lines, so that the child-rearing values of English Canadian and French Canadian parents of the same social class are in many ways more similar to each other than are the child-rearing values of English Canadian working- and middle-class parents or of French Canadian working- and middle-class parents. This is not to negate English Canadian-French Canadian differences, for they do occur, but to place these differences in a wider context. Much of what the casual observer labels as "Englishness" or "Frenchness" may, given the general economic situations of the two groups, more accurately reflect "working-" or "middle-classness."

The Influences of Ethnicity
English Canadian-French Canadian contrasts, although less common in our study than those involving social class, are nonetheless important. Overall differences related to ethnicity emerged in three areas: responses to repeated requests for help with a puzzle, reactions to insolent statements like "You're stupid, Mommy," and approaches to the child's requests to have a friend come in to play. In all three cases, English Canadian parents tended to give tougher or more restrictive replies than did French Canadians. That is, English Canadians were more reticent or less spontaneous in giving help to a child working through a puzzle, they reacted more harshly to insolence, and they were more likely to place restrictions on children's guest privileges.

A number of possible interpretations for these differences come to mind. For example, it may be that the English Canadian tendency to withhold help in the tape-recorded episodes is based on a desire to foster independence and self-reliance. This interpretation agrees with McClelland's data (1961) on independence training in English Canadian and French Canadian areas, and also parallels Rosen's finding (1959) in the United States that independence training is stressed more in Anglo-American than in French-American communities. Although we have no data on the subject, it is interesting to speculate that the English Canadians' harsher response to insolence may reveal an underlying fear that the permissiveness and recent loss of adult control which Bronfenbrenner (1970) has attributed to the United States could come to Canada too, a fear which may be present for French Canadians as well, but which is probably more real to English Canadians who share the American's language and media.

The finding that English Canadian parents were hesitant in granting guest privileges while French Canadian parents maintained an essentially open-door policy can be interpreted in a number of ways. English Canadian parents may again be fostering independence and self-reliance by limiting guest privileges. On the other hand, French Canadians, like other minority ethnic groups in the North American context, may be concerned with maintaining in-group ties and developing children's reliance on a sort of extended family. Having survived as a separate ethnic group in North America, French Canadians have undoubtedly learned to rely on one another, and perhaps have come to place a high value on their children's development of social skills. At least if the parents in our sample act in real life as they do in response to the taped episodes, their children are getting more opportunities to interact with friends than are English Canadian children.

Although the English Canadian-French Canadian differences in harshness or restrictiveness were significant for only three of our twelve scales, for all scales the English Canadian mean is above that of the French Canadians, indicating that our English Canadian respondents were generally harsher than their French Canadian counterparts. Before jumping to the apparently "obvious" conclusion that "of course, English Canadians are more stern, as their English ancestors were" it is important to note that extensions of the Canadian study to both the United States and England have revealed that American and English parents are relatively mild in comparison to our sample of English Canadians. Obviously, we are dealing with a special brand of English Canadians, those living in Montreal where they have economic power but are clearly a minority. Their harshness or restrictiveness may be a reaction to their minority status rather than a general characteristic of English Canadians. Only with additional data collection can we fully evaluate this possibility.

One other interesting English Canadian-French Canadian contrast emerged, this one involving response differences between mothers and fathers. There were greater mother-father differences for English Canadian than for French Canadian parents in response to two scales, one involving the child's fight with a younger sibling and the other concerning his or her attempt to gain comfort for a small injury. In both cases, English Canadian mothers were significantly more lenient than fathers while among French Canadians there were essentially no differences between the responses of mothers and fathers. It should be noted that parental differences did occur for *both* English Canadians and French Canadians on two other scales; one involving the child's attempt to gain attention by exaggerating a small injury, in which case fathers were harsher, and the other involving a squabble between the child and an invited guest, in which case mothers were harsher. What is important here is that, although we observed some attitude differences, perhaps reflecting mother-father role differences for both English and French Canadians, these differences were more frequent among the English Canadians. Further evidence of greater mother-father role differences among English Canadians comes from a recent study of English Canadian and French Canadian children's perceptions of parental roles, conducted by Frasure-Smith and Grenier (1975), who found that English Canadian children see greater mother-father role differences than do French Canadian children. Thus, although French Canadians are frequently depicted as belonging to a more traditional society than English Canadians, there is evidence here that mother-father differences may be more pronounced among the English Canadians.

Although we have observed a number of important English Canadian-French Canadian contrasts in attitudes towards child rearing, these differences have to be placed in perspective in light of the general influence of social class which has proven to be the most powerful variable in our study. Further work is needed before we know whether or not our findings apply to Canadians in general. However, the study has already demonstrated that descriptive statements of English Canadians and French Canadians may be misleading or meaningless unless samples from equivalent social-class levels are compared.

THE ETHNIC IDENTITIES OF FRENCH AND ENGLISH CANADIANS

Reference groups serve two very important social functions. They provide the individual with a standard for comparison and, more importantly in the present context, they inform the individual about the appropriateness of behaviour, attitudes, values, and so forth. There are, of course, a variety of reference groups that are shared by French and English Canadians such as sex, social class, and age groups. Rather than focus on these common identities, we wondered how French and English Canadians identified with various ethnic groups and whether their ethnic identities were essentially distinctive or essentially similar.

Like child-rearing attitudes, the assessment of ethnic identity is not an easy task. For example, one's identity may be influenced by the context in which the assessment takes place. If, for example, you ask a person "What are you?" in a school setting, the response is likely to be "I am in the fifth grade" rather than one that is ethnically relevant (see Lambert and Klineberg, 1967). One can also question people directly about their ethnic affiliation, asking, "Are you a Canadian?" followed by "Are you a Quebecker?" and finally, "Are you a Montrealer?" The problem with this approach is that people have a tendency to acquiesce, and when alternatives are presented in serial order, it becomes difficult to determine which of a variety of possible ethnic reference groups is the most central or most salient.

What is needed then is a procedure that avoids asking vague open-ended questions like "What are you?" while also avoiding direct questioning about ethnic affiliations. Our research on French and English Canadian identity makes use of a procedure which at least partially solves the methodological problems and at the same time is easily adapted for use in any social environment.

The first step in the procedure is the preparation, through informal elicitations, of an over-inclusive list of labels which represents the potential range of ethnic reference groups with which a member of that society could identify (e.g., Canadian, English Canadian, French Canadian, Québécois, etc.). To this list is added the anchor label, "Myself."

Respondents are then presented with these stimulus labels, two at a time, in all possible combinations. For each pair the task is to judge on a scale the degree of similarity or dissimilarity of the two stimulus labels.

Although the judgements required are relatively simple, the data can nevertheless be analyzed so as to reveal important dimensions of ethnic identity. Since respondents make judgements for all possible pairs of stimulus labels, one can generate a mean similarity matrix analogous to a correlation matrix. A multidimensional scaling analysis (Shepard, 1962; Kruskal, 1964) can then be performed. The objective of non-metric multidimensional scaling is to "map a set of objects, or stimuli, into a set of points in a metric space, such that objects which are similar (in some empirical sense) are close together in the space, and objects which are dissimilar are distant from each other in the space" (Spence, 1972, p. 461). In terms of ethnic identity, those ethnic reference groups placed close together are those perceived by respondents to be relatively similar whereas those placed far apart are those perceived as different. By focusing special attention on the position of each of the reference labels relative to "Myself," inferences can be made about the ethnic identity of respondents.

We began our study of ethnic identity by exploring the regional and national identity patterns of first-year high school students in Quebec (Taylor, Simard and Aboud, 1972). The rationale for selecting this age group came from research by Piaget and Weil (1951), and Lambert and Klineberg (1967) which indicates that by the teen years youngsters have begun to crystallize their ethnic identity. Following the procedure described earlier we provided both French and English Canadian respondents with stimulus persons representing both regional (an English Canadian, a French Canadian, a person from my home town) and national reference groups (a Canadian, a person from England, a person from France) along with the anchor stimulus, "Myself." Separate multidimensional scaling analyses were then performed for our samples of French and English respondents.

The responses of the French Canadian respondents fall on one dimension. The concept "Myself" was most closely associated with "a person from my home town," "a French Canadian," or "a person from Quebec." At the opposite end of this dimension were stimuli such as

160

"person from England," "Americans," and of special interest, "English Canadians." Significantly, the concept "Canadian," while not placed in an extreme position, was well removed from "Myself." For our French Canadian respondents, then, regional affiliations dominated feelings of national identity, and English Canadians were judged not only different from but opposite to themselves.

The English-speaking respondents also closely aligned themselves with regional reference groups, but there were important differences in their profile of ethnic identities. Again, the reference groups were judged along a single dimension and, like their French Canadian counterparts, there was a close association between "Myself," "a person from my home town," and "English Canadians." However, the English Canadian respondents place "Canadian" very close to "Myself," reflecting a national identity not found with the French Canadian students.

These French Canadian-English Canadian differences in regional and national identity suggest that factors other than mere geographical proximity dictate reference group selection and hence contribute to feelings of ethnic identity. An informal study of the reasons respondents gave for their judgements revealed that, aside from geography, linguistic and ethnic background factors were especially salient for French Canadian students who gave as these reasons for a lack of identity with Canada. Interestingly, English Canadian students used the same rationale for their apparent lack of affinity with Quebec.

In order to explore further these apparent differences between French Canadian and English Canadian respondents, a systematic study was made of the roles played by ethnic background, language, and geographical location in ethnic identity (Taylor, Bassili and Aboud, 1973). To this end, thirteen stimulus labels were selected to represent different combinations of these three factors. For example, "A French Canadian living in Quebec who speaks French mainly," "An English Canadian living outside of Quebec who speaks English mainly," and all other combinations of the geographic, language, and ethnic background factors were used. This step resulted in twelve items, and to this was added the anchor stimulus, "Myself."

The multidimensional scaling analyses revealed that both French Canadian and English Canadian high school students used two dimensions for judging these stimuli. However, for our present purposes, it is the first dimension, common to both groups, which is of most concern. The placement of each of the reference group labels for the French Canadian and English Canadian samples is reproduced in Figure 1.

For the English Canadian students the stimulus labels form four distinct clusters. The two clusters closest to the label "Myself" involve English-speaking stimulus persons while the two clusters most removed from "Myself" are French-speakers. This basic language dichotomy is further divided according to ethnic background, i.e., persons of English

Figure 1

Results for Dimension 1 of Kruskal-Shepard
Multidimensional scaling for English Canadian
and French Canadian sample.

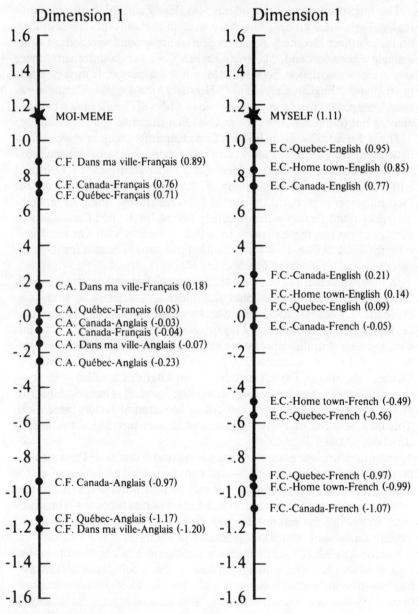

Reprinted from Taylor, Bassili, and Aboud, 1973.

Canadian background are judged more similar to "Myself" than those of French Canadian background. The geographic component of the stimulus labels did not have any important or systematic influence on identity.

The identity of French Canadian students is the converse to that of English Canadians. Again, language seems to be the key issue, with ethnic background playing an important but secondary role. Again, geography had little influence on French Canadian identity.

Our finding that French Canadians and English Canadians identify with different ethnic reference groups has several important implications. At a descriptive level, of course, it might lead us to expect quite different attitudes, values, and orientations for French Canadians and English Canadians. But at a different level the two groups are essentially alike in their ethnic identities since both react in terms of in-group/out-group differences. Although the particular exemplars are different, both French Canadian and English Canadian respondents appear to construct their ethnic identities in terms of those who are like themselves linguistically and to some extent like themselves ethnically. There would appear to be no "cultural" differences in terms of basic psychological structure and process, only in the surface expression of different reference groups.

A second issue emerging from our initial studies is the significance of language as the distinguishing feature of identity. The importance of language for identity is not an isolated finding. It has even emerged as the crucial determinant of ethnic identity in Wales (Giles, Taylor, and Bourhis, in press) where the majority of Welshmen are not fluent in their native tongue. Since language is an acquired characteristic, it would be important to explore how identity is affected by the experience of learning the language of the other group.

With a view to examining this issue, we (Frasure-Smith, Lambert and Taylor, 1975) studied French Canadian and English Canadian parents whose children attended "other" language schools and compared the structure of identity with those parents who send their children to schools where the home language is used as the medium of instruction. The stimulus labels used for this study included monolingual and bilingual reference groups (e.g., a monolingual French Canadian, a bilingual French Canadian, an American, a person from France) along with two anchor stimuli, "Myself" and "My Child."

The results for the two groups of English and two groups of French parents are presented in Figure 2. French Canadian parents whose children attend French language schools show the same pattern of identity that was revealed in our earlier research. That is, there was a clear affinity with the monolingual French-speaking reference group. For this group of parents, bilingual stimulus persons are viewed as being quite distant reference groups. For French Canadian parents whose children attend English schools, on the other hand, we note a much closer identity with bilingual reference groups. It is interesting to note that in the minds of the parents this shift in identity is most pronounced for the children, who are more aligned with bilingual reference groups than are the parents themselves. Finally, both groups of French Canadian parents made little distinction between bilingual English Canadians and bilingual French Canadians. It appears that bilingual people comprise an entirely new reference group regardless of the ethnicity of its incumbents.

Figure 2

Results of Kruskal-Shepard Multidimensional Scaling for: 1. French Canadian parents whose children attend English language school; 2. French Canadian parents whose children attend French language school; 3. English Canadian parents whose children attend French language school; 4. English Canadian parents whose children attend English language school.

LEGEND	
mFC = monolingual French Canadian A = American	
bFC = bilingual French Canadian C = Child	
mEC = monolingual English Canadian F = from France	
bEC = bilingual English Canadian X = Myself	

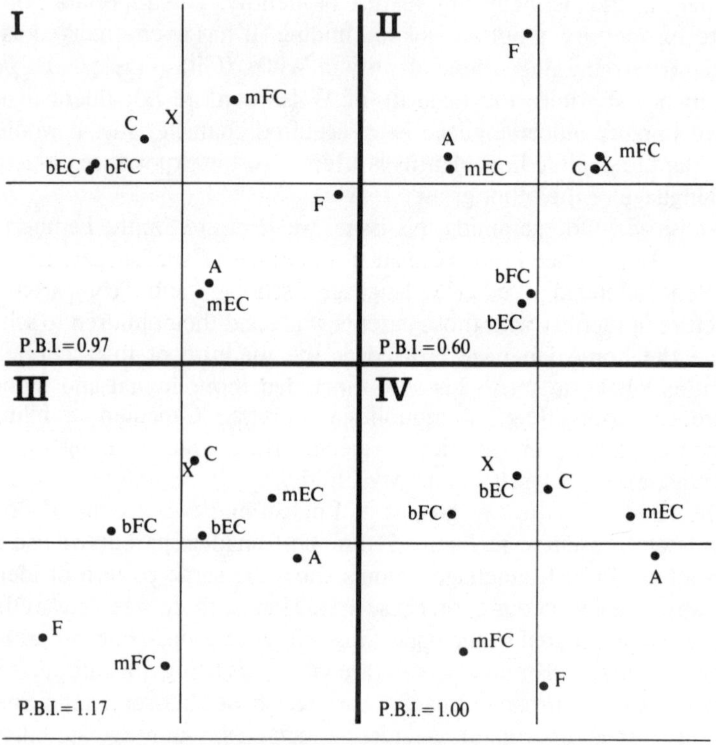

Reprinted from Frasure-Smith, Lambert and Taylor, 1975.

In contrast, English Canadian parents make a distinction between bilingual English and bilingual French reference groups. Nevertheless, both groups of English Canadian parents (those who send their children to the same language school and those whose children attend the "other" language school) identify with bilingual reference groups to the same or to a greater extent than they do with monolingual English Canadians.

Language *per se*, then, may not be a fundamental, dependable basis for "cultural" differences. To the extent that language provides a convenient basis for group distinctions, it may serve as a focus for identity, but it seems that if widespread bilingualism occurred, then either a totally new shared identity would emerge or alternatively separate identities would be confirmed but on a basis other than language.

The fragility of French and English Canadian identity is even more striking when other ethnic groups are considered. A study by Simard, de Broin-Garneau, and Mercier (1975) examined the identity patterns of Grade 6 French Canadian children. The multidimensional scaling procedure was used and since the sample of French children studied had considerable contact with immigrant children, the stimulus labels included not only French Canadian and English Canadian stimulus persons but French- and English-speaking immigrants as well.

There appeared to be two dimensions to the identity of these children. The first, as in all earlier studies, was a language dimension, where a clear polarization of English Canadian and French Canadian reference groups emerged, with immigrant stimulus labels judged closer to the English Canadian than the French Canadian end of the dimension. The second dimension, however, involved both French-speaking and English-speaking stimulus persons clustered around "Myself" at one end of the dimension with immigrant stimulus persons at the other. Thus, while language in this case too seems to promote a separation of reference groups for these French Canadians and English Canadian respondents, there appear to be other aspects of identity that draw the French Canadian and English Canadian together. It seems, then, that it is important for people to have the feeling that they have a unique "cultural" identity. What is not clear is whether these perceptions reflect true "cultural" differences.

SUMMARY and CONCLUSIONS

Our purpose here is to explore just how similar or different French Canadians and English Canadians are by focusing attention on two topics we are currently involved in, namely child-rearing attitudes and ethnic identity. In the process of exploring these similarities and differences we have used innovative methodologies which show promise for further research in this area. Comparing French Canadians and English Canadians on these two social-psychological facets, it appears that many contrasts in child-rearing attitudes that might be attributed to "cultural" differences may be in fact be more the result of social-class differences, making it more difficult to determine just what real "cultural" differences between the two groups may be.

Our studies of ethnic identity demonstrate clear differences between French Canadians and English Canadians in their reference group affiliations. However, these differences can also be seen as basic similarities in terms of each group's own in-group/out-group orientations. Moreover, we found that ethnic identity for both groups was based in large part on the learnable and changeable characteristic of language, and definite similarities in the identities of French Canadian and English Canadian children emerged when these were assessed in an ethnically more complex testing environment. From these exploratory studies, it would appear that some differences do emerge between French Canadians and English Canadians, but whether these represent true "cultural" differences is the crucial question. Trying to determine what constitutes a real "cultural" difference is becoming not only a challenging academic exercise, but also a socially important one (Lambert, 1974). LeVine (1973:10) has recently brought this matter of testing for cultural differences out in the open. A major barrier to dealing with this issue, he argues, is that it "has been obscured by its confusion with popular or folk formulations of national and ethnic differences in behaviour. Popular beliefs concerning foreign groups tend to be stereotyped, which is to say they are simplified, personalized, exaggerated, and highly evaluative." LeVine (1973:10) points out that such stereotyping has been used to "justify policies of national and ethnic competition and conflict in the modern world. Such characterizations have often been dangerous and irresponsible oversimplifications of complex realities." Hopefully, our attempts to grapple with the matter may be of general value.

Note

This paper was written for oral presentation at the Canadian Ethnic Mosaic Conference, Winnipeg, October 1975, and hence many of the details of analyses have been omitted. These analyses are available on request from the authors.

References

Breton, R.
   1972 "Social and Academic Factors in the Career Decisions of Canadian Youth." Ottawa: Manpower and Immigration.
Bronfenbrenner, U.
   1970 *Two Worlds of Childhood.* New York: Russell Sage Foundation.

Frasure-Smith, N., and M.K. Grenier
1975 "English- and French-Canadian Children's Views of Parents."
Canadian Journal of Behavioural Science 7:40-53.
Frasure-Smith, N., W.E. Lambert, and D.M. Taylor
1975 "Choosing the Language of Instruction of One's Children–A
Quebec Study." *Journal of Cross-Cultural Psychology* 6:131-155.
Garigue, P.
1968 "La vie Familiale des Canadiens Français." Montréal: Presse
de l'Université de Montréal, 1962. Translated abstract: The
French-Canadian Family, in B.R. Blishen, F.E. Jones, K.D. Nae-
gele and J. Porter (eds.), *Canadian Society*. Toronto: Macmillan.
Kanungo, R.N.
1976 "Analyses of Employee Behavior in a Bicultural Context." Working Paper No. 76-101, Faculty of Management, McGill University.
Kanungo, R.N., and H.J. Dauderis
"Motivation Orientation of Canadian Anglophone and Francophone Managers." *Canadian Journal of Behavioural Science*. (In
press.)
Kruskal, J.B.
1964 "Multidimensional Scaling by Optimizing Goodness to Fit to a
Non-Metric Hypothesis." *Psychometrika* 29:1-27.
Lambert, W.E.
1973 "Culture and Language as Factors in Learning and Education."
Paper presented at the 5th Annual Learning Symposium on "Cul-
tural Factors in Learning" at Western Washington State College,
Bellingham Washington (November).
Lambert, W.E.; N. Frasure-Smith, and J.F. Hamers
"A Cross-Cultural Study of Child Rearing Values." (In prepara-
tion.)
Lambert, W.E., and O. Klineberg
1967 *Children's Views of Foreign Peoples: A Cross-National Study*.
New York: Appleton-Century-Crofts.
Lambert, W.E., A. Yackley, and R.N. Hein
1971 "Child Training Values of English-Canadian and French-Canadian Parents." *Canadian Journal of Behavioural Science*
3:217-236.
LeVine, R.A.
1973 *Culture, Behavior and Personality*. Chicago: Aldine.
McClelland, D.C.
1961 *The Achieving Society*. Princeton, N.J.: Van Nostrand.
Piaget, J. and A.M. Weil
1951 "The Development of Stereotypes Concerning the Homeland
and of Relations with other Countries." *International Social Science Bulletin* 3:561-578.

Richer, S. and P.E. Laporte
1973 "Culture, Cognition and English-French Competition," in D. Koulock and D. Perlman (eds.), *Readings in Social Psychology: Focus on Canada.* Toronto: Wiley Publishers of Canada.

Rosen, B.C.
1959 "Race, Ethnicity, and the Achievement Syndrome. *American Sociological Review* 24:47-60.

Rothbart, M.K. and E.E. Maccoby
1966 "Parents' Differential Reactions to Sons and Daughters." *Journal of Personality and Social Psychology* 4:237-243.

Shepard, R.N.
1962 "Analysis of Proximities: Multidimensional Scaling with an Unknown Distance Function, I and II." *Psychometrika* 27:125-139; 219-246.

Simard, L.M., I. de Broin-Garneau, and E. Mercier
1975 "Dimensions de l'Identité Ethnique dans une Ville Multiculturelle." Université de Montréal, Mimeo.

Spence, I.
1972 "A Montecarlo Evaluation of Three Nonmetric Multidimensional Scaling Algorithms." *Psychometrika* 37:461-486.

Taylor, D.M., J.N. Bassili, and F.E. Aboud
1973 "Dimensions of Ethnic Identity in Canada." *Journal of Social Psychology* 89:185-192.

Taylor, D.M., L.M. Simard, and F.E. Aboud
1972 "Ethnic Identification in Canada: A Cross-Cultural Investigation." *Canadian Journal of Behavioural Science* 4:13-20.

Yackley, A. and W.E. Lambert
1971 "Inter-Ethnic Group Competition and Levels of Aspiration." *Canadian Journal of Behavioural Science* 3:135-147.

9

Personality Development in Hutterite Communal Society[1]

Shirin and Eduard Schludermann*

Insofar as an individual's personality develops in a social context, it is important to outline briefly some of the major characteristics of the Hutterite society. Detailed information about the Hutterite society is available elsewhere (e.g., Peters, 1965; Bennett, 1967; Peter, 1971; Gross, 1965; Hostetler, 1967, 1969, 1974). The following characteristics distinguish Hutterite colony life from most western life-styles: 1) the Anabaptist ideology of simple living and avoidance of "worldliness"; 2) an ideology of "non-resistant love" and pacifism; 3) abolition of private wealth and the equal sharing of goods; 4) an equalitarian idea of making colony members as equal as possible; 5) communal living; and 6) communal child-rearing.

Hutterites have long recognized the importance of systematic teaching of the young in order to preserve the Hutterite way of life. Thus, Hutterite children and adolescents are subjected to a carefully planned program of socialization in Hutterite values. The Schludermanns systematically studied Hutterite socialization in relation to social role perception, adolescent attitudes towards self and others, adolescents' perception of parent behaviour, as well as attitudes of Hutterite parents towards child rearing (1969 a,b,c,d; 1971 a,b,c,d; 1973, 1974).

Eaton and Weil (1955), Kaplan and Plaut (1956), studied the mental health of the Hutterites, both studies relying heavily on statistical surveys of rate of psychoses and neuroses. Kaplan and Plaut attempted to describe the salient personality characteristics of normal Hutterites and presented a different interpretation of the mental health problems than that presented by Eaton and Weil. However, the Kaplan and Plaut study, though less biased

*Shirin and Eduard Schludermann are both Associate Professors of Psychology, University of Manitoba, Winnipeg.

by culture-related mental health concepts, used basically two projective psychological instruments, the Thematic Apperception Test (TAT) and the Sentence Completion Test. Their interpretations were based on Freudian psychodynamics which do not lend themselves to easy empirical verification. Because of the shortcomings of previous studies, the present study was undertaken to make systematic empirical investigations of normal personality developments of Hutterites.

Theoretical Background of the Study

According to I.R. Child, "Patterns that function as effective stimuli and responses arise in part by cultural definition, and knowledge of the culture may be necessary or at least helpful in understanding what these patterns are and thus knowing what a person is doing and why" (1968: 84). The psychological approach to the study of personality and culture has emphasized the most common or "modal personality." Schludermann and Schludermann (1973) and Inkeles and Levinson (1969) pointed out that the modal personality need not be congruent to the socially required personality. For different societies there may be different degrees of congruence between the modal personality structure and the psychological requirements of a given society. A discrepancy between an individual's personality and the psychological requirements of his society may be less stressful if he shares this incongruity with many other members of his society. For the developmental psychologist it is important to note that different cultures expose the individual to different kinds of stress and different developmental tasks at different stages of the life cycle. Cultures also differ with respect to continuity versus discontinuity of social expectations, and abruptness versus gradual transition in social roles from one developmental level to the next. The interaction between culturally specific developmental tasks and individual peculiarities may best be conceptualized in terms of a "challenge and response" model of individual differences. As the individual proceeds from birth to senescence, his culture presents him with a series of challenges with which he has to cope. The individual's unique personality is determined, to a considerable degree, by how he has dealt with these challenges.

According to "role theory" (Thomas, 1968: 701), "Social change involves alteration of the individual through social agents so as to achieve commonality of the personal characteristics in question." Using role theory concepts, Hutterite socialization may be described as a "prescriptive" system which clearly and unambiguously prescribes the goals and the methods of socializing the young to the Hutterite way of life. The "sanction system" inducing internalization of Hutterite values involves arousing feelings of guilt and remorse in those Hutterites who violate the standards of their society. Therefore, the personality development of Hutterites can be studied through the roles each member is expected to perform, how adequately he performs them, and how much role conflict, role overload, or role ambiguity, discontinuity, and dissonance he encounters in fulfilling his roles in relation to others. Personality development will also depend on the extent to which others facilitate the performance of prescribed roles or hinder their performance. Besides these outward forms of behaviour conformity, one can also ask to what extent a Hutterite adolescent, or child, wants to do what he is required to do. The assumption here is that it is not so much the social sanctions that ensure effective socialization, but rather the appropriate motivations related to socialization. In order to answer some of these questions, a variety of psychological instruments were used. Each type of instrument was geared to answering a specific type of question. Through the multiple approaches to the personality study, an attempt was made to overcome the limitations of the single instrument approach. This paper reports on only three topics selected from a more comprehensive study of Hutterite socialization and personality development: 1) development of ideals; 2) Hutterite attitudes to Hutterite ideology; and 3) general personality traits.

HUTTERITE IDEALS

Havighurst, Robinson and Dorr (1946) pointed out that ideals develop from experiences with people and from reflections on these experiences. These experiences influence the development of self-concepts as well as life aspirations and goals. Ideals are important in directing behaviour, especially when major decisions are involved. Studying ideals through essays written by adolescent boys and girls, Havighurst et al. found that as they become teenagers, American boys and girls show an increased tendency to select romantic and glamorous figures as their ideals. However, as Hutterite adolescents have few opportunities to see, or even to know of glamorous outsiders, their parents, and other adults (more so males than females) continue to hold power and prestige in their age-sex-graded society. Therefore, it is likely that adolescents (and boys more so than girls) will continue to model after parents and other Hutterite adults. Since girls have fewer prestigious models available in the colony, they are therefore more likely than boys to select outside models. Thus it was hypothesized that parents, and parent substitutes, would most often be the preferred ideals over glamorous outsiders. This tendency would be stronger for boys than for girls.

Method and Subjects
Hutterite ideals were studied through essays written by adolescent boys and girls. A sample of 272 adolescents (109 boys and 163 girls), living in fifteen Hutterite colonies in Manitoba, wrote essays describing their ideals. The instructions and method of administering the essay, as well as the category systems to analyze the essays, were according to the system described by Havighurst, et al.[2] Some of the adolescents were asked to

describe their ideals a second time.[3] The essays were subjected to content analyses by three independent raters assessing three aspects of the ideals: 1) types of ideals; 2) attributes of ideals; and 3) occupations of ideals.[4]

Table 1

Essays: Types of Ideals

| | Hutterite | | | |
| | Males | | Females | |
Categories	% Essays	Rank	% Essays	Rank
Parents and older relatives	3	9	11	4
Parent surrogates	29	1	16	2
Glamorous adults	10	5	3	7
Heroes with claim to fame	1	10	1	9
Young adults in colony	13	3	5	5
Young adults outside colony	14	2	36	1
Composite and imaginary characters	11	4	14	3
Age mates or friends	5	6	6	6
Miscellaneous Hutterites	4	7	1	8
Older persons outside colony	4	8	0	10

The results of the first content analysis–types of ideals–are presented in Table 1. Adolescent boys most frequently selected parent surrogates. Next in order of frequency were outside attractive young adults, colonies' attractive young adults, composite and imaginary persons, and glamorous adults. Age mates were rather infrequently mentioned. The most infrequent categories were older persons outside the colony, parents, and famous heroes. In contrast, adolescent girls frequently selected outside attractive and successful young adults. Next were parent surrogates, composite and imaginary persons, and parents. Somewhat infrequently mentioned were the colony's young, attractive adults. The most infrequent categories were age mates, glamorous adults, miscellaneous, Hutterite heroes, and outside older persons. Thus, the type of ideals selected varied on the basis of sex difference.

In describing the attributes of ideals, adolescent boys most frequently mentioned good looks and expressive social traits (e.g., friendliness, kindness). Mentioned somewhat less were qualities like industriousness, wealth, personal moral integrity, actual help-giving, leadership, and contentment. The four attributes most frequently mentioned by adolescent girls were: expressive social traits, good looks, actual help-giving and personal moral integrity. Two qualities mentioned less frequently were self-control and industriousness. The attribute of brotherhood was somewhat

Table 2

Essays: Attributes of Ideals

Categories	Hutterite Males %	Hutterite Females %
Material values (money, property)	11	2
Good looks	47	34
Success due to self-achievement	5	1
Actual help giving	9	28
Expressive social traits (friendly, kind)	23	54
Social traits of self-control (courteous, patient)	4	13
Industrious (hard work)	12	13
Personal moral integrity (honest)	10	18
Brotherhood	0	5
Dominance (leadership)	8	1
Intellectual qualities	6	6
Overall happiness (contentment)	4	6

Note: Categories are not exclusive in the sense that one person may describe his/her ideal in terms of several attributes.

infrequently mentioned. Attributes such as material values, success through achievement, leadership, and contentment were stated very infrequently.

The third content analysis focused on the types of occupations in which the ideal person engaged. Adolescent boys most frequently (41 per cent) selected occupations of Hutterite non-leaders, e.g., farmers, pigmen, poultrymen, carpenters, tractor drivers, etc. People with glamorous occupations, e.g., hockey players, football players, country-western singers, cowboys, horse racers, astronauts, pistol-shooting champions, etc., were indicated with moderate frequency (27 per cent). Occupations of Hutterite leaders, e.g., colony boss, farm foreman, minister, etc., were selected with average frequency (16 per cent). Outside non-professional occupations, e.g., taxi-drivers, policemen, salesmen, mechanics, etc., were mentioned moderately infrequently (11 per cent). Outside professional occupations, e.g., engineers, doctors, "men with great learning," were mentioned very infrequently (1 per cent).

In contrast, adolescent girls selected ideal persons who most frequently (40 per cent) were in outside occupations without higher degrees, e.g., non-university teachers and nurses, untrained social workers, missionaries, stewardesses, and stenographers. The second highest-mentioned (35 per cent) occupational category was that of Hutterie non-leaders, e.g.,

173

housewives. Somewhat less than average (11 per cent) occupations were those of colony women leaders, e.g., kitchenwomen, gardenwomen. Outside glamorous occupations, e.g., cowgirl at stampede, actress, or the queen, were mentioned very infrequently (6 per cent).

Discussion

Three major points may be mentioned: 1) there was considerable variance in the types of ideals selected, based on sex difference; 2) both boys and girls rated highly the expressive social traits and good looks of their ideals; 3) while boys most frequently selected the models and their occupations from inside the colony, the girls, in contrast, selected the models and their occupations from non-professional outsiders.

To the extent that boys most frequently selected as ideals parent substitutes, if not the parents from within the colony, whereas girls chose most frequently outside non-professional persons, the findings tend to support the investigators' hypothesis. As suggested earlier, Hutterite colonies offer greater variety and choice of ideals for boys than for girls. In addition, there is the fact that males enjoy higher prestige and status than do females in the colonies, therefore girls are left with very few alternative role models inside the colony. The other point of interest is that both boys and girls rate highly the expressive social traits, e.g., friendliness and helpfulness. To this extent, the adolescents have accepted the Hutterite values of nurturance, friendliness, and helpfulness. In outside society, the expressive social traits are not emphasized for males, but Hutterite boys tend to accept their colony's orientation in this respect. Emphasis on good looks may be characterized as the adolescents' concern with outward appearance and will likely be de-emphasized as they grow older. Neither boys nor girls tend to select professionals as preferred ideals, which may be due to the colonies' de-emphasis on education and intellectual achievement.

HUTTERITE ATTITUDES

Kaplan and Plaut (1956) studied Hutterite personality structure as a sequence to an earlier study of Hutterite mental health by Eaton and Weil (1955). The purpose of this study was to investigate Hutterite attitudes related to salient Hutterite values, and also to replicate Kaplan and Plaut's study. A sentence-completion form of sixty-five items based on Freudian psychoanalytic personality theory was used by Kaplan and Plaut. A pilot study with this form indicated that the Hutterite adolescents found the sixty-five-item form too long and too demanding. The present study used a short twenty-item, sentence-completion form and kept it "theoretically neutral," in order to make the data scoring and interpretation independent of psychoanalytic biases. The sentence-completion method, although a relatively subjective technique, is often a fruitful device for eliciting first associations to each item. This form can be used from early adolescence to adulthood.

It was hypothesized that Hutterite adolescents would more often show positive rather than negative attitudes toward Hutterite norms and way of life, and that this trend would likely increase with age. Strong reactions to violations of norms would more often be expressed in terms of feelings of guilt and remorse. As mentioned earlier, Hutterite socialization emphasizes internationalization of Hutterite values and norms. While there are external sanctions to reinforce conformity to these values, guilt feelings would be a strong internal restraint against undesirable acts. It was expected that with systematic indoctrination and love Hutterite children and adolescents would increasingly accept Hutterite values as their own and thereby more often show positive rather than negative attitudes towards them.

Method and Subjects
One hundred and seven (42 boys and 65 girls) young adolescents (Y) thirteen to fourteen years of age; 111 (35 boys, 76 girls) older adolescents (0) fifteen to twenty years of age; and 98 (45 men, 53 women) adults (A), completed the short sentence-completion form. The subjects came from fifteen Manitoba colonies. Ten of the twenty items were selected from Wilson's Incomplete Sentence Form designed to assess positive, negative, and neutral attitudes toward education, family, and friends, etc. Ten other items were generated specifically for this study to assess attitudes toward Hutterite values and ideology, e.g., religion, equal sharing of goods, material values (money, power), and political leaders.[5] The twenty items were grouped into eight content areas. The completed sentences were subjected to a systematic content analysis by two independent raters who classified the items into expressions of positive, negative, and neutral attitudes.[6]

Results
Table 3 reports the percentage of positive (P) and negative (N) attitudes for the eight content areas. The overall percentage of positive and negative responses to all twenty items given by all subjects within an age-sex subgroup was used as an index characterizing the general outlook of that group. Such an index (the last column, overall 20 items, in Table 3) was used as a baseline for assessing the responses (higher or lower in P or N) in a given content area.

Taking the overall total average of positive or negative responses, it is apparent that positive responses in each age-sex group were more frequent than the negative responses. Further, the percentage of positive responses tended to increase while the relative frequency of negative responses tended to decrease with age. These overall trends suggest systematic shifts in general attitudes toward many aspects of the subject's envi-

175

Table 3

Hutterite Attitudes: Percentages of Positive (P) and Negative (N) Responses

	No.	Family (3 items)		Religion (1 item)		Money (4 items)		Power (2 items)		H. Values (3 items)		Education (4 items)		Other Sex (2 items)		Pol. Leader (1 item)		Overall Baseline (20 items)	
		P	N	P	N	P	N	P	N	P	N	P	N	P	N	P	N	P	N
MALES																			
13-14 Years	42	52	2	68	6	38	42	29	41	64	9	35	14	34	18	35	24	44	20
15-21 Years	35	62	4	89	4	49	34	30	32	76	7	47	15	54	15	37	11	55	17
22 & Above	45	76	2	93	0	72	17	55	21	87	6	73	7	62	15	81	0	74	10
All males	122	64	3	83	3	54	30	39	31	76	7	53	12	50	16	53	12	58	15
FEMALES																			
13-14 Years	65	73	4	88	2	42	41	35	39	78	6	49	13	57	16	58	11	57	18
15-21 Years	76	79	2	93	1	50	33	30	43	83	5	64	10	65	12	54	10	64	15
22 & Above	53	81	0	96	0	69	17	45	24	87	3	73	9	69	11	71	5	73	9
All females	194	77	2	92	1	53	31	36	36	82	5	62	11	63	13	60	9	64	15

ronment. Both sexes showed a sharp increase in positive attitudes and a moderate decrease in negative attitudes with increase in age. Even though both sexes showed very similar developmental trends, there tended to be greater differences in attitudes according to sex during the adolescent period than during the adult period. Adolescent girls, on the whole, were more positive than were adolescent boys.

Next, focusing on these content areas which are officially approved of by Hutterite ideology, e.g., family, religion, Hutterite values, some common trends were observed for both sexes. During adolescence (Y,O) the percentage of positive responses to each of the content areas was much higher than the averaged baseline indices for that particular age-sex subgroup. For girls, the percentage of positive responses was even higher than that of boys. The percentage of negative responses for each of these content areas was consistently low (less than 1 per cent) for both sexes.

Attitudes of adolescents toward those content areas which were specifically disapproved of, e.g., money, power, or not especially encouraged, e.g., education, political leadership, were also interesting. In these content areas adolescents (Y,O) gave positive responses which in percentages were consistently well below the baseline indices for these age groups. In many cases–especially with money and power–there was also a substantially high percentage of negative responses; more so among the younger adolescents. The responses of adults, in terms of percentages of positive responses, tended to converge toward the averaged baseline index (e.g., adult males on money and education). Thus, the Hutterite adolescents disapproved more strongly than Hutterite adults of those things considered not desirable in Hutterite ideology.

Discussion

Four major trends emerge from these results and may be summarized as follows:

1) The frequency of positive responses tended to increase with age, suggesting that Hutterites develop more favourable attitudes toward all aspects of their environment as they get older. The age-graded social structure of Hutterite society–where older persons have more status and privileges than younger persons–would make such a trend meaningful.

2) There were greater differences in attitudes based on sex during adolescence than during adulthood–adolescent girls expressing more positive attitudes. This trend may express the tendency of Hutterite society to tolerate more non-conformity to Hutterite values and more rebellious attitudes in the case of adolescent boys than they do in the case of adolescent girls. After adolescence is over, Hutterite males tend to identify with Hutterite society as closely as females.

3) For content areas considered "desirable" in Hutterite ideology, adoles-

177

cents more frequently gave positive responses to each area than the overall averaged positive responses of that age group. The results do not provide any indication that Hutterite adolescents were disenchanted with the values of their society.

4) For content areas considered "undesirable" in terms of Hutterite ideology, the percentage of positive responses of adolescents (Y,O) to each content area dropped below the group's averaged baseline. Hutterite adolescents (especially Y) more strongly disapproved of "undesirable" content areas than did adults. Such a developmental trend was parallel to trends in North American society where there is a gradual shift in attitudes from an "absolutistic idealism," during early adolescence, to a "compromising realism" during adulthood.

The results tend to support the original hypothesis of this study. The developmental trends tend to indicate that the Hutterite socialization practices do seem to succeed in instilling and helping to internalize Hutterite ideology by the time the adolescents become adults.

HUTTERITE PERSONALITY TRAITS

It is generally assumed that different socialization experiences in different cultures also result in group differences in behaviour which can be assessed by personality tests. Cultural differences may be observed in the frequency distribution of personality measures, that is, differences in the "modal personality" (Inkeles and Levinson, 1969). Some scores of personality measures tend to be more common in one culture than in others. A basic assumption justifying cross-cultural studies of personality postulates that within-culture variations and between-culture variations in socialization experiences may result in analogous behavioural differences. However, the real-life correlates of a personality score may be different in different cultures.

It is helpful to remember that a given score on a personality test may have a different meaning for the assessment of individuals than for cross-cultural studies. Personality–almost by definition–refers to within-culture variability of behaviour. A given individual's personality is usually assessed against the norms (statistical or ideal) of his own culture. In contrast, cross-cultural research on personality involves the determination of whether or not there are systematic differences in personality measures between samples from different cultures. The interpretation of cross-cultural differences, where they occur, requires knowledge of the cultures compared (e.g., cultural differences as to the social desirability of a given behaviour, differences in frankness about admitting one's weaknesses, etc.).

This study attempted to assess general personality characteristics of normal Hutterite children. Even though personality assessment usually refers to individuals, this study focused on group characteristics which may be a function of their cultural variables. Such group characteristics would also give an indication of the "modal personality" in Hutterite colonies. It was postulated that Hutterite children would tend to show personality characteristics that are congruent with the Hutterite ideals, social structure, and socialization practices. Characteristics such as submissiveness, dependency, seriousness, guilt-proneness, introversion, conformity, etc., would more often be developed among Hutterite children than would the bipolar opposites of these characteristics. The comprehensiveness and intensity of Hutterite socialization practices would induce most children to internalize Hutterite values.

Method and Subjects

A sample of 72 Hutterite children (37 boys, 35 girls) nine to twelve years of age completed the 1963 revised form of the Children's Personality Questionnaire (CPQ) (Porter and Cattell, 1963). Both test forms A and B were administered in the standard way.

Cattell's Children's Personality Questionnaire (Porter and Cattell, 1968) is an inventory based on a trait theory of personality. Personality traits are conceptualized as bipolar measurable continua along which samples from different cultures, and individuals within a culture, differ from one another. The Children's Personality Questionnaire was designed for normal children in the age range of nine to twelve years. It is a comprehensive personality test which assesses personality along fourteen dimensions (factor-analytically derived). Psychometrically, the instrument is highly reliable and valid.

Results

Means and standard deviations on fourteen dimensions of personality traits were obtained for boys and girls separately. In order to compare the Hutterite personality characteristics with those of outsiders, the investigators made use of Cattell's large normative sample of American children. Deviations of Hutterite means from American means were expressed in terms of standard scores (Z-scores), reported in Table 4. Positive standard scores indicate higher Hutterite mean scores, and negative standard scores indicate lower Hutterite mean scores than the corresponding American mean scores. A standard score of ± 0.40 Z was taken as indicative of a "substantial" difference ($p < 0.001$ level) between the Hutterite and American groups.

The personality scores of corresponding Hutterite and American children were compared by t-tests. Substantial differences ($p < 0.001$) between Hutterite and American children were obtained on four scales for boys and on three scales for girls. On most other scales the Hutterite means were very close to the means of American children. The substantial differences are described as follows.

B- Less intelligent vs. more intelligent. Hutterite boys, but not Hutterite

Table 4

Hutterite CPQ Data Versus Cattell's Norms

Scale Name[a]	MALES			FEMALES		
	Hutt. Means	Catt. Means	Z[b]	Hutt. Means	Catt. Means	Z[b]
A Reserved vs. warm-hearted	11.9	12.5	-0.02	13.1	13.8	-0.22
B Less intelligent vs. more intelligent	10.2	12.5	-0.61***	11.8	13.1	-0.37*
C Affected by feelings vs. emotionally stable	11.8	11.7	+0.03	10.9	11.7	-0.21
D Phlegmatic vs. excitable	8.2	8.7	-0.12	6.9	8.1	-0.31*
E Obedient vs. assertive	9.8	10.7	-0.29*	6.4	7.3	-0.29**
F Sober vs. happy-go-lucky	7.0	11.4	-1.44***	5.7	7.1	-0.46***
G Expedient vs. conscientious	11.5	12.5	-0.31*	13.8	14.3	-0.14
H Shy vs. venturesome	11.4	10.6	+0.06	10.4	10.2	+0.05
I Tough-minded vs. tender-minded	8.7	6.7	+0.62***	13.2	11.2	+0.48***
J Vigorous vs. circumspect	9.3	8.7	+0.20	10.3	9.0	+0.46***
N Forthright vs. shrewd	8.5	7.7	+0.22	5.7	5.3	+0.14
O Self-assured vs. apprehensive	9.3	7.7	+0.42***	9.7	8.4	+0.34**
Q3 Casual vs. controlled	11.8	12.0	-0.05	12.7	14.0	-0.35*
Q4 Relaxed vs. tense	8.2	8.8	-0.17	6.5	7.6	-0.27*

[a]Low scores refer to the left side, and high scores refer to the right side of bipolar scales. Standard deviations of these scales can be obtained from the authors.
[b]Deviations of Hutterite means from Cattell's norms expressed in terms of Z scores (standard scores).
*p<0.05 on 2-tailed *t*-test between Hutterite and Cattell means.
**p<0.01 on 2-tailed *t*-test between Hutterite and Cattell means.
***p<0.001 on 2-tailed *t*-test between Hutterite and Cattell means.

girls, performed at a substantially lower level than American boys on this test of general intellectual ability. One main reason for this low level of performance may be attributed to the lack of adequate motivation among Hutterite children to excel in intellectual tasks. Lack of adequate motivation is attributable to the lack of encouragement in and low esteem for booklearning that adult Hutterites pass on to their children. Young boys are constantly told that they are going to be farmers, and booklearning has no place there. Hutterite girls are somewhat more positive in their attitudes than boys in matters of school and education.

I+ Tough-minded vs. tender-minded. Hutterite boys and girls were significantly more "tender-minded," less "tough-minded, and realistic" than the norms. In Cattell's sample I+ individuals with scores as high as those of the Hutterites were described as coming from overprotected and fastidious homes. Characteristics associated with I+ are sometimes associated with neurotic behaviour in American society: in Hutterite society such traits seem quite compatible with good adjustment.

F- Sober vs. happy-go-lucky. Both Hutterite boys and girls were more "sober" and less "happy-go-lucky" than norms. Individuals with high F-scores tend to be serious and self-depreciating. In America, F- individuals frequently come from homes with severe, sobering standards. Among neurotics, F- tends to be associated with headaches, worrying, and depressive reactions. The soberness of Hutterite children seems to be consistent with official Hutterite socialization goals and also with previous mental health information on Hutterite neurotics (Eaton and Weil, 1955; Kaplan and Plaut, 1956).

O+ Self-assured vs. apprehensive. Hutterite boys, but not the girls, were observed as more "apprehensive" and less "self-assured" than the norms. In American society, O+ individuals are described as worrying, depressed, troubled, and insecure. The items describing the O+ scale are based on admissions of subjective distress and feelings of insecurity. Such admissions of subjective feelings may have different meanings for individuals in different cultures. American and Hutterite societies may differ as to the extent personal and subjective negative feelings are allowed to be admitted openly without any adverse reactions from others. For American boys and men it is considered important to project an image of being happy, self-confident, and secure. Admission of "negative feelings" is stigmatized as weakness and lack of masculinity. Only when subjective distress becomes too intense to be covered up—as in neurotics—would Americans admit to feeling "low." In Hutterite society no stigma is attached to admitting feelings of unhappiness some of the time. Therefore, an average Hutterite boy would feel comfortable about admitting feelings of distress or unhappiness, and this open tendency does not necessarily imply that the average Hutterite has "neurotic tendencies."

J+ Vigorous vs. circumspect. Hutterite girls, but not the boys, were more "circumspect and internally restrained" and less "vigorous" than the norms. The content of items comprising the J+ scale suggests that Hutterite girls were more "inner-directed" and less "outer-directed" than the norms. The findings of high J+ scores among Hutterite girls is consistent with the Hutterite socialization of girls emphasizing the internationalization of cultural values, non-assertiveness, and being conscientious. This emphasis is less evident in the case of boys.

Discussion

When Hutterite and American children were compared, the number of personality traits of negligible difference was greater than the number of those with substantial differences. This would argue against the view that one cannot obtain any meaningful information by administering to Hutterite children personality tests standardized on American children. And those few cases where there were substantial differences in traits between Hutterite and American children could be explained in terms of known differences of socialization goals or in terms of cultural differences such as the acceptability of admitting subjective distress.

Compared to American children, Hutterite children were more tender-minded, sober, apprehensive (or timid), and circumspect (girls only) than American children. These characteristics, along with the low intellectual performance of Hutterite boys, reflect closely what is and what is not valued in Hutterite society. As was mentioned before, the low self-assurance (O+ score) usually associated with neuroticism and depression in American society need not be interpreted as a sign of personality weakness in Hutterite society. A trait measured by responses to admitting unhappy feelings, for example, has different meanings depending upon the particular culture, and whether it does or doesn't condone frank admissions of personal feelings. The results of mental health studies suggesting that Hutterites have strong tendencies towards psychotic depression (e.g., Eaton and Weil, 1955) should be interpreted with caution, because the indicators of these "depressive tendencies" may not have the same meaning in Hutterite culture as they do in American. In general, the results tended to confirm the working hypothesis of this study.

At the end of the multi-test, multi-approach personality study of Hutterite children, adolescents, and some adults, what conclusions may be drawn? Taking the "Challenge and Response" model to personality development, the findings may be summarized as follows:

1) Hutterite adolescent boys more frequently selected as ideals parent substitutes, i.e., other adults in Hutterite colonies, than they selected attractive and glamorous outsiders. Adolescent Hutterite girls more frequently selected outside non-professionals, adult females in services, e.g., nurses, teachers, etc., than they selected the attractive and glamorous outsiders. In both cases, the adolescents tended strongly to select

ideals which are congruent rather than incongruent to the Hutterite ideology.

2) In all cases, the number of positive attitudes increased and the number of negative attitudes decreased with an increase in age. Thus, Hutterite adults tended to have more positive outlooks than Hutterite adolescents. This can be indicative of greater life satisfaction among adults than among adolescents. In those areas which reflect Hutterite ideology, e.g., values, religion, family, etc., adolescents showed very positive attitudes, but, again, adults even more so. However, those things which are disapproved of by Hutterite ideology, e.g., money, power, education, politics, etc., found adolescents more in line with official Hutterite ideology than adults. Thus, one may regard the attitudes of the adolescents as "idealistic," and those of the adults as "realistic," perhaps as a result of their everyday experiences.

3) Hutterite children (nine to twelve years) were similar in many personality traits to the same age-sex American children. However, they differed in three or four specific areas. Hutterite boys were not interested in intellectual tasks and tended to score low on intellectual performances. Hutterite boys and girls were more "tender-minded" than "tough-minded," and both were more "sober" than "happy-go-lucky." Hutterite boys were less "self-assured" than the American normative sample, and the Hutterite girls were more "circumspect" and "inner-directed" than the normative sample which was more "vigorous" and "outer-directed." Here again, one sees the development of those patterns of behaviour which are adaptive to the Hutterite way of life, though not to the American way of life.

Thus, the overall conclusion is that Hutterite attitudes, behaviour development, and personality patterns are intimately linked to Hutterite socialization practices, values, social organizations, and ideologies. Hutterite children and adolescents have adapted to the challenges in their environment, and as a result have developed ideals, attitudes, and personalities that enable them to live a contented life in the colonies.

Notes

1. The authors gratefully acknowledge financial assistance from the Laidlaw Foundation and from the Research Board of the University of Manitoba. Only part of the paper presented at the 1975 Canadian Ethnic Studies Association conference is reported here. Copies of the complete paper presented can be obtained by writing to the authors.

2. The adolescents were given a sheet of paper with the following instructions written on the top: "Describe in one page or less a person you would like to be when you grow up. This may be a real person or an imaginary person. He/she may be a combination of several people. Tell something about this person's age, character, appearance, occupation, and recreations. If he/she is a real person say so. You need not give his real name if you do not want to."

3. A few months later (approximately five to six months) a subgroup of the original sample (N=73, 29 boys and 44 girls) were asked to rewrite the same essay. The retest group method was selected to obtain test-retest reliability and consistency of ideals over time. The ideals reported on, and their characteristics, proved to be very stable.

4. The inter-rater reliabilities for three analyses ranged from 80 per cent to 85 per cent agreement. The criterion for assigning a given essay into a given category was that at least two out of the three raters must agree on a certain category.

5. All items had a short stem suggesting a given issue. The subject was asked to complete the sentence, e.g., "The rules around here...."; "To share everything...."; "After all, religion....".

6. The inter-rater reliability was more than 80 per cent.

References

Bennett, J.W.
  1967 *Hutterian Bretheren: The Agricultural Economy of a Communal People.* Stanford, California: Stanford University Press.
Child, I.R.
  1968 "Personality in Culture," in E.F. Borgotta and W.W. Lambert (eds.) *Handbook of Personality Theory and Research.* Chicago: Rand McNally, pp. 82-145.
Eaton, J.W., and R.J. Weil
  1955 *Culture and Mental Disorders.* Glencoe, Illinois: Free Press.
Gross, P.S.
  1965 *The Hutterite Way.* Saskatoon, Sask.: Freeman.
Havighurst, R.J., M.Z. Robinson, and M. Dorr.
  1946 "The Development of the Ideal Self in Childhood and Adolescence." *Journal of Educational Research*, 40:241-257.
Hostetler, J.A.
  1967 "Sources on Child Rearing and Socialization: The Hutterian Brethren." Unpublished manuscript containing translations from early Hutterite documents. Philadelphia, Penn: Department of Anthropology, Temple University.
Hostetler, J.A.
  1969 "Amish and Hutterite Socialization: Social Structure and Contrasting Modes of Adaptation to Public Schooling," in J.A. Hos-

tetler (ed.), *Conference on Child Socialization.* Washington, D.C.: NIMH, pp. 283-308.

Hostetler, J.A.
1974 *Hutterite Society.* Baltimore: The Johns Hopkins University Press.

Inkeles, A., and D.J. Levinson
1969 "National Character: The Study of Modal Personality and Socio-Cultural Systems," in G. Lindzey and E. Aronson (eds.), *Handbook of Social Psychology, Vol. 4.* Reading, Mass.: Addison Wesley, pp. 418-506.

Kaplan, B., and T.F.A. Plaut
1956 *Personality in a Communal Society.* Lawrence, Kansas: University of Kansas Publishers.

Peter, K.
1971 "The Hutterite Family," in K. Ishwaran (ed.), *The Canadian Family.* Toronto: Holt, Rinehart & Winston, pp. 248-262.

Peters, V.
1965 *All Things Common: The Hutterian Way of Life.* Minneapolis: University of Minnesota Press.

Porter, R.B., and R.B. Cattell
1963 *Children's Personality Questionnaire. Forms A and B Ages 8 Through 12.* Published by the Institute for Personality and Ability Testing, 1602-04. Coranado Drive, Champaign, Illinois.

Porter, R.B., and R.B. Cattell
1968 *Handbook for the IPAT Children's Personality Questionnaire "The CPQ."* Champaign, Illinois: Institute for Personality and Ability Tests. With tabular supplement with norms for 1963 edition of CPQ.

Schludermann, S., and E. Schludermann
1969a "Social Role Perception of Children in the Hutterite Communal Society." *Journal of Psychology,* 72:183-188.

Schludermann, S., and E. Schludermann
1969b "Developmental Study of Social Role Perception among Hutterite Adolescents." *Journal of Psychology,* 72:243-246.

Schludermann, S., and E. Schludermann
1969c "Scale Checking Style as a Function of Age and Sex in Indian and Hutterite Children." *Journal of Psychology,* 72:253-261.

Schludermann, S., and E. Schludermann
1969d "Factorial Analysis of Semantic Structures in Hutterite Adults." *Journal of Psychology,* 73:267-273.

Schludermann, S., and E. Schludermann
1971a "Adolescent Perception of Themselves and Adults in the Hutterite Communal Society." *Journal of Psychology,* 78:39-48.

Schludermann, S., and E. Schludermann
1971b "Adolescent Perception of Parent Behavior (CRPBI) in the Hutterite Communal Society." *Journal of Psychology,* 79:29-39.

Schludermann, S., and E. Schludermann
1971c "Paternal Attitudes in the Hutterite Communal Society." *Journal of Psychology*, 79:41-48.
Schludermann, S., and E. Schludermann
1971d "Maternal Child Rearing Attitudes in the Hutterite Communal Society." *Journal of Psychology*, 79:169-177.
Schludermann, S., and E. Schludermann
1973 "Developmental Aspects of Social Role Perception in the Hutterite Communal Society," in L. Brockman, J. Whiteley and J.P. Zubek (eds.), *Child Development: Selected Readings.* Toronto: McClelland and Stewart, pp. 412-426.
Schludermann, S., and E. Schludermann
1973 "A Conceptual Model for the Study of Individual Development in Different Cultures." Contribution to a symposium organized by H. Thomas (Psychology, University of Bonn, Germany) on "The Individual in Developmental Theory: Cross-Cultural Perspectives." Biannual meeting of the International Society for the Study of Behavioral Development, Ann Arbor, Michigan, August 21-25.
Schludermann, S., and E. Schludermann
1974 "Adolescent Perception of Themselves and Others in Hutterite Communal Societies." Contribution to a symposium organized by J.A. Hostetler (Anthropology, Temple University) on "Socialization Theory and Practice in Communal Societies." Meeting of the American Anthropological Association in Mexico City, November 20-24.
Thomas, E.J.
1968 "Role Theory, Personality and the Individual," in E.F. Borgotta and W.W. Lambert (eds.), *Handbook of Personality Theory and Research.* Chicago, Rand McNally, pp. 691-727.

10

Ecology, Culture, and Cognitive Development: Canadian Native Youth[1]

Russell S. MacArthur*

Though the title of this paper is broad, its topic will be illustrated by more focused attention to relations of some selected aspects of ecology and culture to the development of some particular cognitive abilities for selected samples of Canadian native youth. Psychological differentiation theory will be emphasized as one of its conceptual bases; its data will report some of the writer's recent work with Inuit samples, referring also to earlier work with Indian-Métis.

For several years, as part of the Human Adaptability Section of the International Biological Programme (Biesheuvel, 1968), the writer has been conducting a project concerned with two general questions: a) what intellectual abilities are least and what are most related to differences in cultural backgrounds? and b) what particular cultural influences are related to the development of what intellectual abilities? These questions were approached through field work with 750 subjects in four main ethnic groups: Central Canadian Inuit or Eskimos (Igloolik and Frobisher Bay), Nsenga Zambians (Sandwe and Petauke), West Greenlander Eskimos (Augpilagtoq, Kraulshavn and Upernavik), and Alberta Whites (Strathcona County). One less general question was concerned with the extent to which predictions from psychological differentiation theory would be confirmed in these contrasting ethnic groups (MacArthur, 1973c).

RATIONALE

A general rationale to guide consideration of such questions has been suggested in MacArthur (1968b). In brief, it views intellectual abilities or processes as if organized in an oblique hierarchy, from specific abilities at

* Russell S. MacArthur is Professor of Educational Psychology, University of Alberta, Edmonton.

the bottom to general intellectual ability at the top. From a developmental viewpoint, patterns of individual differences in abilities develop through cumulative transfer of learning as innate predispositions interact with environmental conditions; local demands strongly influence what abilities or processes are learned and how they pattern.[2]

Psychological Differentiation Theory
Psychological differentiation theory (Witkin, 1967; Dawson, 1967, 1974; Berry, 1971, 1974) is consonant with this general rationale, and has been reviewed recently in cross-cultural context by Witkin and Berry (1975). The concept of differentiation refers to the complexity of a system's structure, a more differentiated system being in a relatively more heterogeneous state. Since progression in psychological differentiation is consistent over several domains within the organism as a whole it has several "indicator areas": a) more articulated (as contrasted with global) perceptual and intellectual functioning; b) more articulated body concept, where the body is experienced as having definite boundaries separate from its surround, and the parts within as discrete; c) more sense of separate self-identity as reflected by more autonomous functioning in the social area and less dependence on external reference for guidance; d) more structured and intellectualized defences and controls for channeling impulses in the emotional area.

In the perceptual and cognitive area, articulated or field-independent style is exhibited by the individual who is able to perceive an item as discrete from organized ground when the field is structured (analysis), to impose structure on a field and so perceive it as organized when the field has little inherent organization (structuring), and to take some element out of the context presented and use it in a different context to solve a problem. Commonly-used measures of field-independence include the Rod and Frame Test, the Body Adjustment Test, Embedded Figures Test, Block Design, and Human Figure Drawing. Research in Euro-American settings has indicated that psychological differentiation (including field-independence) is fostered by socialization practices which encourage separation of children from family control, and which impart in children standards for self-regulation of impulse.

The relation of socialization practices to the development of field-independence provides one link between Euro-American theory and various cross-cultural contexts. Barry, Child, and Bacon (1959) demonstrated a tendency, in subsistence-level peoples adapting to the demands of their ecological settings, for subsistence hunting and gathering peoples to emphasize self-reliance and independence in the upbringing of children, and for subsistence agricultural and pastoral peoples to emphasize compliance and obedience. At the level of social organization within the community, hunting peoples tend to form loose social structures fostering relatively independent small groups adaptive to their nomadic way of life, whereas

188

subsistence agricultural peoples tend to create much tighter and more complex stratified social structures to which the individual is pressed to conform. Concerning more directly physiological adaptation to the ecology, hunting and gathering subsistence economies require ability to extract key information from the surrounding context for the location of game, and ability to integrate these bits of information into awareness of the hunter's location in space for safe return home; subsistence agricultural economies do not require the same minute differentiation and spatial integrations of the farmer repeatedly working the same soil of his/her valley or plateau. Dawson (1974) has provided some evidence for the relation of protein availability to the development of field-independence.

Thus, at least in subsistence-level economies, a syndrome of contrasting characteristics needed for survival seems to have evolved in man's adaptation to ecologies favouring migratory hunting versus ecologies favouring sedentary agriculture. The syndrome comprises: a) pressure toward minute perceptual and cognitive discrimination, with integration into spatial awareness versus less pressure toward these abilities; b) family upbringing stressing self-reliance versus one stressing obedience; c) loose societal structure and little social pressure versus more structured society with pressure toward social conformity; and d) adequate protein versus perhaps inadequate protein. Psychological differentiation theory, as developed in the Euro-American context, would predict, from this syndrome of influences, higher differentiation in subsistence hunting peoples, especially as exemplified in tests of field-independence versus field-dependence.

Spatial Ability and Field-Independence
There is currently considerable question concerning the relation between spatial abilities and field-independence. Witkin and Berry (1975:75) clearly view field-independence and spatial abilities as discrete dimensions. But three of the tests often referred to by Witkin as markers for field-independence (Embedded Figures Test, Block Design, and Human Figure Drawing) are considered by others as good measures of spatial abilities. Horn (1975), in an extensive review of recent research on human abilities, finds the Embedded Figures Test (flexibility of closure) usually clustering with spatial and visualization tasks in a broad general visualization factor (Gv). He concludes in this connection that it is wise to drop the theory of field-independence when the measure of this is the Embedded Figures Test, and to direct research along lines of identifying determinants of Gv (p. 25). There is some agreement, then, that in Euro-American contexts, field-independence and spatial abilities are not synonymous; it is not yet clear as to what should be encompassed in each, or how they are related.

Since, in the main project outlined herein, a broad spatial/field-independence factor was clearly recognizable for most samples, al-

189

beit for some samples splitting into several correlated factors, psychological differentiation theory will here be postulated to extend to a broad general visualization (Gv) or spatial-practical (k:m) factor, though not necessarily to all supposedly spatial measures for all samples.

Of the many hypotheses inherent in this study, those concerning psychological differentiation theory in a cross-cultural context may be made explicit here as expecting field-independence measures to be positively associated with: some spatial abilities, hunting rather than agricultural communities, open and homogeneous vistas rather than closed and variegated vistas, upbringing encouraging initiative and autonomy rather than obedience and conformity at the family level, and limited social and political stratification rather than extensive social and political stratification at the level of the larger community.

Two points concerning the writer's position should be made very clear at this juncture. First, no ultimate value judgements are placed on high versus low differentiation; both are seen as evolving because they have been valuable for adaptation to differing circumstances. Second, while genetic selection for high or low differentiation in contrasting ecologies, with their accompanying cultural characteristics, has been inferred, no attempt whatever has been inferred to apportion the relative influences of ecology or culture between before and after "moment-of-conception."

SUBJECTS AND MEASURES

Samples

While a number of other theoretical and practical considerations entered into the choice of samples, from the viewpoint of psychological differentiation theory the Central Canadian Inuit and West Greenlander hunters provided contrast with the Nsenga Zambian agriculturalists, with the Alberta Whites aiding in interpreting constructs from Euro-American psychology. Table 1 shows the number of cases and sample identification numbers for the sixteen samples in four age groups, ranging from children to middle-aged adults for each of the four ethnic groups. Within each sample there was balance by sex, and (except for Whites) by less/more transitional orientation, less transitional representing subsistence hunting (for the Nsenga subsistence farming), and more transitional representing wage-earning parental or own occupations. Chronological age is accurate for all but the Nsenga group, for whom stated age, checked by such school and other records as were available, was used. Further demographic descriptive data for the samples are reported in MacArthur (1973c).

Central Canadian Inuit. The ecology and culture of the traditional Inuit, as they may relate to cognitive development, have been well reviewed by Kleinfeld (1973), Graburn and Strong (1973), and Briggs (1974). These reviews demonstrate among the Inuit both cultural homogeneity

Table 1

Identification Numbers and N's of Sixteen Samples

By Age Group and Ethnic Group

	Sample No.	Age 9 to 12	Sample No.	Age 13 to 16	Sample No.	Age 17 to 26	Sample No.	Age 27 to 140	Total
Number of Cases									
Central Inuit	11	61	12	62	13	29	14	25	177
Nsenga Africans	21	65	22	65	23	31	24	31	192
West Greenlanders	31	65	32	64	33	23	34	24	176
Alberta Whites	41	70	42	64	43	36	44	36	206
TOTAL		261		255		119		116	751

Note: Within each sample balance by sex, and (except for Whites) by less/more transitional orientation.

and a variety of adaptations to local circumstances. Most of the Igloolik Inuit had, until two or three years prior to the field work from which data are herein reported, lived in nomadic family-sized hunting camps; many of those on wage-employment in Igloolik and Frobisher Bay hunted on weekends. The land they inhabit is bleak and bare, characterized by visual uniformity, far above the tree-line, and underlaid with permafrost. To hunt they must be sensitive to visual detail, and in finding their way back to a few homes in the tundra, the smallest unique features become important landmarks, often in rotated visual patterns since the hunter may return from a different direction. The mean occupational level (Blishen, 1967) was 30 with a standard deviation of 6.2 (compared with a Canadian mean of about 39 and a standard deviation of twelve); the more traditional occupations were hunting and fishing (seal, caribou, walrus, char, white fox, wolf, bear) while the wage-earners ranged from unskilled labourer to foreman, secretary, teaching aid, and mechanic. Traditional arts and crafts have included soapstone carving and intricately ornamented clothing; women are able to cut out skins and cloth for boots and parkas using a minimum of measurement, while men have long made and used maps.

Control of aggressive and other impulse stresses the general theme that a mature and good person is one who is governed by reason and who demonstrates this by consistently considerate, permissive, and unaggressive behaviour to everyone. Such emotional control is taught to children in the family by adult example, and by scolding or teasing or refusing requests or persuasions, but the child is seldom, if ever, hit; instead, he is treated lovingly, with care and consideration. Children have learned more from examples of adults than from verbal instruction. In traditional occupational education, boys have learned to hunt by going on the hunt from age nine or ten, while girls have been instructed on home skills by their mothers. While differential sex roles are clear, these roles are interchangeable, as need arises, and are afforded relatively equal status. A syllabic script has been in use since the 1930s. Now, almost all school-age children attend school (sometimes sporadically), taught in English by Euro-American teachers.

In social organization at the community level, the traditional nomadic life forced by low natural production of food stuffs has precluded large aggregations of population having rigid class structures and descent groups. There are no tribes in the sense of territorially and politically unified groups; social groups split and re-form throughout the year with membership in flux. Such loose groupings include: a) the band, the largest group of sixty to 300 persons having kinship connections; b) the camp, a smaller focal unit of several households under a camp leader; and c) the household, usually including the nuclear family, grandparents, and newly married couples. The camp leader's role is earned, because it bestows economic benefits on the followers; the leader's advice is usually heeded, but is not obligatory; within social groups sharing of food is universal. The role of the shaman (religious leader) balances the power of the camp leader (though sometimes both are from the same family). Another important small unit is the partnership, based on friendship and economic co-operation. In Igloolik, at the time under consideration here, though the camps had just located together in a village of band (or rather two-band) resemblance, all of the above loose structures were still very clear.

West Greenlander Eskimos. At a very general level the West Greenlander ecology and culture (exemplified by the hunting villages of Augpilagtoq and Kraulshavn, and the wage-earning town of Upernavik) resembled those of the Central Inuit outlined above. Some main differences were: a) the physical setting, rather than being flat, was essentially rocky with deep fiords, islands, and icebergs. It was still relatively low in natural food production, necessitating small-group nomadic life; b) the indigenous Eskimos have been in touch with permanent European settlement since the early 1700s, this fostering slower and less traumatic fusion of the two cultures (and perhaps gradual fusion of gene pools). There has been a written Greenlandic language since 1750; European schooling has spread slowly, allowing some communities to have evolved Danish-type education, with others, until recently, focusing on the local "kateket" speaking the Greenlandic language; economic activities have contributed to a fusing of the two cultures—where modern powered boats have been combined with traditional kayaks, for example, and in cases where wage-earners are working in fish-canning plants; c) wooden frame housing has been usual for some time, though stone and sod dwellings are still seen in villages. But in the villages the essentials of family upbringing, and loose social structure at the community level, still closely resemble those of the Central Canadian Inuit.

For the particular samples of this study (Augpilogtoq, Kraulshavn, and Upernavik) the mean occupational level (Blishen, 1967) was 30 with an S.D. of 5.3; the more traditional occupations were hunting and fishing while the wage-earning ranged from unskilled labour to heavy equipment operator, midwife, secretary, and ship captain.

Nsenga Zambians. The ecology and culture of the traditional Nsenga, as they may relate to cognitive development, have been outlined by Brelsford (1965), and Coster (1958). Again we see cultural homogeneity combined with a variety of adaptations to local circumstances. The Sandwe Nsenga live a village life of sedentary subsistence farming (tsetse fly precludes raising of cattle). The valley they inhabit has deciduous woodland vegetation, providing a variegated vista; no navigational skills are required in traversing the same paths daily from the village to the small plots of farmland, and little spatial ability is required in the cultivation of the land, which is done mainly by women using a hoe and axe. Main crops are maize, "kaffir" corn, bananas, sweet potatoes, pumpkins, and groundnuts; some chickens are raised (and should we mention further protein supplement in the form of buffalo and eland poached from overflow in the nearby game preserve?). The more transitional group was composed of Nsenga background wage-earners in the "boma" (administrative centre) town of Petauke, with occupations varying from unskilled labour and house servant to postmaster, secretary, teacher, principal, medical assistant, and school manager. The mean occupation level (Blishen, 1967) for this whole Nsenga group was 35 with an S.D. of 11.5.

Mwanakatwe (1968) describes the traditional education of the people living in what is today called Zambia. In the training of young children in the home, much emphasis was placed on obedience and respect for elders, specific rituals of good manners, assertion of the authority of society over the individual, and usefulness in the household. In the initiation of a girl to puberty she was instructed in her future role as wife, and told of her obligations to her future husband, and his relatives, for whom she was required to provide food regularly, and of the absolute importance of accepting the authority of her husband and respecting her mother-in-law. During such instruction, if the girl was impertinent, beating was not uncommon. In general, the traditional education in the family sought to prepare children for conforming to life in a static community, stressing at every stage adherence to the accepted moral code, hospitality to friends, co-operation in common tasks, and practical occupational skills. Since independence in Zambia there has been great growth in the structure of formal education, but much of teaching in the early elementary school years is in the vernacular by teachers of little academic background, and secondary residential school places are still limited.

At the level of the larger community traditional social organization was tribal and stratified, with paramount chiefs, chiefs, sub-chiefs, and village headmen, a system adapted to governance of a relatively static society with each tribe and village occupying a definite territory with boundaries. Frequently the lesser dignitaries were younger sons or close kinsmen of the higher, so that the tribe was governed by a set of rulers from one clan. The basic unit of organization was the village, composed of groups of kinsmen linked to the village headman within matrilineal succession, the core of the village being a group of kinsmen who could trace their descent through women from a common ancestress. Another set of officials or councillors had a good deal to do with selecting new chiefs; some of the councillors were advisors, by heredity, and some were selected for merit. Kinship was essential for social relationships, with land-holding, modes of production, political action, and religious ceremonies depending directly on co-operation of close kinsmen. Since independence, though tribal feelings are still strong, many of these loyalties have been transferred to the stratified structures of the new state, encouraging obedience to the laws of the country and adherence to the dictates of the new leaders. The president's slogan is "One Zambia, one nation."

Alberta Whites. This sample from Strathcona County, just outside of Edmonton, was, in many ways, representative of the dominant present-day Canadian society. Its mean Blishen occupational level was 41 with an S.D. of 11.5, and occupations ranged from subsistence farmer and labourer to electrical engineer and university professor.

Measures

Cognitive measures considered here are listed in Table 2, and are further described in MacArthur (1973c) and references therein cited. These measures were selected mainly from those recommended in the *IBP Handbook 10* (Biesheuvel, 1969), or from those used by Vernon (1969), or by Ord (1970). They range from tests of educational achievement to adaptations of a variety of cognitive tasks, essentially from Euro-American psychology, which have been found usable in a number of parts of the world. (There are, of course, no "culture-free" tests.) Back-translation procedures were used for the West Greenlanders, and several markers for field-independence were included. The twenty-nine psycho-social variables included a number of the usual demographic or social status measures, and also a number of what Bloom (1964) calls process variables, i.e., variables in the psycho-social environment which may be related to cognitive development.

SOME RESULTS

Ability Factor Patterns

Oblique higher-order factor analysis (Hendrickson and White, 1966) of cognitive measures for the Canadian Inuit indicated three main first-order common factors (MacArthur, 1973a, 1973c): 1) a verbal-educational factor (here called v:ed and resembling Horn's Gc) marked by such tests as Arithmetic and English Vocabulary; 2) a spatial/field-independence factor (here called k:m and resembling Horn's Gv) marked by such tests as Wechsler Intelligence Scale for Children (WISC), Block Design, Witkin Embedded Figures, and New Guinea Performance Scale Form Assembly; and 3) a factor of inductive-reasoning-from-nonverbal-stimuli (here called i and resembling Horn's Gf) marked by such tests as Standard Progressive Matrices.[3] All three factors were highly correlated and showed high loadings on a single third-order factor. This suggests that the spatial/field-independence and inductive-reasoning tasks tap abilities not merely at a concrete level, but at a level of abstract symbolic representation.

As expected from the developmental rationale behind the study factor patterns of abilities among the various other samples differed considerably (MacArthur 1973b, 1973c, 1974a). But since the above three factors are recognizable for other samples – either with some splitting, or in some combination – they may be used to structure discussion of cognitive abilities here.

Differential Abilities Relative to Ethnic Groups

Table 2 shows t-ratios for differences of means on common ability tests between adolescent and child Whites and the respective Inuit age groups. The horizontal dotted lines group the ability tests according to factor patterns for the adolescent Inuit, Tests 1 to 9 representing a spatial/field-independence cluster, Tests 10 to 19 representing inductive-reasoning-from-nonverbal-stimuli, and tests 20 to 30 representing verbal-educational tasks. There is a clear progression through these three groupings of tests in relative bias against native pupils; for the Inuit adolescents the median t for differences of means with Whites is 1.94 over nine spatial/field-independence tasks, 4.84 over ten induction tasks, and 11.15 over eleven verbal-educational tasks. For the West Greenlanders the results were very similar (MacArthur 1974a, 1973b). On the other hand, the Nsenga adolescents and children were about the same distance below the Whites on all three clusters of abilities.

Table 2

T-ratios of Differences of Means on Ability Tests for Canadian Inuit and Alberta Whites

	Adolescents Alberta White Sample 42 minus Canadian Central Inuit Sample 12 (d.f. 124) t	Children Alberta White Sample 41 minus Canadian Central Inuit Sample 11 (d.f. 129) t
1. Draw Man Witkin	-6.61	-7.54
2. Emb. Fig. AID 1	.40	2.03
3. 2	1.22	2.18
4. Block Design WISC	1.82	.10
5. Memory Designs Benton	1.94	3.17
6. Emb. Fig. Vernon	2.45	.98
7. Form Assembly NGPS	2.54	1.47
8. Passalong NGPS	2.57	-1.32
9. Emb. Fig. Witkin	2.93	.50
10. Progress. Matrices A	2.38	1.52
11. B	2.45	.81
12. C	4.54	5.48
13. D	4.40	5.51
14. E	6.41	
15. SCRIT Scale 2	4.56	4.89
16. MAC 2	5.31	5.84
17. Lorge-Th. NV3 1	6.04	
18. 2	6.09	
19. 3	5.12	
20. Word Learning	5.83	3.01
21. Spelling	7.27	
22. Shipley Abstraction	7.99	6.23
23. Arithmetic Computation	8.64	8.62
24. Eng. Rdg. & Usage	10.11	
25. Information Learning	11.15	
26. Otis Beta	12.76	
27. Grade in School	13.00	8.31
28. Eng. Vocab. Oral	13.28	15.18
29. Eng. Vocab. Written	13.85	
30. Arithmetic Problems	15.61	7.80

		Adolescents	Children
		Alberta White Sample 42 minus Canadian Central Inuit Sample 12 (d.f. 124)	Alberta White Sample 41 minus Canadian Central Inuit Sample 11 (d.f. 129)
		t	t
31. Illusions	T	-1.96	-4.32
32.	L	.89	-3.21
33.	Sander	-2.70	-2.91
34.	M-Lyer	1.23	1.55

Note. T of 1.96 sig. at .05 level; t of 2.60 sig. at .01 level; t of 3.30 sig. at .001 level (approximately).

In this connection, Figure 1 summarizes data over all four ethnic groups of children. T-score norms based on the Canadian Central Inuit adolescents were prepared for each of the ability measures. Mean t-scores, based on norms of this reference sample, were obtained for each of the other samples on each test. Medians of these mean t-scores, taken over each of the three groups of ability measures, are shown in Figure 1 for the Inuit, West Greenlander, Nsenga, and Alberta children. Though all four of the child samples were of the same stated age, parental occupations for the Whites were of a much higher level (by Canadian standards), the Whites had had more years of schooling, and for the Nsenga, the teachers, by Euro-American standards, were less well prepared. Thus, in relation to these tests, evolved mainly from Euro-American culture, it is of no theoretical interest that in Figure 1, the graph for the Nsenga parallels that for the Whites, but at a much lower level. (This simply repeats, *ad nauseam* that on our tests Africans of lower parental occupations and less schooling score lower than Whites.) But as indicated by the oval at the left, on the spatial/field-independence tasks the Central Canadian Inuit and West Greenlander Eskimos, with their hunting background, their ecology demanding minute visual discrimination, and upbringing encouraging initiative and resourcefulness, perform at the same level as that of the Whites. On these same tasks, the Nsenga, with subsistence farming background, closed vistas, and upbringing which encourages conformity to authority, perform much lower. For adolescents of stated age 13 to 16 years, the graphs resemble, remarkably, those for children (MacArthur, 1975). Hypotheses in this connection from psychological differentiation theory, then, are clearly confirmed.

Differential Abilities Relative to Transition
Factor analyses of sixteen likely indices of transition toward a more technological way of life, for each of the samples, resulted in selection of the four transition markers shown in Table 3, which presents correlations

Figure 1

Medians, over clusters of ability measures, of mean t-scores for child ethnic groups. (Based on Central Eskimo adolescents as reference group.)

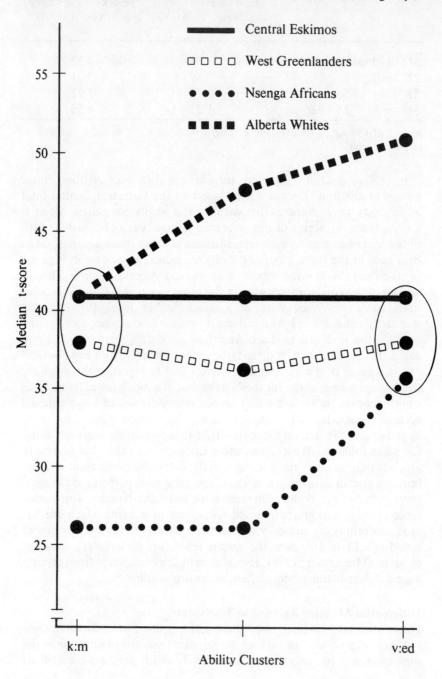

between the ability tests and these transition markers for the Inuit school samples. For the Inuit, there is a clear trend for the spatial/field-independence group of abilities to be related almost not at all to degree of transition, for the inductive-reasoning group to be related somewhat, and for the verbal-educational group to be related, to a much greater extent, to degree of transition. The West Greenlanders showed a similar trend over the three groups of ability tests, again with small relation of spatial abilities to transition. For the Nsenga, on the other hand, there was considerably more relation of spatial abilities to degree of transition (MacArthur, 1973a, 1973b, 1974b).

Differential Abilities Relative to Age

Within each indigenous group an inverted U-shaped relation was expected between age and level of ability on tests common to the four age groups. However, as Table 4 shows, for the central Inuit and West Greenlanders on the spatial/field-independence tasks there were almost no significant differences in means between the adolescents with six years of schooling and the middle-aged adults with little schooling. There were highly significant differences for other tests common to the two age groups. For the Nsenga the trend was similar but not as clear.

Abilities Relative to Sex

On the basis of Eskimo sharing of responsibilities between the sexes and of previous research (MacArthur, 1967), no sex differences in the cognitive tasks were hypothesized for the Eskimos. On the basis of previous research (MacArthur, et al., 1964) and traditional suppression of females, male superiority on all cognitive tasks was predicted for the Nsenga. Some male superiority in spatial tasks, and female superiority in verbal tasks, was expected for the Whites. One of the striking findings of this study was almost no sex differences in any of the ability tests for any of the age groups in any of the ethnic samples (MacArthur, 1974b). The lack of sex differences for the Nsenga is especially noteworthy since extensive male superiority had been expected; the explanation seems to be offered by corresponding lack of sex differences for these Nsenga samples, now, in status or environmental process variables (including occupational plans in terms of Blishen occupational levels, school achievement motivation, and parental aspirations for child's education). This sex non-differences finding strongly suggests that on this broad battery of cognitive tasks for these samples such sex differences as do occur are not likely to be of biological origin, but related, rather, to circumstances in the upbringing of a particular age group in a particular setting at a particular time.

Indian-Métis and Inuit of Western Arctic and Alberta. In many instances, studies of North American indigenes have tended to treat our Native Peoples as if they were homogeneous, with little regard for the great ecological and cultural diversity characterizing the various groups. How-

Table 3

Relations of Ability Tests With Some Transition Markers for Inuit Adolescents (age 13 to 16): (Sample 12) and Children (Sample 11)

Sample	Wages vs. Land (Head)		Appliance Owner- ship (Home)		English Use with Friends		Time in School (Self)	
	12	11	12	11	12	11	12	11
1. Draw Man Witkin	01	16	-15	08	10	09	-01	28*
2. Emb. Fig. AID 1	03	20	17	17	18	20	14	48*
3. 2	06	26*	19	25*	13	21	32*	48*
4. Block Design (WISC)	-06	-03	00	-07	12	20	14	15
5. Memory Designs Benton	05	12	20	06	13	20	26*	17
6. Emb. Fig. Vernon	-03	08	07	14	14	29*	20	33*
7. Form Assembly NGPS	-14	07	-01	-16	09	-14	06	-01
8. Passalong NGPS	-05	04	-10	-10	11	12	07	13
9. Emb. Fig. Witkin	11	19	-09	04	15	24*	16	47*
10. Progress. Matrices A	-04	-06	-05	01	13	04	09	18
11. B	34*	08	16	07	27*	16	29*	29*
12. C	21	25*	13	26*	28*	11	20	47*
13. D	30*	21	23	17	25*	23	31*	47*
14. E	14		29*		31*		23	
15. SCRIT Scale 2	12	26*	24*	16	12	20	26*	36*
16. MAC 2	24*	12	03	19	21	34*	14	30*

17. Lorge-Th. NV3 1	13		13		17		16	
18. 2	15		17		22		38*	
19. 3	17		29*		30*		57*	
20. Word Learning	15	29*	-05	30*	15	19	11	55*
21. Spelling	28*		44*		42*		57*	
22. Shipley Abstraction	21	33*	31*	30*	33*	42*	49*	67*
23. Arithmetic Computation	33*	51*	44*	51*	35*	16	60*	85*
24. Eng. Rdg. & Usage	23		42*		42*		68*	
25. Information Learning	21		32*		32*		43*	
26. Otis Beta	10		34*		57*		38*	
27. Grade in School	27*	60*	54*	56*	46*	36*	72*	89*
28. eng. Vocab. Oral	13	25*	35*	52*	43*	24*	47*	57*
29. Eng. Vocab. Written	13		33*		43*		52*	
30. Arithmetic Problems	05	38*	32*	42*	35*	13	53*	65*
31. Illusions T	-04	08	07	13	12	07	-06	06
32. L	15	02	16	09	-24*	-08	01	11
33. Sander	-11	04	-22	09	-24*	13	-08	13
34. M-Lyer	00	12	13	06	02	14	17	12

*Significant at .05 level. Decimal points omitted.

Table 4

Significance of Differences of Means on Common Ability Tests

Young Adolescents vs. Middle-Aged Adults

Test	Central Inuit Sample 12 minus Sample 14 d.f.85		West Greenlanders Sample 32 minus Sample 34 d.f.86		Nsenga Africans Sample 22 minus Sample 24 d.f.94	
	t	Prob. less than	t	Prob. less than	t	Prob. less than
1. Passalong NGPS	-1.27	.30	-2.35	.05	.14	.90
2. Block Design WISC	1.16	.30	-.57	.60	1.48	.20
3. Form Assembly NGPS	1.79	.10	.18	.90	.39	.70
4. Emb. Fig. Witkin	2.16	.05	1.21	.30	4.20	.001
5. Emb. Fig. AID	8.23	.001	2.70	.01	5.75	.001
6. MAC 2	3.21	.01	2.55	.02	8.18	.001
7. Progress. Matrices Total	5.70	.001	5.83	.001	8.13	.001
8. Eng. (Dan.) Vocab. Oral	5.77	.001	3.89	.001	5.69	.001

ever, results very similar to those just given have been previously obtained by MacArthur with Indian-Métis and Inuit of the Western Arctic and Northern Alberta. Data on which the following is based are for two groups of samples. The Mackenzie Norming sample consisted of 795 Indian-Métis, 510 Eskimos, and 709 Whites, who were representative of pupils attending Grades 1 to 8 of the Mackenzie District of the Northwest Territories. More intensive study was made of smaller groups of Inuit and Whites at Inuvik and Tuktoyaktuk, and Indian-Métis at Faust, Alberta and Ft. Simpson, N.W.T. (MacArthur, 1962, 1965, 1968a, 1968b, 1969, 1972). A similar but more limited battery of cognitive tests were used in these earlier studies, except that no supposedly spatial tasks were included.

For all age groups of each of the three ethnic groups, the two correlated factors, verbal-educational and inductive-reasoning-from-nonverbal-stimuli, were clear and prevailing (there was, of course, no spatial/field-independence factor). In the Mackenzie District Norming Project

(MacArthur, 1965) there were no significant differences on the ability tests between the Indian-Métis and the Inuit for any of the age groups. Abilities least affected by differences in native and white backgrounds were assessed by the inductive-reasoning-from-nonverbal-stimuli factor and those most affected were loaded on the verbal-educational factor (except that spelling and visual word memory showed little bias against the native pupils). Vernon's Embedded Figures showed least differences and Reading Comprehension most differences between native and white pupils. There were no significant correlations of any of the ability tests with sex for any of the samples (MacArthur, 1969), and no significant correlations of the inductive-reasoning tests with parental occupation for the native samples.

Vernon (1969) found that for Indian boys from southern Alberta and Inuit boys of the Mackenzie Delta, age ten to eleven years, the main ability factors underlying his battery of tests were much the same as in his English group, though particular tests differed in their loadings. Relative to his English norms, the Indian groups fairly closely resembled the Inuit, particularly in showing good spatial performance. Both Indians and Inuit were relatively higher in practical-spatial tasks than in school achievement and English comprehension, but both his Ugandan and Jamaican boys were lower in practical-spatial than in verbal memorization. Bowd (1973), using samples of Indian and Métis boys, age twelve to fourteen, from southern and northern Alberta, found among all his Indian groups that spatial-mechanical skills appeared to be high relative to Calgary Whites, while there was widespread linguistic deficit.

This brief review of some previously reported studies by MacArthur, Vernon, and Bowd indicates that, with relatively minor differences in patterning of abilities, and in level of performance on particular tests, the results outlined in the first part of this paper concerning Central Inuit can be generalized with some confidence to Mackenzie Inuit of the Western Arctic and to Indian-Métis of the Mackenzie District and of Alberta.

SOME IMPLICATIONS

Cognitive Strengths of Canadian Native Pupils

Cognitive strengths of our Inuit peoples (and Indian-Métis of Mackenzie District and Alberta) relative to their white age-mates, lie clearly in the spatial/field-independence cluster of abilities. Within Inuit samples, this ability cluster is little related to degree of transition toward technological society, and middle-aged adults with little schooling have developed these abilities as well as have young adolescents who are in school. Anecdotal evidence has long praised the navigational and mechanical skills of the Inuit. Across-ethnic-group, across-age-group, and within-age-group data confirm, in terms of well-known standard psychological tests, and even for child samples, the relatively highly developed spatial/field-

203

independence abilities which the Inuit have developed in their traditional life. It should be noted that in Euro-American society such tests as Block Design, Form Assembly, and Embedded Figures are widely established indicators of technological aptitude.

A second level of cognitive strengths of these Inuit samples is represented by the tasks involving inductive reasoning from nonverbal stimuli. This factor's emergence and strength over v:ed abilities agrees closely with previous results for two samples of Mackenzie Inuit and two Indian-Métis samples living well over 1,000 miles from the Central Inuit. It is in the verbal-educational group of abilities that our native pupils have demonstrated their greatest weakness relative to their white age-mates.

Educational Implications
In terms of practical implications for Inuit and Indian-Métis pupils in formal educational settings, the relative weakness of native pupils in verbal-educational abilities, as defined by our schools, has usually led to the conclusion, even by Vernon and Bowd, that the greatest need in such a context lies in special training in the English language as the main tool for communication, comprehension, and thought. This writer presents a, perhaps, more balanced proposal, demanding adaptation by school as well as by pupil—namely that our native pupils' relative strengths in k:m and i abilities suggest: a) a clear distinction between subjects or *content* of instruction, and methods or *media* of instruction; b) the *content* of instruction is a value matter, of course, in this writer's view, best decided by the Native Peoples directly concerned, but the evidence suggests development of *both* spatial/field-independence and verbal abilities as goals for subjects of instruction; and c) the evidence suggests much more emphasis than is usually present in schools and other educational institutions on the use of nonverbal stimuli and spatial abilities as *media* of instruction. Cross-cultural psychologists have gone some distance in developing principles and practices for helping people of other cultures learn how to do essentially Euro-American tests. These same approaches can be used in helping people from other cultures to learn—whatever they may wish to learn.

From a psychologist's viewpoint, these main principles may be summarized as follows: a) the use of intrinsically interesting materials, perhaps starting with essentially western materials, but progressively seeking exemplars from local practices of the constructs under instruction or test; b) making stimulus problems and responses less dependent on verbal or pictorial communication, with more emphasis on manipulating materials and gesturing as a means of communication; c) explicit instruction via small steps with immediate feedback to tester and testee, and with immediate testee reinforcement; d) reduction of extraneous stimuli, so that the problem stands out as a clear "figure" with as little as possible "background noise" such as printed instructions, or other items on a page or table top; e) assistance in pacing; f) emphasis on clinical more than technical standardization of test administration procedures, including warmth and personal attention; and g) respect for the testee as a person, not just as a subject.

Such principles can be adapted for teaching at the level of centralized production of so-called audio-visual educational materials and directions for their use, but perhaps more important is implementation of the attitudes they imply in day-to-day teaching by the classroom teacher in using varied approaches in the same lesson or lesson sequence. As simple examples, in current approaches to curriculum development in the Northwest Territories, photography is being taught in connection with recording local histories (Devitt, 1975), and the "yellow pages" of the handbook for elementary curriculum development lists many activities for use in day-to-day teaching which can help the native pupil use and build on the cognitive strengths he has brought to the classroom.

Some Occupational and Social Implications
The perceptual accuracy and spatial and visualization abilities of our Native People suggest high aptitudes for such occupations in the current overall Canadian economy as clerical, technical jobs in general, and pilot. One can speculate on the contributions they may make to such fields as higher mathematics and physics. In illustration, consider helping native foremen to read blueprints for crews constructing houses in Indian-Métis housing projects, or in construction for the development of the Athabasca tar sands. How could such nonverbal skills and media be utilized and developed in this context? But more challenging, how about encouraging the development of both the aesthetic (e.g., carving) and the engineering abilities the Inuit have demonstrated in creating blueprints towards the architectural profession? The suggestion here is that encouragement of the spatial/field-independence aptitudes of our Native Peoples has value not only in helping individuals realize a potential within them, but also in enriching the lives of the rest of us through their potential contribution to a Canadian mosaic.

Psychological differentiation theory, and the findings reported here, suggest that adaptation to the complex hierarchical structures of modern technological society is for the Nsenga a relatively simple matter of transfer from conformity to traditional authoritative social structure to conformity to modern Euro-American-type social structures; for the Canadian Native Peoples an adaptation to any authoritative social structure, including modern Euro-American, meets resistance.

In Summary
Patterning of abilities on a wide battery of cognitive measures was examined for child, adolescent, and adult samples of Canadian Central Inuit, Nsenga Zambians, West Greenlanders, and Alberta Whites. As pre-

dicted by psychological differentiation theory, cognitive strengths of the Inuit samples relative to their white age-mates lay clearly in a spatial/field-independence cluster of abilities. This conclusion may be generalized to Inuit and Indian-Métis of the Western Arctic and Alberta. Implications for Canadian native pupils in formal educational settings suggest emphasis on: a) nonverbal and spatial abilities as *media* for instruction; and b) development of both these abilities as aims for *content* of instruction.

Concerning adaptation to modern technological society, the ecology and traditional hunting culture of the Canadian Inuit and Indian have evolved relatively high perceptual and cognitive skills suited for such adaptation–but also affective resistance to conformity to its social complexity; the ecology and traditional agricultural culture of the Nsenga have evolved relatively lower perceptual and cognitive skills in some areas favoured by technological society, but higher affective aptitude for such adaptation. These propositions, of course, in no way suggest that non-Euro-Americans *should* adapt to Euro-American technology, and remind us of the wide range of individual differences in both cognitive and affective aptitudes of our Inuit, Indian, and Nsenga samples.

Notes

1. Grateful acknowledgement for help in the main MacArthur projects outlined here is made: for financial support to the Canada Council, the University of Alberta, and the Education Division of the Department of Indian Affairs and Northern Development of the Canadian Government; for research assistance in the field to Simona Arnatiaq, Bernadette Immaroitok, Kaunak, Elizabeth Blowers, Keith Wilkinson, Albert Tembo, Callisto Nkazi, Marcella Banda, Doreen Bale, Helen McLeod, Anne Pontoppidan, Niels Lynge, and Arne Lynge; for help in data analysis to the many students who participated therein; for permission to conduct research and facilitation of logistic matters to personnel of DIAND; the Educational and Occupational Assessment Service of the Ministry of Labour and the Ministry of Education of the Zambian Government, the Ministry for Greenland of the Danish Government, and the County of Strathcona, Alberta for their collaboration with my colleagues in the Canadian and Danish projects associated with the International Biological Programme Human Adaptability Section, and especially for their time and patience with the 3,000 Canadian Inuit and Indian-Métis, West Greenlanders, Nsenga Zambians, and white Canadians who co-operated as subjects.

2. Statically, this model resembles Vernon's (1965, 1969) orthogonal

206

group-factor hierarchy, or more closely, Cattell's (1963) or Horn's (1970) oblique higher-order hierarchy. Developmentally, Hebb (1949), Piaget (1964), Gagné (1962), and Messick (1972) all outline versions of abilities developing as cumulative effects of transfer of learning. Psychosocially, Ferguson (1954) and Cole et al. (1971, 1974) emphasize environmental effects on learning and patterning of cognitive abilities or processes.

3. Block Design is the test of highest communality in the performance part of the very widely used Wechsler Intelligence Scale for Children; problem-solving takes place through the medium of wooden blocks painted in different colours along the diagonal of one or more sides, which have to be arranged to produce a particular pattern; early items require four blocks and later items nine blocks each. Witkin Embedded Figures is a main marker for field-independence in Witkin's theory; the task set by each item is to hold in mind a simple two-dimensional geometric figure and to pick it out within the distracting context of a much more complex line figure in which it is embedded. NGPS Form Assembly is an adaptation of Form Boards, which have been used for more than a century to assess spatial abilities; items are revealed by placing successive black plastic templates, with progressively more complexly-shaped holes, on a grey background; the holes can be filled by one, two, or three of seven geometric shapes which are glued down so that manipulation of shapes must be done mentally; two-dimensional shape, size, rotation, and orientation must be visualized. In Progressive Matrices, each item is a two-dimensional analogies problem, using nonverbal figurative stimuli, in which the subject is required to select the design that completes a given pattern; each figure is altered from left to right according to one principle and from top to bottom by another principle; the subject must induce these principles and select the completing design which satisfies both principles. Each of the above tests starts with very easy items; learning of both procedures and content is sampled as items become progressively more difficult.

References

Barry, H., I. Child, and M. Bacon
  1959   "Relation of Child Training to Subsistence Economy." *American Anthropologist* 61:51-63.
Berry, J.W.
  1971   "Ecological and Cultural Factors in Spatial Perceptual Development." *Canadian Journal of Behavioural Science* 3:324-336.

Berry, J.W.
1974 "Ecology, Culture and Psychological Differentiation." *International Journal of Psychology* 9:173-193.

Biesheuvel, S.
1968 "Psychology and the International Biological Programme." *International Journal of Psychology* 3:199-207.

Biesheuvel, S. (ed.)
1969 "Methods for the Measurement of Psychological Performance." Oxford: Blackwell.

Blishen, B.R.
1967 "A Socio-Economic Index for Occupations in Canada." *Canadian Review of Sociology and Anthropology* 4:41-53.

Bloom, B.S.
1964 *Stability and Change in Human Characteristics.* New York: Wiley.

Bowd, A.D.
1973 "A Cross-Cultural Study of the Factorial Composition of Mechanical Aptitude." *Canadian Journal of Behavioural Science* 5:13-23.

Brelsford, W.V.
1965 *The Tribes of Zambia.* Lusaka: Government Printer.

Briggs, J.L.
1974 "The Origins of Nonviolence: Aggression in two Canadian Eskimo groups." in *The Psychoanalytic Study of Society*, vol. 6, New York: International Universities Press, 134-203.

Cattell, R.B.
1963 "Theory of Fluid and Crystallized Intelligence." *Journal of Educational Psychology* 54:1-22.

Cole, M., J. Gay, J.A. Glick, and D.W. Sharp
1971 *The Cultural Context of Learning and Thinking.* New York: Basic Books.

Cole, M., and S. Scribner.
1974 *Culture and Thought: A Psychological Introduction.* Toronto: Wiley.

Coster, R.N.
1958 *Peasant Farming in the Petauke and Katete Areas of Northern Rhodesia.* Lusaka: Government Printer.

Dawson, J.L.M.
1967 "Cultural and Physiological Influences Upon Spatial/Perceptual Processes in West Africa," pts. 1 & 2. *International Journal of Psychology* 2:115-128; 171-185.

Dawson, J.L.M.
1974 "Ecology, Cultural Pressures Toward Conformity and Left-Handedness: A Bio-Social Psychological Approach," in J.L.M. Dawson

& W. Lonner (eds.), *Readings in Cross-Cultural Psychology.* Hong Kong: University of Hong Kong Press 124-149.

Devitt, W.G.
1975 Personal communication.

Ferguson, G.A.
1954 "On Learning and Human Ability." *Canadian Journal of Psychology.* 8:95-112.

Gagné, R.M.
1962 "The Acquisition of Knowledge." *Psychological Review* 69:335-365.

Graburn, N.H.H. and B.S. Strong
1973 *Circumpolar Peoples: an Anthropological Approach.* Pacific Palisades, California: Goodyear Publishing.

Hebb, D.O.
1949 *The Organization of Behavior.* New York: John Wiley and Sons.

Hendrickson, A.E., and P.O. White
1966 "A Method for the Rotation of Higher-Order Factors." *British Journal of Mathematical and Statistical Psychology* 19:97-103.

Horn, J.L.
1970 "Organization of Data on Life-Span Development of Human Abilities," in L.R. Goulet and P.B. Baltes (eds.), *Life-Span Developmental Psychology.* New York: Academic Press 423-466.

Horn, J.L.
1975 "Human Abilities: A Review of Research and Theory in the Early 1970's." Unpublished manuscript. (Long draft of article prepared for *Annual Review of Psychology.*)

Inhelder, B., and J. Piaget
1964 *The Early Growth of Logic in the Child.* New York: Harper and Row.

Kleinfeld, J.S.
1973 "Intellectual Strengths in Culturally Different Groups: an Eskimo Illustration." *Review of Educational Research* 43:3, 341-359.

MacArthur, R.S.
1962 Assessing the intellectual ability of Indian and Metis pupils at Fort Simpson. Ottawa: Department of Northern Affairs and National Resources.

MacArthur, R.S.
1965 Mackenzie District Norming Project. Ottawa: Department of Northern Affairs and National Resources.

MacArthur, R.S.
1967 "Sex Differences in Field-Dependence for the Eskimo." *International Journal of Psychology* 2:139-140.

MacArthur, R.S.
1968a "Educational Potential of Northern Canadian Native Pupils." In

Boreal Institute's "Educational Process and Social Change in a Specialized Environmental Milieu." Edmonton: University of Alberta Bookstore 73-81.

MacArthur, R.S.
1968b "Some Differential Abilities of Northern Canadian Native Youth." *International Journal of Psychology* 3:43-51.

MacArthur, R.S.
1969 "Some Cognitive Abilities of Eskimos, Whites and Indian-Métis Ages 9 to 12 years." *Canadian Journal of Behavioural Science* 1:50-59.

MacArthur, R.S.
1970 "Cognition and Psychosocial Influences for Central Eskimos and Nsenga Africans: Some Preliminaries," in Cross-Cultural Symposium. St. John's: Memorial University Institute for Research in Human Abilities, pp. 83-98.

MacArthur, R.S.
1971 "Mental Abilities and Psychosocial Environments: Igloolik Eskimos." International Biological Programme Human Adaptability Project (Igloolik, N.W.T.) Annual Report No. 3. Toronto: University of Toronto, Department of Anthropology, pp. 161-186.

MacArthur, R.S.
1972 "Cross-Cultural Psychology," in J. Schubert (ed.) *Research in Cross-Cultural Psychology.* Regina: University of Saskatchewan (Regina) Division of Social Sciences, pp. 30-60.

MacArthur, R.S.
1973a "Cognitive Strengths of Central Canadian and Northwest Greenland Eskimo Adolescents," in L.H. Storms (Chm.) Patterns of Cognitive Abilities. Symposium presented at Western Psychological Association, Anaheim, California, April.

MacArthur, R.S.
1973b "Cognitive strengths of Central Canadian and Northwest Greenland Eskimo children," in G.A. Ferguson (Chm.) The development of cognitive abilities. Symposium presented at Canadian Psychological Association, Victoria, B.C., June.

MacArthur, R.S.
1973c "Some Ability Patterns: Central Eskimos and Nsenga Africans." *International Journal of Psychology* 8:239-247.

MacArthur, R.S.
1974a "Construct Validity of Three New Guinea Performance Scale Subtests: Central Eskimos and Nsenga Africans," in J.L.M. Dawson and W. Lonner (eds.) *Readings in Cross-Cultural Psychology.* Hong Kong: University of Hong Kong Press, pp. 51-60.

MacArthur, R.S.
1974b "Differential Ability Patterns: Inuit, Nsenga, Canadian Whites."

Paper presented at Second Meeting of International Association for Cross-Cultural Psychology, Kingston, Canada, August.

MacArthur, R.S.
1975 "Differential Ability Patterns: Inuit, Nsenga, Canadian Whites." in J.W. Berry and W.J. Lonner (eds.) *Applied Cross-Cultural Psychology.* Amsterdam: Swets and Zeitlinger, 237-241.

MacArthur, R.S., S.H. Irvine, and A.R. Brimble
1964 Northern Rhodesia Mental Ability Survey. Lusaka: Rhodes-Livingstone Institute.

Messick, S.
1972 "Beyond Structure: In Search of Functional Models of Psychological Processes." *Psychometrika* 37:357-375.

Mwanakatwe, J.M.
1968 *The Growth Of Education in Zambia Since Independence.* Lusaka: Oxford University Press

Ord, I.G.
1970 *Mental Tests for Pre-Literates.* London: Ginn.

Vernon, P.E.
1965 "Ability Factors and Environmental Influences." *American Psychologist* 20: 723-733.

Vernon, P.E.
1969 *Intelligence and Cultural Environment.* London: Methuen.

Vernon, P.E.
1972 "The Distinctiveness of Field Independence." *Journal of Personality* 40: 366-391.

Witkin, H.A.
1967 "A Cognitive-Style Approach to Cross-Cultural Research." *International Journal of Psychology* 2:233-250.

Witkin, H.A., and J.W. Berry
1975 "Psychological Differentiation in Cross-Cultural Perspective." *Journal of Cross-Cultural Psychology* 6:4-87.

PART FOUR

The Quest for Identity:
The Native People

PART FOUR

The Quest for Identity: The Native People

There is a tendency to begin a discussion of Canadian identity with the French and the British because they were the earliest European immigrants and the two charter groups. We often neglect the earliest Canadians, the Indians and Inuit, who are still the majority in about three-fourths of the Canadian territory: the Northwest Territories, the Yukon, and about two-thirds of the most northerly parts of the six western provinces. Some of Canada's Native People are seeking to continue their early ways of life, but many others are turning to other occupations in white settlements, and large numbers of Indians are beginning to migrate south to the cities. According to Vallee and DeVries (1975), 69 per cent of the population in these northerly areas are of native origin, and over half of them still speak their native languages at home. Few immigrants of European origin have had influence, or have cared to have influence on the Native Peoples in the northern lands, although this may be changing. Multilingualism and multiculturalism are evident everywhere in these territories.

The native residents were the first to settle in these northerly areas and they occupy the majority of the land space; in many parts treaties have not yet been made. On the other hand, they are actually a very small percentage of the Canadian population as a whole, and economically and politically they are powerless. It is to this situation that five authors in this volume address themselves. Frideres discusses the evidence of conflict; the Matthiassons describe a community which is segregated in the far North; and Burshtyn and Smith discuss the evidence of occupational changes.

Identity and Social Conflict

Simmel and Coser maintain that collective conflict is functional for group cohesion: it tends to strengthen ingroup bonds and tends to create a sense of identity distinct from the outgroup. Through conflict, group consciousness is reinforced so that members of the ingroup feel that they are different, or set apart. Some minorities feel this separate identity so keenly that they perceive themselves as an antithesis to the larger society. When a minority's values or way of life are threatened, such conflicts can become violent, because, at all costs, that individual identity and existence must be defended.

In his study, Frideres examines a sample of nine daily newspapers to determine the extent of social conflict in which Canadian Indians were involved over a period of twenty-five years. Since the newspapers represent all the regions of Canada, Frideres tries to consider whether there are regional variations in courses of action, whether the tactics used by the Indians were facilitative or obstructive, whether the extent or nature of the conflict changed over time, and whether these incidents received local or national coverage.

Frideres concludes that "conflict is being used by Indian people to attain a sense of sacred identity." Since they are relatively powerless politically and economically, as well as numerically, the Indian people seem to utilize conflict as the most practical and viable technique to gain group identity and to change the relationship between Whites and Indians. He feels that since Indians are collectively oriented rather than self-oriented, conflict is likely to become more intense and violent. These people will reject the very assumptions upon which our society is built, and since the structure of our society is fairly rigid, the potential for conflict is increased. Whether this will contribute to adjustment or to systematic changes in our institutional structures remains to be seen. In the meantime, conflict seems to facilitate coherence among the Indians, creating greater group consciousness which is functional for group identity.

Ethnic Segregation

One of the important factors in the maintenance of a separate identity is residential segregation. Perhaps the most ecologically segregated people are the Inuit, although this too is changing. In their essay, the Matthiassons describe an Inuit community located at Pond Inlet on the northern tip of Baffin Island. Few communities could be found in Canada which are more isolated, and these people are very much set apart from other Canadians, ecologically, culturally, and in many other ways. The Matthiassons propose that the Inuit have only very recently adopted a posture of ethnicity, and that this has resulted in a stance of social separation from non-Inuit inhabitants.

The authors suggest that the Inuit image described by some scholars is misleading and thus they seek to correct it. Although the Inuit are chang-

215

ing as they come into contact with other Canadians, the Matthiassons demonstrate that these people are retaining their heritage and consolidating a new power base in order to retain their identity. In most northern communities, the Native People and other Canadians are residentially segregated, and "the absence of close social interaction between the two" is evident. The Matthiassons suggest that the Inuit of Pond Inlet have developed a boundary-maintaining technique which has discouraged Euro-Canadian interaction with themselves while in the closed and private environment of their homes. The authors conclude that within a short period of time, the Inuit population at Pond Inlet has been transformed from a people who perceived themselves, and were perceived by outsiders, as being different, primarily in terms of racial characteristics, to an ethnic group which has indelible and sustaining ties with the larger society in which it finds itself, and has the internal resources to manage its own affairs. Whereas anthropologists in the past have often lamented the impending demise of the Inuit way of life and identity, the authors suggest that more recent evidence does not confirm this seeming demise. The Inuit may have suffered exploitation in the past, but this seems to have led to a sense of ethnic identity, which ultimately suggests that they will survive.

Ethnicity and Occupational Evaluations

A highly important feature of status identification in an industrial society is occupational prestige. Occupations for urbanites are badges of distinction, and ranking of the work force into valued and less valued categories is common. These rankings usually imply higher education and income which is especially valued in our society. The question is, do Native People and northern Europeans have the same set of values as those of Canadian southerners? One would expect that the northern heritage of Native Peoples would place greater value and prestige on other occupations, such as successful hunting, fishing, and on those that require physical stamina, courage, and endurance. Education and cash income would seem to be less important.

Burshtyn and Smith, when comparing northern students with a national Canadian sample, found that "despite a general similarity to that of the South, there is a different prestige structure of occupations in the North." They found that "the degree to which northern students give relatively low ratings to professional occupations on the list such as Doctor, Lawyer, Banker, Scientist, Teacher, and Minister" is striking. In addition, northerners give higher ratings to clerical, store sales, unskilled, and semi-skilled occupations, while the average Canadian gives low ratings to the same occupations; on the other hand, the northerner gives lower ratings than does the southerner to entrepreneurial occupations. The factor analysis indicated important differences in at least two situation-specific factors: "traditional native occupations," and occupations associated with "moral tone/alcohol use."

216

11

Indian Identity and Social Conflict[1]
*James S. Frideres**

The social forces in Canadian society have, in the past, excluded Indians from participation in the general society. In addition, Indians as a group have lacked organization and co-ordination. Consequently, the feeling of belonging and achieving a sense of purpose could not be attained from the larger society or through participation in voluntary associations within their own group.[2] Collective conflict can produce group cohesion and a sense of identity (Simmel, 1964; Coser, 1956). As Himes (1966) points out, group based conflict functions to facilitate socio-psychic linkage between the individual and the inclusive social system, and thereby produces collective identity.

Collective identity is produced and maintained through an interactive process of history, ritual, and interaction (Klapp, 1972). History refers to events that have taken place in the past which are "stored" in the group memory. Each of these events (information) has a secondary symbol status which can serve to unite people. One major component of this history concerns itself with "group superselves" (group heroes and leaders).

The second component, ritual, is the process by which the "memory" is fed back into the group. As Klapp (1964) points out, all such ritual feeds back to the group some essential part of the collective identity. Because events of the day, called news, continually put new information into this feedback, public drama needs to be continually studied as a crucible for the forming of collective identity.

Encompassing both ritual and history is the process of interaction. Interaction includes both verbal-nonverbal, and inter-intra-group interaction. This paper attempts to focus on a specific form of interaction-intergroup conflict and its relation to collective identity.

*James S. Frideres is Associate Professor of Sociology, University of Calgary, Alberta.

Movements which do not have economic, political, or status goals, are not directly traceable to relative deprivation.[3] They are more likely to be attributable to a "shortcoming in meaning" or the absence of any firm conception of the self, a lack of meaningful sentiments with which to make sense of the surrounding world, and a feeling that major social values are becoming increasingly irrelevant as ultimate guides to the way in which one should live and as ideas which should give meaning to one's life. Man thus searches not only for advantage or equity but for meaning in his life, for an identity which he is able to attach to himself, through which others see him, and by which he becomes socially situated (Wilson, 1973).

Klapp (1969) points out that: "A society fails to supply adequate identity when symbols are disturbed to the extent that they no longer give reliable reference points (in such things as status symbols, place symbols, etc.) by which people can locate themselves socially, realize themselves sentimentally, and declare (to self and others) who they are." This issue seems supported by the research completed by Braroe (1975). He argues that Indians possess two identities simultaneously: the first, sacred identity (positive self-evaluation) which is largely invisible to whites; the second a profane identity (negative self-evaluation) which whites impose upon Indians. In the present study it will be argued that conflict may be a technique utilized by Indians to allow for the sacred self to become publicly validated, concurrently rejecting the profane self-identity (Denton, 1975).

Indians in Canada have in recent years become activists and social protesters. This is not meant to suggest that Indians have never participated in protest or collective aggressive tactics. What it does suggest, however, is that the search is taking place for suitable situations in which to exercise action and strategies to further the concept of "Indians controlling their destiny."

The above theoretical orientation suggests that more and more conflict will be generated by Native People. While most people feel that conflict will "split" or "destroy" a society others suggest that conflict can, in fact, be a useful strategy for minority groups (Coser 1956). Himes (1966) for example, argues that "realistic" conflict produces four positive functions. Because racial conflict situations are defined in power terms, the status differential between the conflicting partners is reduced. Thus, status coordination is one consequence of power equalization. As a result, conflict defines adversaries in terms of self-conception as status equals. Hence: a) conflict alters the social structure from a vertical to a horizontal relation between dominant and subordinate; b) social communication is enhanced. As a result of conflict, core values of society are brought into focus and national attention. People are forced to think about the basic societal values and to consider their meanings. Participants in the conflict are united by the process of the struggle itself; the controversy is a shared social possession in which social interaction occurs since the traditional

218

structures of limited contacts have been broken; c) social solidarity is extended. Because conflict forces the combatants into in-group social consensus, it therefore acts to reaffirm the ultimate values around which the consensus is organized. Thus, conflict sews the society together; d) social identity is facilitated. Our present research will focus on the latter of these four functions.

At the most general level, ethnic identity (sometimes called race consciousness) can be defined as having allegiance to a particular group which is seen as conflicting with the group dominant in Canada (White). It should be pointed out at this time that identities are not static. They are generated over and over again as the cultural context changes. As Hurst (1972) points out, this implies Indian togetherness and/or an anti-assimilation attitude, certainly since the early sixties. People who are attempting to develop an ethnic identity have a shared conscience regarding their group. They feel they must serve it, fight for it, and at all costs, be loyal to it (Brown, 1931).

The role of conflict and its relation to identity must begin with alienation. Indians are crowded into reserves and/or lower-class urban areas. They are relegated to jobs of low prestige and occupy marginal positions in the occupational labour force as well.

Isolated, discriminated against, and defined as useless by the dominant White group, Indians are now searching for the meaning of "Indian" and how to "belong." The sense of an ethnic identity or race consciousness has been missing; the search for it goes on. This is evident in the content and in the increasing number of Indian newspapers being published. Price (1972) and Price and McCaskill (1974) have shown that a dramatic increase in Canadian Indian periodicals has occurred in recent times. This fact becomes important when one recognizes that "communication" is an integral part in developing group self-awareness. For example, from 1971 to 1974 the number of periodicals published increased from thirty-seven to sixty-seven. Fifty-seven per cent are published in cities, although the orientation is still primarily toward the rural Indian. This search for ethnic identity is also evident in the attempt by Indian leaders to create "histories." Books and articles by such leaders as George Manual, Harold Cardinal (1969) and David Courchène (1971) are examples.

Other researchers suggest that media (e.g. television) communication can make minority groups lose their sense of ethnic weakness (Singer, 1973). Meyer (1969) and Marx (1967) argue more specifically that exposure to mass media increases militancy. Their conclusion is that no matter what the medium, being "plugged" into the channels of communication is associated with increased militancy. In conclusion, one could argue that rather than having a fragmenting effect, mass communication can help forge and strengthen identity for minority ethnic groups (Singer, 1973).

Organizations such as the National Indian Brotherhood (NIB), and the American Indian Movement (AIM), as well as a variety of local and re-

219

gional organizations, provide an ego-enhancing rallying point. The National Indian Brotherhood is a political lobbying organization which attempts to co-ordinate and act for Indian people and organizations throughout Canada. It was established in 1968 and receives part of its operating budget from the federal government. The American Indian Movement is also a political lobbying group which began in the United States in the 1960s. It is a militant civil rights movement which has now extended its influence to Canada. However, its function in Canada has been to provide local Indians with organizing and leadership expertise. Whiteside (1973) and Price (1974) have shown that the number of native associations in Canada has increased dramatically in the past few years. In the time period 1900-1919, seven political native associations were created in Canada. During the next decade, an additional twenty were created while from 1940 to 1959 twenty-four were started. Then, in the 1960-1969 period thirty-five came into existence. From 1970 to 1973, nearly fifty different native associations were started. The data revealed by the above authors also show that an additional 230 organizations have been formed in the past seventy-five years but cannot be "dated."

Significantly, membership in these organizations is based upon ascribed status. Indian organizations can be labelled as "brotherhoods." In brotherhoods, moral obligations are owed to others because of their ascriptive relationship, i.e. a man is either one of the group or an alien. The ascriptive brotherhood idea militates against experiments in voluntary associations beyond the boundaries of the "in-group." As Light (1972:187) points out:

> Brotherhoods also organize all strata of a population. They are not like voluntary associations selective in their membership. These ascriptively bounded groupings also uphold a sense of ethnic, tribal, clan, territorial, racial and family honor. Racial honor is exclusive. When a sense of racial honor is joined to an ascriptive associational framework, the maintenance of racial honor becomes a demand capable of disciplining individual conduct.

In other words, the sense of racial and/or ethnic honour is the specific honorarium for all the masses. That is, it is accessible to anyone who belongs to the "subjectively" defined community of descent. In addition, it should be pointed out that these organizations are beginning to produce "leaders." Just as significant is the fact that the focus of these organizations is becoming more political. Price and McCaskill (1974) show that of the more than 400 Indian organizations currently in existence, nearly one-fourth have a "political primary function." Of these, fifty are local oriented, forty provincial-regional directed, and six nationally oriented. An additional one-fourth are "social" in function, with the remaining organizations showing a diversity of orientation, e.g. women's associations, school clubs, arts, crafts, religion, education.

Another indicator of increasing Indian identity is in young Indians attiring themselves in traditional fashion with beads, head bands, braided hair, etc. Still others attempt to reinterpret Christianity as an ideology of Indianness. In addition, the degree of residential "homogeneity" of Indians is becoming significant because of increased urbanization. However, because of the pervasive institutional racist structure in Canadian society, Indians still see themselves, and are viewed, as existing outside the Canadian social system. As a result, they continue on the quest for ethnic identity. One technique that has traditionally served as a means of achieving a sense of belonging (or ethnic identity) is that of conflict, and it has emerged as one successful method of producing the group cohesion necessary for a sense of identity. We are not suggesting that the initial engagement of conflict by Indians was based on such a rational decision-making process but rather the engagement of conflict has been the result of a process which has been going on for some time. Up until recently, most of the collective activity engaged in by Indians has been pursued through what Waskow (1966) defines as "politics of order." However, it would seem that today this strategy is changing. Boldt (1975) argues that there is growing evidence that Indians are willing to engage in "politics of creative disorder," i.e., extra-legal activities. Boldt (1975:22) concludes his study by stating:

> My study indicates that enlightened Indian leaders reject white society's comfortable notions of slow and steady progress toward the achievement of basic human rights for their people and most are inclined not only to approve of extra legal activity as a justifiable means for achieving their conception of the "good society," but are also willing to participate and, if necessary, suffer the consequences of such actions for their cause.

Indians have learned over time that conflict tends to enhance group solidarity. It does this through the establishment and sharpening of group boundaries. This means, of course, that a differentiation between in-group and out-group members is made. Likewise, the emergence of conflict produces an explicit definition of aims and goals of the group. It becomes clear, then, that a grievance has emerged along with a belief that in order to redress this grievance and lessen group dissatisfaction, another group must change. Hence the identification of an adversary. In the case of Indian-White relations, the structure has emerged into a zero-sum situation.

The distinctive feature of the zero-sum game is that one player always gains precisely what the other player loses, and vice versa. In other words, the game is purely competitive. This is in distinction of the non-zero-sum game in which one person's gain is not necessarily the other person's loss. In addition, these goals are communicated to the rank and file. Participants find their position in the collective action and receive internal as well as social rewards for acting out certain behaviours. (This is reinforced by the fact that if in-group members begin to suggest aims at variance with the group's overall aims, they will be severely sanctioned–i.e., being defined as "one of them" or "being duped.") To maintain oneself in the group facilitates linkage between the individual and his/her local reference group. As Pettigrew (1964:195-196) has stated:

> Recruits willingly and eagerly devote themselves to the group's goals. And they find themselves systematically rewarded (by the group) ....They are expected to evince strong racial pride, to assert their full rights as citizens, to face jail and police brutality unhesitatingly for the cause. Note that these expected and rewarded actions all publicly commit the member to the group and its aim.

Himes (1966:10) also argues:

> In the interactive process of organized group conflict self-involvement is the opposite side of the coin of overt action. Actors become absorbed by ego and emotion into the group and the group is projected through their actions. This linkage of individual and group in ego and action is the substance of identity.

As a result, the sense of alienation experienced by many Indian people is dispelled by a new sense of significance and purpose. The personal ethnic identity of Indians is thus significantly enhanced. It is important to remember, as Pitts (1974) points out, that ethnic identity is a social product. It is a result of purposive actions and an interpretation of actions operating in social relationships (Paige, 1971). As Brown (1935) points out: "A race consciousness group...is a social unit struggling for status in society. It is thus a conflict group, and race consciousness itself is a result of conflict. The race of the group, though not intrinsically significant, becomes an identifying symbol, serving to intensify the sense of solidarity." During the past years, Canadian Indians seem to be utilizing more and different forms of collective action. In an attempt to assess the validity of this observation and its relation to identity, we attempted to validate the observation empirically.

Method

A content analysis of news releases published in nine Canadian newspapers[4] was undertaken. Since 73 per cent of all daily news circulation in Canada is controlled by group publishers, the selection of the newspapers was based upon the nine largest chains.[5] The selection, then, represented each region of Canada and included the major newspaper chains.

The analysis of news items relating to Indians covered the period 1950-1974. Each paper was selected at three-year intervals. Thus, paper 'A' was sampled for 1950, 1953, 1956, etc. Within each year sampled, four months were selected as a random sample. Then each paper was read for every day of those four months. All items relating to Indians were selected and coded. However, for the purposes of this paper, we will only report on activities that revealed "collective action" utilized by Canadian Indians.

We attempted to cross check the reliability of our data by content analyzing the CBC radio program "Our Native Land." This program was analyzed for three months in 1975. It was felt that collective activities carried out by Indians not deemed "newsworthy" by newspapers might be carried on the program. On the basis of our content analysis of the radio program, we then checked our selected newspaper to see if the "issue" was covered. The result was that a systematic underrepresentation of reporting of collective incidents was evident in newspapers when compared to the program "Our Native Land."

The collective actions utilized by Canadian Indians in the time period being considered were broken into two major categories: obstructive and facilitative (Day, 1972). When Indians challenged provincial, federal, or municipal laws or violated existing legal structures (formal and informal), the action was labeled "obstructive." On the other hand, if the action involved legal activities, and promoted positive action programs, it was labelled "facilitative."

Using this strategy (operationalization), the following specific activities were classified as obstructive or facilitative:

Obstructive
1. Delaying or halting construction programs, etc.
2. Seizing control of buildings, parks, roads, etc.
3. Picketing, sit-ins, marches, boycotts, etc.
4. Public attacks on governmental officials or their policies

Facilitative
1. Promoting economic development of Indians
2. Organizing conferences
3. Promoting, organizing educational, cultural, religious programs
4. Initiating legal proceedings concerning land rights, aboriginal rights, etc.
5. Initiating of complaints and investigations against violations of "civil liberties"

Obviously the examples given above are not exhaustive but are only to be considered representative of the activities that would be coded and assigned a value. In addition, the activity was defined as directed toward provincial or national issues.

The data collected then represent both an incident and content analysis. We checked carefully if a particular incident was given press coverage for several days, to make sure that the activity was only counted once.

Checks were also made to ensure that a story covered by two newspapers would only be counted once.

It should be made clear that the author is quite aware of the biases and errors that can enter into data collection techniques being utilized in the present study. However, because we feel that the data will provide us with "trend" data, and the fact that if an event was reported, the outside world considered it "important," it was felt that this procedure could best be utilized. One nominal check was to ascertain the positions of news stories related to collective action undertaken by Indians. It is currently fashionable to assert that the press, like other social institutions, represents a White man's point of view (Beiser and Swift, 1972). In order to get an unbiased perspective, each paper was divided into four quartiles. Newspapers were then checked, over time, to see whether or not the content of the stories changed.

Results

With regard to the content of articles in newspapers, we found that very little change has occurred in the past quarter century. On the average, over the past twenty-four years, a majority of the stories appeared in either the second or third quartile. While a few stories have appeared in quartile one, they still remain in quartiles two or three. Only recently (1974) were stories published on the front page. It seems that only if the stories are "sensational" are they placed on the front page and thus make up a majority of the incidents of quartile one.

The Frequency of Collective Action

In attempting to address the central issue of this paper, the overall rate of collective action involving Canadian Indians since 1950 is presented in Table 1. It shows the average number of incidents reported by the press. With two exceptions, the results show an increasing incidence of reporting suggesting that collective action is beginning to become more acceptable to Indians as a strategy and perhaps more acceptable to a wide variety of social groups as well. It should also be pointed out that some regional differences are noticeable in the following data.

Table 1 also shows that a decrease in reported activities occurred from 1950-53 and from 1959-62. We may attempt to explain these decreases in activity by looking at and analyzing external factors. For example, in 1951, the Indian Act was revised for the first time in over half a century. This may have reflected a feeling by Indians that "control" of their identity was within their grasp. The second decrease in Indian conflict activity (1950-62) could be a result of the collapse of the moral order of the Indian Affairs Branch (IAB) during the early 1960s. From the late fifties to early sixties, more and more authority and responsibility were being delegated to Band Councils. Dosman (1973) points out that other structural

224

Table 1

Average Number of Indian Incidents Instigated Per Month

Reported In Selected Newspapers of Canada, 1950-74[a]

	1950	1953	1956	1959	1962	1965	1968	1971	1974
	X̄	X̄	X̄	X̄	X̄	X̄	X̄	X̄	X̄
Montreal Star	.25	.25	.50	1.00	.50	.00	1.00	2.00	2.00
Regina Leader Post	1.20	.25	.75	2.00	.75	1.50	1.20	1.50	1.50
Toronto Daily Star	.50	.25	.25	.75	1.70	1.70	2.00	2.50	2.75
Toronto Globe & Mail	.25	.25	1.25	.25	.50	.00	1.00	1.00	2.00
Vancouver Province	.00	.25	.75	1.20	1.00	.50	.50	.75	1.00
Winnipeg Free Press	.00	.25	.25	1.00	.50	3.50	2.00	3.20	4.00
Calgary Herald	1.50	.25	1.20	1.00	1.20	1.75	3.00	3.00	2.50
La Presse (Montreal)	.50	.25	.50	1.00	.75	.75	1.20	1.50	1.75
Saint John Telegraph-Journal	.25	.25	.75	.75	.50	1.00	1.50	.75	1.50
X̄	.50	.25	.69	.99	.82	1.18	1.49	1.80	2.10

[a]The "per-month" average is based on a sample of four months and then projected over the entire year.

changes such as: a) the commissioning and publication of two major socio-economic studies of Indians in British Columbia and Manitoba; b) the appointment of an Indian as a senator; c) the extension of the federal franchise to Indians; and d) the establishment of a National Indian Organization were taking place. The result was that the Indian Affairs Branch progressively lost whatever legitimacy it possessed. Indians felt they were making headway in determining their destiny. However, it soon became clear that this was not the case. This is clearly denoted by the "spiralling plans and polemics of the IAB climaxed by the government's New Policy of July 1969 which outlined a policy of termination" (Dosman, 1973).

Table 1 also reveals that in the time period of 1962-65 an upsurge in the reported incidents is evident. After 1962 the number of reports slowly begins to increase to its present level.

However, other events that took place during the mid-1950s had serious consequences for Indian peoples and affected their involvement in conflict behaviour. This is clearly reflected in the increased number of obstructive tactics utilized by western Indians (see Table 2). For example, in western Canada the agitation for better educational and social opportunities has exposed the role of church-operated schools. The first result was that the Indians have attacked the churches and the churches have withdrawn all support of Indian organizations and created their new Catholic Indian league. Second, the IAB invoked a rule which stated that bank funds could not be used for travel which involved conferences. During this same time, the provincial and federal governments set up conferences which they controlled and for which they would pay Indians' expenses (Cardinal, 1969).

As a result of the above activities, we find a substantial decline in the number of Indian organizations and their activities during the middle and late 1950s. Yet we find a slight upsurge in the number of reported incidents, and an increase in the number of obstructive tactics. This might suggest that Indians chose to work extra-legally when the "appropriate" (Indian organization) institutional structures were not available.

From the 1960s on, the development of organizations once again increased. The National Indian Council was created and eventually replaced by the National Indian Brotherhood. Also during this time, the government established the Regional Advisory Council, which was to consist of Indian leaders who would be consulted by government when major legislation concerning Indians was being considered. Coincidental was the moral collapse of the old order of Indian Affairs and an attempt by the government to reorganize. Likewise, by 1960 a majority of Indian bands had municipal-type councils elected for two years (Davis and Krauter, 1972). For movements of protest to be effective, they must show evidence of widespread support—hence, the frequent resort to mass rallies, demonstrations, etc. These can be called identification moves. They are proof that the leaders and their demands have large-scale support and should therefore be recognized by the authorities (Oberschall, 1973). It would seem that more and more of these identification moves are being engaged in by Indian people.

Strategies of Collective Action
Table 2 shows the relative proportion of strategies of action reported in the newspapers. It becomes obvious when viewing the conflicts that a majority of events are facilitative. However, upon careful analysis, we find that a greater percentage from 1950 become obstructive. It is also noticeable in Table 2 that the "West" reflects the greater proportion of obstructive tactics. Price and McCaskill (1974) point out that Indian communities in the prairie cities have arrived relatively recently and are extremely hostile to Whites.

The above would tend to indicate that more and more collective events utilized by Indians are obstructive in nature. These data might suggest that Indian people have provided themselves with a rationale for engaging in conflict, that of "a last resort." This rationale provides a legitimacy for Indian people to engage in obstructive tactics.

Focus of Collective Action
Table 3 reflects the proportional distribution of reported conflicts by whether or not the conflict reflects a provincial or a national focus. For example, if the actions taken by Indians were directed toward establishing a new training centre in a province, the issue was considered provincial. On the other hand, if the action concerned changes in IAB housing policy, the action is defined as national. Table 3 shows that in the early 1950s a majority of the action was directed toward provincial issues. However, a shift has occurred in later years, and a greater percentage of the collective action focuses on national issues.

Conclusion
Goals differ in the amount of time and effort required for their realization and certainty of attainment. Thus, Indians hope in some future generation to achieve a "grand purpose," but meanwhile seek only a limited goal. The argument is that in order to reach the "end," one must try and attain limited ends now. A succession of goals must be related to the group's capacities. Clearly, in the present case, Indians' capabilities have increased. Local and/or provincial goals were more manageable and "easier" to attain. However, Indians are now expanding their goals (Kriesberg, 1973).

All of the changes seem to reflect basic changes in Indian-White relations. During the early 1950s, the Indian Act was substantially revised for the first time in several decades. During the sixties, Indians received the right to vote; Indian organizations got off the ground and regional advi-

Table 2

Proportion of Collective Action Defined as Facilitative or Obstructive
Reported in Selected Newspapers for Years 1950-1974[a]

		1950	1953	1956	1959	1962	1965	1968	1971	1974
Montreal Star	Facilitative	100%	100	100	50	100	100	100	100	100
	Obstructive	0%	0	0	50	0	0	0	12	20
Regina Leader Post	Facilitative	80	100	100	100	100	84	100	50	55
	Obstructive	20	0	0	0	0	16	0	50	45
Toronto Daily Star	Facilitative	50	0	0	100	100	85	80	90	80
	Obstructive	50	100	100	0	0	10	20	10	20
Toronto Globe & Mail	Facilitative	100	100	100	0	0	0	75	25	20
	Obstructive	0	0	0	100	100	0	25	75	80
Vancouver Province	Facilitative	0	100	66	60	100	50	100	66	60
	Obstructive	0	0	34	40	0	50	0	34	40
Winnipeg Free Press	Facilitative	0	100	100	0	25	50	70	75	60
	Obstructive	0	0	0	100	75	50	30	25	40
Calgary Herald	Facilitative	100	100	66	56	90	85	66	40	50
	Obstructive	0	0	34	44	10	15	34	60	50
La Presse (Montreal)	Facilitative	100	90	80	100	100	70	60	75	75
	Obstructive	0	10	20	0	0	30	40	25	25
Saint John Telegraph-Journal	Facilitative	100	100	100	80	85	100	75	80	60
	Obstructive	0	0	0	20	15	0	25	20	40

[a] A ratio of facilitative/obstructive techniques to total number for the four months was calculated. A similar strategy was used to distinguish national/provincial focus of the activity. The N for each paper (and each year) can be calculated from Table 1.

Table 3

Percentage Of Conflict Exhibiting Facilitative/Obstructive Tactics by Focus–Provincial vs. National From 1950-1974

		1950	1953	1956	1959	1962	1965	1968	1971	1974
Montreal Star	Provincial	100%	0	50	100	50	0	75	38	30
	National	0%	100	50	0	50	0	25	62	70
Regina Leader Post	Provincial	100	100	100	100	34	90	60	40	40
	National	0	0	0	0	66	10	40	60	60
Toronto Daily Star	Provincial	50	100	100	100	90	100	80	34	30
	National	50	0	0	0	10	0	20	66	70
Toronto Globe & Mail	Provincial	100	0	40	100	50	0	100	25	34
	National	0	100	60	0	50	0	0	75	66
Vancouver Province	Provincial	0	0	100	100	100	0	50	75	100
	National	0	100	0	0	0	100	50	25	0
Winnipeg Free Press	Provincial	0	0	100	25	30	75	55	40	55
	National	0	100	0	75	70	25	45	60	45
Calgary Herald	Provincial	90	100	80	100	100	65	60	65	50
	National	10	0	20	0	0	35	40	35	50
La Presse (Montreal)	Provincial	90	100	100	80	80	75	80	70	80
	National	10	0	0	20	20	25	20	30	20
Saint John Telegraph-Journal	Provincial	100	100	50	65	50	80	80	75	60
	National	0	0	50	35	50	20	20	25	40

sory councils were created. Then, in the late 1960s, Indian people began to organize nationally concerning the White Paper presentation in 1969. In addition, at this time the NIB was created (along with other national organizations) which provided Indian people outlets on national issues.

The results presented in the present paper suggest that conflict is being used by Indian people to attain (and validate) a sense of sacred identity. Whether or not it continues to be used will depend on how quickly Indian people are able to develop a sense of race consciousness. Until then, conflict-oriented behaviour is being utilized as the most practical and viable technique for Indian people to gain a sense of group identity. Beyond this achievement, conflict has additional benefits in that it is beginning to change the relationship between Indians and Whites from a vertical to a horizontal one. However, it should be pointed out that because the members of the minority group (in this case Native Indians) are collectively oriented rather than self-oriented (and thus super-individuals), conflicts, as they arise, are likely to be more intense and violent. Because the struggle is for the group and not for the individual, the participants can justify their involvement and move forward more radically and mercilessly with "good conscience." The impact of conflict on social structure will vary depending on the type and interrelationships of the institutions.

In a society that is rigid in terms of structure, i.e., where a group of people are permanently excluded from participation in its benefits, the chances of conflict are great. In addition, many excluded people will reject the very assumptions upon which the majority society is built.

Whether conflict within our society will lead to adjustment or to systematic changes of our institutional structures depends on the degree of flexibility of the social structure. If Canada maintains its present rigid structures, it is likely to maximize the chances of more violent outbreaks attacking the consensual structure and lead to structural changes of the existing social system.

It must be pointed out that the current "strategy" for engaging in conflict by Native People may change over time and become what has been called the "politics of confrontation" (Howe, 1968). This is a kind of politics that is improvised and moulded within a temporal context by the group using it. The general purpose is to prod and incite an insensitive society to recognize and redress its failures toward minority groups. However, the political philosophy held by members who adhere to Howe's perspective declares that since we live in a capitalistic society and have a social system which, through oppressive tactics, has removed all opposition, we will never see an end to the social and economic oppression of various minority groups.

It is further argued that efforts introduced by the dominant group to introduce reforms in the social system are superficial and are really devices for maintaining the status quo. Hence, neither a traditional Leninism nor a social democratic philosophy will change the structure of society. Thus, the only alternative is to launch a series of "raids," "riots," or "armed attacks," against the larger society to usurp or unsettle the power "establishment." As Ed Burstick, a leader of the American Indian Movement, pointed out in a recent speech, "We must now move to armed confrontation if progress is to be achieved."

The view is that society can only be "shaken" and consequently changed through attack by marginal groups. Changes will take place because the result of confrontation politics is "polarization." In other words, through the constant harassment of the "middle class," some will be driven to radicalism (and thus to the marginal group's side) and the end is an apocalypse.

The result is a series of actions, dramatic, desperate and provocative, which keep the society in a state of constant turmoil. For a while, confrontation politics works because the opposition is caught off guard and has no clear line of defence. However, in the end, a defence is devised by the dominant group and a backlash against the subordinate group by the dominant group will result, placing Native People in an even more subordinate position than they presently hold.

Notes

1. I would like to thank John Price who spent a considerable amount of time criticizing an early draft of this paper. I would also like to thank Leo Driedger, Bill Reeves, and Doug House for helpful suggestions on an earlier draft.

2. Price (1975) argues that the social forces in Canadian society have tended to perpetuate the continuation of native societies in Canada within a decultivating context of neo-colonialism. However, he also argues that this is irrelevant (particularly for reserve-rural) to the native daily life until recently.

3. For a more explicit and expanded discussion relating the notion of relative deprivation to social movements, the reader should consult T. Gurr (1970). Gurr discusses the three dimensions of relative deprivation (material, power, and interpersonal values) and relates them to status, identity, and communal association.

4. *Toronto Daily Star*, Saint John *Telegraph-Journal*, *La Presse*, Calgary *Herald*, *Winnipeg Free Press*, Montreal *Star*, Regina *Leader Post*, *Globe and Mail*, and Vancouver *Province*.

5. Toronto *Star*, Bassett-Eaton, Desmarais, Southam, Thomson, F.P. Publications, McConnell Group, Armadale, and K.C. Irving.

References

Beiser, J., and R. Swift
1972 "Leadership Roles and the Forms of Red Power Movement Among American Indians." Unpublished manuscript.

Boldt, M.
1975 "Native American Leaders' Attitudes Toward Extra Legal Actions." Unpublished manuscript.

Braroe, N.
1975 *Indian and White.* Stanford, California: Stanford University Press.

Brown, W.C.
1931 "The Nature of Racial Conflict." *Social Forces* 20:90-97.
1935 "Racial Conflict Among South African Natives." *American Journal of Sociology* 40:569-581.

Cardinal, H.
1969 *The Unjust Society.* Edmonton: Hurtig Publishing.

Coser, L.
1956 *The Functions of Social Conflict.* Glencoe: Free Press.

Coser, L.
1968 "Some Sociological Aspects of Conflict." *International Encyclopedia of the Social Sciences,* David Sills (ed.), vol. 3. New York: Crowell Collier and Macmillan.

Courchène, D.
1971 *Wahbung: Our Tomorrows.* Winnipeg: Manitoba Indian Brotherhood.

Davis, M., and J. Krauter
1971 *The Other Canadians: Profiles of Six Minorities.* Toronto: Methuen.

Day, R.
1972 "The Emergence of Activism as a Social Movement," in H. Bahr, B. Chadwick and R. Day (eds.), *Native Americans Today: Sociological Perspectives.* New York: Harper and Row.

Denton, T.
1975 "Migration from a Canadian Indian Reserve." *Journal of Canadian Studies* 7:54-62.

Dosman, E.
1972 *Indians: The Urban Dilemma.* Toronto: McClelland and Stewart.

Gurr, T.
1970 *Why Men Rebel.* Princeton: Princeton University Press.

Himes, J.
1966 "The Functions of Racial Conflict." *Social Forces* 45:1-10.

Howe, I.
1968 *The New Confrontation Politics is a Dangerous Game.* New York: New York Times Co.

Hurst, C.
1972 "Race, Class and Consciousness." *American Sociological Review* 37:658-670.

Klapp, O.
1964 *Symbolic Leaders, Public Dramas and Public Men.* Chicago: Aldine Press.

1969 *The Collective Search for Identity.* New York: Holt, Rinehart and Winston.

1972 *Currents of Unrest.* New York: Holt, Rinehart and Winston.

Kriesberg, L.
1973 *The Sociology of Social Conflicts.* Englewood Cliffs: Prentice-Hall.

Light, I.
1972 *Ethnic Enterprise in America.* Richmond, California: University of California Press.

Marx, G.
1967 *Protest and Prejudice: A Study of Belief in a Black Community.* New York: Harper and Row.

Meyer, P.
1969 "Aftermath of Martyrdom: Negro Militancy and Martin Luther King." *Public Opinion Quarterly* 33:160-174.

Oberschall, A.
1973 *Social Conflict and Social Movements.* Englewood Cliffs: Prentice-Hall.

Paige, J.
1971 "Political Orientation and Riot Participation." *American Sociological Review* 36:810-819.

Pettigrew, T.
1964 *A Profile of the Negro American.* Princeton: D. Van Nostrand Co.

Pitts, J.
1974 "The Study of Race Consciousness: Comments on New Directions." *American Journal of Sociology* 80:665-687.

Price, J.
1972 "U.S. and Canadian Indian Periodicals." *The Canadian Review of Sociology and Anthropology* 9:150-162.

1974 "U.S. and Canadian Voluntary Associations: An Evolutionary Synthesis." Unpublished manuscript.

Price, J., and P. McCaskill
1974 "The Urban Integration of Canadian Native People." *Western Canadian Journal of Anthropology* 4:29-47.
Simmel, G.
1964 *Conflict and the Web of Group Affiliation.* New York: Free Press.
Singer, B.
1973 "Mass Society, Mass Media, and the Transformation of Minority Identity." *British Journal of Sociology* 24:101-119.
Waskow, A.I.
1966 "Creative Disorder in the Racial Struggle," in R. Murray and H. Elison (eds.), *Problems and Prospects of the Negro Movement.* Wadsworth, California.
Whiteside, D.
1973 "Historical Development of Aboriginal Political Associations in Canada: Documentation." Ottawa: National Indian Brotherhood.
Wilson, J.
1973 *Introduction to Social Movements.* New York: Basic Books, Inc.

12

A People Apart:
The Ethnicization of
the Inuit of the Eastern
Canadian Arctic

*John S. and Carolyn J.
Matthiasson**

During the past half-decade or so, the study of ethnicity has increasingly captured the interest of social scientists, probably due in no small way to the high visibility of ethnic groups in this country. As John Porter illustrated in *The Vertical Mosaic*, Canadians have traditionally rejected the "melting pot" concept which has been so vigorously perpetuated at an ideological, if not practical, level in the United States. In this paper we will examine some recent socio-cultural trends among the Inuit of northern Canada which are transforming them from a population traditionally identified as a racial category to a *bona fide* ethnic group. As an ethnic group, the modern Inuit stand alongside other ethnic groups in Canada who are struggling to ensure that their personal identity continues to be a part of the Canadian mosaic, whether vertical, horizontal, or both.

This is not the first time that the Inuit have been labelled an ethnic group, but we think that it is one of the first times they have actually been treated as one. This is not meant as a criticism of other observers of the Inuit, but instead as a recognition that the forces which have made them into an ethnic group are very recent. By adopting the posture of ethnicity, the Inuit have also adopted a stance of social separation and, indeed, one of self-imposed or voluntary segregation from the non-Inuit inhabitants of the Canadian Arctic. To a considerable extent this stance has been fostered by pan-Inuit voluntary associations such as the Inuit Tapirisat of Canada (ITC), but not completely.

The data which will be presented in this paper are largely settlement-specific, in that they have been collected primarily in the environs of one

John S. Matthiasson is Associate Professor of Anthropology, University of Manitoba, and Carolyn J. Matthiasson is Assistant Professor of Anthropology, University of Winnipeg.

235

Arctic community, but the conclusions drawn from them can be applied to several other Inuit settlements in the Canadian Arctic.

The community in question is Pond Inlet, located on the northern tip of Baffin Island. John S. Matthiasson spent thirteen months living in a small hunting camp approximately fifty miles from the settlement in 1963-64 and later spent six weeks in the community in the summer of 1973. In the intervening decade the Inuit of Pond Inlet had experienced what were almost cataclysmic changes. During the earlier period almost all of them lived "on the land," making their living from seal hunting and trap lines. A number of factors have contributed to what became a virtually complete migration of the people into the settlement. For example, the building of a school brought children into the settlement, and their parents were not long in following them. A new federal housing program, although planned initially for the hunting camps, was introduced in the settlement, and those who wished to take advantage of it were forced to leave the land. New non-traditional employment opportunities for men added to the incentive to move to town. By 1973 the camps were virtual ghost towns, visited only by the occasional weekend hunter. Many of the younger men had found employment with oil exploration companies, and were flown back and forth from the work sites on a regular basis. Others drove heavy machinery in the settlement, worked on garbage disposal, or, in a few cases, worked as clerks in government offices. The local Settlement Council, composed entirely of Inuit, was working towards the achievement of "hamlet" status for Pond Inlet, which would decrease the amounts of federal and territorial monies available to it, but would also give it greater autonomy. By 1975, Pond Inlet had been incorporated as a hamlet, and what had at times been derisively termed the "Eskimo Council" had become a full-fledged town council, which oversaw and directed the future development and growth of the community. It is in this context, and largely because of these developments, that the Inuit of Pond Inlet have taken on characteristics of an ethnic group.

The Inuit population of Pond Inlet has had a long history of exposure to the outside world, going back to visits by Scottish whaling ships in the late 1800s. Many of these ships wintered in the protected waters of Admiralty Inlet. Contact with the outside world has been continuous ever since, but before examining the nature of that contact, and its influence on the emergence of the people of Pond Inlet as an ethnic group, we would like to examine in broader terms the type of involvement the Inuit people have generally had with Euro-Canadians, and the image that involvement perpetuated in much of the anthropological literature on Arctic Canada. In doing so, we hope to help correct a consistent distortion in that literature, which has characterized the Inuit as an oppressed and exploited people. They have in fact been badly treated by many of the people with whom they have had contact during the last century, but to portray only that is to ignore their capacity to continue to manage their own affairs in effective ways. A decade ago we would have been pessimistic about the Inuit condition and their prospects for the future. Their actual history has belied anthropologists' efforts to predict the course of human events.

Much of the image of Inuit circumstances today has been projected by an influential reader edited by Jean Elliott (1971). At the time of its publication it filled a void in Canadian studies. It was the first book on minority peoples in Canada, done from an anthropological perspective, which included articles on Inuit, Indians, and Métis. Because of these facts, it received wide classroom adoption by anthropologists and sociologists across Canada. In it, Jack Ferguson writes as follows about the contemporary position of the Canadian Inuit:

> In the traditional Eskimo community power had been in the hands of the band leaders who could sway public opinion through their role as pater-familias and the respect that it engendered, and also in the hands of those men whose ability, daring, and ruthlessness were greater than average; men who were willing to take considerable changes with public opinion and were willing to risk public censure and possibly physical assault (Ferguson, 1971:21).
>
> To this day, any Eskimo who wishes to injure another usually gets drunk first...It is not accidental that the best hunters are usually the biggest gamblers and the heaviest drinkers...(Ferguson, 1971:22).

The implication seems to be that Inuit have little organizational abilities, and in the post-contact environment find themselves psychologically and socially adrift. Ferguson goes on to write that:

> Cut off from purposeful economic activities and living from various kinds of welfare activities, the typical Eskimo community will become more, and not less, part of a satellite society. For this is the last and certainly the most important factor in the maintenance of such a society—the lack of meaningful work for adults. Attendant with this will be other social problems and one could expect that differing forms of deviance will develop. If one could develop a picture of what the society will be like, it would have to include a healthy, well-housed, population growing at a very high rate, fed only reasonably well on canned foods, having an enormous amount of leisure time, and little purposeful or gainful activity. To top off this picture, one would add that they would have almost all administration done for them, they would not get sufficient education to compete for the available civil service jobs, nor would they participate in politics. Accordingly, their resentment would increase proportionately to their status as second-rate citizens (Ferguson, 1971;27).

In the same volume we find John and Irma Honigmann writing: "Although much learning is taking place in Frobisher Bay, it tends to be one-sided; the Eskimo receives instruction from and mimics the Euro-Canadian.

What might this trend portend for the future of the Eskimo as a culturally distinctive and viable ethnic group?'' (Honigmann and Honigmann, 1971:55). In her reader, Elliott herself comments on Ferguson's article that:

> Although the Eskimo must adapt to a changing socio-cultural environment, the gravest problem facing him may well be symbolized by the presence of his southern caretakers...Viewed within the context of paternalism, the plight of the Eskimo as a powerless minority is clear. In the arctic townsites, the Eskimo tends to be physically segregated and have poorer housing than the Euro-Canadian, but more important, "The government is not indigenous to the population." The Eskimo, therefore, is subtly exploited and his culture systematically "debased and pauperized" (Elliott, 1971;15).

Inuit housing was indeed inferior to that of Euro-Canadians in the Arctic a decade ago. It is not typically so today. Inuit culture has been neither debased nor pauperized. Ask any Inuit who is a member of the Inuit Tapirisat of Canada. To imply that it has been either is to demean the Inuit. Anthropologists have identified a category of society which they refer to as a "band" form of organization. It is a loose form of political structure. As nomadic hunters Inuit seem to fit the description for the pre-contact period. However, in this paper we will attempt to demonstrate that during the contact-traditional period, Inuit of northern Canada have developed skills of organization that have made them more than capable of coping with the modern world. Instead of being passively exploited, they have discovered new techniques for handling bureaucrats and others who would keep them in a pauperized and cultureless situation. Much of their capacity to do so has its roots in traditional Inuit society, but we will not examine that here. However, it is worth noting, although it will be unpopular to do so, that an implicit assumption made by writers like Ferguson and Elliott is that Inuit culture is being lost, and this is to be bemoaned. Yet the retention of it, in political terms, would work against the acquisition of a new power base in northern communities by the Inuit. It seems that such writers want it both ways. The Inuit, on the other hand, are too busy finding methods of retaining their cultural heritage and consolidating a new power base to be as concerned as the social science observers. It also seems that a definition of culture is being used which is devoid of any political content. This, of course, is a carryover from the band society concept with its stereotyped image of nomadic peoples and their life-styles.

It we are to be fair to the Inuit, we must recognize their right and, more importantly, perhaps, their capacity to carve a position for themselves within what is commonly called the Canadian mosaic. As they do so, they adopt the techniques and mechanisms employed by other ethnic groups which seek separateness and yet unity within this national and still

238

poorly understood experiment in multiculturalism. If we as academics, and those who are the children of modern-day Inuit, are to understand how these people who are admired around the world as among the most adaptable members of our species, having learned centuries ago to live in the harsh environment of the Arctic, achieved the ends in the Canadian national context which they have defined for themselves, we must, it seems to us, study their present behaviour, however much out of fashion social science research in the Arctic regions may be today. The results of their activities will in all probability change the legal and political structure of large geographical portions of this nation. Furthermore, if the Inuit are successful in their efforts to achieve satisfaction in the matter of their land claims, for example, other indigenous peoples in other parts of the world may learn from their experiences.

Ethnicity as a concept is only relevant in settings where populations of people find themselves to be in a minority position and, in realizing that status, create devices to preserve their identity. As such they become, unless severe political suppression is used against them, quasi-political groups which establish boundary-maintaining mechanisms that enhance and support their distinctiveness from the social majority. Not all minority populations behave in this way, but those who wish to retain ethnic identities do. They maintain a reserve *vis-à-vis* the larger society. Inuit in northern Canada have done so, and quite consciously, but historical factors as well have encouraged their adopted stance.

The Canadian Arctic is huge geographically but small socially. It is not uncommon for an outsider to make a friend in an isolated settlement on Baffin Island in the eastern high Arctic and then, a year or so later, meet the same person in a western community such as Yellowknife. This is likely a fairly typical pattern in frontier regions around the world. The Inuit also maintain their own communication networks, and information is often rapidly transmitted from one area to another. Our reason for discussing this is that trends and news events in one part of the Canadian Arctic are usually passed from settlement to settlement, or by individuals passing through an area for reasons of illness, employment, etc. (Matthiasson, 1975). Patterns of segregation practised in communities such as Rankin Inlet, then, have been described and discussed by Inuit across the Arctic.

Rankin Inlet and Resolute Bay are two examples of imposed segregation between Euro-Canadians and Inuit during the early 1960s. Both settlements were artificial creations, and Inuit residents were brought to them from other settlement areas. Rankin Inlet, which is on the west coast of Hudson Bay, was born in 1954, when a mine was established at a lode of nickel which had been found in 1928. Earlier a few Inuit had lived at the site, but, as Dailey and Dailey have reported, they identified themselves with the larger settlement of Chesterfield Inlet, where they did their trading. In 1956 and 1957, however, more than seventy Inuit men were brought to the settlement to work in the mine. They came from several coastal and inland regions of northern Canada (Dailey and Dailey, 1961).

In an attempt at benevolent paternalism, the mining company, with the approval of the Department of Northern Affairs and National Resources, kept the Inuit miners and their families segregated from Euro-Canadian residents. "Most whites at Rankin Inlet have absolutely no idea of how the Eskimo lives. White personnel are forbidden to enter the Eskimo settlement without the permission of the superintendent, and any Eskimo woman who seems at all 'familiar' is warned by the mine" (Dailey and Dailey, 1961;95). In a chiding reference to Farley Mowat's popular books on the inland Inuit of the interior barren-lands behind Rankin Inlet, the Daileys claimed that, "contrary to what Mowat says, the Eskimo is not a part 'of the society which dominates the Western world.' There is no real Eskimo-White social interaction of any kind" (Dailey and Dailey, 1961;95).

Their description of Rankin Inlet of the late 1950s was accurate, and the social separation of the two populations in the settlement continued after the closing of the mine. When we spent a summer in Rankin in 1967, teaching a course on field techniques, we insisted that students, many of whom worked in Arctic settlements as teachers, visit each home in the community and ask a series of specified questions. Most felt awkward in carrying out the task, including those who had Arctic winter jobs. The Inuit, on the other hand, although gracious in their reception of the students, found the interactions to be uncomfortable, and this intensified the desires of the students themselves to find other projects, or to spend their time interviewing only those whose families were most outgoing. The Inuit in the community were unfamiliar with having Euro-Canadians visit in their homes. The pattern established during the time when the mine was in operation had been perpetuated and stabilized. These same Inuit were among the most mobile in the Canadian Arctic of that time period, several of them later having found employment in Yellowknife and other mining communities. Their experiences, one would expect, were communicated to other Inuit still struggling to understand their own relationships with the suddenly large number of Euro-Canadians living in their North.

Resolute Bay, on Cornwallis Island, has become in many respects a nerve centre of activity in the high Arctic. Today it is the centre for air traffic in that region. To reach most settlements in the high Arctic, one must travel from Edmonton or Montreal by commercial airline, and then either arrange a charter into more isolated settlements or wait for one of the irregularly scheduled flights from Resolute Bay. Oil exploration activities in the high Arctic are centred in Resolute Bay, and it has been claimed by some residents that the landing strip there has more daily landings and take-offs than any other airport in Canada.

Inuit were relocated from Pond Inlet on northern Baffin Island and from Spence Bay to Resolute Bay in the 1950s to service the Department of Transport (DOT) and Royal Canadian Air Force (RCAF) bases. There were no women in residence at the bases, and Inuit women were not permitted access to them. Two popular sayings at Resolute in the early 1960s were, "The Nordair stewardesses never leave the aircraft in Resolute," and "Any White caught in the Eskimo settlement will be shipped south on the next aircraft out." Once again, an Inuit settlement which had been artificially produced for either commercial or governmental reasons, and members of which had contact with several other, more natural and traditional Inuit settlements, had had a policy of severe and policed segregation imposed on it. In the case of Resolute Bay, the Royal Canadian Mounted Police detachment was built in the Inuit community.

The benevolent paternalism practised in Rankin Inlet and Resolute Bay may not have been totally in error. The many, but often undocumented, cases of rape of Inuit women which occurred in settlements where Euro-Canadian males were quartered are mute testimony to the providential nature of such housing arrangements and social policies. Nevertheless, they did contribute to a set of conditions that have encouraged Inuit to identify themselves as different, socially, physically, and often, we fear, politically and legally, from other Canadians. These policies have, then, contributed to the formation of the Inuit into an ethnic unit.

The separation of the two populations in Rankin Inlet and Resolute Bay was imposed, institutionalized, and formal. But these two situations did not deviate extensively from historical conditions in virtually all Canadian Arctic settlements. Traditionally, these communities had as non-Inuit residents missionaries, policemen, and traders. Free traders were rarely found in high Arctic regions, and the traders who were there were almost always employees of the Hudson Bay Company, a monolithic organization that dominated Arctic commerce for decades. Free traders often developed close interaction patterns with the Native People with whom they conducted business, and they frequently married native women. Hudson Bay traders were forbidden by company *fiat* to marry local women. Missionaries interacted closely with their Inuit parishioners in most Arctic settlements, but they were often more concerned with competition with missionaries from other denominations than with their Inuit converts. The police (RCMP) usually learned the Inuit language, and provided a variety of services for the Inuit as para-medical practitioners, novice social workers, and so on, but socially they maintained a distance from them.

As so often occurs in colonial situations, members of the Euro-Canadian community in most settlements turn to one another for recreation and social interaction. Patterns were commonly established whereby, for instance, Inuit visitors to Euro-Canadian homes carried out their business, such as it may have been, in vestibules or offices, rarely being invited to sit down. In fact they rarely removed their parkas. We do not mean to criticize the Euro-Canadians, for we know far too many members of all three segments of the typical Arctic *troika* with sensitivity and compassion, who are, or were, dedicated to Arctic life and living. Our point is simply that the Inuit, regardless of whether or not they desired to form close bonds with Euro-Canadians, were denied the possibility of doing so. Interaction settings were severely circumscribed. Such circumstances are not, of course, limited to colonial settings. It is not at all uncommon in many rural areas of North America and elsewhere for shopkeepers, for example, to be from a different ethnic group than the majority population. This may be because social and cultural contexts in which there is limited role differentiation are more compatible to the use of "outsiders" in non-typical and non-traditional roles. In any event, this was a common occurrence in Arctic communities in Canada until recently.

In the 1950s and early 1960s the picture changed in virtually all Canadian Inuit communities. This was the period when massive efforts were carried out by the federal government to "develop" the Arctic settlements. They were joined by civil servants (Northern Service Officers and Area Administrators) school teachers, mechanics, and, in many instances, their families.

In the past, most Inuit had lived in camps located some distance from the settlements. They would visit the nearest trading post once a month or so to trade, and then return to their camps. With the encroachment of government personnel on the settlements, new housing had to be provided for these same government employees. To attract them to isolated and remote settlements, the housing provided had to be fairly substantial. Shortly after they arrived, their presence in settlements and their actions began to attract Inuit settlers as well. Some Inuit men found employment on construction teams, others received training as heavy equipment operators and built and maintained roads. Others moved to town simply because their children were enrolled in schools and they wished to be near them.

Older and/or disabled Inuit moved to the settlements to be nearer medical and other services and facilities, and government housing. All migrants to town, of course, needed housing, and virtually all received it – almost always provided by government housing agencies. The reasons for this massive and rapid change in residence patterns varied somewhat from one settlement to another, but these were essentially the ones which were most important for the people of Pond Inlet and its environs. In Pond Inlet during that period, Inuit housing was to some extent spatially integrated with Euro-Canadian housing. Today, it is difficult to tell an Inuit home from that of a Euro-Canadian in that settlement, but in the early 1960s the differences between them were readily apparent to even the most casual observer. Inuit housing was far inferior then; while Euro-Canadians usually had two- or three-bedroom bungalows, Inuit typically had small, one-room dwellings. The interior layout of furniture in the latter was sparse, and similar to that found in traditional homes in the camps the Inuit had recently vacated.

The wives of newly arrived Euro-Canadians in Pond Inlet, and in particular the wives of Area Administrators and school teachers, often attempted to create arenas of possible interaction between themselves and the Inuit women in the settlement. However, their attempts to do so stood in sharp contrast with the traditional patterns of social interaction between the two populations, formed over several decades by members of the *troika*, and implicitly accepted by most Inuit. In addition, the only two possible arenas for such new social involvement were the homes of Inuit and those of Euro-Canadians. Overtures by Euro-Canadian wives of government personnel were usually accepted by Inuit women, although often with some temerity on the part of younger ones, but invitations to coffee get-togethers and other social gatherings in Euro-Canadian homes were difficult to return for Inuit women, who often felt uncomfortable hosting their Euro-Canadian counterparts in their smaller and far less attractive homes. The initial advances by Euro-Canadian wives of government personnel, then, did not lead to long-term interactions between the two populations, and soon these women found themselves part of a closed Euro-Canadian community which included wives of members of the *troika*. Parties held by members of this community rarely included Inuit couples, although on odd occasions one or more might receive invitations. Periodic dances held by the Inuit at the local school in Pond Inlet would be attended for the first hour or so by Euro-Canadians. After their early departures, the dances would usually continue through the night.

Even in cases in which close friendships were formed between Inuit and Euro-Canadians in Pond Inlet after the introduction-of-government period, they were difficult to maintain over long periods of time due to the typically short time of residence in the settlement of the Euro-Canadians. Teachers, nurses, and other government personnel rarely remained in a settlement for more than two years. Of course, the difficulties of creating such cross-population bonds were aggravated by the fact that during the early 1960s, when the movement into the settlement occurred, neither group spoke the language of the other, with only the odd exception.

During the 1960s and 1970s many Inuit children were sent out of their home settlements to Frobisher Bay, Northwest Territories or Churchill, Manitoba for high school education. (Today most settlements, including Pond Inlet, have their own high schools, but this is a recent trend.) In these consolidated schools they met children from other settlements, and almost certainly compared their experiences with their own. Also, in the two communities in which the schools were located they saw what many of them probably interpreted as discriminatory, or at least segregated, housing patterns for resident Inuit peoples. In Churchill, for example, the Inuit residents lived in Akudlik, a residential area separated from the main townsite. The only non-Inuit allowed to live there were personnel of the Department of Northern Affairs and National Resources (DNANR, now Department of Indian Affairs and National Resources). In fact, the Inuit housing was possibly the best in the town, but its physical separation was probably noted by Inuit schoolchildren from more northern settlements. In the 1960s a less marked but still real housing separation between the majority of Inuit and Euro-Canadians also existed in Frobisher Bay. Finally, children from many settlements met, in either Churchill or Frobisher Bay, children from Rankin Inlet and Resolute Bay, the two northern settlements in which geographical separation between the two populations was most noticeable and enforced.

We reject the notion that there has ever been a conscious effort on the part of any segment of the Euro-Canadian population resident permanently or temporarily in the Canadian Arctic to impose patterns of social segregation on the Inuit, with the exception, perhaps, of some groups of missionaries who feared that exposure to external and southern influences would lead to secularization and hence corruption of their converts, and of those agencies who created the Rankin Inlet and Resolute Bay settings. Nevertheless, it does seem that there have been several historical precedents and factors which may well have led Inuit in many Arctic settlements to perceive segregation, or at least limited and circumscribed interaction between the two groups, as natural and inevitable. Experiences in their own settlements may have been reinforced through contact with other Inuit from other settlements whose experiences may have been similar.

It may be that patterns of non-involvement of social groupings, culturally defined as being different from one another, have roots within traditional Inuit society. There are some suggestions that this was the case. In Rankin Inlet, which was composed of Inuit who had been relocated there from several other settlements across the eastern and central Arctic, interaction patterns, and even housing, when families were given the opportunity to select their own, were sharply demarcated along settlement of origin lines, until at least the late 1960s. Grise Fiord, in the high eastern Arctic, was created by the federal government in the 1950s. The aim was to relocate several families from Port Harrison, Quebec, to a new hunting area in an effort to relieve the over-hunting which was occurring around Port Harrison. To assist them in adapting to this new ecological zone, several Inuit families were also relocated to Grise Fiord from Pond Inlet. Although neither of us has visited Grise Fiord, several informants who know the settlement have told us that the two populations lined themselves and their homes up on either side of it, and little interaction other than of an occupational nature transpired between them until as late as 1970. We recall an RCMP Inuit special constable from Port Harrison who was stationed in Pond Inlet for more than a year in the early 1960s, and neither he nor other members of his family were ever invited into a local

Inuit home. The last two references are admittedly anecdotal, but we suggest that they do imply a pattern of social separation of Inuit in situations in which the Inuit perceive two or more ethnic groups to be present.

Regardless of the motivations of participants in the situation, then, we feel that there is historical evidence for an emerging form of separation of Inuit and Euro-Canadians into two distinct groupings in most Canadian Arctic settlements, and that this may have found a convenient cognitive niche within traditional Inuit culture. Northern Euro-Canadian residents come and go, some staying for years and others for only a few months. Many of them move about from one part of the Arctic to another, and so learn to work within the emerging social patterns, but they rarely have a strong allegiance to any one settlement. The Inuit remain, and although increasing mobility is to be found among the younger Inuit, most regard their own settlements as home. They are bound to an outside economy for goods and services which they desire and now believe they require, and for the employment which will provide them with these. They must interact with Euro-Canadians, then, in the market place and in other institutionally defined areas. The way in which they manage these arenas is, we suggest, based on the historical events we have described. Such social patterns have transformed the Inuit into an ethnic group within the Canadian national context, as part of the Canadian mosaic.

By 1973, life in Pond Inlet had changed in a variety of ways from the period in the early 1960s shortly after the Inuit of the area had moved into the settlement and ended a way of life based on hunting and trapping. The settlement had been established and new life-styles created which were both responses to the new conditions and attempts, conscious or otherwise, to retain some traditional patterns. To a considerable extent the new responses were predicated on the extensive experiences the Pond Inlet Inuit had had with outsiders over a period of more than a century. These responses, then, were shaped at least partially by the events we have described.

John Matthiasson lived for six weeks in an Inuit home in Pond Inlet during the summer of 1973. One of his first and later most compelling observations was the absence of close social interaction between the Inuit and Euro-Canadian populations. During that six-week period, not one Euro-Canadian entered the Inuit home in which Matthiasson was a guest. While he was visiting another Inuit home one evening–that of friends from a decade before–several young adolescents entered the home and challenged him in a friendly way as to what he was doing there. They were not used to seeing a Euro-Canadian in an Inuit home on other than official business, and were rather startled. We suggest that the Inuit of Pond Inlet have developed a boundary-maintaining technique which discourages Euro-Canadian interaction in the closed environment of their homes. The home is their private rather than public world, and they seek to control it.

Most of the younger Inuit in the settlement had received extensive formal education, and could read, write, and speak English quite fluently. The older people knew only a few practical words and phrases. English was almost never spoken in Inuit homes, although young people would use it on occasion in a joking or semi-mocking manner, usually mimicking Euro-Canadians in positions of authority. The settlement radio station, under the control of the Settlement Council (which consisted completely of Inuit), broadcast exclusively in the Inuit language. Radio was a medium for the exchange of information, gossip, and so on, and was one mechanism for linking the Inuit population together. The use of the telephone was another. The settlement was a long strip of buildings along the coast, with some clustering of houses on the two hills which stood behind. The twenty-minute walk from one side to the other was obviated by the use of the telephone, and regular use was made of it. It served to preserve and enhance social ties between friends and relatives across the settlement. Conversation was carried on in the Inuit language.

Food sharing between members of the Inuit population—a basic characteristic of traditional Inuit culture—was perpetuated in 1973. Although virtually all adult men had full-time employment, and many at high salaries, they would sometimes be required to hunt in the evenings or on weekends, because the Hudson Bay Company store, which had a trade monopoly in the settlement, often ran out of commonly purchased food stuffs such as meat and vegetables during summer months. They would often bring back cuts of seal, which would be distributed among friends and kinsmen. This practice also acted as a bond which linked the members of the Inuit community and excluded Euro-Canadians.

It is difficult in the confines of a paper to identify and analyze the changes that occurred in Pond Inlet and in other Canadian settlements like it between 1963 and 1973. These changes transformed the Inuit population from a people who perceived themselves and were perceived as outsiders, primarily because of racial characteristics, to an ethnic group which has indelible and sustaining ties within the larger society, but at the same time has its own internal resources for the successful management of its own social affairs.

Some of the changes experienced by the Inuit population during the past century have been slow and orderly; for example, the period of centralization of the people into the settlement in the 1960s. Anthropologists and other observers who have looked at the situation of the Canadian Inuit at one or the other of these periods of gradual or rapid change have come up with different models of acculturation, its directions and its consequences, and almost all have made predictions about the ultimate fate of the Inuit. Most have been doom-sayers. On the basis of more recent evidence drawn from one fairly typical Arctic settlement, we tend to reject earlier predictions. We maintain with strong emphasis that the image of the Canadian Inuit of today as an oppressed and exploited product of the whims and vagaries of commercial and governmental priorities is a false image indeed, and one that demeans rather than describes the Inuit.

Had the history of Inuit contact with the European and later Canadian worlds been different, of course, without the events and processes of social separation we have described here, the contemporary situation might be quite different. Then, the Inuit might not have so actively turned in on themselves. On the other hand, had that history been different, the efforts of the Inuit of today to preserve elements of their traditional culture might not have been either as intense or successful. Also, they might not have developed, as they were forced to do by history, the skills which have enabled them to successfully adopt the stance of an ethnic group within Canada. Euro-Canadians in the Canadian Arctic have come and gone. The Inuit have stayed, and plan to continue to do so. While they have bided their time, they have discovered and developed skills which enable them to manage events and situations by which, in the past, they have been controlled.

With the creation in 1972 of the Inuit Tapirisat of Canada the Inuit have found a nationwide voice for their concerns. Its regional organizations now link the national organization with local settlements, no matter how isolated. With their own voluntary associations such as ITC, the Inuit of Canada have taken on one more of the distinguishing marks of other ethnic groups in Canada. The ITC is a quasi-political organization which seeks to gain more advantages for its constituents from the larger society, and its commercial and political institutions, while also lobbying for the right to preserve the distinctive identity of the Inuit within a society which claims to value multiculturalism.

The Inuit may have suffered oppression and exploitation in the past. Most other ethnic groups in Canada have as well, and that may be exactly why they have retained ethnic identities, and now do so in an unself-conscious manner. The Inuit have also survived, and will continue to do so. Long-range predictions are difficult to make. If their position as an ethnic group within Canada is uncertain, the same must be true of other ethnic groups. In conclusion, we suggest that whatever may be the future of the Canadian Inuit, they will survive, and Canadians and the Canadian government will find it to their advantage to accept that fact. They will survive as an ethnic group or not at all.

References

Dailey, R.C., and L.A. Dailey
1961 *The Eskimo of Rankin Inlet: A Preliminary Report.* Ottawa: Northern Coordination and Research Center, N.D.A.N.R.
Damas, D., and J. Helm
1962 "The Contract-Traditional All-Native Community of the Canadian North." *Anthropologica*, 5:1.
Elliott, J.
1971 *Minority Canadians*, Volume I. Scarborough: Prentice-Hall.
Ferguson, J.
1971 "Eskimos in a Satellite Society," in Jean Elliott (ed.) *Minority Canadians*, Volume I. Scarborough: Prentice-Hall. Pp. 15-28.
Honigmann, J., and I. Honigmann
1971 "The Eskimo of Frobisher Bay," in Jean Elliott (ed.) *Minority Canadians*, Volume I. Scarborough: Prentice-Hall. Pp. 55-74.
Matthiasson, J.S.
"Their Fathers Were Hunters." Unpublished manuscript.
Matthiasson, J.S.
1975 "You Scratch My Back and I'll Scratch Yours: Continuities in Inuit Social Relations." *Arctic Anthropology* 12:12-36.
Porter, J.
1965 *The Vertical Mosaic.* Toronto: University of Toronto Press.

13

Occupational Prestige Ratings Among High School Students in the Canadian Arctic

Hyman Burshtyn and Derek G. Smith*

Patterns of occupational prestige ratings have now been widely studied in a large number of countries and across a large number of cultural groups (Inkeles and Rossi, 1956; Hodge, Treiman, and Rossi, 1966). In addition, a considerable number of studies examine intrasocietal patterns and correlations of occupational prestige ratings between different class, status, and ethnic groups (Armer, 1968; Burchinal, 1961; Gist and Bennett, 1963; Haller and Sewell, 1957; Kuvlesky and Ohlendorf, 1968; Kuvlesky and Pelham, 1966; Middleton and Grigg, 1959). The study of occupational prestige ratings is well established in the United States, and the work of Pineo and Porter (1967) has yielded significant understanding of Canadian national patterns. However, in Canada relatively little attention has been given to similarities and differences in occupational prestige ratings between ethnic groups, especially the Native Peoples, and the wider Canadian society. Elliott (1970) has provided a study of an Indian group in this field and Smith has done some preliminary work in the Canadian Arctic, comparing the responses of Inuit, Indians, Métis, and Euro-Canadians attending northern high schools (Smith, 1971, 1974).[1]

International and intercultural comparisons have yielded a consistent pattern of high intercorrelations (Hodge, Treiman, and Rossi, 1966) which have stimulated considerable debate as to whether cultural factors play any significant role in determining occupational prestige patterns. The fundamental similarities in occupational prestige ratings apparently encountered across national, class, ethnic, regional, rural-urban, and "modernized" versus "traditionalistic" boundaries argue strongly against

* Hyman Burshtyn is Associate Professor of Sociology and Derek G. Smith is Assistant Professor of Sociology and Anthropology, both at Carleton University, Ottawa, Ontario.

249

a relativistic "culturalist" explanation, and strongly suggest that the high degree of similarity across many kinds of groups is a "structural" phenomenon arising from widespread exposure to a fundamentally similar structure of industrial society now widespread in the modern world (Inkeles and Rossi, 1956:339; Hodge, Treiman, and Rossi, 1966:310).

Yet an argument has been building on the other side. Haller and Lewis (1962) have called attention to methodological artifacts which could inflate correlations and conceal societal differences. Few samples have been drawn from populations with really simple divisions of labour. Lists tend to be biased toward comparable occupations and ones whose names can be confidently translated between languages. Lists are biased in other ways because the practice of random sampling of occupations has not been followed: indeed, the whole question of how to define the universe of occupations, and to construct a listing of that universe of occupations, although crucial, has hardly been touched. Most studies have used disturbingly short lists, usually purposely selected to include occupations well spread over the hierarchy found to exist in the United States, which is not the same as a representative list.

Nosanchuk, in a perceptive methodological note, has shown that precisely such lists will inflate correlation coefficients. Moreover, he has shown how high correlations can leave room for considerable variations in the way in which groups rate individual occupations relative to one another, possibly concealing "extremely divergent views of the occupational structure" (1972:358). Following Benoit-Smullyan's (1944) distinction between *strata* (aggregates of like-status occupations) and *situses* (sets of occupations in one functional area such as construction, health care, education, finance, etc.), he demonstrates that an extremely high correlation can exist between two societies' rankings so long as they rank broad strata similarly, even if, within each stratum, one inverts the ranking of the other for each situs.

In fact, some studies, such as those by Reiss (1961), Burshtyn, and Pineo and Porter, have not only noted variations, but have investigated some of the systematic ways in which individuals with similar background characteristics rate occupations in ways that are different from the average. Pineo and Porter, for example, point out that French Canadians in Canada rate blue collar, sales, and small managerial jobs higher than English Canadians do, and rate "superior white collar jobs" lower (1967:32). Nosanchuk, more closely inspecting the Pineo and Porter tables, finds that "French raters rank occupations in the medical and construction situses more highly...and those in the educational and government situses consistently lower" (1972:361). Burshtyn found, among other things, that the ratings assigned to menial jobs varied with the socioeconomic status of the respondents, that the ratings assigned to professional and scientific occupations varied directly with the size of city respondents grew up in, and that the ratings assigned to entrepreneurial occupations varied inversely with age (1968:173-180). While Burshtyn did express dissatisfaction with the extent of his ability to predict variations with the variables included in his study, the emergence of strong, interpretable factors shows that there are subgroups in the population that have views of certain *kinds* of occupations that are different from the average. All of this suggests that although the structuralist thesis[2] that structural factors cause great similarity in prestige hierarchies cannot be rejected, interesting variations across groups are to be expected, and groups may project aspects of their uniqueness in the way they rate occupations.

In this paper we shall be asking in what ways the people of the Canadian western North view the prestige of occupations. Unfortunately for this paper we do not have ratings performed by adults and shall be using data from the sample of northern high school students collected and partially analyzed by Smith (1971; 1974).[3] Fortunately, we know that other studies have found that children learn rather early the ranking of occupations (Simmons and Rosenberg, 1971:236-239).[4] Moreover, these data have validity in their own right as an index of the way in which this generation sees the occupational structure.

Smith's[5] previous analyses of these data found high correlations among the rankings produced by the Inuit, Indian, Métis, and Euro-Canadian students, as well as between the whole northern sample and the sample of the whole Canadian society reported by Pineo and Porter on the twenty-six comparable titles, suggesting little northern or ethnic group uniqueness.[6] In this study, we engage in procedures aimed at better detecting whatever differences there might be. First, we will carry out a more detailed comparison with the Pineo and Porter national sample ratings. Second, we shall present the results of a factor analysis of the prestige ratings, and compare the results with those of a similar study made by Burshtyn (1968) to see to what extent the underlying dimensions affecting rating differ. Finally, we shall examine how the factors are related to the ethnicity of the raters, to see to what extent the different northern groups hold different views on occupations. Because there are considerable differences in the ways in which males and females evaluate occupations, we present the data so as to reveal this.

The schools selected for this study were chosen because a) they were among the largest in the North, ensuring reasonable size for analysis, and b) because they were known to contain heterogeneous populations along the dimensions of age, sex, settlement of origin, and, most important for this study, ethnic affiliation.

The portion of the questionnaire analyzed in this study presented the students with forty-eight occupational titles randomly selected from a list of over 200 occupations encountered or known in the North. Respondents were asked to rate the occupational titles on a five-point scale, writing a number 1 beside "those jobs which you think are the best or are the

Table 1

Number of Cases by Ethnicity and Sex

| Ethnicity | Sex | | |
	Males	Females	Total
Métis	32	40	72
Indian	37	30	67
Inuit	203	128	331
European	231	208	439
Total	503	406	906

kinds of jobs you would most like to do," and so on through number 5, to be placed beside "those jobs which you think are the worst or are the kinds of jobs you would least like to do."

The Occupational Prestige Ratings

Table 2 compares the ratings given by the northern students with those given by the national sample. The discrepancies are unusually large for this kind of data.

Probably the most striking feature is the degree to which northern students give relatively low ratings to professional occupations on the list, such as Doctor, Lawyer, Banker, Scientist, Teacher, and Minister or Priest. Part of the explanation may lie in the way in which the rating task was put to the northern students. The question was phrased so as to elicit not only the "general standing" or prestige associated with the occupation, but also to elicit the degree to which raters might aspire to the occupation. Although *perceived prestige* and *desirability for self* can be expected to correlate highly, they are not identical. Therefore, our comparison of northern students' ratings with the Pineo-Porter results is not strictly justified. Nevertheless, on other grounds we feel the low ratings for professional occupations do indeed reflect the positions of these occupations in the North. Lawyers and bankers, for example, are almost unknown in many areas of the North, and many respondents would be trying to guess the characteristics of these occupations on the basis of very little information. The medical profession, while rated highly relative to other occupations, does not get the reverence it gets in the South. In addition, the prestige difference between doctors and nurses in the South (some 20 points), based on large differences in education, skills, authority, responsibility, and remuneration, are little perceived in the North. It can be expected that as southern institutions spread to the North, the ratings given these occupations by Native People will rise. The impact of television will probably be great.

It is difficult to tell precisely on what basis the northern students are allocating ratings from the present data. However, our guess is that the bases are probably not essentially different from those of southerners, and that the northerners simply did not know very much about the training required, the authority and responsibility vested in the professionals, and, probably most important, the upper reaches of earnings. We would expect rapid changes in ratings allocated to the professions as acculturation proceeds. In fact, we feel that the degree of congruence between a northerner's ratings and those of the national sample is a powerful index of acculturation.

Another interesting feature of the comparison is the extent to which northerners give higher ratings to clerical, store sales, and menial unskilled or semi-skilled occupations. In the North these are good, steady, safe, and desirable jobs to which many Native People aspire, but do not always obtain easily. Even the minimal education these jobs require is still scarce among Native People. In addition, there is the effect of the absence of large numbers of middle-level occupations in that, in the North, these jobs place in the 40 to 55 range as compared to 25 to 40 in the South. Even the "worst" jobs rate 3 to 14 points higher in the North.

Almost all clerical, service, skilled trade, and menial occupations are rated more highly by the northern students. In the North, these jobs are valued because they are relatively well paid, and because many of them provide comfortable working conditions. While the menial jobs are rated low relative to other jobs by northerners, there is no clear consensus that these are jobs which should receive a rating of 5. For example, only Garbageman gets an index value below 20. Again, it will be interesting to see what happens to the position of these occupations as knowledge of their extremely low status in the South spreads to the North. This is probably one of the mechanisms by which Native Peoples and other minorities are degraded even as they are becoming acculturated and assimilated: the occupations that once were reasonably rewarding, if attainable only with difficulty, ironically become less rewarding as the very process which better equips one for these jobs also teaches that the occupations are not valued.

It should also be noted that northern students give a lower rating than southerners do to entrepreneurial occupations (such as Contractor). This is consistent with the northerners' marked aversion to self-employment (Smith, 1974:16,18). Employment with large corporations is the most preferred since such occupations are the most secure.

Finally, it is noteworthy that northerners do not give any occupation consistently high ratings. Only three occupations have index values above 60.00, and only one above 61.00. Two of these occupations are at the top of the occupational hierarchy in the North and are associated with the aircraft industry. These are the occupations northerners view as glamorous and rewarding, and the ones to which they most aspire.

Table 2

Comparison of Ratings by Northern Student
and National Canadian[a] Samples

		Samples		
Northern Student				National Canadian
Title	Score	Difference	Score	Title
Airplane Pilot	67.00	.09	66.1	Airline Pilot
Radio Operator	60.60	22.60	38.0	Disc Jockey
Doctor	60.20	-27.00	84.2	Physician
Electrician	58.60	8.40	50.2	Electrician
Airline Stewardess	57.80	.80	57.0	Air Hostess
Lawyer	57.00	-25.30	82.3	Lawyer
Typist & Office Worker	56.00	14.70	41.9	Typist
Typist & Office Worker	56.00	21.00	35.6	Office Clerk
Banker	56.40	-14.50	70.9	Bank Manager
Banker	56.40	14.10	42.3	Bank Teller
Game Officer	56.20			
Nurse	56.00	- 8.70	64.7	Registered Nurse
Airplane Mechanic	55.80	5.50	50.3	Airplane Mechanic
Scientist	54.00	-18.60	72.6	Biologist
Scientist	54.00	-19.50	73.5	Chemist
Teacher	53.80	-12.30	66.1	High School Teacher
Teacher	53.80	- 5.80	59.6	Grade School Teacher
Settlement Admin.	53.60	-15.20	66.8	Administrative Officer
Settlement Admin.	53.60	-15.20	66.8	Federal Civil Servant
Clerk in Store	53.00	26.50	26.5	Sales Clerk in Store
Policeman	52.40	.80	51.6	Policeman
Carpenter	52.20	13.30	38.9	House Carpenter
Nurse's Aide	51.80			
Post Office Job	51.80	14.60	37.2	Post Office Clerk
Diesel Mechanic	50.60			
Contractor	50.20	- 6.30	56.5	Building Contractor
Skidoo Repairman	46.40			
Truck Driver	46.20	13.40	32.8	Trailer Truck Driver
Bulldozer Operator	44.00			
Cook	43.60	13.90	29.7	Cook in Restaurant
Barber Or Hairdresser	42.80	3.50	39.3	Barber

| Samples | | | | |
| Northern Student | | | | National Canadian |
Title	Score	Difference	Score	Title
Barber or				
Hairdresser	42.80	7.60	35.2	Beauty Operator
Sailor in Navy	42.60			
Soldier in Army	39.80	11.40	28.4	Private in the Army
Hunter & Trapper	39.20			
Baker	39.00	.01	38.9	Baker
Carpenter's Helper	39.00	15.90	23.1	Carpenter's Helper
Boat Builder	36.80			
Road Bldg. Crew	36.60			
Miner	35.80	8.20	27.6	Coal Miner
Minister or Priest	34.60	-33.20	67.8	Protestant Minister
Minister or Priest	34.60	-38.20	72.8	Catholic Priest
Trader	34.00			
Waitress	34.00	14.10	19.9	Waitress in Restaurant
General Labourer	33.40	6.90	26.5	Construction Labourer
Railway Worker	33.40	- 3.70	37.1	Railroad Brakeman
Railway Worker	33.40	6.10	27.3	Railroad Sectionhand
Fur Garment				
Worker	33.20	4.40	(28.8	Textile Mill Worker
Bartender	32.00	11.80	20.2	Bartender
Barge Crew	32.00			
Warehouse Man	31.80	10.50	21.3	Warehouse Hand
Tannery Worker	29.20			
Laundry Worker	28.80	9.50	19.3	Laundress
Janitor	26.80	9.50	17.3	Janitor
Reindeer Herder	24.60			
Garbageman	17.80	3.00	14.8	Garbage Collector

[a]Peter C. Pineo and John Porter, "Occupational Prestige in Canada," *Canadian Review of Sociology and Anthropology* IV, 1 (February, 1967).

Table 3 exhibits the ratings as they are related to the sex and ethnicity of the northern respondents. Most of the information in the table will be discussed in the section on factor scores.

Table 3

Occupational Prestige Ratings by Ethnicity and Sex

Title	Ethnicity							
	Métis		Indian		Eskimo		Euro-Canadian	
	M	F	M	F	M	F	M	F
Lawyer	66.0	66.2	60.6	54.7	42.5	35.0	63.6	73.5
Barber/Hairdresser	42.7	63.3	39.0	67.1	31.8	50.5	34.4	51.5
Janitor	37.6	18.4	29.4	25.7	30.3	29.5	27.5	20.0
Policeman	50.7	69.5	51.9	57.9	53.3	41.3	52.8	54.8
Garbageman	22.0	12.1	17.3	12.9	24.0	21.6	16.1	12.6
Nurse's Aide	43.8	69.5	49.3	67.9	41.4	73.8	34.6	61.2
Truck Driver	63.3	32.8	62.8	35.7	65.1	36.8	48.0	29.7
Waitress	30.0	34.1	33.2	47.9	31.5	50.6	24.1	35.5
Sailor in the Navy	48.0	41.9	50.6	45.0	44.9	30.0	48.1	39.6
Carpenter	66.0	48.4	62.6	54.3	61.1	40.6	51.2	48.5
Radio-Operator	66.0	68.9	73.0	61.7	60.4	53.0	61.9	59.3
Reindeer Herder	26.7	15.4	27.5	24.3	28.8	21.7	26.1	22.2
Clerk in a Store	46.7	53.2	48.2	61.0	58.8	71.4	39.9	51.4
Boat-Builder	43.8	31.6	43.1	38.6	43.3	28.9	38.1	32.7
Teacher	50.6	70.5	54.2	63.6	37.3	60.4	47.7	68.8
Tannery Worker	35.3	27.8	33.1	26.3	30.4	30.2	27.2	29.4
Post Office Job	53.3	62.8	55.0	64.5	51.1	65.5	38.0	53.0
Airline Stewardess	51.4	78.7	50.7	81.0	44.0	66.6	42.5	75.7
Bulldozer Operator	61.6	37.6	62.5	36.7	57.6	31.1	46.8	32.1

Doctor	54.0	71.1	55.6	67.9	48.5	51.9	59.4	75.4
Trader	41.3	29.5	39.7	35.0	36.5	33.3	36.5	28.2
Scientist	50.7	54.7	53.8	52.1	46.1	42.3	59.4	62.8
Electrician	74.7	64.2	66.0	57.4	64.3	38.9	61.1	57.4
General Labourer	45.3	27.4	44.4	29.3	39.2	27.1	33.5	29.7
Laundry Worker	34.0	28.0	34.4	34.3	29.3	41.5	22.5	25.4
Cook	47.2	43.7	45.0	52.1	41.2	50.7	40.9	42.2
Carpenter's Helper	57.3	28.9	50.6	39.3	51.3	32.4	37.3	30.2
Banker	47.3	66.3	59.4	65.7	49.7	53.5	53.6	65.4
Soldier in the Army	48.0	34.4	51.2	40.7	42.6	26.7	48.1	34.4
Barge Crew	50.0	24.7	46.3	30.7	38.6	24.7	35.5	23.2
Miner	56.7	32.2	45.6	28.6	43.8	28.2	35.9	29.7
Nurse	45.2	76.5	48.7	70.0	38.9	69.2	43.1	73.3
Bartender	38.7	38.1	36.3	28.6	28.5	25.3	38.8	29.9
Repairman–Skidoos & Kickers	56.0	36.3	56.9	35.0	68.4	38.9	45.2	31.7
Hunter & Trapper	44.7	28.9	46.0	37.1	54.8	37.2	38.5	26.6
Diesel Mechanic	65.3	57.7	61.6	47.9	62.2	34.9	52.9	41.7
Railway Worker	37.3	30.0	43.1	34.3	38.4	27.6	35.9	28.1
Fur-Garment Worker	34.7	33.7	40.6	42.9	32.7	34.2	26.9	37.2
Church Minister or Priest	27.3	40.8	32.4	45.0	39.7	42.5	22.1	37.6
Typist and Office Worker	48.1	77.5	59.4	79.3	51.9	69.4	36.3	68.3
Airplane Pilot	66.2	68.0	70.0	65.0	69.2	48.5	72.8	69.3
Baker	40.8	39.3	37.1	52.1	34.8	42.4	35.9	42.0
Road Building Crew	26.7	56.0	43.8	34.3	45.7	26.9	38.5	30.9
Contractor	50.5	67.9	53.2	44.3	49.3	34.8	55.9	52.1
Airplane Mechanic	56.5	66.0	60.9	45.7	60.8	36.6	63.9	52.8
Game Officer	62.6	74.0	68.8	57.6	52.7	42.5	60.7	57.1
Warehouseman	26.8	38.3	37.3	26.4	38.4	29.4	32.3	26.1
Settlement Administrator	66.9	62.3	73.8	63.6	57.8	53.0	43.5	52.4

The Factor Analysis

A successful factor analysis will identify all (or, at least, the important) properties of the objects which underlie variations in the way in which they are rated by the respondents.[7]

The factor structure is of interest because it can reveal aspects or dimensions of occupations to which members of a group are differentially sensitive. Factor analysis provides another tool for the examination of inter-ethnic and intercultural prestige ratings of occupations. Traditionally, the way of examining inter-ethnic and intercultural differences in occupational prestige rating has been to look for differences in the average ratings assigned to the occupations by different groups. This has been the tradition of Reiss (1961), and Pineo and Porter (1967), to mention but a few. However, factor analysis of occupational prestige ratings may be a more sensitive indicator of group similarities and differences. For example, Burshtyn (1968) found that only seven interpretable factors in an analysis of occupational prestige ratings by a sample of Ottawa heads of households accounted for most of the co-variation in the ratings. He named these factors Lower-Class, Professional, Entrepreneurial, Apparent Autonomy, Official Power, Skilled Trades, and Quasi-Professional. The finding that one or more of these factors did not emerge, or that other factors did emerge in the analysis of the Arctic data, could help to identify significant similarities or differences in orientations to occupations between southern and northern Canadian populations. These might relate to ethnicity. Even if the same factor structure did emerge in both the Ottawa and the Arctic samples, particular occupations might load on different factors, indicating that the meanings of the occupations were different for Arctic high school students, even if their places in the prestige hierarchy were the same.

Table 4 shows the results of the factor analysis after rotation.[8] To facilitate interpretation, Table 5 was constructed, showing the ten highest loadings for each factor and the name assigned. For the most part, it was not difficult to name the factors on the basis of what seemed to distinguish jobs that had high loadings from those that did not.

The title of Factor 10 probably calls for some explanation. We called it "Moral Tone/Alcohol Use" mainly because the only title with a really high loading was Bartender, and partly because other occupations loading moderately, such as Barge Crew and Miner, may be associated with drinking for many respondents. The other piece of information used to name the factor was that the title Minister or Priest had a *negative* loading on this factor.

There are both striking similarities and differences when the northern factor structure is compared to the one reported by Burshtyn for the Ottawa area. Some of the differences are clearly attributable to differences in the lists of occupational titles used. Others may be due to differences in instructions, as previously noted. Finally, some are probably due to real

258

differences between the way northerners and southerners view occupations.

The most striking similarity is the emergence of the factors "Professional," "Skilled Trades," and "Menial" (or "Lower-Class")[9] in both analyses. Obviously these are major dimensions in terms of which occupations are perceived and which form the basis of individual differences in the evaluation of jobs in *both* the North and the South. (Table 6 indicates that this factor does not arise simply because of differences between Euro-Canadians, on the one hand, and Métis, Indians, and Inuit on the other.) Probably these are such basic dimensions that they will always appear in any group that has a system of differentiated occupations, and what will be of significance for cross-cultural analysis will be not their presence or absence but, rather, the *relative* strength of the three.

In fact, one of the major and most striking differences between the North and South lies in the factor which emerges as the strongest: in the South it is the Menial factor, while in the North, it is the Skilled Trades factor.

Part of the reason for this is that among the northern students, there are greater differences in how perceived skill of jobs is evaluated than among southerners. But this is not the whole story. Just as important, and highly significant for our search for cultural differences, is the fact that *other* dimensions of jobs take on a salience in the North they lack in the South. A detailed examination of the factor analysis shows this. Many of the jobs which load strongly on the Lower-Class factor in the South load strongly on other factors in the North—factors which do not emerge at all in the South. Janitor and Garbageman, which load so strongly on Lower Class in Ottawa they help to define the factor, form the basis for a new factor in the North. Other "menial" occupations loading (moderately) on the same factor as Janitor and Garbageman are Truckdriver, Laundry Worker, Labourer, Warehouseman, and Barge Crew. Truckdriver loaded virtually exclusively on the Menial factor in the South; in the North, its heaviest loading is on the Skills factor, and the rest of its strength is dissipated among several other factors. Clothes Presser, Laundry, in the Ottawa list (comparable to Laundry Worker on the northern list) similarly loaded virtually exclusively on the Menial factor. It still loads on that factor in the North, but not nearly so strongly.

Finally, there is the emergence of the factor we have named Traditional Occupations. This factor could not emerge in the South because the occupations were not included in the list. Yet it is not likely that their inclusion would have resulted in such a strong factor—or any at all—in the South. The southerner would probably perceive them primarily as menial jobs, and his rating of them would be a function of how he tended to rate menial jobs generally. He would probably also respond to the fact that they involve specialized skills of the type that characterize skilled trades or crafts. Northern students respond to these two aspects of these jobs, but

Table 4

Ten Factor Orthogonal Simple Structure Solution

Variables	h²	Factors									
		1	2	3	4	5	6	7	8	9	10
LAWYER[a]	.67	-.02	.78	.07	-.05	-.13	.08	.09	.00	-.05	.08
BARBER	.44	-.10	.21	.47	.06	.25	.08	.19	.21	.05	.01
JANITOR	.65	.17	-.00	.06	.06	-.03	.05	.17	.16	.73	.02
POLICEMA	.54	.18	.47	-.00	-.03	.12	.48	.04	.04	.09	-.11
GARBAGEM	.67	.13	-.12	-.03	.09	.08	-.06	.00	-.04	.78	.03
NURSEAID	.73	-.07	.10	.80	-.01	.16	-.03	.02	.07	.09	-.14
TRUKDRIVER	.58	.59	-.21	-.12	.17	.03	.21	.06	-.02	.25	.08
WAITRESS	.55	.02	-.17	.63	.02	.30	.02	.05	.11	.07	.09
SAILOR	.70	.22	.17	.04	.13	-.05	.76	.07	.04	-.07	.01
CARPENTR	.52	.59	.14	-.09	.11	.04	.00	.17	.25	.06	-.15
RADIOOPR	.38	.40	.35	.15	.03	.20	.10	.01	.02	-.10	.08
RRNDRHER	.53	.17	-.01	-.00	.65	-.10	.07	.21	.04	.04	-.00
STORCLERK	.62	.03	-.19	.20	.05	.71	-.01	.01	.10	.12	-.00
BOTBLDER	.48	.46	.16	-.01	.35	-.03	-.00	.26	.08	.03	-.16
TEACHER	.51	-.24	.55	.22	-.08	.24	.00	.07	.07	.06	-.02
TANNERYWORKER	.53	.14	.12	.09	.34	.10	.01	.59	-.01	.03	.01
POSTOFFJ	.63	.04	.09	.19	.02	.70	-.02	.24	.13	.06	.07
STWRDESS	.67	-.04	.20	.76	-.00	.09	.01	-.01	-.00	-.14	.08
BLLDZRO	.60	.73	-.04	-.08	.12	-.00	.14	.03	-.01	.09	.08
DOCTOR	.68	-.03	.77	.20	.07	.07	.08	-.08	.01	-.04	-.03
TRADER	.53	.15	.13	-.02	.62	.08	.10	.04	.12	.11	.22

SCIENTIST	.56	.05	.72	.08	.04	-.06	.08	.04	.02	-.01	-.07
ELECTRCIAN	.60	.58	.48	.00	-.06	.00	.06	-.03	-.01	-.05	-.06
LABOURER	.40	.34	-.00	-.05	.04	.07	.12	.46	-.01	.18	.09
LAUNDRYWOKER	.51	.01	-.12	.19	.08	.19	.07	.47	.35	.20	-.11
COOK	.76	.04	.01	.13	.12	.06	.05	-.00	.83	.11	.01
CARPENTER'SHEL	.57	.53	-.12	-.17	.15	.12	-.05	.27	.29	.17	-.05
BANKER	.55	-.00	.56	.13	.06	.37	.10	.07	.13	-.13	.10
SOLDIER	.74	.20	.15	-.07	.04	-.06	.80	.05	.02	.01	.08
BARGECREW	.55	.48	-.09	.00	.21	.02	.25	.22	-.00	.17	.32
MINER	.37	.47	-.00	.07	.07	-.04	.10	.04	.03	.19	.27
NURSE	.73	-.10	.34	.75	-.00	.06	-.07	-.03	.10	-.03	-.04
BARTENDR	.63	.13	.11	.03	.12	.05	.07	-.00	.09	.09	.74
SKDRPRM	.63	.68	-.12	-.15	.26	.14	.05	-.08	.00	.14	-.04
HUNTRAP	.67	.34	-.20	-.12	.66	.04	.04	-.10	.10	.16	-.05
DIESMECH	.62	.76	.90	.00	-.01	-.00	.09	-.04	-.06	-.04	-.02
RAILWRKR	.51	.52	.04	.04	.11	-.00	.20	.41	.02	-.01	.06
FURGATWR	.51	.08	.15	.26	.53	.14	-.03	.29	.06	-.07	-.00
MINPRIST	.56	-.02	.21	.17	.29	.29	.20	-.05	.09	.20	-.46
TYPSTOFF	.60	-.06	.16	.34	-.05	.65	-.05	.03	.00	-.11	-.08
AIRPILOT	.59	.40	.51	.09	.07	-.16	.22	-.25	-.00	-.07	.05
BAKER	.70	.05	.17	.17	.10	.14	.01	.06	.76	-.05	.10
ROADCREW	.55	.61	-.05	-.01	.13	-.07	.00	.33	.05	.06	.15
CONTRACTOR	.51	.47	.43	-.03	.06	-.01	-.04	.21	.00	-.05	.19
PLANMECH	.61	.62	.40	.02	.01	-.06	.12	-.16	-.05	-.02	.06
GAMEOFFC	.52	.32	.39	-.09	.26	.07	.07	.00	.11	-.00	.22
WAREHSMN	.45	.39	.05	-.10	.23	.25	-.11	.17	.01	.29	.17
SETADMIN	.55	.25	.45	.00	.13	.47	-.07	-.15	.01	.00	-.05

aSee Table 3 for Occupational Titles exactly as presented to respondents.

261

Table 5

Ten Highest Loading Items on
Each Factor, Ten Factor Solution

Factor 1. Skilled Trades
.77 Diesel mechanic
.74 Bulldozer operator
.69 Skidoo/Kicker repairman
.62 Airplane mechanic
.61 Road building crew
.60 Truck driver
.60 Carpenter
.59 Electrician
.53 Carpenter's helper
.52 Railway worker

Factor 2. Professional
.78 Lawyer
.78 Doctor
.73 Scientist
.57 Banker
.56 Teacher
.51 Airplane pilot
.48 Electrician
.47 Policeman
.45 Settlement administrator
.44 Contractor

Factor 3. Female Occupations
.80 Nurse's aide
.77 Stewardess
.75 Nurse
.63 Waitress
.48 Barber or Hairdresser
.34 Typist and officeworker
.26 Fur-garment worker
.22 Teacher
.21 Clerk in a store
.20 Doctor

Factor 4. Traditional Native
.66 Hunter and Trapper
.66 Reindeer herder
.63 Trader

Factor 6. Military
.81 Soldier
.76 Sailor
.49 Policeman
.26 Barge crew
.22 Air plane pilot
.22 Truckdriver
.21 Railway worker
.20 Minister or priest
.12 Airplane mechanic
.12 General labourer

Factor 7. Menial
.59 Tannery worker
.47 Laundry worker
.46 General labourer
.33 Road building crew
.42 Railway worker
.29 Fur-garment worker
.27 Carpenter's helper
.26 Boat-builder
.25 Airplane pilot
.24 Post office job

Factor 8. Kitchen Work
.84 Cook
.77 Baker
.35 Laundry worker
.29 Carpenter's helper
.25 Carpenter
.22 Barber or hairdresser
.17 Janitor
.13 Post office job
.14 Banker
.12 Trader

Factor 9. Janitor/Garbageman
.78 Garbageman
.74 Janitor
.30 Warehouseman

.54 Fur-garment worker
.36 Boat-builder
.35 Tannery worker
.27 Skidoo/Kicker repairman
.26 Game officer
.29 Church minister or priest
.24 Warehouseman

Factor 5. Clerical
.72 Clerk in a store
.70 Post office job
.65 Typist and office worker
.47 Settlement administrator
.37 Banker
.30 Waitress
.30 Church minister or priest
.25 Barber or hairdresser
.26 Warehouseman
.25 Teacher

.26 Truckdriver
.21 Church minister or priest
.20 Laundry worker
.18 Carpenter's helper
.18 General labourer
.17 Barge crew
.20 Nurse

Factor 10. Moral Tone/Alcohol Use
.74 Bartender
.46 Church minister or priest
.32 Barge crew
.27 Miner
.23 Game officer
.19 Airplane mechanic
.18 Warehouseman
.16 Carpenter
.16 Boat-builder

---

in addition to, and independent of this, some give these jobs relatively high ratings *as a set*, while some do the opposite, which is what gives rise to the emergence of the factor. The factor analysis, in other words, is sensitive to the polarization, in the North, of "traditionalists" and "non-traditionalists"–an issue which would not have much relevance in the South.

The emergence in the North of the Moral Tone/Alcohol factor is also of interest. It is dominated by the occupation Bartender, which in Ottawa loaded mainly on the Menial factor. Clearly, in the North, some occupations, because of their moral connotation, are being evaluated differently than in the South. In the South, an occupation such as Bartender is being evaluated according to how respondents react to its "meniality" rather than to its association with alcohol or its "moral tone."

Besides Public School Teacher, Restaurant Cook, and Nightclub Singer, there were no occupations that one could readily identify with "female" occupations.

The factor analysis, we feel, suggests rather strongly that northerners are sensitive to a variety of aspects of occupations which reflect emphases and concerns current in the culture. It does this by indicating that the "meniality" of jobs is not nearly so important an aspect in the North as it is in the South and that other aspects, such as associated skills, the relationship to alcohol use, or the relationship to the traditional way of life, figure more prominently. Thus, some unique features of orientations of northerners to occupations are reflected.

The factor analysis thus far also suggests some of the continuities or points of articulation with southern culture: not only is the general hierarchy of occupations broadly similar to that of the South, but the major dimensions along which variability of judgements develop are also similar.

Ethnicity, Sex, and Orientations Towards Occupations

Table 6 shows how the factors are related to the ethnicity and sex of the respondents.[10]

The most striking feature of Table 6 is the lack of any kind of clear-cut patterns. No two groups show consistent similarities. Moreover, the size of the standard deviations and of the differences between the sexes in the same groups indicates that the within-ethnicity variability is large. Finally, the variability is difficult to explain even in an *ad hoc* fashion. The following may be noted:

Native respondents prize Skilled Trades more than Euro-Canadians do, and, within each ethnicity, males prize them more than females do. For reasons we cannot discern, Inuit females are especially negative on this factor.

Females consistently rate the Female Occupations factor high. This must be due at least partly to the instructions suggesting that the task was to rate in terms of how desirable the job would be to the respondent. It is rather interesting that Euro-Canadians rate these jobs considerably lower than the Natives do, and that Euro-Canadian males rate them especially low.

Most of the variation in ratings of Traditional Native Occupations is within groups. Indians and Inuit value them more than Euro-Canadians and Métis do, but the differences are not large.

It is not surprising to find that Natives score Clerical Occupations considerably higher than Euro-Canadians do, and that females score it higher than males do.[11] This reflects definitions of desirability of jobs in the North. Among the Native groups, only Métis males score this factor below average. The very low scores of Euro-Canadian males stand in stark contrast to the way in which the Indian and Inuit males and Native females define these jobs.

There is little that is noteworthy for the next three factors. Indians are a little more positively oriented toward Military Occupations than are the other groups; Métis males are more positive on Menial Occupations than other groups–although Indian males are somewhat above average–and Indian females are positive on Kitchen Work. Inuit positively evaluate the Janitor/Garbageman Occupations factor. Other female groups give it low ratings, but Métis males rate it high. Inuit negatively evaluate Alcohol Use Occupations, as do Indian females, but Indian males score somewhat above average, while Métis and Euro-Canadian males score considerably above average.

Table 6
Means of Factor Scores, by Ethnicity and Sex

1. Skilled Trades

	M.	F.	Total	Diff.
Métis	+.79	-.17	+.25	.96
Indian	+.58	-.25	+.17	.83
Inuit	+.66	-.63	+.17	1.29
Euro	+.04	-.44	-.19	.48
Total	+.38	-.46	-	.84

6. Military

	M.	F.	Total	Diff.
Métis	-.09	+.04	-.02	-.13
Indian	+.22	+.19	+.21	+.03
Inuit	+.09	-.22	-.03	+.31
Euro	+.16	-.19	-.01	+.35
Total	+.12	-.15	-	+.27

2. Professional

	M.	F.	Total	Diff.
Métis	+.06	+.49	+.30	-.43
Indian	+.03	+.00	+.04	+.03
Inuit	-.46	-.61	-.52	+.15
Euro	+.19	+.53	+.35	-.34
Total	-.09	+.13	-	-.22

7. Menial

	M.	F.	Total	Diff.
Métis	+.44	-.17	+.10	+.16
Indian	+.22	+.06	+.17	+.16
Inuit	-.18	+.00	-.11	-.18
Euro	-.02	+.13	+.04	-.15
Total	-.04	+.05	-	-.09

3. Female Occupations

	M.	F.	Total	Diff.
Métis	-.26	+.57	+.20	-.83
Indian	-.22	+.67	+.19	-.89
Inuit	-.38	+.65	+.01	-1.03
Euro	-.50	+.41	-.07	-.91
Total	-.42	+.52	-	-.94

8. Kitchen Work

	M.	F.	Total	Diff.
Métis	+.14	-.03	+.04	+.17
Indian	-.03	+.44	+.15	-.47
Inuit	-.16	+.17	-.03	-.33
Euro	+.00	-.01	+.00	+.01
Total	-.06	+.08	-	-.14

4. Traditional Native

	M.	F.	Total	Diff.
Métis	-.13	-.38	-.27	+.25
Indian	+.17	+.09	+.10	+.08
Inuit	+.22	+.05	+.15	+.17
Euro	-.02	-.15	-.08	+.13
Total	+.08	-.09	-	+.17

9. Janitor-Garbageman

	M.	F.	Total	Diff.
Métis	+.36	-.34	-.03	+.70
Indian	-.08	-.38	-.20	+.30
Inuit	+.24	+.30	+.27	-.06
Euro	-.05	-.29	-.16	+.24
Total	+.09	-.09	-	+.18

5. Clericals

	M.	F.	Total	Diff.
Métis	-.24	+.50	+.17	-.74
Indian	+.20	+.58	+.34	-.38
Inuit	+.20	+.62	+.36	-.42
Euro	-.67	-.03	-.37	-.64
Total	-.23	+.27	-	-.50

10. Moral Tone/Alcohol Use

	M.	F.	Total	Diff.
Métis	+.48	+.03	+.23	+.45
Indian	+.16	-.25	-.07	+.41
Inuit	-.35	-.26	-.32	-.09
Euro	+.43	-.04	+.21	+.47
Total	+.10	-.09	-	+.19

Note: The bottom rows (total) of each sub-table may be read to indicate the relationship of sex to the Factor, with ethnicity not controlled; the last column may be read to indicate the relationship of ethnicity to the Factor, with sex not controlled.

Another way to summarize the visible patterns is to attempt to describe the factor profiles for each group. Compared to Native groups, Euro-Canadians tend to rate low the Skilled Trades, Female, and Clerical factors. They do not rate any factor particularly high, except perhaps the Professional factor. Euro-Canadian males tend especially to rate low the Female and Clerical factors, and to rate high occupations associated with alcohol. Euro-Canadian females rate the Professional factor especially high and the Menial factor low.

Inuit show the greatest similarity between males and females. They both score the Professional and Alcohol-associated occupations low, and rate highly the Clerical and Janitor/Garbageman factors. However, they diverge greatly on the Skilled Trades, with the males elevating it, the females depressing it. The opposite happens on Female Occupations.

Indian males tend to be close to the average for the Native groups on most factors. They elevate Skilled Trades, as do all Native males, and they value the Military factor more than any other Native group does. Indian females are noteworthy only for the extent to which they elevate the Kitchen Work factor.

Métis males probably have the strongest factor profile of any group. They react very positively to the Skilled Trades, Menial occupations, and those associated with alcohol. Métis females elevate Professional occupations, but are fairly negative to Traditional, Menial, and Kitchen Work occupations.

Overall, there is no particular pattern discernible, let alone interpretable. In general, there is no consistent tendency for males and females from the same ethnic group to score occupations in similar ways. If structural position affects how one perceives the prestige of occupations, then it is clear that neither sex nor ethnicity is of overriding importance. Rather, it would seem that it is the conjunction of sex *and* ethnicity that defines unique structural configurations influencing the rating of occupations.

Discussion and Conclusion

Traditionally, cross-cultural or cross-national comparisons of occupational prestige ratings have relied on simple correlation of the prestige profiles. Such studies have consistently yielded high correlations, regardless of the cultural or national groups being surveyed. On the basis of this, it has been argued that there is a basic occupational prestige structure which, with the advance of industrialization and its effects even in "underdeveloped" areas, has become a world-wide phenomenon. The opinion is that there has been a homogenization of attitudes towards occupations that is the result of essentially similar responses to essentially the same widespread occupational structure. As a corollary, it is argued that the local cultural peculiarities have no major effect on the evaluation of occupations. The consistently high cross-national and cross-cultural correlations of occupational prestige structures, however, since they usually rely on one simple measure of correlation, may in fact be concealing real cultural or local differences. We have argued that a comparison of factor structures may reveal local cultural and/or structural effects.

The national prestige ranking of occupations for all of Canada is now well established (Pineo and Porter, 1967). Few comparisons of subsocietal entities, such as ethnic groups, and particularly Native Peoples, to the national occupational prestige ranking, have been made. Exceptions are Elliott (1970) and Smith (1971:1974) who have made first attempts at studies of this kind. Smith (1974) has already shown that there is high intercorrelation among the hierarchies produced by Arctic Indian, Métis, Inuit, and Euro-Canadian high school students, and a high correlation between the northern hierarchy and the one produced by the Pineo and Porter national sample (Smith 1971:436-437). On the basis of such evidence, one might readily conclude that there was little room for variation.

In this study, however, the occupational prestige ratings of the northern respondents were factor-analyzed and compared with the results of a factor-analysis of ratings of a southern group. Despite the great similarities indicated by simple correlation techniques, the factor analyses show important differences. We argue that factor analysis is a technique sensitive to local differences in the ways in which occupations are rated, and that factor analysis is a useful technique in the exploration of ethnic (or cultural and national) differences.

In the case of northern high school students, ten interpretable factors emerged. Significantly, three factors, Professional, Skilled Trades, and Menial, were similar to the factors in the southern sample. These indicate that, in general, the *basic* underlying dimensions of occupations along which variation in ratings can develop is shared. Also significant, and to a degree qualifying this statement, is the fact that whereas among northern ethnic groups the Skilled Trades factor was strongest, in the southern group the Menial or Lower-Class factor was strongest. In short, while the northern groups share the same general perspectives on occupations as southerners do, the northerners seem more sensitive to, and exhibit more variability with regard to, the degree of skill involved than to the meniality of an occupation.

Also significant is the emergence in the northern sample of at least two situation-specific factors: Traditional Native Occupations and occupations associated with Moral Tone/Alcohol Use. The Traditional Native Occupations factor is of considerable interest, indicating that among Native People there is considerable polarization of attitude towards these occupations—some esteeming them highly, some giving them a very negative evaluation. Although Métis score this factor below average, this variation is not strongly related to ethnicity: most of it is within ethnicities. Of particular note, more females than males give these occupations a negative rating. This variation probably reflects the transitional nature of the present northern occupational structure.

Given the prominence of alcohol problems in today's North, it should not be surprising that a number of occupations associated with alcohol should emerge as a distinct factor. Loading on this factor are certain occupations, such as Miner and Barge Crew, which are held by transient workers in the North who often engage in rowdy and public displays of drinking. Again, for this to emerge as a factor, there must be polarization of attitudes within the northern community to the association with alcohol. Significantly, Indian and Inuit females tend to give such occupations a negative rating, while Euro-Canadian males give it a positive rating.

The other factors which emerged in the northern sample, Female Occupations, Military, Kitchen Work, and Janitor/Garbageman, are a little more difficult to interpret. The Female Occupations factor is probably in part an artifact of the instructions, in part a reflection of differences between males and females in the evaluation of occupations identified with females. The Military factor probably emerged because, in places where the military have been prominent in the North, they are held in low esteem. The Janitor/Garbageman factor has probably emerged because, while some Native People disdain the meniality of these jobs, others value the security or the comfort of working indoors associated with them, compared to the other unskilled or general labour occupations available.

In short, despite general similarities in the South, there is a different patterning of orientations to occupations in the North, significant for understanding the aspirations and frustrations of the people living there. For example, our study clearly suggests that Native northern male students aspire to skilled trades and females to clerical occupations. Especially in the more traditional northern settlements, such occupations are few in number and, in the past at least, have not typically been held by Native persons. What appears to be happening now is that Native People are valuing and aspiring to occupations to which they as yet have limited access. This discrepancy between aspiration and reality is a fertile breeding ground for the social malaise and disorders shown to exist, for example, in Clairmont (1963).

The trend appears to be for Native People to end up in general labour, unskilled, and semi-skilled occupations, with only a few achieving the valued skilled trades. One can readily predict that since northern Native students have occupational prestige patterns and aspirations beyond what they are likely to achieve, much dissatisfaction will result. Whatever Native People actually acquire by way of occupations, they will tend to judge the rewards and satisfactions by the prestige and aspirational criteria they hold and which are revealed by this study.

Notes

1. Smith and Burshtyn have also collected more extensive data of this kind on adult males in the western Arctic region, which unfortunately are as yet insufficiently analyzed to include in this paper.

2. There are actually two variants of the "structuralist" argument. One is that all industrial societies will show similar hierarchies regardless of local culture because of the functional requisites of such societies. When it was discovered that non-industrialized societies also apparently produced hierarchies strongly correlating with those of the United States, the argument was extended to cover "national societies of any degree after complexity and even to all societies, whether industrialized or not, because of similar constraints placed on evaluation by the structure of work, the system or rewards for work, and the need to maintain at least a gross consistency in the distribution of different kinds of rewards" (Hodge, Treiman and Rossi, 1966:310). There does not seem to be much consideration given to the argument that the similarities in industrialized societies may stem not from functional and structural constraints but rather from the diffusion of western values–i.e. cultural factors. The Inkeles and Rossi (1956) heritage seems to dictate that only *deviations* from the American pattern shall be regarded as the result of the operation of "cultural" factors. For the sake of consistency we use this terminology, but it should be pointed out that cultural variation is often explained through the invocation of structural factors. It would probably be best to recognize that "structuralist" explanations could be invoked to explain both cross-societal similarities and differences, and reserve the term "cultural explanation" for an explanation which invokes the operation of local *values* which have some degree of freedom from a structural base. See Smith (1971; 1974) and Nosanchuk (1972) for other kinds of critiques of the polarization of the "structuralist" and the "culturalist" positions.

3. The data examined in this paper were collected in a questionnaire study of over 1,000 high school students in six schools in Aklavik, Inuvik, Fort McPherson, Yellowknife, Churchill, and Frobisher Bay between 1971 and 1976. The respondent population accounted for nearly all students in grades 7 through 12 (including the Inuvik "occupational class"). The data in the Mackenzie area were collected by Smith during field research for a doctoral dissertation at Harvard University, and the data at Yellowknife, Churchill, and Frobisher Bay were collected by a research assistant, Michael H. Capelle, under Smith's direction. The cooperation of the school staff and the respondents is gratefully acknowledged. All of the research was supported by the Department of Indian Affairs and Northern Development, to which we owe our thanks. In particular, we owe much to the support and encouragement of A.J. Kerr, Chief of the Northern Science Research Group in that department.

Hyman Burshtyn became involved in later stages of the data analysis, especially the factor analysis, since he has made a similar study in the Ottawa area (Burshtyn, 1968).

4. Simmons and Rosenberg (1971:238), using thirteen occupations well spread over the prestige continuum, found the Pearsonian product moment correlation between the 1963 American adult ratings and elementary, junior, and senior high school students' ratings to be .96, .97, and .98 while the Spearman rhos were .93, .92, and .92: Baxter and Nosanchuk (1975:40) report Spearman rhos between Pineo and Porter ratings and those of a sample of Vancouver children range from only .52 for the 9-10 group to .83 for the 17-18-year-olds. However, they used only nine matching occupations which had relatively low variance in prestige, and included Policeman, which ranked first among the youngest children, sharply reducing the correlation. With Policeman removed, rho for the remaining eight occupations is .70.

5. In the 1971 and 1974 reports by Smith, *median* ratings for various subgroups were computed, and the correlations coefficients were reported as Spearman rank order rhos between subgroups across median ratings, showing the degree of similarity between groups in the way in which they "arranged" titles on an occupational prestige scale. In the present study, means, rather than medians, were computed, and the correlations were Pearsonian product moment coefficients of correlations, among occupations, across individual ratings. This rendered the results comparable to other studies of occupational prestige ratings, especially those of Pineo and Porter (1967) and Burshtyn (1968).

6. Ratings were made in terms of a 1-9 scale in the Pineo-Porter study, and 1-5 in the present study. A rating of 1 represented the highest rating in both studies. The mean ratings in the Pineo-Porter study were then transformed to a 10-90 scale, with 90 now representing the highest possible prestige. To render comparable the mean ratings (M) in the present study, they were transformed through the formula $Y = (5-M) 20 + 10$.

7. For good introductory treatments of factor analysis see Nie, et al. (1976:ch. 24) or Harmon (1960); for a discussion of the interpretation of the results of the factor analysis of occupational prestige ratings, see Burshtyn (1968:161-173).

Factor analysis may be used to isolate aspects of objects being rated towards which the raters have complex or multidimensional attitudes. Often these attitudinal dimensions are latent, in the sense that the raters may not be conscious of the fact that they are responding to those properties of the rated objects. Usually (although not necessarily) the factors correspond to subsets of objects whose ratings are highly intercorrelated. Such intercorrelations tend to arise because some raters tend to give all members of the subset higher than average ratings, while others tend to give all members of the subset lower than average ratings. It is assumed that they do this because they perceive a commonality to the subset to which they react either positively or negatively. For example, it may be that some occupations are perceived to be primarily "for females." If, in addition, some raters consistently give "female" occupations above-average ratings, while some give them below-average ratings, a factor would arise with high loadings for "female" occupations. This, in fact, happens in the data examined in this paper. It is of course possible for some occupations to have more than one property towards which attitudes differ. The occupation will then "load" on more than one factor.

Factors are named through an artful inductive process: the name reflects what occupations which load strongly on a factor share that differentiates them from occupations which do not load strongly on that factor.

Factor scores may be computed for each rater on each factor. A high score on a factor would typically mean that the individual tends to give occupations having the characteristics named by the factor higher than average ratings on that account, i.e., he positively evaluates that characteristic.

8. A Principal Components factor analysis was performed using the PA1 option of SPSS, Nie, et al. (1976:479-480). The ten factors with latent roots (eigenvalues) larger than 1.00 were rotated to orthogonal simple structure using the Varimax criterion. The ten factors account for 57.6 per cent of the total variance of the forty-eight variables.

9. Burshtyn (1968:164) called the factor "Lower-Class Connotation." What is obviously the same factor emerges in the present study, but is here called "Menial" because the patterning of the loadings suggests it reflects more of a "menial" than of a "lower-class" connotation in the North.

10. This factor might not have emerged had the instruction in the North not contained such phrases as "the kinds of jobs you would most like to do." The instructions containing such phrases were also followed by a paragraph requesting males to respond to female jobs in terms of whether they would like their female relatives to have them, and vice versa. One wonders how well the device worked. The variability of means of factor scores, however, indicates the factor would arise even if the analysis were done separately for males and females.

11. This is not due to a "female job" connotation, since, in effect, that aspect has been "partialled out" by the emergence of Factor 3.

References

Armer, J.M.
1968 "Intersociety and Intrasociety Correlations of Occupational Prestige." *American Journal of Sociology*, 74: 1, 28-36.

Baxter, E.H., and T.A. Nosanchuk
1975 "The Learning of the Occupational Hierarchy." Pp. 28-50, in *Socialization, Social Stratification and Ethnicity,* Robert A. Pike and Elia Zureik (eds.) Toronto: McClelland and Stewart (The Carleton Library).

Burchinal, G.
1961 "Differences in Educational and Occupational Aspirations of Farm, Small-Town and City Boys." *Rural Sociology,* 26:107-121.

Burshtyn, H.
1968 "A Factor-Analytic Study of Occupational Prestige Ratings." *Canadian Review of Sociology and Anthropology,* 5:156-180.

Clairmont, D.H.T.
1968 *Deviance Among Indians and Eskimos at Aklavik,* Ottawa: Department of Northern Affairs and National Resources, Northern Coordination and Research Centre.

Elliott, J.G.
1970 *Educational and Occupational Aspirations and Expectations: A Comparative Study of Indian and Non-Indian Youth.* Antigonish, N.S.: St. Francis Xavier University.

Haller, A.O., and W.H. Sewell
1957 "Farm Residence and Levels of Educational and Occupational Aspirations." *American Journal of Sociology* 72:210-216.

Haller, A.O., and D.M. Lewis
1962 "The Hypothesis of Intersocietal Similarity in Occupational Prestige Hierarchies," *American Journal of Sociology,* 72:210-216.

Harmon, H.
1960 *Modern Factor Analysis.* Chicago: University of Chicago Press.

Hodge, R.W., D.J. Treiman and P.H. Rossi
1966 "A Comparative Study of Occupational Prestige." pp. 309-321 in *Class, Status and Power* 2nd. ed., Reinhard Bendix and Seymour M. Lipset (ed.) New York: Free Press.

Hodge, R.W., P.M. Seigal and P.H. Rossi
1966 "Occupational Prestige in the United States: 1925-1963." Pp. 322-334, in *Class, Status and Power,* 2nd ed., Reinhard Bendix and Seymour M. Lipset, (eds) New York: Free Press.

Inkeles, A., and P.H. Rossi
1956 "National Comparisons of Occupational Prestige." *American Journal of Sociology,* 61:329-339.

Kuvlesky, W.P., and G.W. Ohlendorf
1968 "A Rural-Urban Comparison of the Occupational Status Orientations of Negro Boys." *Rural Sociology*, 33:2,141-152.
Kuvlesky, W.P., and J. Pelham
1966 *Occupational Status Orientations of Rural Youth: Structured Annotations and Evaluations of the Research Literature.* College Station: Texas A. & M. University, Department of Agriculture, Economics and Sociology, Technical Report No. 66-3.
Middleton, R. and C.M. Grigg
1969 "Rural-Urban Differences in Aspirations." *Rural Sociology*, 24:347-354.
Nie, N.H., *et. al.*
1975 *SPSS: Statistical Package for the Social Sciences*, 2nd. ed.. Toronto: McGraw-Hill.
Nosanchuk, T.A.
1972 "A Note in the Use of the Correlation Coefficient for Assessing the Similarity of Occupational Rankings." *Canadian Review of Sociology and Anthropology*, 9:357-365.
Pineo, P.C., and J. Porter
1967 "Occupational Prestige in Canada." *Canadian Review of Sociology and Anthropology*, 4:24-40.
Reiss, A.J., *et. al.*
1961 *Occupations and Social Status.* New York: Free Press.
Simmons, R.A., and M. Rosenberg
1971 "Functions of Children's Perceptions of the Stratification System." *American Sociology Review, 36:235-250.*
Smith, D.G.
1971 "Natives and Outsiders: Poverty, Marginality, and Pluralism in the Mackenzie River Delta." Ph.D. Thesis, Harvard.
Smith, D.G.
1974 *Occupational Preferences of Northern Students.* Northern Economic Development Branch Social Science Notes-5, Information Canada: Ottawa.

PART FIVE

The Quest for Identity: Ethnic Minorities

PART FIVE

The Quest for Identity:
Ethnic Minorities

In a volume of this nature, it is difficult to decide which studies of the many minority groups should be included. The selection is often determined by studies of minority groups that have been extensively researched. In Part Five, the first two studies, which deal with the Mennonites and the Chassidic Jews, represent small religious minorities. Jansen's study of Italians in Toronto is a study of one of the larger minority groups in Canada. Other larger minorities which might have been included in this category are the Germans, Ukrainians, Dutch, and Poles. Cappon's study deals with the relationship between Francophones and new immigrants who come to Montreal. It illustrates the potential conflict between majority and minority groups within one province.

The four papers included in this section each emphasize a different dimension of ethnic identity. Epp, an historian, traces the complex history of the Mennonites over 450 years. His historical analysis provides a longitudinal view of the struggle of a small minority. Shaffir focuses intensively on the socialization process of Chassidic Jews in one urban community. By participant observation over several years, he is able to report the depth processes that are involved in attracting and holding adherents. Jansen's study of the Italians also focuses on one group within an urban setting, but he describes the social organizations this community has developed in order to show how such institutions support group identification. Cappon's study of new Canadians in Montreal illustrates the kinds of conflicts which can arise when the aspirations of minorities within a community tend to vary with those of the Francophone majority. Each of these approaches and units of study illustrates a variety of methods applicable in the study of ethnic groups.

Historical Identification of Minorities

From the description of the Mennonites by Epp, many readers might wonder how such a small minority, which has proliferated into some twenty sub-groups, could have managed to exist for 450 years. Epp describes their migrations through many countries and their many conflicts, and suggests that the story of the Mennonites could be told in terms of identification, separation, and struggle for survival. This struggle included the maintenance of unpopular religious beliefs in an intolerant sixteenth-century Europe; it included frequent forced migration into other countries, further misunderstandings of their beliefs and negative public images as a result, and besetting internal fragmentation. Because of their position of non-resistance, conflicts between Mennonites and the state create problems in times of war and urbanization creates problems for those people because they are from a predominantly rural background. Sociologically, many might have expected this minority to have disappeared long ago, but instead they have survived and flourished. Conflict may have been functional for their survival.

Many groups that have survived for a long time through considerable struggle have developed mechanisms for the maintenance of communities: religion would seem to be a major factor in the cohesiveness of the Mennonites. The forces of both identification and assimilation are in evidence among them. However, because they have survived for 450 years, will they continue to maintain a separate identity in the Canadian technological society?

Socialization into a Community

The Jews, like the Mennonites, have depended a great deal upon their religious community for the socialization of their offspring into the ethnic enclave. Shaffir suggests that the "management of persons by institutions may be viewed as a process of status passage." One outcome of such processing is a change in how the person is seen by others, and it results in the transformation of the person's identity. In his paper, Shaffir examines the religious transformation of newcomers into a religious community of Orthodox Jews, a process which involves the giving up of one ordered world view for another. A certain series of procedures is employed by the chassidic community to ease the newcomer's transition into his new status.

Social and cultural insulation from the larger community is used in order to maintain a distinctive way of life. A series of steps are used to induct the newcomer into the new community, and these are clearly outlined so that the socialization of the newcomer can take place step by step. First, the degree of Jewishness needs to be established in order that disassociation from the previous life-style can be transformed into a commitment to a new life. Shaffir describes how the Lubavitcher Chassidim have co-ordinated a series of proselytizing activities to draw non-observant

Jews closer to orthodox Judaism. Since there are dropouts from the community, attracting newcomers is a necessity for ensuring and maintaining dynamic growth. Any minority that seeks to develop a separate identity must learn to cope with setbacks, but it must also be able to socialize its offspring and newcomers into their ethnic enclave. In Shaffir's study, respondents describe their identification process and how they became members of a new community.

Ethnic Community Organization

Whereas the two papers already mentioned deal with historical group maintenance and the socialization process into an ethnic community, Jansen's paper deals with the social structure and institutions of an ethnic community. A community is frequently identified with a territory, and the members who inhabit that space usually identify with the culture and institutions of that region. To some extent, the Italians of Toronto live in partially segregated communities where they promote their culture and institutions. Professor Jansen attempts to describe such an urban Italian ethnic community.

The 250,000 Italians in Toronto are maintaining considerable institutional completeness, as Breton would describe it. The Roman Catholic Church plays an important role in shaping the Italian identity, although church attendance and participation in church organizations is not very high. Social assistance organizations, such as the Italian Immigrant Aid Society, are especially helpful to new immigrants. Italian newspapers, and radio and television programs are also in evidence in Toronto. Over sixty ethnic clubs provide opportunities for social interaction; leadership, which appeared to be weak in the past, now seems to be developing within the group.

Jansen concludes that the variety of ethnic institutions in the Toronto Italian community demonstrate that multiculturalism is a reality. As a result, many more Italians are identifying with the ethnic community in the 1970s.

Inter-Ethnic Conflict

The development and maintenance of minority communities are, to a great extent, dependent upon the attitudes and behaviour of the majority community. Politically and economically, the majority can control and even shape the minority community. If the majority does not feel greatly threatened by minority competition, and if the minorities easily accept a lower-status position, then ethnic relationships are often quite congenial and co-operative. However, when the aspirations of minorities conflict with majority interests, there is potential for conflict.

In his essay, Cappon describes the conflict between Francophones in Quebec, who represent the majority political power, and recent immigrants to Montreal who choose English schools rather than French. The study includes evidence of violent confrontations between Italian New Canadians and Francophones, and describes how the two groups were reluctant to communicate directly about their mutual hostility and aggressive attitudes. Francophones were concerned about preserving their cultural identity, while the new immigrants were concerned with the upward socio-economic mobility they perceived could best be attained by learning the English language.

Cappon concludes that inter-ethnic co-operation in Montreal will be severely limited unless greater opportunities for the mutual benefit of all groups are pursued. In the first part of this volume Isajiw explored the potential for co-operation between majority and minority groups in Canada. In Cappon's study there is evidence that the French, the weaker of the charter group partners, are inclined to use their dominance in Montreal for their own advantage, which tends to create severe problems for the successful integration of minority groups. Such groups as the Italians in Montreal feel that their own identity is severely threatened when their opportunities for an English education are limited. As a result, ethnic co-operation is difficult, and the potential for conflict is increased.

The question of the extent to which conflict is inevitable, when Canadians wish to build a multicultural ethnic mosaic, needs more research. Will the French, one of the two majority groups, accept the multicultural model? There is evidence that many French Quebeckers do not accept such a mosaic because they feel it threatens their own survival. Must more powerful groups dominate to preserve their own interests, or is it possible to permit all Canadians to pursue their own identities and thus create a genuine ethnic mosaic?

14

Problems of Mennonite Identity: A Historical Study

Frank H. Epp*

The quest for identity has certainly been the experience of 168,160 Mennonites in Canada (1971 census), not only for the present time but for their entire 450-year history, going back to the times of the Reformation in the northern and southern parts of Germanic Europe.

This quest is one of several themes that has become useful in understanding these people whose presence in this country dates back to 1786, or nearly 200 years. Two other themes are the experience of separation, and in common with many other minorities, the struggle for survival (Epp, 1974; 19-20, 415-418). While these motifs have been applied to particular periods in the last two centuries, none of them has, in reality, an exclusive application. On the contrary, all of them apply to a greater or lesser degree to the entire Mennonite story, which began with the Anabaptists, the radical left wing of the Reformation (Klaassen, 1973).

Origins and Identity
The issue of identity existed for all the dissenters within the Holy Roman Empire. But for the Lutherans the problem was minimized by the strong leadership of Martin Luther, who became the rallying point not only for religious dissent but also for political revolt. Further help came from a war, which defined Lutheranism not only in terms of a religion but also in terms of geography and demography. After 1555, in addition to a Lutheran creed, there were Lutheran lands and regions, Lutheran peoples and princes, and, not to be overlooked as a significant identity symbol, Luther's German Bible. Other "Reformed" peoples had similar "advantages."

* Frank H. Epp is Associate Professor of History, Conrad Grebel College, University of Waterloo, Ontario.

The Mennonites, first known by themselves as Brethren and by their enemies as *Wiedertaeufer* (Anabaptists), had no such "luck." Not only was their early leadership diffuse, but it was soon put to the sword. One of the earliest gatherings of Anabaptist leaders came to be called the Martyrs' Synod, precisely because most of those present paid with their lives soon after.

Representing a radically different understanding of the Christian faith, the Mennonites rejected the positions and symbols which had fused together church and state, either in the old synthesis of the Holy Roman Empire or in the new alliances. The latter included those forged not only by men like Luther, but also by such widely different characters as Henry VIII, the self-proclaimed head of the Church of England, and by Ulrich Zwingli, the priest who helped a Swiss canton assert its independence from Rome.

The Anabaptists insisted that the state had no mandate with respect to religious ordinances, appointments, and authority over the religious conscience. Their position led them to reject both infant baptism and the sword, the two instruments of social control which all the other Reformers had in common with the Catholics (Klaassen, 1973; Epp, 1974). This rejection produced a series of reactions which greatly complicated the matter of identity. Anabaptists were often named anarchists and associated with Joseph Muentzer, the revolutionary priest-leader of rebelling peasants, and also with the Muensterites, violent radicals who sought to establish the kingdom of God at Muenster by force. Quite understandably, these dissenters from the old order were also suspected, not always falsely, of being friends of the Turks. Persecuted by both church and state, they were driven in many directions. Often leaderless, they fled into hills, isolated river valleys, and caves where essential contact with a sizable group of other like-minded people was denied them.

This "baptism" with blood, however, soon became one of their identity symbols. Martyrdom marked the Anabaptists as a voluntarily disciplined and suffering community of believers, who felt themselves called to establish the kingdom of God not on the grand political design of holy empires but as small non-resistant groups who might be prototypes of the coming kingdom of God. Their songs of martyrdom, eventually collected in the *Ausbund* hymnal, and the stories of martyrdom, compiled after a century into the encyclopaedic *Martyrs' Mirror*, became the marks by which the Anabaptists were known to themselves and to others.

Menno and the Mennonite Commonwealth
The northern wing of this European movement, the Dutch-North German Anabaptists, had an outstanding leader in the person of Menno Simons, after whom they were named Mennists. Appropriately so, because few worked as tirelessly and fearlessly as Menno to identify and nurture

the Anabaptists, not as revolutionary Muensterites but as peaceful and non-resistant dissenters. Noblemen on the frontier of the empire now welcomed these *Mennisten* into their estates as useful craftsmen, builders of dykes, and tillers of the soil. It is doubtful whether the name Mennonite would have gathered and retained as much strength as it did, without its utilitarian value in distinguishing at least some Anabaptists from the Muensterites, which distinction had to be made in history rather frequently (*New York Times*, 1929; Bender, 1929).

Menno Simons gave a scattered and insecure people more than a name. Like Luther he gave them a literature, tracts, and treatises on the fundamentals of the faith as well as congregational organization, and exemplary leadership as a shepherd of a flock (Wenger, 1956). The lowlands of the Vistula, where Simons found a temporary haven, provided the environment and the opportunity for the Dutch *Mennisten* to establish themselves. So solid did they become in their congregational communities here and so identified with the wider German culture that when Catherine the Great of Russia made even larger tracts of land available near the Black Sea, they developed what became known as "the Mennonite commonwealth of Russia" (Francis, 1955; Rempel, 1974; Urry, 1975).

Set against a vast sea of Russian peasantry, they experienced themselves as a germanic people of superior breeding and culture. But adult baptism and non-resistance had become sufficiently part of their self-understanding that they identified themselves as Mennonites over and against the German Catholics and German Lutherans who lived next to them. The Mennonites were also known for excellence in agriculture, ingenuity in industry, and, by the end of the eighteenth century, as great lovers of education in particular and self-improvement in general.

Since this development occurred in the context of a self-contained land area and a relatively complete social system, the religious meaning of "Mennonite" was supplemented, and sometimes overshadowed, by a new cultural and ethnic meaning. It was this fact that largely accounted for several attempts at religious renewal in which birthright membership in the Mennonite society was rejected as secondary, if not irrelevant, to the church and the kingdom (Toews, 1975).

Thus, when the first Mennonites came to Canada (specifically, to Manitoba) from Russia in the 1870s, they brought with them a self-image that was quite confusing. They were at the same time Dutch, German, and Russian, yet not really any one of these. They were marked by both ethnic and religious characteristics, but their superficial definitions of both their own ethnicity and their own religiosity tended to invalidate each other and to be mutually exclusive. Additionally, the designations of the competitive religious "denominations" within the Mennonite family were becoming increasingly important. In their religion, the Mennonites were no longer Mennonites but *Brueder* or *Kirchlich* or *Allianz* or *Krim-*

mer or *Altkolonier* or *Bergthaler*, the latter names being derived from the colonies with which the church structures had been coterminous (Gerbrandt, 1970).

Immigrations, of course, were helpful to the restoration of a common identity. In the confrontations and negotiations with governments, either in the countries from which they emigrated or in the countries of their immigration, the Mennonite nomenclature once again emerged as preeminent. In Russia Mennonites were known by vocation as farmers, by language as German (they felt so German that that language had to be preserved at all costs) (Epp, 1965), and in citizenship committed to obedience yet refusing the oath of allegiance. In their religion they insisted on freedom of conscience and on exemption from military service.

The Swiss as Pennsylvania Dutch

The Swiss Mennonites, who had come to North America as part of William Penn's holy experiment in Pennsylvania, and who preceded the Russian Mennonites to Canada by nearly 100 years, had similar characteristics. They had been invited into Upper Canada by its Lieutenant Governor precisely because they were known to be stable settlers of the soil and because they were loyal to the British crown (though not as loyal as their fighting predecessors, the United Empire Loyalists of history). The invitation was extended in full recognition of their pacifist position. As with the Dutch Mennonites from Russia, there were internal divisions among the Swiss in Pennsylvania. In the latter group, the Amish in particular had obtained a cultural identity so distinct that many decades would pass before the Amish would find themselves again under the Mennonite umbrella (Fretz, 1967; Gingerich, 1972).

Some important differences between the two Mennonite families, the Dutch-German and the Swiss-German, should be noted. The Mennonites in Pennsylvania, to a larger degree than those in Russia, had become part of a much wider German community (popularly known as Pennsylvania Dutch, meaning *Deutsch*, after the unique German dialect which had developed among the thousands of German sectarians who had found their freedom in Penn's haven). To this day, Mennonites in Ontario are full and eager participants in activities of the Pennsylvania Dutch societies, whose memberships reach far beyond the Mennonite borders.

This identification with the larger community was helped along in another way. In Pennsylvania, the Mennonites were related to other pacifists. Not only did Penn's state have pacifist inclinations, but among its leading citizens were his religious cohorts the Quakers, plus the German Baptists and related sects who joined the Mennonites in the trek northward, and thus it happened that the Mennonites, Quakers, and Tunkers (Church of the Brethren) became an inseparable pacifist "trinity" in the laws of nineteenth-century Canada. But beyond this pacifist fellowship, the Swiss Mennonites in Ontario were hospitable also to the immigrating Catholics and, indeed, to all strangers. Not all opened their schools and churches to all in the community, as did the Erbs and Ebys, but Mennonite breadth of heart and generosity of spirit became proverbial in the land. These favourable relations and identification with the wider community were for the Swiss Mennonites a very advantageous feature in time of war.

Negative Public Images
The Mennonites from Russia who settled in western Canada did not, at least in their opinion, fare so well. In the First World War period and indeed since the late 1870s, they became identified in Canadian law with two other immigrant groups whose public image had unfortunately and undeservedly become essentially negative. These were the Doukhobors and the Hutterites, who entered Canada for the first time just before the turn of century. Since they too required exemption from military service, and since the orders-in-council exempting them were modelled after the Mennonite precedent of 1873, the three groups tended to appear together, inseparably linked, first in the legal literature, then in political rhetoric, and finally in the sensational and confused, but widely believed, coverage in the newspapers.

Since all three groups were pacifist, since they all came from Russia, and since they all spoke a foreign language and lived in well organized communities of one kind or another, the public mind easily confused them, especially in the patriotic heat of the Great War. Among all the enemy aliens, these "shirkers" of national duty with "communistic" tendencies were the most alien and the most "enemy" of all. A single stroke of the federal legal pen in a 1919 order-in-council barred all three from immigration, until 1922, when Prime Minister Mackenzie King, responding to a Mennonite "lobby," had the order revoked (Epp, 1962: 93-105; 1974: 391-414).

The Mennonites, of course, resented this identification. Respectable as they thought themselves to be, they would not be associated with Doukhobor protests or for that matter with the Hutterite colonies, in which all property was held communally. Mennonites believed in community and neighbourliness, but only on the basis of private property.

Progressives and Conservatives
The public image of the Mennonites in Canada was further complicated by migrations in the early 1920s. How were the Canadian people to make sense of a situation in which one group of Mennonites was leaving the country in protest, and at great sacrifice, for Mexico and Paraguay (Sawatzky, 1971; Fretz, 1953), while another group, composed of thousands of would-be *émigrés* from the Bolshevik Revolution, were, speaking figuratively, beating down the Canadian door. Their advance men ex-

plained that the new arrivals were not only *émigrés* from the Communist Revolution but had been participants in the "golden age" of Mennonite culture in Russia, which had just come to an end. In other words, they were "progressive" in their ways, supportive of public schools and higher education, and ready to learn the ways of the English world, in contrast to the "conservatives" who refused even the slightest accommodation to the Canadian environment (Redekop, 1969).

The newcomers from Russia were promptly named *Russlaender* by those who had already been in the country for fifty years, who in turn now were known as *Kanadier*. It was ironic that both terms stuck. The *Russlaender* of the 1920s, though they knew more of the Russian language than the immigrants of the 1870s, due to a half-century of russification, were actually more German, with greater sophistication, than were their conservative predecessors. To add further to the irony, during the Great War, when Germans in Russia were "aliens," the Russian Mennonites mounted a considerable *Hollaenderei* campaign to identify themselves not as Germans but as Dutch. And the people now known as *Kanadier* were, of all Mennonites in Canada, the least "Canadian" in their mentality and identification. Yet, as inaccurate as identity symbols may be, they can adopt connotations which, in particular contexts, serve the intended purpose of differentiation rather well.

Although the *Kanadier* offered hospitality to the *Russlaender*, little love was lost between them, and differentiations made on the basis of progressivism and conservatism became a painful and rather bitter experience for the *Kanadier*. How deep the feelings of the conservatives ran with respect to the labels applied by the progressives was discovered by the present writer on a visit in 1972 to Bolivia, the latest haven of Mennonites who have been alienated not only by Canada but recently by Mexico.[1]

Among the Swiss in Ontario, the conservative-progressive imagery expressed itself in terms of "old Mennonites" and "new Mennonites." Among the former, the Old Order Mennonites, like the Old Order Amish, virtually froze nineteenth-century culture, as they refused to use products of the new technology, including cars, radios, and telephones. Ridiculed for the longest time not only by Canadians generally but also by their more accommodating Mennonite kinfolk, the Old Order had to await the day of ecological awareness and energy crises, when city-dwellers by the thousands flee telephone and television every weekend, to discover how up-to-date they really were.

Germanism and Anglicization
The 20,000 immigrants from Russia, the largest mass Mennonite movement ever, were not as ready to assimilate and anglicize as had once been assumed. True, they urbanized more readily and moved more easily through the public schools into non-agricultural careers, but anglicization

was viewed as negatively by many in Canada as russification had been viewed in Russia. The anti-Communism and pan-Germanism of Hitler's Third Reich helped to strengthen the Germanist cause among the *Russlaender* (Epp, 1965).

When the war came, and with it a wartime census, the Mennonite identity was hard-pressed. Not only did they have to decide, as in Russia in the First World War, whether their cultural origins were German or Dutch (it was obviously advantageous to claim the latter), but they also needed to give some indication of loyalty to Canada (Britain), even while their empathy for things German tended to carry over into the political realm. But loyalty was hard to prove when the proof was accompanied by an insistence on exemption from military service. The high percentage of *Russlaender* youths (c. 50 per cent) joining the armed forces in the Second World War has been explained in part as the reaction of the sons to a Germanism which was wed to pacifism in the value system of the fathers. For the rebellious sons, the choice of Britain over Germany seemed also to require the choice of militarism over pacifism (Juhnke, 1974).

This twinning of anglicization and militarism was not only an immediate product of wartime patriotism, but also, and perhaps more significant, a result of educational acculturation through the public schools. It might be remembered here that the "conservative" *Kanadier* opposed the public schools precisely because they saw them as agents of the British imperium, as well as the harbingers of the evil world in general. After the First World War thousands of them left for Mexico and Paraguay to escape those Canadian pressures, which to them ultimately meant assimilation and the loss of their identity. After the Second World War additional thousands left the country for similar reasons, again for Paraguay, and as late as the 1960s for Bolivia, joined by others from Mexico and British Honduras. Not all of them stayed, and the returnees brought to Canada additional features which further enriched (or besmirched, depending on the point of view) the Mennonite kaleidoscope (Martens, 1975).

Separation and Accommodation

Emigration, isolation, and the insistence on separation thus became ways in which the Mennonite effort to retain identity expressed itself in the post-war era of Canadian life. The manifestations of the separation model were many: emigration from Canada, as already pointed out; migration within Canada to isolated frontier areas; congregational and conference rulings against movies and television and other encroachments of mass culture; very determined efforts among the *Russlaender* to retain the German language and among the Swiss to keep the head covering, the plain coat, and other indispensable symbols of nonconformity.

An opposite response, equally strong in the post-war era, may be described as the accommodation model. Its earliest representatives were the Mennonite Brethren in Christ, who among the Swiss were the "new Mennonites" of the late nineteenth century. Having been embarrassed during the Second World War by Mennonite identity for ethnic-cultural reasons, as well as on theological grounds–the Mennonite Brethren in Christ had made nonresistance an entirely optional tenet–they saw their future differently. On the one hand, their movement brought Mennonites closer to an assimilation with Canadian society in general. On the other hand, religious identity was sought with other common North American denominators, of evangelicalism and the missionary enterprise. The new name chosen by the group was the United Missionary Church (Storms, 1958).

None of the other Mennonite groups went to this extreme in disassociating themselves, but the accommodation model, expressing itself in urbanization, professionalization, anglicization, Canadianization, evangelicalization, and a host of other ways, became a strong option for many Mennonites (Driedger, 1972, 1968). Adjustments in nomenclature were made in many places. The (Old) Mennonites, not to be confused with the Old Order Mennonites, officially dropped the "Old." The "progressive" Amish, who had already become Amish Mennonites, became the Western Ontario Mennonite Conference. The *Kleinegemeinde* became the Evangelical Mennonite Conference and the *Rudnerweider*, a break-away group from the conservative *Kanadier Sommerfelder* in the 1930s, became the Evangelical Mennonite Mission Conference.

Names became very long as efforts were made to have nomenclature reflect all the desired imagery. For not a few Mennonites, language, names, and other symbols had become of the essence. Things German were both rejected and defended, as opposing sides assumed fundamental significance in forms. The *Bruderthaler*, who had already become Evangelical Mennonite Brethren, were reaching for an even more modern identity, but new names representing a consensus were not easily found. A schismatic Mennonitism and a fundamentalistic evangelicalism had just about exhausted the possibilities.

The name changes came slowly and with much difficulty in the conferences. Small new urban congregations, however, had little difficulty in dropping "Mennonite" from their names, reducing it in its printed size, or bracketing it, as they adopted such main designations for their churches as Fellowship, Community, Bible, Word of Life, etc., etc. Some Mennonite family names were anglicized also, by changing either the spelling or the pronunciation.

Accommodation Without Total Assimilation
The majority of the Canadian Mennonites found themselves somewhere along a spectrum between the extremes of separation and accommodation, as on the one hand they made those adjustments to Canadian society which they deemed necessary and desirable, and at the same time tried to preserve those values they considered desirable and retainable (Kauffman, 1975; Driedger, 1972).

288

This was essentially the approach pioneered in the early decades of this century by H.H. Ewert, the principal of the Mennonite Collegiate Institute (MCI) of Manitoba, who was also the government-appointed inspector of schools in Mennonite districts at a time when the *Kanadier* were opposed to the introduction of public schools. Ewert accepted the public school as a necessary, and not wholly undesirable, phenomenon. But all his energies were directed toward placing Mennonite teachers in those public schools, teachers who became qualified at the Mennonite Collegiate Institute to teach both the German language and the Mennonite catechism.

The option of accepting Canadian society, moving into it and even embracing it while at the same time introducing Mennonite institutions and values into it, is the one that most Mennonites are pursuing, though to varying degrees and at various speeds. The result of this approach in the post-war era has been an unprecedented amount of institution-building and program activity of all kinds. The past twenty-five years may some day be known as the "golden age" of Canadian Mennonitism for that very reason. The building and expansion of schools, the proliferation of organizations of all kinds, professionalization, and some bureaucratization have all been spawned by the Mennonite desire to be in the world in a respectable way and yet not totally of the world. Studies in Winnipeg, the largest urban concentration of Mennonites anywhere in the world, have shown that large groups of people can maintain and perhaps even strengthen their sense of peoplehood in an unaccustomed urban environment if they are fortified by the necessary institutions and structures (Driedger, 1973).

Both kinds of responses to the identity problem–separation and accommodation–are, for the most part, sincere responses. Representatives of both assume that theirs is the best way to preserve for the future the best of the Mennonite past. Both, however, have tended to disparage the opposite approach as being unworthy of that past and in the long run as counterproductive in preserving cherished values.

Internal Fragmentation and Differentiation
The lack of an internal consensus, always an Anabaptist weakness, has been accented by the multiplicity of post-war options. This weakness may prove to be the biggest handicap of all in maintaining a Mennonite identity which can survive influences and pressures from the outside. Certainly, the internal strength of a group does not depend, at least not in the Anabaptist tradition, entirely on numbers. Inner strength, which comes from an uncompromising commitment to a noble ideal, is sufficient to overcome many handicaps, but in the modern world, a minority group, or groups, can become too small to survive even in isolation. Modern mass cultures may not persecute minorities by killing them physically, but so powerful and relentless are they in their attack that the real life-blood of

all but the strongest minorities is poured out in the interest of conformity.

Some numerical strength is not only a helpful supplement to the convictions held by a group, but it may actually become indispensable to the sustenance and nurture of those convictions. After all, a certain constituency is required to maintain a separate school at whatever level, or to make viable those publications which have become essential spiritual lifelines or vehicles for a minority surrounded by the mass media. As one considers the Mennonite future in Canada, one cannot, therefore, overlook the many ways in which internal Mennonite fragmentation or differentiation remains a problem. To be noted are the following:

1) The two main cultural families of Canadian Mennonitism: the Dutch-German, and the Swiss-German. While they relate in many ways, they still represent two distinct families. Added to these are the converts from many different backgrounds.

2) The many immigrations, which have not yet come to an end, all of which represent, to greater or lesser degrees, particular identities. In addition to the coming of the *Schweizer*, the *Ammaner*, the *Kanadier*, the *Amerikaner*, and the *Russlaender* before the Second World War, one can identify the *Deutschlaender*, *Mexikaner*, *Paraguayer*, other *Amerikaner*, and the *Umsiedler* since then, in immigrations extending to this very day.

3) The continuing denominational fragmentation, which seems to run at least as strong as Mennonite ecumenicity. Mennonites know themselves more in terms of their particular denominational identities than in terms of a general Mennonite image. There are at least ten of these denominational families in each of the two main traditions, Swiss-German and Dutch-German.[2]

4) The varying relations to and attitudes toward the state, always an important factor in establishing Mennonite identity. Here, again, we have a plethora of understandings. They range all the way from the extreme of the separation model to the extreme of the accommodation model. On the one hand, there are Mennonites vigorously resisting the state on big issues like public education while co-operating readily on minor issues like the postal code, even in faraway Fort Vermillion where the code may never be used. On the other hand, there are Mennonites uncritically embracing every facet of public education (and perhaps state service!) while being completely indifferent to minor issues like postal codes and traffic lights.

5) The relation to society in general covers a similar spectrum, all the way from a very simple, austere, and separated life-style to a complete acceptance of every technological innovation and luxury.

6) Urbanization and other geographic scattering. Apart from the German Block and German Land Company Tracts in Ontario, and the reserves in Manitoba and Saskatchewan, Mennonites have scattered

widely and often very thinly. Urbanization has vastly accelerated this trend, though several larger Canadian cities have large and strong Mennonite communities (Driedger, 1968).

7) Disparate definitions of religion and ethnic culture. To the extent that they are narrowly and superficially defined, the two main meanings of Mennonite become mutually exclusive with a consequent rending apart within the Mennonite body.

8) Outside influences, including mass culture, mass education, and mass religion, resulting in a widespread redefinition and transfer from Mennonite ethnic culture to Canadianism and from Mennonite religion to a variety of forms, both old and new, in evangelicalism.

Conclusion

Not all of the forces at work within and upon the Mennonite minority group contribute to fragmentation and sectionalism. Total group feeling and a general Mennonite identity has been helped along in recent years not least of all by the development of such inclusive Mennonite institutions as Mennonite Central Committee (Canada) and its provincial counterparts. A wide variety of public events and celebrations, including the traditional song fests, the more recent dramatic presentations and art exhibitions, and all kinds of mass gatherings which have cut across many of the dividing lines, have contributed substantially to a new sense of Mennonite peoplehood.

The significance of a favourable Canadian social climate, nurtured by an official multiculturalism supportive of minority groups, must not be overlooked either, though it can be overemphasized. On the one hand, a separate Mennonite identity has found the public support which it was denied for many years. Mexican Mennonites, for instance, returning to Canada after a fifty-year absence, may have difficulty recognizing the country. A government and a society which could not tolerate them earlier in the century are now coming to their defence, even though the cultural gap between the two has widened during the Mexican sojourn.

On the other hand, multiculturalism's lumping together of Mennonites, presumably as ethnics, with all other ethnic minorities presents a problem to a minority group whose essence is not integration but separation and which has seen itself as something more than ethnic even in its most "ethnic" moments. Also, and here lies another contradiction, Mennonites have in some ways tended to survive better as Mennonites when state and society were hostile or indifferent than when state and society were over friendly. For that reason, multiculturalism can, for the Mennonites, be a wolf in sheep's clothing. What it may really represent in the long run is a Canadianism as devastating of minority values as all proud nationalisms have been. Unless multiculturalism is profound and honest it is but a new word for the old melting pot of the dominant culture.

Today, Mennonite identity remains a problem both for those who seek to cultivate it and bring it to a new maturity and for those who seek to deny or even to destroy it. For the former, the internal and external forces contributing to disintegration are too strong to offer much hope. The latter, on the other hand, must be quite discouraged by the strong recovery of Mennonite peoplehood, manifested particularly in the last several years of anniversaries and celebrations and in the mammoth projects undertaken and successfully executed on the basis of a consolidated and continuing national Mennonite community. The foreseeable future is likely to provide a good deal of evidence that both sides are both winning and losing.

Notes

1. This visit followed the Ninth Mennonite World Conference in Curitiba, Brazil. My host, I will call him Mr. Fehr, chided me for using the word "Conservative" (Epp, 1972). "Who are the true conservatives and who are the true progressives?" he asked me, as he reviewed Mennonite immigration history for me. In every instance, the first to go to new countries like Russia, Canada, Mexico, and Paraguay, he pointed out, had been the so-called conservatives. The so-called progressives had followed, enjoying the advantage of others having prepared the way. He was unfailingly correct in his interpretation of history.

2. Ten groups in the Swiss-German tradition are: (old) Mennonites; Missionary Church; Western Ontario Mennonites; Conservative Mennonites; Old Order Mennonites; David Martin Old Order Mennonites; Waterloo-Markham Mennonites; Reformed Mennonites; Old Order Amish; Conservative Amish. Ten groups in the Dutch-German tradition are: the General Conference Mennonites (Conference of Mennonites in Canada); Mennonite Brethren; Old Colony; Sommerfelder; Bergthaler; Reinlaender; Chortitzer; Evangelical Mennonite Brethren; Evangelical Mennonite Conference; Evangelical Mennonite Mission Conference. The Church of God in Christ Mennonite (Holdeman) is a strong mixture of people of both traditions.

References

Bender, H.S.
   1929 Letter to the editor on Mennonites. *New York Times.* December 11:28.
Driedger, L.
   1972 "Urbanization of Mennonites," in Henry Poettcker and Rudy A. Regehr, *Call to Faithfulness: Essays in Canadian Mennonite Studies.* Winnipeg; Canadian Mennonite Bible College.

Driedger, L.
1973 "Impelled Group Migration: Minority Struggle to Maintain Institutional Completeness." *International Migration Review* 7:257-
259.
Driedger, L.
1968 "A Perspective on Canadian Mennonite Urbanization." *Mennonite Life* 28:147-152.
Epp, F.H.
1974 *Mennonites in Canada, 1786-1920: The History of a Separate
People.* Toronto: Macmillan of Canada.
Epp, F.H.
1972 "Conservative Colonists on the Bolivian Frontier." *Mennonite
Reporter II* (October 30, 1972):9-11.
Epp, F.H.
1965 "An Analysis of Germanism and National Socialism in the Immigrant Press of a Canadian Minority Group, the Mennonites, in
the 1930s." Ph.D. dissertation. University of Minnesota.
Epp, F.H.
1962 *Mennonite Exodus: The Rescue and Resettlement of the Russian
Mennonites Since the Communist Revolution.* Altona: D.W.
Friesen & Sons.
Francis, E.K.
1955 *In Search of Utopia: The Story of the Mennonites in Manitoba.*
Altona: D.W. Friesen & Sons.
Fretz, J.W.
1967 *Mennonites in Ontario.* Waterloo: Mennonite Historical Society
of Ontario.
Fretz, J.W.
1953 *Pilgrims in Paraguay: The Story of Mennonite Colonization in
South America.* Scottdale: Herald Press, 1953.
Gerbrandt, H.J.
1970 *Adventure in Faith: The Background in Europe and the Develop-
ment in Canada of the Bergthaler Church in Manitoba.* Altona:
D.W. Friesen & Sons.
Gingerich, O.
1972 *The Amish in Canada.* Waterloo: Conrad Press.
Hoeschen, S.
1975 "The God Life." *Weekend Magazine,* September 27, 1975.
Juhnke, J.
1974 *A People of Two Kingdoms.* Newton: Faith and Life.
Kauffman, J.H. and L. Harder
1975 *Anabaptists Four Centuries Later.* Scottdale: Herald Press.
Klaassen, W.
1973 *Anabaptism: Neither Catholic Nor Protestant.* Waterloo: Conrad
Press.

Martens, H.
 1975 "Mennonites from Mexico: Their Immigration and Settlement in Canada." A Research Report for Canada Department of Manpower and Immigration.
New York Times
 1929 Editorial on Mennonites. December 6:26.
Redekop, C.
 1969 *The Old Colony Mennonites: Dilemmas of Ethnic Minority Life.* Baltimore: John Hopkins Press.
Rempel, D.G.
 1974 "The Mennonite Commonwealth in Russia: A Sketch of its Founding and Endurance, 1789-1919." *Mennonite Quarterly Review*, 48:5-5447: 259-308.
Robertson, H.
 1973 *Grass Roots.* Toronto: James Lewis & Samuel.
Sawatzky, H.L.
 1971 *They Sought a Country: Mennonite Colonization in Mexico.* Berkeley: University of California Press.
Storms, E.
 1958 *History of the United Missionary Church.* Elkhart: Bethel Publishing Company.
Toews, J.A.
 1975 *A History of the Mennonite Brethren Church: Pilgrims and Pioneers.* Fresno: General Conference of Mennonite Brethren Churches.
Urry, J.
 1975 "The Closed and the Open: Social and Religious Change Amongst the Mennonites in Russia (1789-1889)." Oxford, England. (Ph.D. dissertation).
Wenger, J.C., (ed).
 1956 *Complete Writings of Menno Simons.* Scottdale: Mennonite Publishing House.

15

Becoming an Orthodox Chassidic Jew: The Socialization of Newcomers to a Religious Community

William Shaffir*

Sociological accounts have analyzed how institutions socialize their charges to become specific kinds of people. Such accounts, for example, have examined the institutional influences in prisons (Baum and Wheeler, 1968; Clemmer, 1958), educational institutions (Cicourel and Kitsuse, 1963; Mercurio, 1972), hospitals (Goffman, 1963), and agencies for the blind (Scott, 1972), and have analyzed how the institution shapes and alters the person's sense of who and what he is. One outcome of such institutional processing is a change in how the person is seen by others, resulting in a transformation of the person's identity (Kitsuse, 1970). The management of persons by institutions may be viewed as a process of status passage (Glaser and Strauss, 1971).

The phenomenon of religious transformation may also be conceptualized as a status passage. The process by which such transformation occurs has received attention in the literature (DeSantes, 1927; Lofland, 1966; Gordon, 1967). This paper focuses on the process of the transformation of newcomers to a religious community of orthodox Jews, Lubavitcher Chassidim; the giving up of one perspective or ordered view of the world for another (Lofland and Stark, 1965). The procedures employed by this chassidic community to ease the newcomers' transition to their new status will be discussed.[1] Viewing the community as an institution which attracts non-observant Jews to orthodox Judaism and to the Lubavitch community, we will highlight the transition of newcomers into the community from outsiders to fully-fledged members. A brief analysis of the intentions and consequences of this proselytization process will be included.

* William Shaffir is Assistant Professor of Sociology, McMaster University, Hamilton, Ontario.

The individual's movement to orthodox Judaism and to the Lubavitch community may be regarded as a status passage with the following key properties: a) the voluntary nature of the passage; b) its occurrence over a period of time; and c) the community's lack of formal control over its shape (Glaser and Strauss, 1971:57-88). In that newcomers learn about and are eventually expected to conform to specific laws and practices, the status passage is prescribed. The passage's scheduling, however, is not institutionally determined but is instead organized to fit the particular needs of the individuals concerned.

Background

The Chassidim are a religious movement within the framework of Jewish laws and practices, but have their own customs and traditions. Their everyday way of life is circumscribed by religious ideas and principles which differentiate them from other Jewish minority groups, both orthodox and non-orthodox. Not unlike other religious communities studied in the literature (Hostetler, 1968; Redekop, 1969), all chassidic groups attempt to insulate themselves both socially and culturally from the larger community in order to maintain their distinctive way of life. The commonly referred-to "chassidic community" (Poll, 1962) consists, in fact, of a number of different chassidic groups, each with a loyalty and devotion to its own leader, or *Rebbe*. With their headquarters in Brooklyn, New York, and communities in many parts of the world, the Lubavitcher comprise one segment of the chassidic community. Whereas other chassidic groups have minimized contact with the larger non-orthodox Jewish community, Lubavitcher, under the leadership and guidance of their *Rebbe*,[2] have organized a series of activities to inform non-observant Jews about the principles underlying orthodox Judaism.

The discussion is based on observation of a community of Lubavitcher Chassidim in Montreal.[3] The Lubavitch community in this city dates back to 1941 and today numbers roughly one hundred families. In order to maintain relations with Jews in the larger community, Lubavitcher have shifted their residential and institutional concentration in line with the demographic changes in the Jewish community. Today, this community is located in a neighbourhood with a high proportion of Jews.

The data were gathered through participant observation in the community from late 1969 to 1971. During this period as much time as possible was spent with Lubavitcher, participating with them in a wide range of activities. Although most of the observation was spent in the community's spiritual and social centre–the Yeshiva–it also included travel with Lubavitcher to New York, visiting them in their summer camps, and meeting with them in their homes. Information about newcomers was obtained from two principal sources: lengthy interviews with fifteen newcomers (eight males and seven females) at their homes, and time spent with the men at different community activities. In addition, we interviewed seven Lubavitcher (four males and three females) who were actively engaged in helping newcomers integrate into the community's way of life. The interviewed newcomers ranged in their involvement with the community from three to ten years, and comprised approximately 80 per cent of the newcomers to the community. When successive interviews confirmed that the analysis accurately reflected the typical sequence of steps by which newcomers were socialized into the community, the data collection was discontinued.

The General Approach
In many institutions there exists a typical sequence of steps by which a newcomer is inducted. Available to the newcomer is a clear conception of the direction of the socialization process. The scheduled passage sets forth how he is to be moved along at a prescribed rate by indicating the number of transitional statuses, in what order or sequence they fall, and the duration of time to be spent in each (Glaser and Strauss, 1971). In contrast, a newcomer to the Lubavitch community enters each new status voluntarily. While aware of the direction they wish the passage to assume, the community socializers do not exercise formal control over the passagee's movement but, instead, allow the latter to largely determine his direction and scheduling.

The initial central organizing principles of Lubavitch's approach with a newcomer are to make him a more observant Jew and to bring him along at his own pace. Since the newcomer submits himself to such processing voluntarily, Lubavitcher realize that he is not committed to continuing and can back out at any time. Since, at least in the beginning, Lubavitcher exercise little if any control over a newcomer, to insist that he follow a rigid initiation schedule does not seem a successful way to draw people into the orthodox fold and Lubavitch circles.

Lubavitcher do, however, encourage newcomers to follow certain basic precepts immediately. One of the first of these for males is the donning of phylacteries (*tefillin*), while married females are impressed with the importance of attending the ritual bath (*mikveh*). The newcomers are then themselves called upon to determine when they are willing and prepared to begin observing additional religious precepts.

As such, there is no definite time period during which the newcomer must be ready to adhere to the many laws and customs regulating an orthodox Jew's life. A Lubavitcher comments:

> I can think of a Lubavitch family right off, right off like this, that, I think ten years ago, they became interested in Lubavitch. And her sons were wearing beards and this woman, just last year, maybe a year and half ago, she finally covered her hair. It took her ten years to cover her hair, but I'm sure that now she is doing it....You see, it's real. Now she's not doing it just to be like everybody else.

Lubavitcher have discovered that fanatical recruits who try to alter their life-style immediately and completely in conformity with orthodox laws and chassidic traditions and customs are more likely to experience personal and familial difficulties as a result of the abrupt disassociation. It is not surprising, then, that Lubavitcher suggest to newcomers who are eager to observe as many religious precepts as possible to wait some time before accepting additional ones. A Lubavitcher explains the reason for this:

> We don't want to come and then label you...here, this is our group and you have to dress this way, and you have to put on this and that....As long as it doesn't come from his own feelings...what's the purpose? Don't grab too many *mitzvess* [religious commandments] together because then it will be too hard on you. So then you're going to drop them off. It'll be double hard to take them on again.

The Lubavitch strategy calls for the recruit to "make a beginning," to start observing at least one religious commandment:

> I would say to a person...it wouldn't make any difference which *mitzveh* you want to do. Whatever appeals to you, whatever is easiest, and just the opposite, you never pick a hard *mitzveh* because then you're very discouraged.

In fact, the recruit is initially encouraged to select a commandment which will not interfere drastically with his present way of life. Although the recruit is permitted to progress at his own pace, he is, nonetheless, encouraged to perform additional ones. Such encouragement only occurs, however, when the newcomer is considered ready for advancement. While he selects those commandments he feels confident to begin observing, the Lubavitcher in contact with him has a planned "*mitzveh* route" which he hopes the recruit will eventually follow:

> ...and we hope that...the next main step will be *kashress* [the observance of Kashruth] and *Shabbess* [the observance of the Sabbath] and we hope we wouldn't push him to *Shabbess* like we push him to *Tefillin*.
> This person himself...will decide to come [to synagogue] on *Shabbess*.
> Smoking will be difficult for him to stop. Movies will be more difficult. To maybe not drive his car...on *Shabbess* might be easier for him....

The Lubavitch approach just described is a consequence of having newcomers who are neither committed to nor identified with traditional Judaism. They are not committed because they can leave at any time and, at least in the beginning, lose nothing. They may not be strongly identified because they are not seeking to become fanatics but rather to become more observant; they may in fact have been approached through recruitment activities rather than through self-selection. As a result, Lubavitcher recognize the advantages of not exacting too many demands of newcomers since such demands may lead them to terminate their involvement with the chassidic group:

> I know when I deal with people...there are some things which I don't tell them to do because I know that he's not ready to do it, and he's just going to get up and take the next bus home. You cannot push anything on a person until he is ready.

Determining the Level of Jewishness

The Lubavitch philosophy stresses that each Jew is, at any time, at a particular level of *Yiddishkayt* (orthodox Judaism) and his objective is to raise himself to the next higher level. No Jew must become complacent with his degree of religious observance but must continually strive to achieve even more. A Lubavitcher expresses this philosophy as follows:

> ...Actually, it is a chassidic philosophy that what you do with a person is you recognize that every person is on a level and his job is to get to the next level. Not to get ten levels ahead, and not to get on someone else's level, but it's his particular level. So when you're with a person you try to get him to take the next step, to go to the next level. For a person who doesn't keep *Shabbess* [observe the Sabbath] at all, maybe for that person to give up smoking puts that person on a different level.

The Lubavitchers' initial concern with a newcomer is to determine his level of *Yiddishkayt*. This entails seeking certain information about his history, including type and extent of Jewish education and degree of religious observance. Such information, which is vital for determining the shape of the person's passage, is elicited in several ways. First, a newcomer's appearance might provide some clues. For example, a young man's entering the Yeshiva without a head covering, or a woman's attending a Lubavitch women's meeting in a sleeveless dress, would indicate that they are unaware or unconcerned about the impropriety of their appearance. Yet gathering clues from a person's appearance is unreliable. The manner of dress does not give sufficient information about, for instance, observance of the laws of *Kashruth*. Also, the person may dress appropriately only when in the presence of Lubavitchers. For example, a woman might lower the hemline on a few of her dresses which she will then wear only to Lubavitch functions. A more reliable way of learning about background and religious practices is conversation, for in the course of such conversation the person will be asked whether he observes the donning of phylacteries on the Sabbath. Acquiring such information about the individual helps Lubavitcher determine how best to encourage him to become more observant.

Socialization of the Newcomer

The newcomer is familiarized with certain religious practices that are expected to instil in him an identification with traditional Judaism. This is best accomplished when the newcomer begins to practise *Yiddishkayt* immediately. To link the person to Lubavitch he is gradually informed about the Lubavitcher *Rebbe* and his views, and about events sponsored by this chassidic group. As a newcomer, he is engaged in a simultaneous process of socialization into the Lubavitch way of life and disassociation from much of his previous life-style. It is hoped that this will begin to both identify him with and commit him to Judaism from a traditional and Lubavitch perspective. At first, male and female newcomers generally learn much the same precepts, for example the laws regulating *Kashruth*, but, as they become more observant, certain features of the socialization process assume greater relevance for men or women.

A basic starting point for both is that they practise being more observant. While they will eventually become familiar with and understand the traditions and customs linked to orthodox Judaism and Lubavitch, they are initially encouraged to behave as much as possible like an orthodox Jew. With the male, this may take the form of beginning to pray, or praying on a more regular basis. As the newcomer becomes familiar with the precepts of orthodox Judaism, he is encouraged to choose among those precepts he will find less demanding to observe initially: "I remember when I stopped writing on *Shabbess*. I didn't do anything else. I didn't *davn* [pray]. I listened to the radio, I answered the telephone, but I didn't write."

While he is becoming acquainted with the details of Jewish law, the newcomer is expected to incorporate as many precepts as he sees feasible into his everyday life. He is impressed with the idea that orthodox Judaism is a way of life and not a mere series of acts to be performed at specified times. In time he becomes increasingly observant by performing additional religious commandments or performing the same ones more devoutly. Here is an account of the former:

> ...and we just decided to do one thing at a time. We started *benching* [saying grace after the meal]. That was the first thing that we did. Then we stopped driving on *Shabbess*. Then we took one additional step—we built a *Sukkeh* [a temporary structure in which meals are eaten during the holiday Feast of Tabernacles]. We started to keep *Kashress* properly. We stopped turning out the lights on *Shabbess*.

One may also become more sincere and serious in performing the same *mitzveh*:

> Since I got married, I've taken a lot of things more seriously. I didn't care too much the time I was learning before I was married. Now it seems more important to me....I put on a *talless* [prayer shawl] when I

300

davn and I guess I'm more serious. I think more of what I say when I *davn* than I did then.

In Lubavitch circles, and among all chassidic and orthodox Jews, the woman's place is in the home, for which she is held primarily responsible. Consequently she must familiarize herself with those laws which will ensure an orthodox home and family life. Two important sets of laws are those pertaining to *Kashruth* and to family purity (*taharas hamishpocheh*) Married female newcomers must learn certain things to help them manage their homes and themselves in an orthodox manner.

In keeping a kosher home, one must see to it that all food products, including the utensils in which the food is cooked and served, are pure. This involves learning how to be certain that a particular food product is kosher and where it might be purchased. For those who have not previously observed *Kashruth*, kosher food products will have to be substituted for those normally used. As one female newcomer remarked:

> I wanted to know what butcher they [Lubavitch women] buy from and where to buy fish and things like that....Some things were hard, like, I used to use these cheeses, this Kraft sliced cheese, and now there is this kosher cheese....

Keeping informed about kosher food products is a continuous learning process. New kosher products continually appear but, more important, old ones may disappear; that is, the ingredients of the product are altered so that it is no longer kosher. A newcomer describes some of her experiences:

> ....You bring in a product sometimes and you find out about it, and all of a sudden someone will tell you that this product is really dairy and it's not really kosher. So, it's a matter of learning every single day, and always watching what you bring into the house because there will always be something new that they'll change and you don't know when they're going to change a product....

Along with the laws pertaining to *Kashruth*, female newcomers must familiarize themselves with laws relating to family purity. They begin to attend the *mikveh* and study the laws accompanying attendance.

In the process of becoming more observant, newcomers learn not only about Jewish laws and traditions but about the Lubavitcher *Rebbe* and the kinds of attitudes and feelings his chassidim display toward him. They are impressed with the *Rebbe*'s special powers and will hear accounts testifying to his extraordinary attributes. From the outset they will be encouraged to write to the *Rebbe*, either for a blessing (*brocheh*) or for specific advice. In addition, the newcomer may be asked to consider the possibility of travelling to New York for a private audience with the *Rebbe*. A newcomer remarks:

Their [Lubavitch] main objective is to influence you to become religious, and after [you are] religious, to become a Lubavitcher. A Lubavitcher is someone who has contact with the *Rebbe.* They got me to write. Writing is the next step. Then, personal contact, or at least to go to New York where the *Rebbe* talks....

It appears, however, that initially newcomers experience difficulty in accepting the *Rebbe* as other Lubavitcher do. This can sometimes result in a reluctance to arrange for a personal audience with him. For example:

For some reason or other, I don't know what it was, it was something I just couldn't quite accept, because in my knowledge of Judaism it doesn't mean that just because you become an observant Jew you have to accept a *Rebbe.* With the chassidim it's almost part and parcel....

The newcomer soon realizes what other Lubavitcher would like to see of him and his eventual consent to a personal audience with the *Rebbe* is taken both by him and others to indicate the beginning of a commitment to the Lubavitch orientation to orthodox Judaism.

Upon contact with Lubavitch, the person is taught laws, customs, and traditions relating to Judaism and Lubavitch. As he applies what he learns to his everyday life he begins to identify with *Yiddishkayt* and sees himself trying to practise and observe traditional Judaism. The Lubavitch approach recognizes the importance of first offering the newcomer activities to build his identification with *Yiddishkayt.* In time, however, after becoming immersed in a Lubavitch milieu, the latter finds himself increasingly committed to this different, orthodox way of life. The transition from mere identification to identification with commitment is very gradual and is signalled by certain kinds of activities.

Disassociation From Previous Life-style and Commitment to Lubavitch

As newcomers learn to be more observant, they begin to feel compelled to display evidence indicating that they are taking this new way of life seriously. This often takes the form of reallocating their time to allow more opportunity for religious-related activities.

Along with the observance of Jewish laws and participation in Lubavitch activities, the newcomer is encouraged to establish a relationship with the *Rebbe.* This relationship is likely to assume a different intensity depending on the newcomer's level of identification with traditional Judaism and the Lubavitcher Chassidim. At the outset of his contact with Lubavitch, he inevitably discovers the reverence Lubavitcher display toward their leader and the central role he occupies in their lives. He becomes acquainted with this information not merely through formal instruction but because the *Rebbe*'s ideas, attitudes, and actions are a constant topic of conversation in Lubavitch circles. The newcomer recognizes the *Rebbe* to be a holy man but remains sceptical of the powers that Lubavitcher claim are vested in his person. Since Lubavitcher regularly travel to New York to attend the *Rebbe*'s *Farbrengens* (Lubavitch chassidic gatherings) and encourage the newcomer to experience a *Farbrengen* first hand, he usually accepts their invitation, albeit with some trepidation. During the course of his stay with a Lubavitch family in New York, he is again exposed to a series of stories testifying to the *Rebbe*'s superhuman powers. Through contact with Lubavitcher he discovers the intensity of the Lubavitcher's relationship with the *Rebbe* and that the former regularly seeks the *Rebbe*'s advice and blessings before proceeding on any important course of action. In time, the newcomer becomes sufficiently interested in the *Rebbe* to the point of inquiring from Lubavitcher about "what the *Rebbe* said" or "what the *Rebbe* has to say" concerning various topics.

During this period of interest in the *Rebbe*, the recruit might "write in" to the *Rebbe* for a blessing, and might even agree to the arrangement of a personal audience with him. Unlike other Lubavitcher, however, he has not yet entrusted himself completely to the *Rebbe*. When faced with an important decision, for example, he may still rely primarily on his personal judgement for a suitable solution. It is only when the recruit places himself completely under the *Rebbe*'s direction and is prepared to abide by the *Rebbe*'s advice, however contrary it may be to his own and others' thinking, that he is considered to be emotionally and intellectually committed to this chassidic group.

In the beginning, the newcomer's attachment to orthodox Judaism and to Lubavitch is tenuous. If he feels inclined to observe a precept he does; if he does not feel so inclined, he does not. Although he is becoming increasingly preoccupied with orthodox Judaism and Lubavitch, he may still meet with his non-religious friends. In time, however, he begins losing contact with many of them. What separates him from them is the feeling that he has little in common with them. As one Lubavitcher recalled her experience:

> You know, you do lose contact...if I'm visiting Toronto having contact with [previous non-orthodox friends] or trying to renew contact with them is sort of futile because we have so little interests in common other than our family and home and furniture.

The alternative is to choose new friends with whom interests are shared:

> I enjoy the friends that I do have and I have quite a few friends whom I'm quite close to here in Montreal and I enjoy their friendship and I depend on that very much. There is a definite exchange of interests and I think that there are things that we share, and these are very important to me....

The majority of new friends are likely to be from Lubavitch and they teach the newcomer what he wants and is expected to know. Since Lubavitch men spend a considerable amount of their time in the Yeshiva, the male newcomer is likely to do the same. His social life begins to centre around the Yeshiva where he spends much of his time in the presence of Lubavitcher. For the female newcomer, increasing involvement in the Lubavitch community comes by way of participating in various women's activities.

Along with this, certain changes are expected and come about in the female newcomer's appearance. Though she may resist these changes initially, she is made to recognize the importance of conforming to certain standards of dress. She is informed of the *Rebbe*'s emphasis on *tzneeus* (modesty) in appearance and conduct. By seeing others she learns that one's hair is to be always covered in public, that dresses are to be long-sleeved, high-necked, and of approximately knee length. While in the privacy of her home she may not be too meticulous about the length of her dress or sleeves; when before others she tries to present herself appropriately. As one female remarked:

> Well, if I go out and forget my hat, I go back and get it. Or if I go out and realize that I'm wearing a dress that might be bothersome to someone, I will go back and get a sweater. I don't want to be disrespectful.

Males also change their style of dress. The most important features that identify them and commit them to behave like orthodox Jews include wearing a hat and/or *yarmulke* (skull cap) at all times, a dark-coloured suit or appropriate substitute, a *talless kotn* (fringed undershirt), and, in most cases, a beard.

As these newcomers gradually become more committed to *Yiddishkayt* and to Lubavitch, they learn to reallocate their time in accordance with their new way of life. They come to realize that time is a precious commodity that must be spent productively, and concluding that certain activities are either too time consuming or not compatible with a Lubavitch life-style, they try to refrain from them. For example, men grow to feel that time spent at movies ought to be put to more valuable use. As one male newcomer said: "You're not supposed to go to a movie....If you had the time...you could learn or do a good deed...." Beginning to think of himself as a religious Jew fitting into the Lubavitch community, and anxious to be so regarded by others, the newcomer stops taking part in activities which may lead himself and others to question his sincerity.

The newcomer's intensified contact with Lubavitcher is accompanied by a process of disassociation from his previous life-style. He gradually assumes the Lubavitch attitude to the role and purpose of an orthodox Jew and realizes that continued participation in some of his previous activities is not in conformity with his new self-perception. He is now likely to focus his attention and devote his time practising to be a better Jew;

that is, to elevate himself to a higher level of *Yiddishkayt*. He becomes increasingly aware that he is drifting away from his past way of life, and while a complete break may never occur, his degree of involvement with his former non-religious friends and relatives slowly diminishes. His everyday social life is heavily influenced by Lubavitcher, and they become his reference group and constitute the significant others in his immediate world (Shibutani, 1955). At this point, the newcomer can be said to be socially committed to Lubavitch. The perceived costs of terminating involvement with the chassidic community or deviating sharply from the expected orthodox way of life are too great and the newcomer becomes structurally locked into the community's way of life (Becker, 1960).

Dropouts
Since passage into Lubavitch is a voluntary act, individuals are free to terminate the process whenever they wish. In fact, only a minority of those who come into contact with Lubavitch agree to change their lifestyle and begin observing Jewish law. While these newcomers travel the route of the status passage by gradually conforming to the kinds of expectations made of them by others in the community, most begin and continue to show progress but then reverse their field, either by failing to progress or by discontinuing the observation of those precepts practised to date. Thus, another property of the status passage into Lubavitch is reversibility.

Those who reverse their field give various reasons to justify their decision. A common feature is the inability or lack of desire to accept and maintain what are perceived as restrictions on life-style. A Lubavitch woman, regarded as an experienced teacher of newcomers, told of a typical incident about a girl with whom she studied Jewish law. The two had studied together for six months when one day the girl announced that a good Jew can only be a committed Jew and that henceforth she would observe the Sabbath and other laws she learned in the course of her studies. The woman said:

> Recently, she decided to go away from it all. She had realized, she thinks at least, not to completely divorce herself but certainly to retreat. She feels that it had posed too many problems, and given her an insecure feeling and has made her belong nowhere almost. So there was only one answer for her—recede. I don't know how long she'll stay at that point. I think she's typical.

Lubavitcher recognize that most of the people they encounter are not already observant Jews and that few will become so. They are also aware that there is no guarantee that those whom they impress with the importance of traditional Judaism will live a fully Jewish life. Even so, Lubavitcher are unanimous in their belief that one should not feel discouraged in efforts to draw people closer to orthodox Judaism, that a person's observance of even one precept, if only for one occasion, is superior to no observance at all, and can be viewed as a great accomplishment. A person, then, does not have to become an orthodox Jew and a Lubavitcher to be considered a successful case. As one woman put it: "Every little bit is better than nothing...."

Conclusion

Unlike other chassidic communities studied in the literature (Gutwirth, 1969; Poll, 1962; Rubin, 1972; Sobol, 1965), the Lubavitcher Chassidim have co-ordinated a series of proselytizing activities to draw non-observant Jews closer to orthodox Judaism. One consequence of such activities is that outsiders are attracted to this community's way of life, and of these a small number become Lubavitcher Chassidim. The absence of a prolonged and sustained drive to process non-orthodox newcomers into Lubavitcher indicates that these activities are not intended primarily to attract newcomers.

System theorists have argued that recruitment of new members is a functional prerequisite of any social system (Aberle et al., 1950). If the community cannot maintain its ranks through internal production, it will seek outsiders as newcomers to maintain itself. The purpose of proselytization, then, is to attract new members to enlarge the community or to maintain its size. Although the Lubavitcher proselytize, they do not do so in order to expand, and few members have been attracted to the community in this manner. In addition, the community does not need to attract new members, as it experiences a high enough birth-rate to maintain its numbers. As a result, the argument usually mounted for proselytizing does not apply to the Lubavitch community under study.

Another reason why many religious groups need to recruit outsiders is that their numbers are depleted by members lapsing from the faith. To help retain a stable population figure, the community has to shop in the larger community for interested people to join it. The community's size may decline, then, as adults become dissatisfied and disappointed with the community's life-style and leave. The Lubavitch community under study, however, is able to provide its members with a tenable way of life and few, if any, leave the community. If, as I have suggested, the manifest consequences of proselytizing do not pertain to this particular community, why, then, is this activity pursued? I maintain that it is rather the latent consequences of proselytizing that are important to the community's persistence.

Festinger, et al., in their presentation of cognitive-dissonance theory in *When Prophecy Fails*, suggest that a consequence of a group's successful proselytizing is reduced dissonance (1956:28). If the group's central beliefs are either questioned or disbelieved by others, proselytizing becomes an effective means of reaffirming the members' identity with the group. As the writers assert, "If more and more people can be persuaded that the system of belief is correct, then clearly it must, after all, be correct" (1956:28). In spite of the fact that they recognize that a large proportion of Jews in Montreal do not share their convictions about orthodox Judaism, Lubavitcher do not become discouraged and continue ordering their lives according to their version of precepts underlying traditional Jewish law. It is precisely the act of proselytizing in the larger Jewish community that reinforces the members' beliefs and enables the Lubavitch community to retain its distinctive identity. When a Lubavitcher attempts to influence and convince a non-observant Jew of the relevance of orthodox Judaism, and the importance of the Lubavitcher *Rebbe*, he is, in fact, becoming influenced and convinced himself (Mead, 1934:199-246).

It appears that Lubavitchers' proselytizing in the larger Jewish community would threaten the preservation of their distinctive identity by diluting the community's boundaries and thus the distinction between insiders and outsiders. This threat does not, however, appear to decrease the Chassidim's proselytizing zeal, nor in fact to weaken the community. In spite of theories to the contrary, proselytizing appears to have beneficial consequences for the community that are almost incidental to most of its professed aims.

Notes

1. I am indebted to Berkeley Fleming for his valuable suggestions on an earlier draft of this paper.

2. From the Lubavitch headquarters in Brooklyn, New York, the Lubavitcher *Rebbe* directs the affairs of the Lubavitch movement throughout the world. To his Chassidim the *Rebbe* represents the essence of Lubavitch. The *Rebbe*'s followers recognize him as a central figure in their lives and are eager to accept his views and practise his directives. An appreciation of any chassidic group requires that the reader understands the Chassidim's relationship to their *Rebbe*. Some recent studies about the Chassidim deal with the *Rebbe*'s importance to his followers. Mintz (1968), for example, presents an analysis of the *Rebbe*'s functions and suggests that the *Rebbe* serves as a mediator between his followers and God. In his chapter on "The Lubavitcher Movement," Weiner (1969) describes his personal audience with the Lubavitcher *Rebbe*. For a discussion of the Satmarer *Rebbe*, see Rubin (1972), pp. 56-62. Gutwirth's study (1970) of the Belzer Chassidim includes discussion of the Belzer *Rebbe*.

3. My doctoral dissertation was written on the Lubavitch community in Montreal. A discussion of how this chassidic community maintains a dis-

tinctive way of life while actively engaging in proselytizing work in the larger Jewish community is presented in William Shaffir, *Life in A Religious Community: The Lubavitcher Chassidim in Montreal.* Toronto: Holt, Rinehart and Winston of Canada, Limited, 1974.

References

Aberle, D.F., et. al.
   1950 "The Functional Prerequisites of Society." *Ethics*, 60: (January) pp. 100-11.
Baum, M., and S. Wheeler
   1968 "Becoming an Inmate," in S. Wheeler (ed.), *Controlling Delinquents*, New York: John Wiley and Sons.
Becker, H.S.
   1960 "Notes on the Concept of Commitment." *American Journal of Sociology*, 66 (July):32-40.
Cicourel, A.V., and J.I. Kitsuse
   1963 *The Educational Decision-Makers.* New York: The Bobbs-Merrill Company, Inc.
Clemmer, D.
   1958 *The Prison Community.* New York: Holt, Rinehart and Winston.
De Sanctis, S.
   1927 *Religious Conversion.* London: Routledge and Kegan Paul.
Festinger, L., H.W. Riecken, and S. Schachter
   1956 *When Prophecy Fails* New York: Harper and Row.
Glaser, B.G., and H.L. Strauss
   1971 *Status Passage.* Chicago: Aldine Atherton.
Goffman, E.
   1961 *Asylums.* New York: Doubleday.
Gordon, A.I.
   1967 *The Nature of Conversion.* Boston: Beacon Press.
Gutwirth, J.
   1970 *Vie Juive Traditionnelle: Ethnologie d'une Communauté Hassidique.* Paris: Les Editions De Minuit.
Hostetler, J.A.
   1968 *Amish Society.* Baltimore: The John Hopkins Press.
Kitsuse, J.I.
   1970 "Editor's Preface." *American Behavioural Scientist* 14: (November-December):163-65.
Lofland, J. and R. Stark
   1965 "Conversion to a Deviant Perspective." *American Sociological Review*, 30 (December):862-75.

Lofland, J.
  1966 *Doomsday Cult: A Study of Conversion, Proselytization, and Maintenance of Faith*. Englewood Cliffs, N.J.: Prentice-Hall, Inc.
Mead, G.H.
  1934 *Mind, Self and Society*. Chicago: The University of Chicago Press.
Mercurio, J.A.
  1972 *Caning: Educational Rite and Tradition*. Syracuse: Syracuse University Division of Special Education and Rehabilitation and the Center on Human Policy.
Mintz, J.
  1968 *Legends of the Hasidim*. Chicago: University of Chicago Press.
Poll, S.
  1962 *The Hassidic Community of Williamsburg*. New York: the Free Press of Glencoe, Inc.
Redekop, C.W.
  1969 *The Old Colony Mennonites: Dilemmas of Ethnic Minority Life*. Baltimore: The John Hopkins Press.
Rubin, I.
  1972 *Satmar: An Island in the City*. Chicago: Quadrangle Books.
Scott, R.A.
  1969 *The Making of Blind Men*. New York: Russell Sage Foundation.
Shaffir, W.
  1974 *Life in a Religious Community: The Lubavitcher Chassidim in Montreal*. Toronto: Holt, Rinehart and Winston of Canada, Limited.
Shibutani, T.
  1955 "Reference Groups as Perspectives." *American Journal of Sociology*, 60 (May):562-69.
Sobol, B.
  1956 "The Milochim: A Study of a Religious Community." Unpublished Master's Thesis, New School of Social Research.
Weiner, H.
  1969 *Mystics*. New York: Holt, Rinehart and Winston.

16
Community Organization of Italians in Toronto
Clifford J. Jansen*

What qualifies a group of persons of common ethnic origin to be referred to as a community? What distinct organizations or institutions tend to be created within the ethnic group? Who are the ethnic leaders and what roles do they play? These are some of the questions considered in this paper with special reference to Italians in Toronto.

Ethnic Communities
The concept of an ethnic community is best captured by J.P. Fitzpatrick when he states that an ethnic community is:

> ...a group of people who follow a way of life or patterns of behaviour which mark them out as different from the people of another society, or from other people in the larger society in which they live or to which they have come. They...have generally come from the same place, or...identified with the particular locality where they now live....They speak the same language, probably have the same religious beliefs. They tend to "stick together," to help and support each other. They have expectations of loyalty one to the other and methods of control (Fitzpatrick, 1966:6).

But the label "community" is often given to a group even when some of the basic conditions described above are not present. In these cases the label is usually given by persons outside the group in question. The community referred to may *not* be "concentrated...in a limited territory." Persons of German origin who live in Toronto tend to be well dispersed

* *Clifford J. Jansen is Associate Professor of Sociology, York University, Toronto.*

through the city with very little concentration, yet daily newspapers, government agencies, and the population in general often refer to the "German community." Similarly, the above definition refers to a "sense of loyalty" to the group, when in fact quite often there are strong dissensions within the group giving rise to a number of sub-groups. Because of these rivalries one may question whether the label "community" is appropriate. On the other hand, some groups may have a common ethnic and historical background and seldom be referred to as a community. The British, who comprise the largest proportion of post-war immigrants to Canada, or immigrants from the United States who have been increasing in numbers in recent years, are hardly ever referred to as "communities."

At what point, then, does an immigrant or ethnic group tend to be referred to as a community? It seems to occur only when the ethnic group creates distinctive institutions which are specific to its members which fulfil functions similar to those of institutions of the wider society. When there is an obvious need for such sub-group institutions and a considerable degree of participation of sub-group members in these institutional activities, one can speak of community organization.

But most ethnic institutions face a dilemma, for it has been proposed that the degree of institutional completeness of a particular group (i.e., the number of ethnic institutions) may affect the integration of the group into the wider society (Breton, 1964). Many ethnic institutions are designed to assist immigrants in the transition from the old country to the new one. However, such an aim implies the eventual self-destruction of the institution itself, once it is felt that the community is sufficiently integrated to participate in the institutions of the wider society. The problem is accentuated by the fact that the children of imigrants will most likely receive their education in the new country and therefore relate more easily to institutions of the new society than to the old ones.

Another area of concern is that of ethnic leadership. All sub-groups give rise to some leaders or representatives of the group. Leaders are usually either heads of one or more community institutions, "locals" to whom a number of persons in the community turn for advice, or persons involved in a number of important community decisions.[1]

The role of the ethnic leader in a community is described by S.N. Eisenstadt when he states that the existence of a distinct (ethnic or immigrant) community need not necessarily be a sign of a lack of adaptation, provided its members perform the universal roles of society, its particularist tendencies agree with the normative premises of the absorbing social structure, and its structural peculiarities fall within the wider society's legitimate institutional limits. But in such cases, ethnic associations and leaders play important roles as channels of communication and as mediators of the roles and values of the wider society (Eisenstadt, 1954).

This role, however, places the ethnic community leader in a marginal position and gives rise to divided loyalty. According to Kurt Lewin, this is mainly due to the different structures of the receiving society and the ethnic group. While in the former the forces acting on the individual member are directed toward the central layers of the group (toward integration of the group), in the latter they are directed toward the periphery, and often toward the higher status members of the receiving society. So, the ethnic leader, while displaying his qualifications for acceptance by the receiving society, has to continue to maintain certain characteristics of the ethnic group, so that they too will "accept" him as a leader (Lewin, 1948).

Finally, the larger the ethnic group the more likely will be the possibility of a variety of solutions to problems. Rival groups and leaders may each have their own answer as to what is "good for the group." So leaders are often faced with the added element of competition in their endeavours.

Let us turn to a study of Italians in Toronto to describe an ethnic community in an urban setting.

Community Organization of Italians
According to the Census of 1971, there were 250,190 persons of Italian ethnic origin in Metropolitan Toronto, making them the second largest ethnic-origin group (12.0 per cent) after the British. The number of families who indicated that their mother tongue was Italian (language first spoken and still understood) was 58,300.[2]

Our survey revealed that the average number of persons per Italian family was 4.3 (for Toronto as a whole in 1971 this was 3.4) and the average length of residence in Canada was 13.1 years. Immigration from Italy to Canada has dropped sharply in recent years; 71.8 per cent had been here ten years or more while only 11.8 per cent had been here six years or less.

The principal jobs of heads of households were Craftsmen or Labourers (58.9 per cent); the only other category with more than a tenth was the Managerial (15.9 per cent), presumably manager-owners of small businesses. The average individual income before taxes per week was $209 and for the whole family it was $267.

Toronto Italians originate principally from the poorer southern parts of Italy. The survey showed that 25.9 per cent were from Calabria, 19.3 per cent from Abruzzi, 15.9 per cent from Lazio, and 10.8 per cent from Sicily. All of these are regions south of Rome, and 67.1 per cent said their home in Italy had been a small village. While 53.8 per cent had visited Italy in the past three years, 32 per cent had not left Canada at all during that period.

Over half of respondents (52.5 per cent) owned their homes, and the average down payment was $7,486. Over half (52.8 per cent) said they had no credit cards—not even for gasoline.

Language has often been cited as one of the principal problems facing the group. In conducting our survey, 60 per cent were interviewed in Italian because 64.1 per cent still converse with their spouses in Italian, and while 42.4 per cent of the males had attended English-language classes themselves, only 28.8 per cent of their spouses had done so. Only 26.3 per cent speak Italian to their children, while as few as 4.7 per cent of their children converse in Italian between themselves. Sixty-two per cent converse entirely in English, while 33.2 per cent use both languages. Only 34.5 per cent said their children attended Italian-language classes.

When asked if they preferred living in a predominantly Italian neighbourhood, only 39.5 per cent said they did–37.6 per cent preferred mixed ethnic neighbourhoods, and 22.9 per cent preferred predominantly English-speaking neighbourhoods. When asked about citizenship, as many as 70.1 per cent said they had become Canadians, and another 12.5 per cent intended to become citizens as soon as possible. This figure appears quite high at first, but when one considers that immigration has dropped off considerably in the past few years, most Italians who are here are eligible to become citizens.

In both our 1968 case study[3] and our 1973 survey study,[4] institutions mentioned as playing an important role in the community were: the church; social assistance organizations; the media; and social clubs. While very few said that ethnic leaders play an important role, we feel that they should be discussed also.

The Church

The institution of the church performs a unique function for immigrants, since it is the one institution that provides continuity between their former lives in Italy and their new lives in Toronto. In addition to its manifest religious function, a church ceremony functions as a social gathering where one may meet fellow countrymen, use one's mother tongue, and have a link with the wider society through the priest, who usually is not only bilingual but has a better knowledge of the expectations, norms, customs, and culture of the host society.

Because of the important role of the church, the twenty-two priests interviewed in 1968 were asked whether they felt Italians attended church more often in Toronto than in Italy, the degree to which they participated in the social activities of the church, the role played by the church in the non-religious sphere, and the kinds of contacts these priests had with secular organizations. These same questions were again asked in a 1974 interview with a priest-spokesman of Italian priests in Toronto. Of the seven priests interviewed in 1968 who thought Italians did not attend church more frequently in Toronto, one explained that they were rural persons unable to cope with the highly structured urban services. Among those who felt that these immigrants did attend more frequently in Toronto, one explained that Torontonians in general were more church minded: "...the church is seen as a moral force for good in this country";

"Religious attitudes here are more sincere, since Catholics are only a proportion of all religious groups–unlike in Italy, where everybody is supposedly Catholic." Only one respondent felt that it was "...a means of preserving national ties in an Anglo-Saxon atmosphere."

In the 1973 interviews, however, the reason given for low attendance was a structural one: all churches with Italian-speaking priests and services conducted in Italian are concentrated in the major Italian areas in the city, but more and more Italians are "spreading out" across the city and therefore feel lost in a mainly Anglo-Saxon church structure. This could well be the case. In the 1973-74 edition of the Italian Commercial Guide, where twenty-six Italian Catholic churches are listed, only two are *not* in what is considered to be the principal Italian area of the city. Yet, the 1971 census shows 4,995 families with Italian mother-tongue in Etobicoke (only one church) and 3,165 in Scarborough (only one church), while North York with 17,735 Italians also has large areas where no Italian services are held.

Twelve of twenty-two priests felt there was good participation by Italians in church "societies"–but these were mainly in parishes where the congregation was predominantly (sometimes as much as 80 per cent) Italian. Among the remaining ten, it was felt very difficult to get Italians involved "because Italians were not people for organizations." "Because of the language barrier–even those who could speak English felt at a psychological disadvantage *vis-à-vis* their Anglo-Saxon counterparts," and "it was near impossible to get women involved in anything."

In the 1973 interview it was felt that those men's clubs that did get together were in no way church-related, but that church buildings and facilities (notice boards, bulletins, etc.) were often used by them.

The principal roles played by the church in the social life of immigrants were seen as mainly unintentional: it provided opportunity for people to meet each other; the priest was often knowledgeable about available social services; and the mere existence of a social organization like the church, which had Canadian as well as immigrant parishioners, had to have an effect on helping immigrants to integrate. One respondent felt the church was a form of social security–the priest was usually among the few persons willing to help without having any "ulterior motive." Less than half of the parishioners investigated felt they had been directly involved in non-parish activities.

One important development which has taken place since 1968 is the formation of a committee of priests having large numbers of Italian parishioners. It is composed of sixty-five priests, all but seven of whom are Italians. The priest interviewed in 1974 was an executive member of this committee.

The committee has not had an easy existence to date. This is partly due to the differing opinions among the priests themselves about what issues are to be dealt with, and partly due to the fact that the committee has no "official" recognition from the Catholic hierarchy of Toronto. While the Bishop of Toronto sees the need for greater help for immigrants, many non-immigrant priests fail to see any special problems faced by immigrants. Their general attitude has been "immigrants should assimilate to the Canadian way of life, then we can treat them as any other group."

Achievements of the committee to date (1975) include a television program every Sunday called "Il Samaritano," a radio program discussion, and publication of a weekly bulletin distributed at Italian Sunday masses, *La Voce*.

In conclusion, we may say that the role played by the church has depended largely on the actions of individual priests, has been largely uncoordinated and quite often unintentional.

Social Assistance Organizations

"Social assistance organizations" is a sort of umbrella name given to various organizations which in one way or another attempt to deal with a variety of problems faced by the Italian immigrant in his daily life. These problems may range from the purely material (money problems, getting a job, etc.) to the more cultural (learning the new language, adapting to the new culture, taking steps to becoming a Canadian citizen), and the moral (mainly conflicts of mores between parents and children). The organizations to be discussed here include the Centro Organizativo Scuole Techniche Italiane, the Italian Immigrant Aid Society, Centro Organizativo Italiano, and New Canada.

Centro Organizativo Scuole Techniche Italiane

The Centro Organizativo Scuole Techniche Italiane is a community service organization dedicated to the principle of "integration through education." It was founded in 1961, when because of a recession in Canada, a group of individuals, including Charles Caccia (Liberal member of Parliament for Davenport since 1968) and Father Carraro (founder), wanted to do something to help the most vulnerable groups, e.g., Italians in the construction industry having no other qualifications. On September 7, 1962, Centro Organizativo Scuole Techniche Italiane was officially recognized as a non-profit organization by the provincial secretary and ministry of citizenship. Since its modest beginnings, the centre has expanded very successfully and today offers a variety of services to immigrants, over 80 per cent of whom are Italian.

The work done by the centre can be divided into two principal areas: adult education and social services. In 1973, eighty-six courses were organized for 1,752 students, with the principal objective of upgrading skills in preparation for specific jobs. In addition, 1,350 students attended English-language classes. The centre also has a rehabilitation program for the physically handicapped, employing between forty and forty-five persons on its premises at any one time. This program, sponsored by the Workmen's Compensation Board, principally trains and retrains the handicapped in cabinet-making and furniture finishing.

Under social services, the principal areas of activity are counselling, general assistance, and community work. Most counselling is done in the areas of vocational choice (3,721 cases in 1973), and family problems (603 cases) such as marital discord, value conflict between parents and children, school drop-outs, drug abuse, runaways from home, etc. And it is counselling services that the centre hopes to expand.

Too many Italian youths drop out of the school system at an early age. The centre has thus arranged a project with Atkinson College (part time and night school leading to a degree) of York University whereby interested persons may "try out" their abilities to do university study part time—even though they may have "dropped out" of education at an earlier stage. Then there is a feeling that too many Italian youths are oriented toward vocational-type careers, principally because parents are seldom involved enough in their children's education. A project called "two-way value translations" tries to encourage parents to become more involved in the education process by scheduling meetings of parents and teachers (held in Italian, with interpreters present if necessary).

Attempts are also being made to get Italian women more involved in community matters. Plans are to provide a drop-in centre for women, and a program which will show women how they can participate meaningfully in the community.

Under the rubric of general assistance, the centre helps individuals to deal with bureaucracies like the Unemployment Insurance Commission, the Workmen's Compensation Board, or welfare departments (2,467 cases in 1973); the centre does interpreting (929), and offers legal and information services in the areas of education, health, housing, human rights, work, etc. (5,441).

Community work involves meeting with citizens' groups, helping to set up new services and programs, and meeting with social agencies to discuss the special problems of immigrants.

Principal sources of the centre's income are from fees for services such as work done for the Workmen's Compensation Board, Metro Social Services, etc., as well as from government grants and the United Appeal Fund. The Centro Organizativo Scuole Techniche Italiane also has a membership club to which members contribute.

The Italian Immigrant Aid Society

Founded in 1952, the Italian Immigrant Aid Society was officially recognized in 1956 as a corporation without share capital. Its principal aim is to work "exclusively towards fitting Italian immigrants into Canadian life." Qualified as a charitable organization, it is financed by voluntary contributions received from individuals and business firms, an annual dance event and membership dues.

Principal activities include: finding employment; helping immigrants familiarize themselves with the languages, laws, and customs of Canada; enlightening immigrants in the history, constitution, and legislation of Canada so that as good citizens they may become aware of their rights and duties; helping victims of accident or illness; helping the unemployed and destitute; preparing immigrants for Canadian citizenship; and providing whatever other services may be requested. Specific services provided include: information and referral; interpreting; translation of documents; and specific services similar to those started under the Local Initiatives and Opportunities for Youth programs.

The Local Initiatives grant funded a project which gave additional instruction in the homes of Italian immigrant children attending regular elementary schools, but who were having difficulties because of the language. Carried out by twelve university graduates, this program had the added advantage of getting parents and children to learn English together. Under the auspices of the Italian Immigrant Aid Society two Opportunities for Youth grants were received in 1971. One project called Approach the Italian Poor helped identify the principal problems of the poorer elements of the community while a second, Italian Child Care, assisted children from needy families by providing an opportunity to observe and participate in the Canadian milieu of the city: children were taken to museums, galleries, parks and the like. This project was also handled by university students.

Centro Organizativo Italiano

The impetus for starting the Centro Organizativo Italiano stemmed originally from the concern which the Young Men's Christian Association at Dovercourt and College Streets showed in getting Italian workmen more organized. A study of the problems of the area led to a number of persons obtaining Opportunities for Youth grants for limited projects in the area, which included free movies being shown on a large screen on a dead-end street, summer classes in Italian for children of immigrant parents, and the organizing of a theatre for young people.

With the aid of a Local Initiatives grant a "storefront" was opened on College Street in January 1972. At first, workmen were helped with the filling out of official forms, interpreting, and general problems they faced. One kind of problem tended to stand out: dealing with the Workmen's Compensation Board and unemployment insurance. As a result of these initial efforts, an Action Committee was set up in May 1973 to look into the problem of Italian workers' rights, and from this committee a Union of Injured Workers was formed. In the area of unemployment insurance a committee of 200 members was started and their activities are directed by a policy committee. Among the achievements of this committee is the fact that a number of Italian-speaking immigrants are now employed directly by the Unemployment Insurance Commission.

In addition a Circle for the Aged was started on the premises. It has become a meeting place for the aged in the area, financed by the Department of National Health and Welfare. To date, however, the circle is frequented almost entirely by males, it being very difficult to get women to participate in these activities. The problem of the aged is becoming more acute among Italians since in many families both parents work, young children speak mainly English, and the aged become more and more isolated.

The present aims of the centre as a whole are: interpreting–particularly legal documents and in dealing with various bureaucracies; organization–getting groups with common interests (workers, the aged, etc.) to organize; and cultural–helping a variety of immigrants learn more about their own (Italian) culture and also about Canadian culture. So far, this is carried out mainly through films and the theatre.

The majority of members live within a two-mile radius of the centre and most clients who use services have been in Toronto for ten to twenty years, so that future activities are not likely to decrease as a result of the drop in the number of Italian immigrants to Canada in recent years.

Although funds for starting the project were part of a Local Initiatives grant, sources of income now include the Secretary of State's Office, Toronto City Council, and the United Appeal.

New Canada Project

The second project to get under way with a LIP grant is called New Canada and it started with a very specific aim: to acquaint as many Italian immigrants as possible with the procedures involved in becoming Canadian citizens. At first, project workers simply distributed leaflets to as many Italian households as possible, giving them a number to call if they were at all interested in Canadian citizenship. In addition, the idea was discussed on a radio program "Parliamo Insieme" (let's talk together). Started in February 1972, the program had registered 5,675 persons by mid-1974; 4,000 have applied for citizenship and so far 2,500 have already obtained it through the program. Again, the idea seems to be of greatest appeal to immigrants who came to Canada in the 1950s, and who though eligible had no idea about how to proceed in obtaining Canadian citizenship.

From this single initial goal, the project has developed other areas of interest: more citizen participation on the part of Italians; understanding of various levels of Canadian government and its departments, and simply reinforcing Italian identity, without organizing them into any formal groupings.

Long-term goals, some of which are already under way, include getting various government departments, particularly the Workmen's Compensation Board, the Unemployment Insurance Commission, and the Canada Pension Plan, to deal directly with the clientèle, thus removing the need for "middlemen" who often work to the detriment of the client. Some of these government departments have already taken up offices in the project's building, located in the heart of the Italian area at Dufferin and St. Clair Avenues.

In addition to the Local Initiatives grant, New Canada received funds from the Minister of Multiculturalism and the provincial and metropolitan levels of government.

The activities carried out by these four social assistance groups tend to show how Italians themselves are responding to the principal needs of the community. In many cases their activities overlap, but given the size of the community, its geographical distribution across the city, and the locations of these centres it is likely that they are each rendering a service in their own particular way.

The Media

Italians have a daily newspaper, a weekly newspaper, a monthly magazine, a radio station, and several daily and weekly programs on various television stations. In the recent survey, heads of Italian households were asked about their behaviour and attitudes in this area.

When asked about readership of the daily newspaper *Corriere Canadaese*, 21.9 per cent said they read it daily and another 39.2 per cent read it sometimes. In 1973, the newspaper had an average circulation of about 20,000 per day. In addition, 39.5 per cent said they read the weekly Italian newspaper, *Il Giornale di Toronto*, regularly. With regard to Toronto's three English-language newspapers, almost three in ten read the Toronto *Star* daily, just over a tenth read the *Sun* but only 5.0 per cent read the *Globe and Mail* daily.

While a majority of parents listened principally to the Italian radio station, their children preferred English stations to a much greater extent. Just under half of respondents had bought a television in the past three years; three in ten had a colour set. A brief examination of a television guide for any given week (in this case 5-12 May 1974), reveals that there is at least one Italian program daily on weekdays and that on Sundays there are as many as six. In the survey, a third of the respondents said they watched the daily show every day of the week and just about half watched it every Sunday.

By examining the content of the two newspapers in a three-month period in 1973 we may be able to see the principal interests of the community. This analysis of content will be supplemented by comments from interviews with key persons on the staff of these newspapers.

The *Corriere* generally contains twelve pages per day, extended to fourteen from time to time, while the *Giornale* usually has sixteen extending to eighteen per week.

Each newspaper includes classified advertising. These classified advertisements usually focus on real estate; buying and selling objects; jobs and professional services: repairmen, plumbers etc. A good deal of regular advertising is from Italian owners of local businesses, including an Italian bookstore, movie house, television program, and radio station, but large non-Italian companies also advertise in Italian, including banks, loan companies, funeral parlours, supermarkets, furniture and department stores. The *Giornale* also has a regular column of advertisements from different (mostly Italian) travel agents.

Both newspapers tend to cover Canadian, world, and Italian news. The *Giornale* more often than not has headline news concerning either local Italian events (Toronto) or some event from Italy. One striking difference is the habit of the *Giornale* to publish its principal articles in English with Italian translations from time to time. In an interview, the editor of this paper explained that the paper sees itself as the "guardian" of rights of Italians in Toronto—thus when an important issue presents itself, he wishes "influential" non-Italians to know about it.

In the area of sport both papers cover local and world events, but particular emphasis is placed on Italian sports in the latter context. Since there is a growing interest in soccer in North America and most teams have European origins—players on local teams are mostly European and almost all visiting teams come from Europe—more and more ethnic firms and the media (newspapers, radio, television) are sponsoring matches.

It is probably in the area of special "features" that the two newspapers differ most. The *Corriere* gives daily rates of foreign exchange and the temperature in different places in Italy, as well as brief summaries of world and local news very similar to those found in the English language press of Toronto, the *Giornale* includes times of masses in Italian churches in Toronto weekly—these are but minor differences. The *Giornale* devotes space to letters to the editor while the *Corriere* has a daily column entiled "La Grande Citta" (the Big City) in which it gives brief summaries of different local services.

This short comparison of the two newspapers provides an idea of the role of the media in shaping the future of the Italian community in Toronto. In this period of consolidation of the community (i.e., immigration from Italy dropping to its lowest level in post-war years) the media play as important a role as channels of communication with the wider society and particularly with the various levels of Canadian government as that expected of ethnic leaders. Before turning to the question of leaders, we would briefly like to discuss the role of ethnic clubs.

Ethnic Clubs

In 1970 the Federation of Italian Canadian Associations and Clubs was incorporated as a non-share capital corporation. By 1973 the Federation consisted of sixty organizations. Listed among these are regional clubs based on village or origin in Italy (Abbruzzi Club, Lazio Club, Matera

Club, Molise '70, Pisticci Club), sports clubs, and special interest clubs. Given the large number of clubs, it is surprising to note that in the survey conducted in 1973 only 17.1 per cent said that they belonged to any Italian clubs whatsoever in Toronto.

Since many of these smaller clubs may thus exist more in name than in reality, the focus of this section will be mainly on the activities and aims of the Federation of Italian Canadian Associations and Clubs and on some of its achievements to date.

Membership in the Federation is only granted to those clubs which have shown permanence, seriousness, and determination in their objectives and willingness to co-operate within the framework of a general community design. Among aims of the Federation are: the uniting fraternally of all corporations, associations, and other legal entities with an Italian character; to foster and encourage the integration of Italian immigrants into the Canadian way of life; to cultivate the values of Italian tradition; and to study the problems of various aspects of the Italian Canadian.

The greatest efforts appear to have been made in the area of education. The Federation reacted strongly against the high proportion of Italian students being oriented toward vocational-type schools and suggested that the method used to assess the mental ability of students for higher academic study worked against persons of different language and cultural background. The Federation now has a delegate on a special commission of the Board of Education and was instrumental in getting Italian taught in schools with large numbers of Italian-origin students. Annually, the Federation holds "The Italian Heritage Seminar" for teachers to give them a realistic picture of students of Italian background. It was also instrumental in getting an independent Department of Italian Studies in the University of Toronto and provides bursaries to be awarded to the most proficient students of the Italian language at the University of Guelph.

In areas other than education, the Federation of Italian Canadian Associations and Clubs organized the Italian pavilion for the annual Metro Caravan in Toronto; it organized a visit by the Prime Minister of Canada to the Italian community, in which the Prime Minister was made Honorary President of the Federation; and it is at present planning a home for the aged called "Villa Colombo" in order to "express the gratitude of the new generation of Italians to those who first came to Canada and changed the face of our country through sacrifice and hardship." Other activities include a summer camp for children, an after-school Italian program in public schools, referrals to appropriate social assistance agencies, briefs to various government commissions, for example, on the "unjustifiable bias against Italians" in television programs and the news media, and a campaign to help more Italians become Canadian citizens.

Principal sources of finance are grants from the Citizenship Department of the Ontario government and from the Secretary of State's office in the federal government, while membership clubs pay a yearly fee, although the sum is fairly nominal.

Italian Leadership

In the introduction to this chapter we pointed out the difficulties of identifying leaders in any community. The simplest approach is to ask people being interviewed in the community who the leaders are. This was done both in 1968 when "key" informants were interviewed and in 1973 when a random sample of heads of households were interviewed. The negative aspects of a simple question like "When you think of persons who are leaders in the community which three names come to mind?" can be seen by the fact that in 1968, 37 per cent of the "key" informants failed to mention one name and in 1973, 54 per cent of heads of households did likewise.

The "key" informants quite often preferred giving comments about leadership such as: "There aren't any real leaders but self-appointed men taking the lead"; "You don't talk to Italians about leaders: each Italian speaks for himself–they're individualists"; and "Most leaders here further their own interests and not those of the community."

Despite the high proportion who did not mention any names in the survey of households, there were a total of 426 mentions (each respondent was allowed to mention up to 3 names), referring to a total of 37 different people. But it was soon obvious that in the minds of respondents "leaders" meant the best-known persons in the community. The first five names, accounting for 84.8 per cent of all mentions, included a federal member of Parliament, a city alderman, the Italian consul, an owner of a radio station–long popular in the community–and the president of the Federation of Italian Clubs. What was interesting was that so few of the persons in charge of the organizations, the media, etc. were mentioned. In fact, only two people mentioned the name of a priest and one person mentioned the owner of a newspaper. One must conclude that the persons working actively for the good of the community are not necessarily those whose names are most popular within it.

Given this situation, where "popular" personalities are generally mentioned as leaders, it was not felt appropriate to interview these persons in 1973. However, in the 1968 study, twelve such persons were interviewed about their roles in the community. It was interesting to note when comparing names mentioned by "key" informants in 1968 and heads of households in 1973 that only three names from the former were still considered leaders in 1973 and that these three got the most mentions (108, 105, and 89 respectively).

The twelve original leaders were, respectively, a director of several companies (since disappeared from the public scene through illness), a business owner, a television producer (now returned to Italy after a scandal involving funds belonging to tourists), a real estate agent, a high school teacher, a general insurance agent, a lawyer-politician, an editor-publisher (still at the same job), an executive director of a company, an alderman, an estate planner, and a company president. While most Italians originate from the poorer south of Italy these leaders were evenly split between the north and south. The majority were not living in areas of Toronto where Italians predominated. While the large majority of Italian immigrants had elementary education or less, all but one of the leaders had at least secondary education or higher.

While persons heading organizations of various kinds in the community tend to work with (at least a few) other Italians, most of the "named" leaders tended to be in competition with each other. For example, some felt only the work they were involved in in the community to be worthwhile. Several claimed sole recognition for having started campaigns of various kinds in the community. When asked about their relationships with other named leaders, their remarks were usually derogatory.

The discussion of leadership so far refers to the study carried out in 1968 and one must be careful not to over-emphasize this negative role of leadership because it may be due to the fashion in which sociologists try to determine leadership in the community. Decisions affecting large proportions of the community may be made by persons whose names never appear in the limelight. This certainly tends to be the case for a number of persons involved in organizations of the community today.

From the individual interviews carried out in 1973 with persons in various organizations, one gets the impression that the heyday of the "popular leader" is at an end. There may be many new leaders working "behind the scenes" without community recognition, but carrying out a competent job. As one such person mentioned when interviewed: "We never sign our name to any of the literature we distribute—we use the name of the organization." And he added, "When we first thought of the idea (of helping Italians become citizens) we approached several popular leaders. But they were mostly interested in appending their names to the literature we distributed—so we avoided further contact with them."

Judging by the fact that the general survey of households, as many as twenty-one of the thirty-seven names mentioned were only mentioned once, we must conclude that there are a number of persons doing a good job in the community whose names have not achieved the notoriety of the "popular leader."

Conclusion

After reviewing the many aspects of the Italian community and its institutions, we come to the conclusion that it is reasonable to hope, as a leader in 1968 did, that the immigrants today are "individualistic members of some future Italian community." This is certainly the impression one is left with from the number of organizations which have been created since 1968. In 1973, as compared to 1968, fewer accusations were made and there was much more co-operation between various persons, groups, and organizations serving the community.

The "old-style" popular leader who was "more in it for his own reputation than for the good of the group" seems to be on the way out and there are many lesser known persons genuinely working for the good of the whole community. This maturity of the group has come about for several reasons, including the fact that immigration from Italy has dropped off sharply in the past five years. It is no longer easy to migrate back and forth to Italy; more persons are beginning to "accept" Canada as their home rather than a "stopping place" before retiring in Italy. No doubt this is also due to the fact that their children now have their roots here. More and more Italians have become Canadian citizens, allowing them to fully participate in the political life of the country.

Secondly, the first generation of young Italians are graduating from high schools and to a lesser degree from universities, and they are genuinely concerned about bettering their community—no doubt because of the difficulties and stigmas they have had to face in achieving that level of education. The 1968-74 period was also one where "opportunity" existed in the form of federal and provincial grants to "try out" new ventures. And this was coupled by a firm commitment by the federal government to a policy of multiculturalism, making newcomers really feel that they were "one of us."

Thirdly, since Italians are the largest non-British ethnic group in Toronto they have a "leadership" role to play for groups such as the Portuguese, Greeks, and similar southern Europeans, who because of their later arrival and smaller numbers do not have the same influence in their dealings with Canadians.

This study of the success of Italian institutions in Toronto certainly supports the thesis that multiculturalism in Canada is a reality; many Italians are identifying with the ethnic Italian community in the 1970s. They are part of the Canadian ethnic mosaic.

Notes

1. The data presented here are based on the 1971 census, our case studies work done in 1968 and again in 1973, and a random survey sample of Italian households carried out in Toronto in 1973.

2. Sociologists have used three basic techniques for identifying community leaders: a) positional technique: those who occupy key positions in the major social, economic or political institutions of the community; b)

reputational technique: those who have a "reputation" for power, assessed by the community; c) decision-making techniques: identifying those who were involved in important community decisions (Aiken, et al., 1970:192-358). All three of these techniques were used in this study.

3. For the 1968 study a list of Italian community organizations such as churches, social assistance organizations, media organizations, clubs, trade unions with large numbers of Italian workers, travel and real estate agents, was established from the Italian Canadian Directory. In each of these spokesmen willing to talk about the community were contacted. Interviews were relatively unstructured but while some questions were asked of all groups (e.g., principal concerns of the community, who the leaders were); others were naturally directed to specific problems (e.g., church attendance, attendance at labour-union meetings, travelling between Italy and Canada). The twelve leaders mentioned by these spokesmen were interviewed about community problems, their own roles, and their relations with other named leaders. While these spokesmen gave a good idea of their views of the Italian community they could not be considered as a representative sample.

4. In the 1973 study some key spokesmen (or the persons now holding the same positions) interviewed in 1968 were interviewed again but the 1973 study also included questions to a representative sample of heads of households. The 1971 Census indicated that there were 58,000 households where the head had "Italian" as a mother tongue. The proportion of these heads of households in each census tract of Metropolitan Toronto was calculated. It was decided to try to interview 580 heads of household (1 per cent) and these were selected on the basis of the total number of each census tract. The sample thus covered the whole of the Metropolitan area, even those parts of the city which are not predominantly "Italian."

References

Aiken, M., and P.E. Mott (eds.)
1970 *The Structure of Community.* New York: Random House.
Allodi, F.
1971 "The Italians in Toronto: Mental Health Problems of an Immigrant Community," in W.E. Mann (ed.) *Social Deviance in Canada.* Toronto: Copp Clark.
Boissevain, J.
1970 *The Italians of Montreal: Social Adjustment in a Plural Society.* Ottawa: The Queen's Printer.

Breton, R.
1964 "Institutional Completeness of Ethnic Communities and Personal Relations of Immigrants." *The American Journal of Sociology*, 70: 193-205.

Danziger, K.
1971 *The Socialization of Immigrant Children.* Toronto: York University Ethnic Research Programme. Institute of Behavioural Research.

Eisenstadt, S.N.
1954 *The Absorption of Immigrants.* London: Routledge and Kegan Paul.

Fitzpatrick, J.P.
1966 "The Importance of Community in the Process of Immigrant Assimilation." *International Migration Review*, 1:1.

Jansen, C.J.
1969 "Leadership in the Toronto Italian Ethnic Group." *International Migration Review*, 4:1.

Jansen, C.J.
1971 "The Italian Community in Toronto," in Jean L. Elliott (ed.) *Minority Canadians II.* Scarborough: Prentice-Hall.

Lewin, K.
1948 "The Problem of Minority Leadership," in Gertrude Weiss (ed.) *Resolving Social Conflict.* New York: Harper and Brothers.

Ziegler, S., and A.H. Richmond
1972 *Characteristics of Italian Householders in Metropolitan Toronto.* Toronto: York University Ethnic Research Programme, Institute of Behavioural Research.

17

Nationalism and Inter-Ethnic and Linguistic Conflict in Quebec
*Paul Cappon**

Nationalist ideologies in Quebec have undergone significant changes since the Second World War. These developments have been accompanied by changes in linguistic and inter-ethnic conflict in that province. This paper attempts to demonstrate the very close relationship between these two phenomena in the Quebec context. The studies which form the basis for this paper include the employment of a methodology which, although not rendering data which are statistically significant, constitutes a way of examining that relationship.

It would perhaps be a mistake to study the character of French Canadian nationalist ideologies without reference to the distinct parallels which exist between tendencies in Quebec and those one can perceive in other colonized developing countries, for in many of these countries, as in Quebec, the new growth and acceptance of nationalist ideologies on the left has become an important social fact. Similar developments in Quebec therefore take place within a world context of increasing confrontation with imperialist power.

Fundamental change in the ideological system connected with the study of nationalism has led in recent years to reformulations both of general theories of nationalism and of the analysis of nationalism in the various countries. Texts dealing with Western nationalism since the world wars had commonly treated it as a kind of dangerous deviance associated with extreme right-wing activity. This treatment is closely related to the reaction against fascism, Nazism, and to an ideological imperative for the growth of international capitalism, particularly in the forms of multi-national corporations and of neo-colonialism. The in-

* Paul Cappon is Assistant Professor of Sociology, University of British Columbia, Vancouver.

creasing prominence in modern social history of national liberation struggles on all continents, but particularly in the less industrialized states of Asia, Africa, and Latin America, has of necessity been accompanied by the promulgation of more complex concepts of nationalism, concepts which distinguish at the least between its reactionary and progressive forms. Representative of such formulations is Anouar Abdel-Malek's conception of *"le phénomène nationalitaire"*: nationalist ideologies are differentiated according to the social classes which articulate them. In particular, nationalism associated with anti-imperialist struggles of peasantry and workers cannot be compared with expansionist, rightist, and anti-internationalist perspectives on the role of the nation associated with the old western bourgeoisie, or with the narrow, interested, often racist nationalism of the petty bourgeoisie of Third World states.

These changes in the theory of nationalism with regard to colonized or dominated countries–within which certain classes attempt to move towards independence–are paralleled by recent analysis of French Canadian nationalism in Quebec, an analysis which attempts to relate class to form of nationalism in order to describe the role of each in Quebec's movement towards national independence. According to Bourque and Laurin-Frenette (1972) "Nationalist ideologies can only be class ideologies. A nationalist ideology only makes sense through the class which becomes its propagandist....Several types of nationalist ideology can exist within a social formation." It is mandatory to indicate that the ideological premises for this new structuralist analysis are no less determining than they were for the previous conceptions of French Canadian nationalism formulated by Rioux (1964 and 1965), Dofny (1966), and Dumont (1968). These conceptions centred around the idealist notion that French Canadians constituted an "ethnic class" whose "collective desire to live" creates the objective reality of its existence out of its perception of its existence (Dumont, 1968). This leads thereby "to give priority to the awareness of group consciousness" in the study of French Canadian nationalism (Rioux and Dofny, 1964). Rioux writes a history of Quebec in which "the predominance of one or the other consciousness at any given moment explains the physiognomy of each epoch, the alliances and ideological struggles that appear in Quebec" (Rioux, 1965).

It is not surprising that sociological analysis in the 1960s should have concentrated on the problem of ethnic consciousness to the point of declaring it the moving force behind Quebec history: this implied that, given the extraordinary development of national consciousness following the death of Duplessis, the logical consequence and next phase in Quebec history would and should be constituted by the movement toward political independence. Such a reading of Quebec history and contemporary society lays emphasis upon the communality of interest among the various social groupings whose individual differences are overridden by their identical ethnic class. We must therefore conclude with Bourque and Laurin-Frenette (1972) that the ideological premise of such an analysis "underlies all those political positions that favour joining the Parti Québécois and encourage tactical support for the bourgeoisie, without upholding the need for a specifically working class political organization." Yet the fact that this analysis gained such wide currency during the decade of rapid development of social and political consciousness indicates the strength of the form of nationalism espoused by these writers themselves–a form which we will broadly term "culturalist." The more differentiated theory of Quebec nationalism, promulgated by writers like Bourque, Laurin-Frenette, and Ryerson, and following the essential distinctions made by Abdel-Malek, is no less rooted in the ideological necessity of finding a coherent explanation for the evident cleavages between the interests of working class and petty bourgeoisie within the nationalist movement. The very goal of such an explanation–the determining of the role of each social class within the movement–is premised upon the belief that Quebec must move toward national liberation and independent economic development. As the popularity of the ethnic class theory indicated a general level of ideological development in Quebec during the 1960s, so the acceptance of the *"nationalitaire"* theory reflects recent rapid evolution of nationalist ideology toward a perspective rooted in growing class consciousness and general awareness of Quebec's colonial situation.

Two Model-Types of Francophone Nationalism:
In attempting to elucidate the relationship between nationalism and linguistic and inter-ethnic conflict in Quebec I have not been primarily concerned with a delineation of the full spectrum of types of nationalist ideology. On the other hand, like Abdel-Malek and Bourque (1972), I must indicate the fundamental difference in character and in goals between left- and right-wing nationalism in Quebec. The two contrasting types of nationalism in Quebec may be termed "culturalist" and "economic" or "progressive."

There are two principal reasons for the adaptation of models rather than the exhaustive descriptive of the spectrum of types. First, others, notably Bourque and Laurin-Frenette (1972), have already begun this task by referring to the classes that support each type. Second, it seems somewhat perilous to describe each type with the degree of specificity implied by the categorical association of social class with nationalism. Bourque and Laurin-Frenette (1972), for example, contend that the nationalist ideology concerned with "national liberation and socialist self-management" is primarily that of the working class. Yet it seems clear that this is not presently the dominant form of nationalism among the Quebec working class. It seems more true to indicate that the dominant type of nationalism is in a state of flux between the two forms set up as models, and that ideas which may be claimed to uphold the interests of a class may not coincide with its present ideology. It has therefore been my principal interest to study the tendencies in the movement of the dominant or currently most accepted form of nationalism as between the model-types, not only with regard to Quebec society as a whole but also to the various classes within the social formation. The analysis of linguistic and inter-ethnic conflict within that context will demonstrate the variation in degree and intensity of that conflict according to the current tendencies of the dominant form.

An "Action-Research" Study of Inter-ethnic Conflict

The examination of the precise relationship between linguistic and interethnic conflict and nationalism in Montreal was an object of a study undertaken in 1971 (Cappon, 1974). During the study, an attempt was made to recreate within discussion groups the dynamic of the St. Léonard school crisis situation of 1968-69, during which disagreement between immigrants, particularly of Italian extraction, and French Canadians, on the question of the language of schooling of immigrants' children led to violent confrontation. Each discussion group was small (a maximum of ten participants) and carefully composed, consisting of members of the French Canadian group and of three major immigrant groups of Italian, German, and Greek extraction. Participants in each group displayed an approximately homogeneous "social profile" and, in particular, all belonged to an equivalent social stratum, taken in terms of occupation and income. The writer actively moderated the discussions (each about two and a half hours in length) introducing subjective information concerning the attitudes of each group to the others, thereby consistently orienting the participants towards their differences in opinion regarding linguistic policy and reform. An atmosphere of tension similar to that which prevailed during the school crisis was created. It prevented participants from exercising the cool detachment typical of questionnaire responses, proving propitious to the expression of frank opinion. A total of ten meetings were held, two each involving "professionals and independent businessmen," "white collar workers," "blue collar workers" (including housewives), students, and a "mixed" group. The first group included mainly lawyers and small businessmen, the second upper-level office workers and bureaucrats, the third manual workers, and the last people of various social classes. Big businessmen from Francophone and immigrant communities were not included, their number and power being small relative to that of Anglophone businessmen. Anglophones also were excluded because a principal object of the discussions was the study of the extent of the determining influence of Anglophone domination in Quebec over conflict between Francophone and immigrant groups. The language of the discussion itself was not determined by the monitor, even though most Greek and German Canadians spoke little French. The willingness of Francophone participants to translate their remarks to interested non-French speakers became itself an attitudinal indicator. The monitor introduced new questions in French but spoke English when addressed in that language.

The general (and not unexpected) conclusion from the meetings was that there was very little *direct* communication between the Francophone group on the one hand and the immigrants on the other on the subject of their mutual aggressive or hostile attitudes. Indeed, they communicated largely indirectly, through the reality of the established socio-economic order, dominated by Anglophone capital. Francophone discussion centred around the necessity of cultural preservation in the face of economic realities encouraging immigrants to integrate with the Anglophone community and to adopt its language, whilst immigrants concentrated their remarks on the objective of socio-economic mobility for themselves and their children by adaptation to the same economic realities through the adoption of English. Excluding statements made by Italians concerning discrimination practised against them by Francophones, almost no reference was made to direct relationships between Francophones and immigrants, despite the fact that such a study was the declared intent of the meetings. In a typical meeting, fewer than 20 per cent of Francophone remarks referred to Francophone-immigrant relations, whilst over 75 per cent referred either to the dominance of the Anglophone upper class or to an alliance of Anglophones and immigrants against Francophones. Among immigrants an average of fewer than 30 per cent of statements made referred directly to their relationship with Francophones, most of these being attributable to Italian charges of xenophobia and discrimination. Severe inter-ethnic conflict between Francophones and immigrants therefore had no manifest independent existence, but depended upon the relationship of each group to the Anglophone dominant class. Most conflict between them, including even job competition, as well as the demographic threat posed by immigrants, assimilation to English, was shown to be a corollary of Anglophone domination and of the concomitant necessity for the immigrant to give priority to the language necessary to the procurement of occupational mobility. Furthermore, it was clear from an analysis of immigrants' attitudes that such conflict was likely to continue, for they could not countenance perceived Francophone threats to their economic objectives through the forcible adoption of French. Social class constituted only a relatively insignificant variable affecting immigrants' attitudes towards linguistic conflict with Francophones.

Francophones' attitudes towards immigrants with regard to the language problem were, by contrast, differentiated by social class as it affects the type of nationalism expressed. Economic nationalists (Bourque's "national liberationists"), found mainly among the workers and students at our meetings, consistently demonstrated more tolerance towards immigrants than did culturalist nationalists, most of whom belonged to the upper strata.

Nationalism, Class, and Attitudes Towards New Canadians

The model of a nationalist ideology which we have termed "culturalist" combined the old conservative ideology centred on French Canadian particularism with the more modern dynamic nationalism concentrating on what Rioux describes as "catching up" (*rattrapage*), as well as on special political status or independence. It consists of several elements–that of "catching up" and a questioning of Francophone socio-economic and linguistic inferiority. As Gerald Fortin (1967) indicates the notion of *"la francophonie"*–a kind of vague co-operation among Francophone states–plays an important role in this culturalist ideology. "Vouloir créer une société industrielle et française dans le contexte nord-américain est une sorte de folie collective au moment où l'économie est presque entièrement contrôlée par les États-Unis, et que les Canadiens français, par suite de l'idéologie traditionelle, n'ont pratiquement aucune expérience ni aucun contrôle du monde industriel. Pour essayer de diminuer l'importance des capitaux américains, il fallait chercher à tout prix à attirer des capitaux...par des contacts positifs avec la France et la Belgique." The insistence on the search for "Francophone capital"–on the *"francisation"* of economic life with the maintenance of the social structures of the capitalist state–relates to another fundamental preoccupation of culturalist nationalism: the necessity to create and maintain a native capitalist class or, at the least, much greater access for Francophones to positions of management of foreign (including English Canadian) capital, a position currently occupied almost exclusively by the Anglophone bourgeoisie. This modern form of culturalist nationalism–because it seeks to preserve cultural and linguistic identity and to augment Francophone socio-economic mobility without a fundamental challenge to the socio-economic order–particularly to Quebec's position of appendage to the American economic system–could be formulated only by the new Francophone middle class arising during the "Quiet Revolution" (Guindon, 1964). "Lionel Groulx's was a voice in the desert until the new classes made it theirs. His historical, economic, and social views were academically marginal and politically ineffective until the emergence of the new middle class and its access to political power. His views have become the unifying ideology giving political cohesiveness to this new social class." The policy through which occupational mobility would be obtained for this middle class appeared identical to that which culturalist nationalists promulgated to preserve cultural integrity–the growth of an enterprising Francophone bourgeoisie, the success of *"francophonie"* the establishment of a politically autonomous or independent and unilingual Quebec state, and the immediate imposition of French upon immigrants. The Anglophone group, guarantors of the existing order, would be affected by the change only insofar as it would perforce share its management position with the Francophone elite. In this connection, we must note that those who perceive most clearly the political and economic advantages of the English Canadians are members of the Francophone bourgeoisie and petty bourgeoisie (Roseborough and Breton, 1968).

Culturalist nationalism, having taken root in and being propagated mainly by the petty bourgeoisie in defence of its interests, was expressed predominantly by Francophone participants of the "Professional and Independent Businessman" and "White Collar" categories. Several lawyers and administrators of the Francophone group demonstrated hostility to any nationalization of foreign enterprises, expressing encouragement for foreign capital in corporations which would use the French language in Quebec, thereby allowing access for Francophones to top management positions. Typical statements from petty bourgeois participants regarding the dominance of foreign direct capital investment were the following: "Le capital n'a pas de langue...le capital se conforme aux lois du pays." Without transforming either the modalities of this investment nor the distribution of profits, all petty bourgeois participants indicated support for requesting that Anglo-American corporations "transform your business to a French operation; and you have good contracts and your business will prosper. Aluminum companies set up in Quebec because we had aluminum...American big-shot businessmen in Japan learn Japanese." In this manner economic stability would be maintained whilst Francophones would share administration of enterprises with Anglophones. In order to preserve the entente with Anglophones, according to all but one Francophone petty bourgeois participant, the latter would enjoy "Le privilège de vivre en anglais" but "les autres devront aller à l'école française, comme ça se fait ailleurs. Comme en Ontario, comme au Manitoba."

It appeared clear from the detailed analysis of such attitudes in all meetings in which "middle class" Francophones participated that expression of the culturalist type of nationalism varied positively with the degree of active intolerance of immigrants, or the general hardening of attitudes towards them. Culturalist nationalists tended invariably to take a hard line on the school question, demanding that immigrants forego their material interests by sending their children to French schools. For them, the cultural growth of the French Canadian nation depends not upon socio-economic transformation but rather upon constraining New Canadians to speak French. During the St. Léonard school crisis, culturalist nationalists expressed the view that it was "le devoir strict des immigrants de s'intégrer à la majorité" (Fédération des Ensignants du Québec, 1968). Similar opinions were consistently stated by these nationalists at our meetings: "Nous formons une nation et en tant nous avons le droit d'imposer notre langue aux immigrants," whilst "Les Anglophones ont des droits acquis"; "Pour moi, un Québec francophone, ça veut dire une collectivité francophone qui a décidé de réaliser ensemble un projet collectif qui s'appelle le Québec, c'est-à-dire une culture." It is interesting to note the similarity of this collectivist and idealist view with that of its academic counterpart–the ethnic class theory. Finally, we must note that those Francophones who espoused culturalist nationalism were also those who perceived the problems of immigrant integration to nation and culture at a personal level, depending largely upon individual good will. Thus it is neither a social system nor an economic order which is brought into question but simply the willingness of a certain number of individuals to demonstrate their democratic instinct by their submission to the integrationist resolve of the majority. These Francophones therefore emphasized the linguistic capacity of their New Canadian interlocutors and were often recognizable by their refusal to speak English to other participants who understood no French, reproaching immigrants for their language choice more than did other Francophone participants. Nevertheless, culturalist nationalists were generally careful to maintain the myth of contestation of Anglophone dominance, typically contending that "On ne s'attaque pas aux Italiens (à St. Léonard) mais aux Anglais qui se servent des Italiens comme des paravents."

This attitude is similar to that of many unilingualist groups active during the school crisis–le Mouvement pour l'intégration scolaire, la Société St. Jean Baptiste, le Front du Québec Français, and many members of the Parti Québécois. Yet we have seen that most culturalist nationalists wish to retain the privilege "*des vrais Anglais*": to choose the language of schooling. The desire to preserve the entente with the guarantors of the economic order at the price of linguistic discrimination against new Quebeckers is reflected by the astonishment of many integrationists at the vehemence of Anglophone reaction to the crisis. Hoping to arrive at an agreement with the Anglophone community, culturalist nationalists decry the fact that the latter feels menaced by the pressure exercized by Francophones on the immigrants, and that it attempts to limit Francophones' coercive action against New Canadians: "Éditoriaux sur éditoriaux de la presse anglophone de Montréal se poursuivent pour revendiquer cette liberté de choix de l'école pour les immigrants. A lire ces éditoriaux, on dirait que la puissante communauté anglophone se sent menacée jusque dans son existence par l'affaire de St. Léonard" (*Relations* 1969). An important goal of culturalist nationalism is the reversal of the present use of the immigrant as a perceived vehicle of Francophone linguistic inferiority through a kind of scapegoating. This implies the projection upon New Canadians of aggression engendered by contradictions between the francophone working class and petty bourgeoisie and the Anglophone dominant class. That such a projection serves the interest of the Francophone petty bourgeoisie is demonstrated by the unanimous tendency among petty bourgeois participants at our meetings towards culturalist nationalism.

The modern form of culturalist nationalism, though a product of the Francophone middle class, retains its dominance within the total French Canadian society mainly through its emphasis on the "national" character of the struggle to form "un état français sur le sol nord-américain." This ideology was certain to attract many adherents among a French Canadian population with a level of class consciousness still restricted by extreme ethnic sensibility: even the Francophone working class, whose interests would seem to lie in the direction of a more complete restructuring of the Quebec socio-economic system, exhibits many of the characteristics endemic to culturalist nationalism. It is therefore not surprising that the working class tends to attach blame to immigrants for their choice of language.

Nevertheless, it is also obvious that another type of nationalism is of growing importance within the working class. This form of nationalism, which we have termed "economic nationalism," is closely related to the development of class consciousness. An integral part of this nationalist ideology is the rejection of the American social and economic model, with the implication of the necessity for a genuine decolonization of Quebec, not simply the replacement of one ethnic category within the dominant class by another. Consequently, transformation of the colonial social structure would accompany the termination of foreign economic domination. Political autonomy and unilingualism, often proposed as panaceas by culturalist nationalists, are subordinated by more progressive nationalists to socio-economic transformation, and indeed follow from it. Naturally, this conception of Quebec society implies class contradictions within the Francophone ethnic group between on the one hand the liberal middle class, perceiving contestation as essentially the servant of the interests of socio-professional mobility for members of their class as well as of the national culture, and the working class on the other. Without under-emphasizing the importance of language, the proponents of this new ideology propose social and economic change which would threaten the interests of the Francophone bourgeoisie.

The rapid development of working class consciousness over the past few years, marked by the extension of the union movement and radicalization of the major union centrals, has led to a polarization of nationalists on the political level, where the Parti Québécois is increasingly unable to contain nationalist elements of all social classes and political tendencies. Present positions of Parti Québécois leadership make it clear that the abandonment of culturalist nationalism by part of the working class is perceived as a threat by the middle class, represented on the politico-linguistic level by organizations like the M.I.S. la Société St. Jean Baptiste, and the leadership of the Parti Québécois.

This brief characterization of the "economic" or "progressive" form of nationalism–a type which is still limited, even in Montreal–indicates that the growth of this type would lead to the sharpening of perceived contradictions between the Francophone working class and the Anglophone dominant class. Consequently, conflict between immigrants and Francophones would appear only as the tip of an iceberg of which the base is the contradictions which create that conflict. Projection of aggression upon New Canadians is infrequent because economic nationalists show less tendency to perceive immigrants as the willing Anglophone pawns responsible for the demographic threat. Culturalist nationalists also claim initially that they do not hold New Canadians responsible for the threat. However, the hollowness of such declarations was shown by subsequent opinions expressed by culturalist nationalists at our meetings. A typical example: "Je n'accuse pas les immigrants mais les immigrants se sont trompés de pays. Ils doivent aider les francophones en s'alliant â eux....Je ne blâme pas les immigrants de vouloir la paix. Mais je ne blâme pas les francophones qui ne veulent pas leur laisser la paix. Pourquoi les immigrants auraient la paix et moi j'habite mon pays depuis 200 ans et je ne l'ai pas eue parce qu'il a toutes sortes de circonstances qui m'empêchent de l'avoir. Je ne vois pourquoi ils auraient la conscience tranquille alors que mois je ne l'ai pas." Therefore, the linguistic policies which they promulgate are not discriminatory: Anglophones would be equally affected by any reform or by any change in the language of schooling.

During our meetings, it was evident that those who showed consistently more sympathetic attitudes towards immigrants, particularly regarding the language problem, were representatives of the student group or the working class–despite the fact of job competition. Typical statements displayed some understanding of the immigrants' plight, attaching less blame to them for their choice of language: "We don't ever blame the immigrants, even in St. Léonard....How can we blame the immigrant, when to work he has to speak English? We are blaming the system that creates this situation...Les immigrants de St. Léonard étaient les victimes du système." The tendency of workers to discuss the language problem in terms of a necessary imposition of Francophone culture and language upon New Canadians is an important characteristic differentiating progressive nationalism from the culturalist type. According to Francophone workers at our meetings: "The Anglophones use everything they can; they have the power, the government..."; "La presse anglaise met les immigrants en garde contre la perte de leur sécurité. Mais, en fait, ils ne parlent pas de la sécurité des immigrants mais de leur propre sécurité, qui font partie de l'establishment qui mène tout au Québec, qui sont privilégiés présentement. Notre premier ministre est placé là. La haute finance et la presse anglaise va jouer ce jeu-là et l'immigrant va être porté vers la presse anglaise."

It is nonetheless clear that culturalist nationalism retains a considerable place in the ideology of the Francophone worker, thereby influencing collective attitudes towards immigrant groups. Indeed, the expression of a desire to transform foreign domination is often contradicted by the anxiety of the same participant to preserve economic stability. Parallelling this anxiety, characteristic of culturalist nationalism, is the occasional expression of attitudes towards New Canadians which are less than understanding. A realistic conclusion is that the type of nationalism which dominates collectively the French Canadian working class in the Montreal region contains elements of both model-types of nationalism. To the degree that class consciousness develops among that class, progressive nationalism will also take on increasing importance, and conflicts engendered between that segment of the Quebec social formation and New Canadians will diminish.

Nationalists among the Francophone bourgeoisie and petty bourgeoisie display an ideology very close to the first model-type described, and since this ideology is also rooted in class interest, it seems unlikely to evolve. We can therefore expect continued hostility towards immigrants and perhaps accrued conflict deriving from the attitudes of that social category.

Conclusions

The conclusions which must be drawn from this study are of two types—methodological and theoretical. On the level of methodology, I believe that my research has shown the discussion group method to have definite merits in considering research priorities in the field of nationalism and inter-ethnic conflict in Quebec. If such meetings could be carried on at regular intervals, perhaps including the important Anglophone community in some studies, they would perhaps give a more precise indicator of the development of attitudes towards other ethnic groups than could methods like the traditional questionnaire or interviewing techniques. Although the data would not be statistically significant, it would also furnish valuable information regarding the tendencies of French Canadian nationalism.

The theoretical conclusions, which also have important empirical connotations, relate to the use of the discussion group method in indicating Francophone attitudes. Implicit in the results of this study—including both the discussion groups and the history of inter-ethnic conflict in Montreal—is the idea that the degree of aggression demonstrated by Francophones in their attitudes towards immigrants is so closely related to the dominant form of ingroup nationalism that observation and analysis of those attitudes could constitute a valuable index to analyze the movement of nationalist tendencies. When conflict diminishes and Francophone attitudes show less hostility we may conclude that the dominant form of nationalism among French Canadians as a group is moving in the direction of the economic type. The results of our discussion groups do not, however, allow us to predict the triumph of such a movement in the near future. Although it is true that working-class Francophones tended to demonstrate more components of this form of nationalism, these components were mixed with the culturalist type. We may view the present uncertainty and disunity among union leadership with respect to questions of nationhood and social change as a parallel to this ambivalence.

The Francophone working class still operates under the ideological hegemony of its middle classes; until this ceases to be the case it will not have a completely separate and distinct form of nationalism.

Finally, we must conclude–and this is substantiated by recent political debates in Quebec–that independence inspired essentially by the culturalist nationalism which originated with the middle class could easily lead to an eventual backlash against immigrant ethnic groups. This would be the case especially if that independence were accompanied by serious economic and political difficulties. In this case, we could not be optimistic about the fate of these groups in Quebec.

References

Bourque, G., and N. Laurin-Frenette
1972 "Social Classes and Nationalist Ideologies in Quebec," in Teeple (ed.) *Capitalism and the National Question*. Toronto: University of Toronto press.

Brazeau, J.
1966 "La Question Linguistique à Montréal." *Revue de l'Institut de Sociologie*, Bruxelles.

Brazeau, J.
1968 "Language Differences and Occupational Experience." *Canadian Journal of Economic and Political Science* 24:522-400.

Brunet, M.
1967 "Le Québec et le Canada Anglais." *Recherches Sociographiques*, Montreal.

Caillot, M.
1969 "L'Insertion Sociale des Étrangers," *Hommes et Migrations*, 3ieme Trimestre.

Cappon, P.
1974 *Conflit entre les Néo-Canadiens et les Franchophones de Montréal.* Quebec: Presses de l'Université Laval.

Dofny, J.
1966 "Le Québec et la Sociologie Québécoise." *Revue de l'Institut de Sociologie*, Bruxelles.

Dofny, J., and Audy
1969 "Mobilités Professionnelles au Québec." *Sociologie et Société, 1 (November):277-301.*

Dumont, F.
1968 "Notes sur l'Analyse des Idéologies." *Recherches Sociographiques*, Fédération des Enseignants du Quebec, le. 5 Septembre.

Fortin, G.

1967 *"Le Québec' une Société Globale à la Recherche d'Elle-même."*
Recherches Sociographiques 8 (Janvier-Avril):7-13.

Guindon, H.

1968 "Social Unrest, Social Class, and Quebec's Bureaucratic Revolution," in B.R. Blishen et al (eds.) *Canadian Society.* Toronto: Macmillan.

Légaré, J., and J. Henripin

1969 *Evolution Démographique du Québec et de ses Régions,* 1966-86. Quebec: Presses de l'Université Laval.

Ossenberg, R.J.

1966 "The Social Integration of Post-war Immigrants in Montreal and Toronto," in W.E. Mann (ed.) *Canada-A Sociological Profile.* Toronto: Copp Clark.

Rioux, M.

1964 *Sur l'Evolution des Idéologies au Québec.* Toronto: McClelland and Stewart.

Rioux, M.

1965 "Conscience Ethnique et Conscience de Classe au Québec."
Recherches Sociographiques, 6 (Janvier-Avril): 23-32.

Rioux, M. and J. Dofny

1964 "Social Class in French Canada," in Rioux and Martin (eds.)
French Canadian Society. Toronto: University of Toronto Press.

Roseborough, and R. Breton

1968 "Ethnic Differences in Status," in B.R. Blishen et al (eds.) *Canadian Society.* Toronto: MacMillian.

Postscript on
Ethnic Methodology

As scholars of ethnic research, we are continually seeking new ways to analyze complex ethnic data. In this volume, about a dozen methods are used to do both qualitative and quantitative research. The complexity of ethnic data requires longitudinal macro-studies over time, comparative studies, depth studies of smaller communities and groups, and sophisticated statistical analysis in many cases which require scaling and testing. We are happy to include the whole range of methods in this book because ethnic research requires both qualitative and quantitative methodologies. The ethnic phenomenon is rich and diverse; all the methods devised will be needed to analyze the Canadian mosaic. First, we will review qualitative methods, and then follow with a discussion of the quantitative methods used in this volume.

Qualitative Research Methods
The historical approach is best illustrated by Frank Epp's descriptive study of the 450-year survival of the Mennonites. Events which occurred in the past over long periods of time can be studied only by means of finding what literature is available; often there are only fragmented sources available for study, in the nooks and crannies of libraries and institutions. The historical approach is also perhaps the only method which can cope with such a diversity of information, holding together a multitude of trends and directions. Much of the ethnic literature in Canada is of the historical variety, but unfortunately a great deal of it is poorly documented; as a result the reader is left in doubt about the reliability of the data and also about the validity of the interpretation of events. Fortunately, Epp's study is based on a recently published book by the author, *Mennonites in Canada, 1886-1920*, which is but one of a series he will write based on the

extensive collection of historical data. Historical macro-studies, however, are subject to reliance largely on the interpretation of the data by the authors. Often there is no alternative; research of the past can no longer be designed, and the limited data which is available is the only source of information. Many historians are becoming increasingly concerned about the reliability of their data.

Ethnography, the second qualitative method used in this volume, is best demonstrated by the Matthiassons' study of the Inuit at Pond Inlet. Social anthropologists have developed the method of participant observation by living in a community for considerable lengths of time while they study the occupants of that community. They developed such a technique, especially when they studied illiterate people, people with no written records or information to analyze. Oral tradition, customs, culture, and social organization were studied by learning the language of the group, and by living in their midst. Although the Inuit of Pond Inlet are coming into more contact with outsiders, they are still very much set apart in the far North; thus, the ethnographic approach was used to study the life of these people, an approach which describes one isolated community in considerable depth.

The *community study* approach used by William Shaffir in his study of the Chassidic Jews, and by Clifford Jansen to study the Italians in Toronto, is in many ways similar to the ethnographic study, except that it usually involves contemporary agricultural or urban people who have written records and historical materials which can be examined. Shaffir employed participant observation and personal interviewing in his study (also published in a book titled *Life in a Religious Community*); he studied the socialization process of participants into a small group because this process reveals in-depth attitudes, emotions, and motives, and yields useful information about a few in a small community in Montreal. Participant observation developed trust, and made possible an extended interview with much open-ended probing in a small gemeinshaft-like ingroup. While Shaffir's study is an intensive ingroup study on a primary level, Jansen's study of the Italian community organization in Toronto was done on a much larger scale at a more secondary institutional community level. By means of interviews and questionnaires, he collected the data to describe the religious and social assistance organizations, as well as ethnic clubs and the use of ethnic media.

Comparative studies may be both qualitative and quantitative. One of the four comparative studies in this volume tends to be qualitative and three tend to be quantitative. The advantages of comparing two or more groups are obvious: it provides the opportunity to demonstrate how different groups vary with regard to specific variables in different environments. Paul Cappon's comparison of the attitudes of French Canadians and recent Italian imigrants to the St. Léonard School crisis during 1968-69 demonstrates great differences, and also severe latent conflict potential. Both groups reside in Montreal, but they live in two worlds which have very different social values. Taylor, Frasure-Smith, and Lambert compared the attitudes of French- and English-Canadian parents toward childrearing in the same city, but although they did not find as many differences as they expected, there were some. In this case, the social values of the two ethnic groups tended to be more similar.

In the study of Native People, comparisons are helpful when the cultural contexts are varied, to see whether attitudes will vary. Burshtyn and Smith compared Inuit, Indian, Métis, and Euro-Canadian students, and found some important differences among northern and southern groups in their occupational prestige orientations. Russell MacArthur's comparison of the Central Canadian Inuit, the West Greenlander Eskimos, the Nsenga Zambians, and Alberta Whites who come from very different cultures also illustrates important differences between these four groups.

Quantitative Research Methods
The battle between the qualitative and quantitative scholars continues, but some of us are convinced that especially in the study of ethnicity, all methods of research are needed. Many social phenomena are difficult to quantify; on the other hand it is encouraging that some of these phenomena can be dealt with by more specific quantifiable means.

Demographic descriptions, such as Warren Kalbach's study, are in many ways a quantitative history of describing Canadian immigration during the past hundred years. At first we thought that a historian might provide this historical account; however, the demographic approach is more specific. And perhaps one of the richest sources of data is the Canadian census, which goes back a century, and has been taken every ten years. Census data are, however, fraught with many problems of reliable sampling, comparability, and the like; nevertheless, they are more accurate than fragments of unsystematic data found in letters, journals, and institutions. Thus, census data are the best source for longitudinal studies because, on a national scale, no one has collected so much data over such a long period of time. The cost involved in making such national surveys is enormous, certainly outside the reach of most research scholars.

The census data, however, are very limited in the scope of data collected. They include mainly demographic information on fertility, mortality, immigration, ethnic and religious groups, sex, occupation, education, income, language use, rural-urban populations, and the like. And these findings are usually reported in cross-tabular statistical form. As a result, those who wish to study more subtle social phenomena, such as attitudes, emotions, family relationships, communities, social structures, institutions, and elites, will not get much help from the census.

Social survey research is designed to study specific social phenomena related to specific problems. Burshtyn and Smith make use of two social surveys: a national sample collected by Pineo and Porter on occupational prestige ratings, and a special sample of high school students in northern Canada. Questionnaires were administered in both of these survey samples, and the data were collected for the specific purpose of determining the occupational prestige ratings of Canadians. Even limited surveys of a national sample–or even a sample of ethnic groups in Toronto like that collected by Richmond–are very costly. Burshtyn and Smith's sampling of high schools was somewhat easier and less costly because a sampling of high schools involves fewer units, and questionnaires could be administered to large groupings of respondents in these schools. Jeremiah Allen also made use of two samples in his study of unemployment in Canada: he examines the longitudinal survey reported in *Three Years in Canada*, which is part of the Green Paper on Immigration, and his own study of a case of mass layoff. Both surveys were designed to deal with problems of immigration and successful competition for jobs in Canada. Social surveys are done on a much smaller scale than national census surveys. Some of these surveys are national samples, but, as illustrated by some of the surveys reported in this volume, many are smaller samples of cities, schools, or individuals in smaller communities; and some of these surveys are random samples, while others are purposive.

Content analysis is best described as a method for quantifying qualitative observations, typically in the form of written documents. James Frideres undertook a content analysis of news releases published in nine Canadian newspapers, covering the period of 1950-1974. Within each year sampled, a random sample of four months was selected; then each paper was read for all days of each month selected. All items relating to Indians were selected and coded. The Schludermanns used content analysis in their analysis of essays written by Hutterite adolescents about Hutterite ideals. Content analysis is also used in Hutterite sentence completions related to Hutterites values and attitudes.

In a way all of us do our own unsystematic sampling while reading. Content analysis provides a more objective method for selecting data, but it is very time-consuming, and specific to written and published materials. Data collected in this manner are usually committed to relatively descriptive cross-tabular quantification.

The experimental laboratory. Social scientists often complain that their data are scattered everywhere in a variety of settings, so that it is very difficult to control for the factors which might influence human behaviour. Physical scientists often observe and conduct their experiments in laboratories for greater control and for more careful observation. Unfortunately most social research cannot be done in the laboratory, but occasionally social experiments can be designed and conducted within a small group laboratory. Two of the studies presented in this volume were done in laboratory-type settings.

Paul Cappon tried to create within discussion groups the dynamic of the St. Léonard school crisis situation of 1968-69. During ten meetings

Cappon experimented with French, Italian and other ethnic groups, to observe variations in group conflict. He also controlled for social class by introducing white collar and working class variations.

Taylor, Frasure-Smith, and Lambert elicited spontaneous parental reactions to a tape-recorded version of young children in familiar interaction episodes. The child makes a number of comments and demands of the parent and the parent's task is to imagine how he should respond. Parental responses were coded in terms of a lenience-harshness dimension. The authors interviewed sets of English Canadian and French Canadian parents, and they also controlled for social class (half the parents from each ethnic group were working class and half were middle class) to observe class variations. These experiments were not always made in small group laboratories especially designed for maximum control, but they were laboratory-like studies which illustrate another method of social study.

Statistical techniques are the most sophisticated method of presenting data including factor analysis, analysis of variance, co-variance, regression analysis, and the like. Not all of these techniques are demonstrated in this volume, but Burshtyn and Smith use factor analysis (orthogonal simple structure solution) to measure occupational prestige ratings among high school students in the Canadian Arctic (factor analysis may be used to isolate aspects of objects being rated, aspects toward which the raters have complex or multidimensional attitudes). MacArthur uses the model which resembles Vernon's orthogonal group-factor hierarchy in his comparison of four ethnic groups. MacArthur also uses correlations of ability tests, while the Schludermanns use two tailed t-tests between Hutterite and Cattell means. These are a few of the statistical tests used to measure correlations.

As the readings in this volume suggest, our task was to examine a few of the multidimensional, multicultural, and multidynamic phenomena in the pluralist Canadian society. We explored numerous perspectives and collected a variety of data, hoping to encompass some of the varied phenomena and develop methods to analyze these complex mini-cultures and ethnic structures into a complex whole. That is the challenge in Canadian ethnic research, and that, many of us think, will provide us with new insights into Canadian society. We hope this volume will contribute in a small way to this gigantic task before us.

Author Index

Index